Library of
Davidson College

COURT & GARDEN

Michael Dennis		From the French Hôtel to the City of Modern Architecture

© 1986 by The Massachusetts Institute of Technology

All rights reserved. No part of this book may be reproduced in any form by any electronic or mechanical means (including photocopying, recording, or information storage and retrieval) without permission in writing from the publisher.

This book was set in Trump Medieval by Achorn Graphics and printed and bound by Halliday Lithograph in the United States of America

Library of Congress Cataloging in Publication Data

Dennis, Michael.
  Court & garden.

  Bibliography: p.
  Includes index.
  1. Architecture and society.
  2. Architecture—Philosophy. 3. Space (Architecture) 4. Personal space.
  5. Palaces. 6. Plazas. I. Title.
  NA2543.S6D39   1986   720'.1'03   85-7906
  ISBN 0-262-04082-4

Publication of this book has been aided by a generous grant from the Graham Foundation for Advanced Studies in the Fine Arts.

For my mother and the memory of my father

The Graham Foundation Architecture Series

The Secret Life of Buildings: An American Mythology for Modern Architecture,
Gavin Macrae-Gibson, 1985.

Court & Garden: From the French Hôtel to the City of Modern Architecture,
Michael Dennis, 1986.

Contents

	Preface	viii
	Introduction	1
	The Public Realm	1
	The French Hôtel	3
	The Royal Squares	6
	The Publications	6
	The Anatomy of History, c. 1540–1800	8
1	*Public versus Private*	15
	Theory and Practice	15
	Palladio and the Italian Renaissance: Unity and Continuity	16
	Versailles and Blenheim: Total Design	20
	Louis Le Vau: Differentiation and Discontinuity	20
2	*The Prototypes*	29
	Italian Renaissance Space	29
	The Place Ducale at Vitry-le-François	30
	Le Grand Ferrare	31
	Serlio and Du Cerceau	40
3	*Public Spaces: The Baroque Hôtel*	43
	The Urban Squares of Henri IV	44
	The Baroque Hôtel	52
	Marot	77

4	*Display and Retreat: The Rococo Hôtel*	79
	The Place Louis-le-Grand	82
	The Rococo Hôtel	91
	Blondel and Briseux	118
5	*Private Icons: The Neoclassical Hôtel*	125
	The Place Louis XV	128
	The Neoclassical Hôtel	136
	Krafft and Ransonnette	176
	The Nineteenth Century	178
6	*Le Corbusier and the City of Modern Architecture*	189
7	*Architecture and the Cumulative City*	211
8	*Excursus Americanus*	229
	Plans of Paris	245
	Chronology of Hôtels and Key Plan	263
	Notes	265
	Bibliography	271
	Illustration Credits	275
	Index	281

Preface

The first version of this book was written rather quickly in the late spring and early summer of 1977—the product of frustration with the urban intractability of modern architecture. One hundred copies of French Hôtel Plans were xeroxed, bound, and distributed to friends and students. At the time there was no reason to imagine the degree to which those original copies would multiply thanks to the modern magic of "xerography," but over the next few years "the *hôtel* book" was reproduced and passed on again and again, mostly among students. My own original copy was given away long ago (was it to Leon Krier or Maurice Culot?), and people periodically complain about the unreadability of their eighth-generation copy and inquire about a fresh one. Naturally, the underground success of that first version gives me pleasure second only to the completion, finally, of this one.

There was also no reason to think about how much the original material would expand, how intricate the research could become, and how difficult it would be to hold the true line of the idea. It could easily have become another kind of book, and many painful decisions as to inclusion or exclusion are evident. The operative strategy was that the book could not be, and should not be, the definitive history of the *hôtel*; it also should not (by ostensible completeness) deflect attention from the richness of first sources. I hope in fact that the reader will pass through this work as through a sieve to the finer-grain pleasures beyond. The material included speaks for itself, of course, but some notable exclusions merit acknowledgment. The omission of some famous architects (Peyre, de Wailly, Gondoin, etc.) and *hôtels* (de L'Orme, Bazinière, Aumont, etc.) was simply a matter of redundancy, and information on these architects and *hôtels* is easily available elsewhere. Directly related to the material—especially since it forms half the title of the book—is the topic of the French garden; but again, the French garden is well covered elsewhere, and its specific relationship to the development of the *hôtel* is rather obvious. Far more serious, however, and at once crucial and elusive, is the relationship of the *hôtel* to the French *château* and the English country house. Alas, this subject simply must remain a loose end, for it is beyond the scope of this book. Perhaps it is a topic in its own right, "A Tale of Two Countries" of sorts. Loose ends, omissions, and potential errors are cause for special worry when one transgresses the domain of others, and I am well aware that domestic Parisian architecture is clearly the domain of a very few—mostly French—scholars. I can only hope that enthusiasm for the subject will allow them to suffer my blunders with tolerance and with what Krafft called "that engaging politeness that characterises the French nation."

The initial research for this book was done at Cornell University; that original material was researched again and expanded during a year at Princeton University in 1979–80; and successive drafts were written in Ithaca, New York, and Cambridge, Massachusetts. During that time, lectures at many universities helped clarify and expand various aspects of the subject, and many people and institutions helped bring the work to fruition.

I wish to acknowledge my students first, for they have always been the single greatest source of support, experiment, and speculation. Also, many friends and colleagues in the Department of Architecture at Cornell University contributed to an atmosphere which was, and presumably still is, unpredictably volatile and quietly brilliant, an atmosphere in which odd things could be pursued unfettered by the pressures of public display.

Caroline Constant, Richard Etlin, and Fred Koetter read the draft manuscript and gave invaluable advice at that crucial stage. Ellen Count straightened out the final manuscript, and the editorial and design staff of The MIT Press completed the work with spirit and finesse. During the last hectic months my partner, Jeffrey Clark, covered for my lapses at the office, and Nils, Erika, Julian, Justine, and Jesse learned to tolerate their father's sporadic attention, depression, paranoia, inexplicable exhilaration, and compulsion. I wish to acknowledge an indefinable debt to Colin Rowe. Colin's modesty and generosity with ideas are well known, and although it is impossible to credit many specifics, his spirit has informed the whole. The poet fox could (and should) have written this book long ago. To you all I am deeply grateful.

I also wish to thank the Graham Foundation for Advanced Studies in the Fine Arts for a generous grant for illustrations, and the Harvard Graduate School of Design for support in the form of time and services.

The staffs of several libraries have given patient and indispensable help, and I offer thanks to the Fine Arts Library at Cornell University; Marquand Library at Princeton University; Avery Library at Columbia University; the Loeb, Houghton, and Fine Arts libraries at Harvard University; and the Bibliothèque Nationale in Paris. In addition, the Francis M. Loeb Library and the Houghton Library at Harvard University have kindly given permission to publish material from their collections.

It was an honor, a privilege, and an appropriate conclusion to have delivered the material of this book as the Preston H. Thomas Memorial Lectures at Cornell University on five evenings in October and November, 1985.

Michael Dennis
Cambridge, Massachusetts, 1985

COURT & GARDEN

1
Los Angeles

Introduction

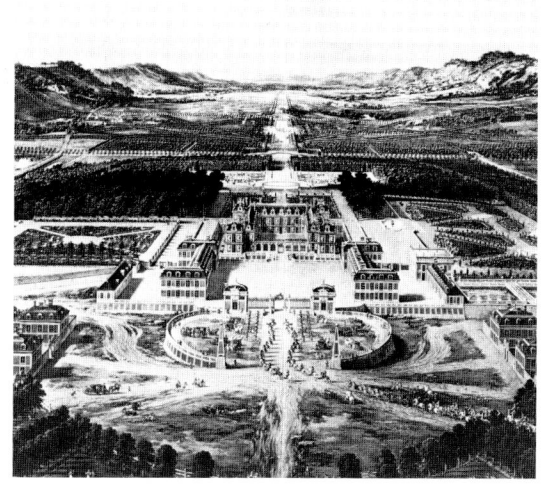

2
Versailles in 1666. Painting by Patel.

The Public Realm

Between the artificial demands of public display at Versailles in the late 1670s and the sincere but no less demanding expressions of private prerogative at Berkeley in the late 1960s lies a phenomenal social transformation. The erosion of public life and the increased preoccupation with personal life during this three-hundred-year period means, according to Richard Sennett in *The Fall of Public Man*, that the "civilized possibility [of the city as] a focus for active social life . . . is today dormant." Parallel to this social phenomenon lies an equally important architectural and urban transformation. For centuries, space was the principle medium of urbanism—the matrix that united public and private interests in the city, guaranteeing a balance between the two. But in the eighteenth century, a process of change—social, intellectual, and formal—began to alter that balance in favor of the private realm. Freestanding object buildings began to replace enclosed public space as the focus of architectural thought, and despite some resistance during the nineteenth century, this formal transformation—from public space to private icon—was finally completed in the early twentieth century. The demise of the public realm was then assured.

If, as Sennett implies, a revival of public man is possible, any form of rebirth must be accompanied by the reconstitution of the formal setting public life requires. The architectural techniques needed for the reconstruction of the spatially rich city and the evolution of a modern conception of space are the central subjects of this book.

Primarily an argument about architecture and the city, as well as a compendium of architectural stimulants, the book has also become a history of sorts. My intention was not to write a history, much less the definitive history of a building type, so the history has a service role and has been assembled, puzzle-like, from the research of others. Without the recent significant additions by Babelon, Blunt, Braham, Gallet, Hautecoeur, Kalnein, Kaufmann, and Thomson to the limited literature on French architecture, my work would have been impossible.

This book also participates in the long tradition of illustrated French architecture books—a tradition in which one work "builds" upon another and in which most works are composed of two texts, one verbal and the other visual. Although here the two texts are interrelated, they may also be read independently of each other. Architects, for instance, should be able to understand the ideas without the words. Today, few architects bother to read the text of Jacques-François Blondel's *Architecture françoise*, but the plates continue to provide a fertile source of ideas. On the other hand, architects have allowed themselves to become dangerously separated from their theoretical literature, and I would encourage reconnection if form is to have any cultural meaning at all.

The angst about distinctions between speculation and history seems to me another symptom of the modern dilemma of excessive isolation and fragmentation. Today the *and* between theory *and* practice, or, for that matter, between architecture *and* the city, implies an almost intolerable degree of self-consciousness, autonomy, and territoriality. In short, *and* in this context now connotes separation rather than articulation.

Nowhere are the effects of fragmentation and isolation so tangible, so visible, as in our cities.

For it is here, in the physical environment, that unseen forces or attitudes show up, and it is the physical environment that in turn redefines our values. The sources and consequences of the modern urban dilemma are most elegantly described by Werner Goehner:

The scientific and analytic mind, with its tendency to break the world into ever smaller parts, has, during the past fifty years of urban and architectural development, finally succeeded in ending a long and fruitful marriage between architecture and the city. Within the modern movement, both the neopositivistic view of architecture as an ahistorical phenomenon, and the view of architecture as exclusively the result of political and economic conditions, dependent on technological and cultural developments (*Zeitgeist* obsession), finally led to the estrangement of architecture from the city.... The reduction of architecture to an issue of the private realm alone stripped architecture of its civic dimension.... In the modern city a meaningful dialogue between the *res publica* and the *res privata* is missing, leading to an impoverishment of the urban spatial morphology.... [W]ithout such spatial articulation of the public realm, the city becomes unintelligible.[1]

Unfortunately, it is difficult to arrest or change an ongoing cycle, and yet that is what is most needed at the moment.

If the roots of this predicament lie, approximately, in the third quarter of the eighteenth century, the results are most clearly visible in the third quarter of the twentieth. Until a confluence of forces following the convulsion of the second world war assured its widespread acceptance, modern architecture was largely an avant-garde phenomenon with limited public appeal. (Indeed, it is now clear that the history of modern architecture is not the history of twentieth-century

3
Houston

architecture.) But after the war, in a spirit of expansive optimism, cities around the world were transformed. Neither "developed" nor "developing" countries could resist. In Europe the destruction of war had prepared the way, while in America it was urban renewal. The results were the same—the fabric of traditional urbanism was ravaged and an antithetical architecture was introduced.

By the late 1960s not just a physical or an aesthetic problem became apparent, but a social, even a cultural one. In spite of affluence and success, nothing seemed to work as planned, and confidence in the rightness of action waned. The excess of private indulgence was in itself indicative of the failure, if not the total demise, of the public realm. Indeed, this period marks the end of a long transformation from public to private hegemony.

Thus, the approximate dates 1775 and 1975, thresholds to two periods of change, vitality, and confusion, are like historical parentheses articulating pre-industrial and post-industrial society. At the very least, they delimit a two-hundred-year period of formal and social development in which societies rushed away from a past marred by class distinction, authority, and, especially in France, unbridled public extravagance.

But if this period produced, ultimately, a kind of tyranny of the private realm, is the result that much less demanding or that much more deserving of endorsement than the tyranny of the public realm it replaced, that of the Louis and the *ancien régime*? And can the absence of a tangible public realm do other than expose the now isolated and vulnerable *res privata* to the possibility of an even more deadly tyranny—that of a covert Orwellian *res publica*?

Whether this reading of history and the present is correct or not, a distinct change in architectural and urban values has come about since the mid-1970s. Today we put a clear, but uneasy, distance between ourselves and the preceding half century and its values, and dissatisfaction with the inadequacies of modern architecture has led to fresh initiatives from many quarters. We are reexamining architecture in its own terms, and, most importantly, in its relation to the city. Changing sensibilities allow new views and new uses of the past, and an emerging idea of the city—one which includes the past as well as the future—is reorganizing the dialogue between architecture and urbanism. The past is alive again as a most valuable resource. The study of architecture and the city are again central to their own restructuring.

The French Hôtel

The study of a single building type, an aristocratic town house, associated almost entirely with one city, Paris, and with a finite period of development, c. 1550–1800, might initially seem to be of limited value today. In the history of western architecture alone, the French *hôtel* is like a very small crack on a very large wall; and this study focuses on only one portion of that crack. On the other hand, architectural *cognoscenti* have long known that the French *hôtel* is to the art of the plan what the Venetian facade is to the art of vertical surface. I hope that looking closely enough at one aspect of the subject, the formal, will expose or illuminate a larger view.

The French *hôtel* has flickered in the shadows of scholarship for too long now, mostly obscured, occasionally oscillating into the useful half-light, but never moving, fully illuminated, on to center stage. Perhaps it has been hidden by the shroud of perversity, or decadence, which seems to envelop the much-maligned Rococo period, with which the *hôtel* is often solely associated. Emil Kaufmann, for example, dismisses the entire era in his *Architecture in the Age of Reason*:

About 1670 a compromise was reached between the never quenched desire for the integral system and the national taste. Then came a period of lull lasting nearly a century. Historically, this period is of less importance than the preceding and following struggles. Its elaborate performances are very attractive and cherished by connoisseurs and people who pose as such. Here on uncontested ground they can show their taste, undisturbed by the pressing problems of growth and death. It is for the historian to see whether life was still going on under the surface in these in-between times.[2]

Little did Kaufmann suspect that the revolutionary architecture of the "following struggles," and indeed he himself, would in time become "cherished by connoisseurs and people who pose as such," but his attitude is typical of most modernists. The *hôtels* and their forgotten architects are to them only part of the "elaborate performances" during the euphoria before the death of the Renaissance and the dawn of modernism. The *hôtels* are also usually seen as the symbols of a previous social order, rather than a prelude to the new, and as isolated displays of decorative virtuosity, rather than as components of a planning tradition that might be of value today. That such a puritanical posture has obscured the French *hôtels'* intrinsic value is unfortunate. With a revised agenda for the city, however, we can see the *hôtel* in a new light—as a sophisticated component of a complex pre-industrial city, as a developed instrument of French urbanism, and as both historically interesting and currently useful.

The *hôtel*, as an aristocratic residence, was directly related to the place of royal residence: the nobility had to be near the king.³ Although during his reign François I resided at Fontainebleau, and therefore so did the nobility, his decision to make Paris the seat of government assured the city's prime role in the development of the *hôtel*. The die was cast for the inhabitation of Paris by future kings and courtiers. Once that union was effected and nurtured by rulers such as Henri III and Henri IV, not even Louis XIV, with his preference for Versailles, could stem the domestic development of Paris. Indeed, during the last years of Louis XIV's reign, at the beginning of the eighteenth century, the construction of *hôtels* flourished in Paris, and with one major interruption continually increased throughout the century.

The number of architects also increased at an astonishing rate between the middle of the sixteenth century and the end of the eighteenth century, reflecting an increase in the number of clients able to afford buildings and the number of buildings being built. Previously architects had been most concerned with public buildings and princely residences, but as society opened up—as more people had access to wealth and taste—the profession expanded to accommodate the need. Specialization even entered the picture as some architects became known almost solely as skilled domestic planners. Thus, in numbers and in function, architects were symptomatic of the coming of modern society. In a word, the architectural profession grew with the expanding socioeconomic order.

The exact origin of the word *hôtel* is not known, but in the sixteenth century it was restricted to the houses of the French nobility and to a few public buildings such as the Hôtel-Dieu and the Hôtel de Ville. A very clear hierarchy existed: the term *palais* was reserved for houses of the king and the princes and princesses of the blood; the term *hôtel* was for houses of the rest of the nobility; and the term *maison* was for the houses of the bourgeoisie. By the late seventeenth century, however, the distinctions had begun to break down, and with the increased blurring of class lines between the nobility and the bourgeoisie in the eighteenth century, the term *hôtel* lost its rigid application. By the nineteenth century it had largely come to mean a single-family town house for bankers, financiers, and even artists. Today the meaning of the word *hôtel* is even more obscure; outside of France it is barely known except to a small circle of scholars and architects, and even then it is rarely used with precision to distinguish between types. This is symptomatic of a larger problem with language and especially with the terminology of architecture.

"The obscurity of terms is one of the greatest obstacles to understanding an art," proclaimed d'Aviler in the introduction to his 1691 dictionary.⁴ When the terms are in a foreign language, the problem is proportionally greater. There are many French words in this book. Some, perhaps most, have disappeared from common usage, and yet at one time they had not only a commonly understood meaning, but frequently a precise one. For that reason I have chosen to use the French words (italicized) where possible. For example, an *antichambre* is not exactly an anteroom or an antechamber or a waiting room; although it is generally each of those, it had a specific meaning in French. A late-eighteenth-century French architect might also ask if one meant a *première antichambre*, *a seconde antichambre*, or a *troisième antichambre*; two hundred years earlier even the simple *antichambre* did not exist. Today, *antichambre* might be confused with *vestibule*.

In addition to the problems posed by a forgotten language, there is the further complication of modern terms and concepts applied to historic projects. To the best of my knowledge the terms *space*, *local symmetry*, and *poché* do not appear in contemporary literature about the *hôtel*; they are modern terms. *Poché* is doubly difficult as it is a nineteenth-century term (a product of the Beaux-Arts) that fell out of favor with the advent of modernism. Technically, in French, it is a verb from *pocher*; meaning to poach (an egg), to black (an eye), or to sketch rapidly. In architecture it means the blacking in of residual areas, such as the thick structural solids of a plan. At the Beaux-Arts, the precise profile of the plan was inked by the designer, while the rougher work of filling in the outlined area could be done by beginning students. The word also came to be used as a noun at the Beaux-Arts, where either *poché pur* (black) or *poché dilué* (gray) could be required. Since the structural system used by the Beaux-Arts was load-bearing masonry, *poché* aided the "reading" of the plan by its direct proportional relationship to the white areas of the rooms it bounded; that is, a large space could be assumed to have a higher ceiling, and its wider span (and greater load) would require larger supports. Thus the volumetric aspects of the design could be read from the two-dimensional abstraction of the plan. With the triumph of the structural frame, the intimate relationship of solid to void—the prized *beau poché*—became meaningless, and was of course scorned by modernists.

The term *poché* has only recently returned to common use, though it is perhaps little understood.[5] In this book it is used as a principle, not as a fact. But this should present no problem; the language of form transcends time and culture. Thus, if we look at a plan by d'Aviler, we easily understand that when he says "the corners of the *chambre à coucher* (G-4) are rounded in order to facilitate the *dégagement* off one corner and a place for the *chaise de commodité* in the *garderobe* off the other,"[6] he is saying that the formal residue, or *poché*, left by the creation of a figural room provides a convenient service passage (disengagement) and a place for the toilet and closet.

In traditional histories of French architecture, the *hôtel* is dispersed among other building types, which are generally arranged chronologically according to architect, thereby obscuring the development of the *hôtel* as an independent type. But because of its chronological and geographical closure and because it was reasonably well documented in illustrated books of the time, the *hôtel* lends itself more to extraction and independent examination than do most building types. If the *hôtel* is isolated from its specific urban and cultural context and from other building types, and if its development is read in chronological sequence, then the *hôtel* can be more easily understood as a continuous morphology within which three general form types may be identified: Baroque, Rococo, and Neoclassical.[7]

The first *hôtel* type, the Baroque type, is a sometimes irregular urban infill, or party-wall, building, which is organized around a stable, geometrically regular exterior court. This court is connected directly to the street, and the service parts of the house are distributed along one or both sides of the court. Sometimes one or more service courts are adjacent and connected to the forecourt. The main living spaces occur at the end of the forecourt, away from the street, and usually face a private garden to the rear. Where the site is extremely limited, the main living quarters may occupy the street side of the court and the garden is omitted. In terms of the traditional city, the Baroque *hôtel* is the most urban of the three types because it allows for a denser, more continuous urban fabric.

The second *hôtel* type, the Rococo, is similar to the first but is a transformation of it. The main living block at the end of the forecourt is articulated in plan and section as an independent element that asserts itself as a pavilion between the court and the garden. This change plus the usually more extensive gardens make this type more suburban than the Baroque type.

The third *hôtel* type, the Neoclassical, is a further transformation of the Rococo and a complete inversion of the Baroque type: a freestanding, geometrically regular solid that sits between the forecourt and the garden. The service elements, such as the stables, are much reduced in size and are located on the street side of the forecourt. With the characteristics of a detached villa or pavilion, the Neoclassical *hôtel* is the most suburban of the three types.

The Baroque, Rococo, and Neoclassical *hôtels* form a typological system related to, but to a certain extent independent from, the mainstream of French architecture during the period c. 1550–1800. As such, they are interesting on several levels. First, they form a separate tradition, which is usefully critical of the public buildings that parallel their development and therefore also of a related and timeless state of mind—that which requires totally unified order. In their *hôtels*, French architects resisted that attitude, and through principles such as discontinuity, they demonstrated a freer one that anticipates modern attitudes: order is relative. Second, as the physical backdrop for what was an elaborate and important society, the *hôtels* reveal social and cultural changes that signal the coming of mass democratic society. Finally, however, it is as a formal instrument of architecture and urbanism that the French *hôtel* assumes its greatest interest for us today.

The transformation of the *hôtel* from positive-space urban "infill"—the essential urban tissue of the traditional city—to freestanding pavilion clearly chronicles the evolution of a modern conception of urban space and therefore of the modern city. If that modern conception is less than adequate, then the *hôtel* may suggest possibilities for the reconstruction of a spatially rich city. At the very least, as a lucid ethical agent in what today is all too often the tenuous commerce between architecture and urbanism, the French *hôtel* offers an indispensable lesson in the architecture of urbanism and a close-up view of the development of one of the world's great cities.

In architectural terms, the *hôtels* illustrate plan techniques and characteristics that offer important conceptual references for an attempt to reconcile modern and traditional modes of building organization and spatial development. These techniques, which combine principles of stability and instability, continuity and discontinuity, symmetry and asymmetry, suggest nothing short of a new kind of architectural space. It is surprising that the French *hôtel* has not already been investigated and exploited since it is a uniquely clear litmus of formal and cultural change and a potent stimulant today.

Parallel to the development of the *hôtel* and relevant to our study are two other traditions: the royal squares of Paris and a series of architectural publications associated with the *hôtel*.

The Royal Squares

We have only to examine the Place Ducale in Vitry-le-François and Paris's Place Royale (later Place des Vosges), Place Louis-le-Grand (later Place Vendôme), and Place Louis XV (later Place de la Concorde) to discover a formal and social transformation related to that of the *hôtel*. The Italian Renaissance notion of conspicuous urban space was introduced into France in the Place Ducale in Vitry-le-François, the prototype for the French residential square. The idea was further developed in the Place Royale in Paris, where there is an easy relationship between the public and private realms and between individual and communal expression. With the Place Louis-le-Grand, a formal rift is visible between the public realm of the statue square and the private realm of lavish houses lying behind the unified facade that separates the two realms. Finally, the Place Louis XV illustrates by the absence of architectural enclosure a changing sensibility related to the suburban Neoclassical *hôtel* type; it symbolizes the demise of the Renaissance urban system of continuous building and articulate space and the beginning of the modern system of articulate objects in a continuous landscape. Because of the French Revolution, no royal square materialized for Louis XVI, so the Place Louis XV is the last one before the markedly different urban experiences of the nineteenth century and the ultimate development of the Neoclassical urban system in the twentieth century.

The Publications

Three kinds of architectural publications are relevant to this study: plans of Paris, illustrated handbooks, and theoretical treatises. Each deals with a different aspect of the subject, and each has its line of evolution.

The plans of Paris, for example, show the urban development and some of the architectural development at critical stages of the city's growth. They also demonstrate graphically the evolution of the relationship between the art and the science of cartography during the period c. 1550–1800. The early plans, such as that called "Aux Trois Personnages" (1540+) and the Merian plan (1614), were bird's-eye views, or pictorial plans, in which the buildings were shown in three dimensions. The Gombust plan of 1652 was the first of a series of basically planimetric views with only important buildings shown in three dimensions. This was the first plan "founded on geometric principles," and it was framed by a border of pictorial views of royal buildings in the environs of Paris.

By the eighteenth century almost all plans were pure planimetric views with major buildings and *hôtels* also shown in plan, and in general the borders of these plans were more restrained. The major exception to the pure plan view during the eighteenth century was the spectacular pictorial view of the Turgot plan of 1739. This famous plan was not a cartographic innovation, but it does offer a remarkable view of the city at one essentially complete stage of development. Two other eighteenth-century plans that are both useful and extremely beautiful are the Delagrive plan of 1728 and the Jaillot plan of 1778.

Both of these distinguish a large number of *hôtels* as well as the major public buildings, and in both the open land and the city blocks are textured. The Jaillot plan in particular shows the gardens of the *hôtels* in great detail. A turning point is reached with the Verniquet plan of 1799. This was the first plan to be geometrically surveyed and was therefore the basis for many later ones. In contrast to earlier plans, it is graphically austere, without a border and with no hatching in the urban blocks; few *hôtels* appear. The successor to the Verniquet plan, the Maire plan of 1808, shows all the Neoclassical *hôtels*, however, and has a legend as well, so it provides valuable information though it is not artistically interesting. The last useful plan for this study is the Vasserot plan of 1827–36. Although outside the time frame of the study, it shows ground plans of all the buildings just prior to the massive interventions of Haussmann during the Second Empire.

The essential distinction between the two other relevant kinds of publications—the illustrated books and the theoretical treatises—is that one illustrates ideas by hypothetical and built examples and is supplemented by a minimal text, whereas the other describes principles via a text, which is sometimes supplemented by illustrations. The illustrated books preceded the theoretical treatises that proliferated in the eighteenth century and thus support the argument made in this study that with the *hôtels*, practice tended to precede theory. Theoretical treatises did appear earlier than the eighteenth century, of course, but those generally focused on the orders and public buildings rather than on the *hôtel*.

The prototype for the illustrated architectural book was Sebastiano Serlio's work, which appeared as several books near the middle of the sixteenth century. With their unprecedented body of illustrated material and their emphasis on both the scientific and the practical aspects of architecture, they served as the model for Palladio and Vignola in Italy and for Philibert de L'Orme and Jacques Androuet Du Cerceau in France. Serlio's unpublished sixth book on town houses is especially important in this respect and must have been known because Du Cerceau's first *Livre d'Architecture* (1559) seems to have derived from it. Du Cerceau's book illustrates town houses of various sizes for different categories of owners, from merchants to princes, and was the predecessor to Pierre Le Muet's *Manière de bien bastir pour toutes sortes de personnes*, published in 1623. Le Muet's book also contained only theoretical plans; it was not until the edition of 1647 that a few examples of built work were included. Du Cerceau's other work, the two volumes of *Les plus excellents bastiments de France*, published in 1576 and 1579, anticipated not only the second version of Le Muet in that they illustrated built works, but most importantly they also anticipated the three major documentations of the French *hôtel*: the two works by Jean Marot, known as the *Petit Marot* (c. 1660–70), and the *Grand Marot* (c. 1670); Jacques-François Blondel's *Architecture françoise* (1752); and Krafft and Ransonnette's *Plans, coupes, élévations des plus belles maisons . . . à Paris* (c. 1802). Unfortunately, neither Du Cerceau's *Bastiments* nor any other publication documented the *hôtels* constructed during the last half of the sixteenth century, most of which did not survive.

Theoretical texts focusing on the principles of the *hôtels* appeared somewhat later than the illustrated handbooks, and as might be expected, most of them were published in the eighteenth century. The earliest was Louis Savot's *Architecture françoise*, first published in 1624. A companion volume to Le Muet's *Manière*, Savot's work is a practical handbook about the considerations affecting the construction of private houses in Paris during the first half of the seventeenth century. Toward the end of the century a series of architectural treatises appeared, but vital to the development of the *hôtel* was the *Cours d'architecture* by C.-A. d'Aviler. The first edition of 1691 was the most important manifesto of academic doctrine after François Blondel's *Cours d'architecture* (1675–98), and it illustrated the major rules governing domestic architecture. The expanded second edition of 1710 (edited by A. Le Blond) was the most popular manual of the early eighteenth century and was the beginning of a rich series of eighteenth-century books about the principles of domestic planning. Two important works that reflected a change in sensibility followed in the 1720s: Jean Courtonne's *Traité de la perspective pratique*, published in 1725, and C.-E. Briseux's *Architecture moderne, ou l'art de bien bastir pour toutes sortes de personnes*, published in 1728. These dealt with the principles of the architecture commonly referred to as Régence and were followed by two other works that outlined the early phase of the Rococo: Jacques-François Blondel's *De la distribution des maisons de plaisance et la décoration des édifices en général* (1737 and 1738) and a work that was modeled after it, C.-E. Briseux's *L'Art de bâtir des maisons de campagne* (1743). Finally, three works by J.-F. Blondel completed the prescription for the mid-eighteenth-century house: the *Abrégé d'architecture concernant la distribution, la décoration, et la construction des bâtiments civils*, an unpublished work (c. 1740?);[8] the *Introduction à l'architecture contenant les principes généraux de cet art*, published in the first volume of the *Architecture françoise* (1752); and the *Cours d'architecture* (1771–77). In the *Abrégé*, domestic planning theory was illustrated by application to a house designed by Blondel, whereas in the *Introduction*, theory was presented independently, as a set of principles that could be seen in the illustrations of notable French architecture that followed.

The articulation of theory and practice in Blondel's *Architecture* thus assigns it to both the tradition of the illustrated handbooks and the tradition of theoretical treatises. (This is in contrast to the works of Serlio and Du Cerceau of two hundred years earlier, in which ideas were illustrated mostly by hypothetical type. It is also unlike the later work by Le Camus de Mézières, *Le Génie de l'architecture ou l'Analogie de cet art avec nos sensations*, published in 1780, in which theoretical principles are not accompanied by any illustrative material.) Blondel's use of real examples and the independent codification of principles reflect the high degree of rationalization and particularization in domestic architecture during the eighteenth century; and if the architecture seems today to lend itself more readily than the text to speculation and reinterpretation, the theoretical principles do expand our architectural understanding of the plans and the society that required them. Both the plans and the principles in Blondel's *Architecture* illustrate the transformation from functionally nonspecific rooms during the sixteenth century to the functionally particularized interiors of the eighteenth century—and therefore the coming of modernism. Although more archival research would be useful in this area, when taken together the plans of Paris, the illustrated books, and the theoretical treatises offer an accessible view of the development of the *hôtel*.

The Anatomy of History, c. 1540–1800

Arranging the parallel developments in the squares, *hôtels*, and publications in correct chronological sequence reveals a surprising set of interrelationships between genres. Like a selective x-ray, the time-line chart reveals an historical anatomy that would otherwise be invisible. For example, despite the apparently continuous morphological development of the *hôtel*, the diagram reveals that production was not continuous but contains significant gaps and that these gaps articulate four major periods of *hôtel* production, each introduced by an urban square and each concluded with a major publication.

The prototype for each category appears in the middle of the sixteenth century, near the end of the reign of François I. The prototypes—the Place Ducale at Vitry-le-François, the Hôtel de Ferrare in Fontainebleau, and Serlio's books—are followed by a proposal for an urban square in Paris, by a considerable number of *hôtels* constructed in Paris in the last half of the century, and by Du Cerceau's *Bastiments*. Unfortunately, however, as a result of the Wars of Religion, the proposed square was not built, almost no visible traces of the *hôtels* remain, and no publication documented either the square or the *hôtels*. The resultant discontinuity is thus apparent, not actual. The *hôtels* of this period, such as the extant Hôtel Carnavalet and the Hôtel d'Angoulême, anticipate the Baroque type.

The next period began under Henri IV with the construction of the Place Royale (now the Place des Vosges) in the Marais district of Paris shortly after 1600. Then came a group of *hôtels* of the

9   The Anatomy of History

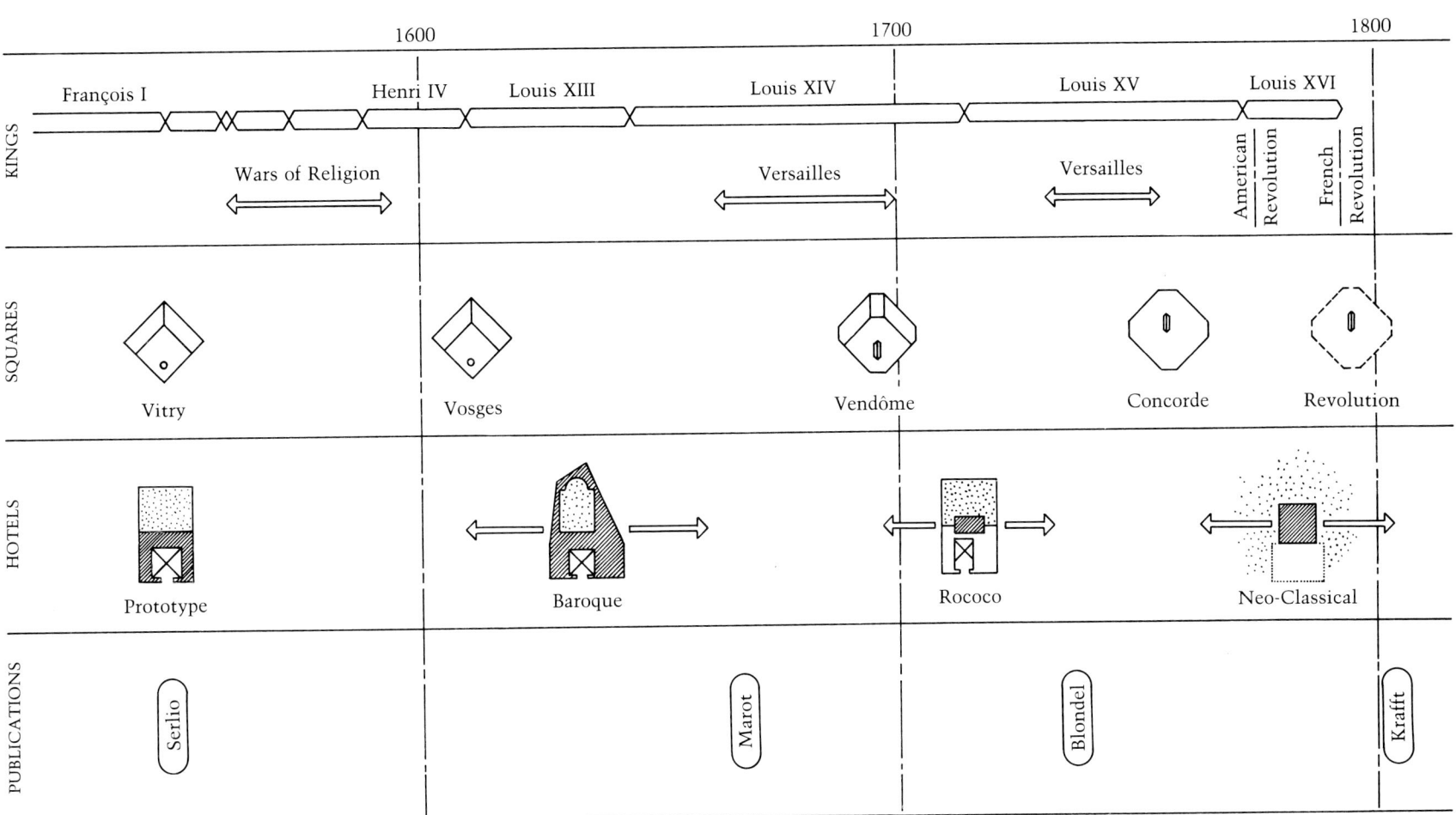

4
Graphic diagram of
the time-line chart,
1500–1800

5
Time-line chart of kings, architects, squares, *hôtels*, and publications, 1500–1800

11 *The Anatomy of History*

6
Paris, the Turgot plan,
1734–39

Baroque type in the Marais and Richelieu districts of Paris. This period of construction ended around 1661, when Louis XIV assumed the rule, and was followed by a gap in production of some forty years. These *hôtels* were published in Jean Marot's *L'Architecture françoise*, known as the *Grand Marot*, in 1670.

The third period of *hôtel* construction began about 1700 with Louis XIV's royal square, the Place Louis-le-Grand (now the Place Vendôme) in the western part of Paris. The *hôtels* of this period were also built in the same general area: in the Faubourg St.-Honoré near the Place Louis-le-Grand on the right bank and in the newly developing suburb of the Faubourg St.-Germain on the left bank. The first *hôtels* constructed during this era continued the Baroque type of the previous period, but there was soon a transformation to the transitional type, the Rococo. By 1723, when Louis XV took the throne and after the court had returned to Versailles, the majority of the Rococo *hôtels* had already been constructed. Also at this time theoreticians such as Courtonne and Briseux observed and articulated a notable change in interior planning, and in society. The last Rococo *hôtels* were constructed in the early 1730s. P. J. Mariette had published most of the Rococo *hôtels* in 1727, and they were republished by J.-F. Blondel, with some additions, beginning in 1752.

After another interruption of domestic urban building construction, the last period began in the early 1750s with the competition for the Parisian royal square dedicated to Louis XV, the result of which is now known as the Place de la Concorde. This square was followed by a large number of *hôtels* of the Neoclassical type in the northern sections of Paris beyond the *boulevards*.

The French Revolution effectively marks the end of the Neoclassical period, whose *hôtels* were published by Krafft and Ransonnette shortly after 1800 (1802?). Krafft's limited text effectively summarizes the last three periods and therefore the three *hôtel* types. He says that the *hôtels* of the first type, the Baroque *hôtels* of the age of Louis XIV, had impressive exteriors but lacked sophisticated interior planning; that the Rococo *hôtels* associated with Louis XV made great advances in convenient internal arrangements, but at the expense of external development; and, finally, that the architects of the late eighteenth century were able to combine the virtues of the two previous eras while eliminating the shortcomings, thus making the Neoclassical *hôtels* of the last period into "masterpieces" of domestic architecture.

It cannot be overemphasized that the gaps or discontinuities in production that separated the various periods did not produce similar discontinuities in the architectural morphology of the *hôtel*. Rather, there is an articulate and essentially continuous sequence of development. Inventions occur within the conventions, and occasionally prophetic or revolutionary works appear, but the sharp focus of our selectivity and the clarity conferred by hindsight enhance their "visibility."

The main body of this book—the part dealing with the *hôtel*—is organized according to the outline described above. There is a chapter for each of the four periods, and each chapter follows the sequence: royal squares–*hôtels*–publication. Next are two chapters on the twentieth century and an excursus about the unique American relationship to the material. The two modern chapters are intended to follow the main body, but they are also somewhat independent and might just as easily be read first. "Architecture and the Cumulative City," for example, could profitably be read as the introduction because it was, after all, the beginning—the reason for a new examination of the *hôtel*.

But a word of caution: although this book deals with fundamental architectural issues, it is not for the beginner, nor can it have much meaning without substantive understanding of modern architecture. To take it alone, to assume it to be a total repudiation of modernism, would be a misinterpretation. After all, the lady may suffer from agoraphobia exacerbated by a kind of architectural anorexia, but she also has many redeeming qualities and seems reluctant to acknowledge reports of her demise.

Finally then, this study is about the art of the plan—the plan as generator, as an abstraction of space, as a precise instrument of urbanism, but above all as an abstraction of the vertical surface. I therefore hope that it will invite speculation not only about the making of plans and cities, but also about the poetry of the wall in a time when it is virtually a lost art.

7
Garches in Venice, montage

8
Frontispiece of Claude Perrault's translation of Vitruvius, 1673. Engraving by Sebastien Mercier. Three of Perrault's principal works are represented: in the left foreground, the triumphal arch for the Porte St.-Antoine (now the Place de la Nation); in the middle ground, the east facade of the Louvre; in the background, the Observatoire.

9
Hôtel de Beauvais, upper floor plan, Antoine Le Pautre, 1652–55

1 Public versus Private

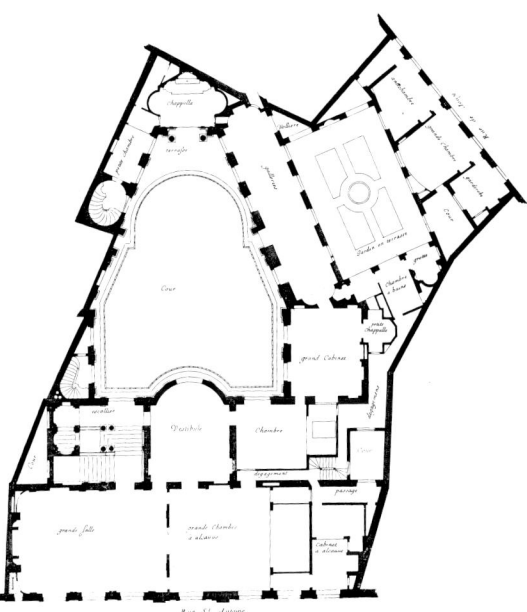

Theory and Practice

From about 1500 until at least 1700 (if not 1750, or even 1790), architectural theory in France was involved with the extension and development of Italian Renaissance ideas in public buildings such as Versailles; but from the middle of the sixteenth century, French practice was involved with private buildings—the *hôtels*—which were based on different principles and which were to prefigure a new style, a new social order, and a new sensibility. As an extension of the Italian Renaissance, the public architecture of Baroque France tended to be based on Palladian ideas and therefore to favor total design, freestanding buildings, overall symmetry, integration between inside and outside, and unity through continuity. The private architecture of the *hôtels*, on the other hand, was derived from French models and developed a completely different system based on asymmetry, articulation, and discontinuity. In contrast to the public buildings, the *hôtels* were initially urban infill, or party-wall buildings; it was only later, as the social order changed, that they began to assume the freestanding characteristics of the public buildings. Thus the French *hôtel* can be seen as an all-inclusive critique of the public architecture of Baroque France and of Palladian ideals as well.

The differences between public and private buildings may be attributable simply to a hierarchy of subject matter—to the architectural equivalent of the genres in classical painting: at the top of the hierarchy were the public and religious buildings; below that in importance were the *hôtels* of the nobility; and still further down were the dwellings of the lower classes. Naturally, most architectural energy was focused at the top of the pyramid, and almost none at the bottom. Even within the upper categories of architectural endeavor, there was sometimes little exchange (especially in the eighteenth century) because the most prominent architects, such as J. H. Mansart, were preoccupied with major public commissions and some, such as Jacques-Germain Soufflot, were not involved with *hôtels* at all. On the other hand, many other architects—Aubert, Mollet, Cartaud, etc.—spent most of their professional lives involved only with domestic buildings.

The point is that it was in the realm of the most important public monuments that the great polemical battles were fought (such as that over the east front of the Louvre), and this may have protected the domestic architecture of the *hôtels* from the white heat of French theory, thus allowing the unfettered growth of another sensibility. In the restricted public realm, theory was indispensable and indeed preceded building, while in the private arena theory was somehow more relaxed, more flexible—here building preceded theory. It is as if tradition and the idea of type were sufficient to sate the French domestic appetite, but the public main course demanded more self-conscious attention and explanation.

The most important difference between public and private buildings was their relation to the ideal and the circumstantial. Public buildings exhibited an almost complete insistence on the classical ideal—on symmetry, regularity, and unity—and a great resistance to any accommodation of the empirical. The *hôtels* were less impervious to the empirical and the particular. It is not that domestic buildings did not subscribe to the ideal, but rather that in the case of the *hôtel*, circumstance frequently necessitated deformation of the ideal, of the type. This new combining of the ideal and the circumstantial was the beginning of an alternative tradition.

These two traditions reflect, more generally, the overlapping of two cultures: the classical world of the *ancien régime* and the beginnings of modern society. As Rudolf Wittkower pointed out in his essay "Classical Theory and Eighteenth-Century Sensibility," it was during the eighteenth century that "deeply rooted classical convictions, maxims and beliefs" were finally demolished, and that "before the eighteenth century[,] sensibility never led to or sanctioned relativity." Wittkower also notes that it was primarily nonartists who were responsible for revolutionary speculations on art during the eighteenth century, while artists and particularly architects never strayed far from theories that were "embedded in a classical-idealist framework of references focused on absolute standards."[1] Since Palladian ideals dominated public architecture, the tradition of the *hôtel* was as close as architecture came to breaking away from the absolute standards of the past.

Palladio and the Italian Renaissance: Unity and Continuity

Italian Renaissance architecture was marked from its inception by a basic tension between attitudes toward order and toward space. The tendency toward cosmic unity was most effectively represented by the centralized plan, with its conceptually pure, finite, ideal order; while practical consideration and enthusiasm for perspective encouraged a worldly spatial continuity, best represented by axial plans, with their pragmatically accommodating and perceptually organized episodes. These opposing tendencies are illustrated by both church and secular plan types. If, for example, the Florentine *palazzo* type with its squarish plan and focus on the central courtyard is the secular version of the centralized church, then, in contrast, the Venetian *palazzo* type with its linear plan and focus at its ends is analogous to the Latin cross church. In both religious and secular cases, the centralized plan tends to forsake sequence for unity, while the linear plans tend to forsake unity for sequence and continuity. Thus, from the early Renaissance of the Pazzi Chapel to the Baroque of Versailles and Blenheim, the architectural quest was for a combination of unity and continuity. The primary issues were the relationship of the part to the whole (a progression from independent and articulate parts to the subjugation of the part to the whole); the relationship of the outside to the inside (a progression toward unification); the problems of centrality and symmetry (a progression from quadrilateral symmetry to bilateral symmetry); and, lastly, the spatial relationship to the environment (a progression from the closed, finite, shallow spatial

10
Rome, plan for St. Peter's, Bramante, c. 1506

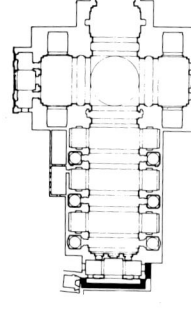

11
Mantua, S. Andrea, plan, Alberti, 1470

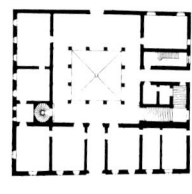

12
Florence, Palazzo Medici-Riccardi, plan, Michelozzo, 1444–64

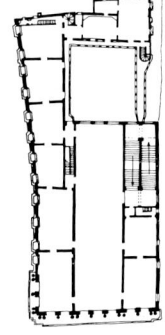

13
Venice, Ca' Pesaro, plan, Longhena, 1676–1710

organizations of the early Renaissance to the open, extended, deep space developments of the Baroque).

Andrea Palladio was a central figure in the quest, for he summed up early and high Renaissance ideals and prefigured the Baroque. He was able to fuse the ideals of unity and continuity by combining the central and sequential plan types and so became the undisputed master of the totally controlled plan. Since the totally ordered plan is the foundation of French public architecture, and is the antithesis of the French *hôtel* plan, just how it is achieved is of some consequence to this investigation.

One of Palladio's most brilliant inventions and the key to his villas is his fusion of the Roman house type with the Venetian plan type. The essence of this invention can be clearly seen in one of his studies for the plan of the Palazzo Barbaran in Vicenza. Here the Roman sequence of atrium, tablinum, and peristyle have, in effect, been compressed laterally and inserted into the *portego*, or central hall, of a Venetian three-part plan, thus qualifying and giving sequence to the otherwise excessively long and inarticulate Venetian hall. From this plan it is easy to see the derivation of the more complex five-part schema for the villas[2] and, in addition, to see the villas as fragments of Roman houses, where only part of the plan is built and the rest of the spatial sequence is only implied.

The primary grid of this prototypical schema and the system of proportions together control and order both the figural central space and the secondary rooms of the typical Palladian villa plan. In addition, there is a secondary system of gridding which further subdivides the plan and contributes to the relationship of the inside to the outside. While the central space is reflected directly on the facade by the portico or loggia, the windows in the solid side portions of the facade align with the doors of the secondary rooms, which are themselves arranged in series, or *enfilade*. These axial relationships then produce a secondary grid of slots, or zones of space, which unites the rooms and relates them to the exterior. In the Villa Foscari, *La Malcontenta*, the system is carried even further by the frescoes of the walls: a trabeated system of painted columns and beams actually frames not only the real windows and doors, but also painted landscapes and architectural details. Thus each room is gridded phenomenally and literally in a manner similar to the overall building. This control of plan, section, and elevation results in a unity rarely achieved until Palladio.

Indeed, with the typical Palladian plan it is difficult to imagine that a problem ever existed. If, as Wittkower has suggested, "classical aesthetics saw beauty and truth in the simple and typical,"[3] then the Palladian plan was surely an inspiration to the classical-idealist mentality. As such, it differed in four important ways from the plan of the French *hôtel:* in the ordered gridding of the plan, section, and elevation; in the use of only rectangular and functionally generalized rooms; in the insistence on bilateral symmetry; and in the open sequence of space along a central axis. These are also precisely the characteristics so cherished by French architects of Baroque public buildings.

The axial implications of Palladio's interpretation of the Roman plan, and his use of layered space and facades, made it possible to build up more complex compositions using loggias and out-buildings to extend the axes and spaces of the central block deep into the landscape and, at the same time, to frame the central block and tie it to the land. Of his many schemes for both flat and hilltop sites, the unrealized project for the Villa Trissino at Meledo is somehow the most compelling and influential. Its combined implications of central focus and spatial extension must have appealed to Baroque architects in general and certainly influenced the *château* at Versailles and Blenheim Palace.

18 Public versus Private

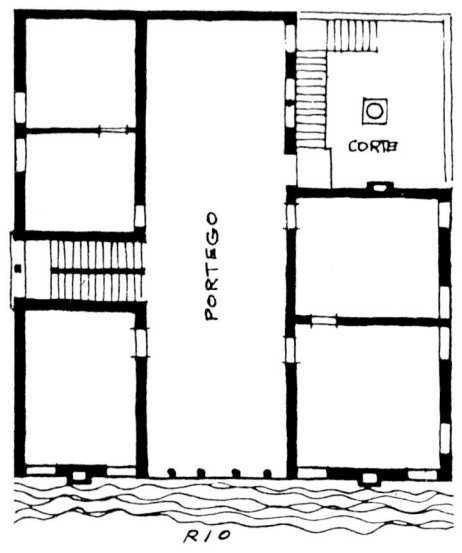
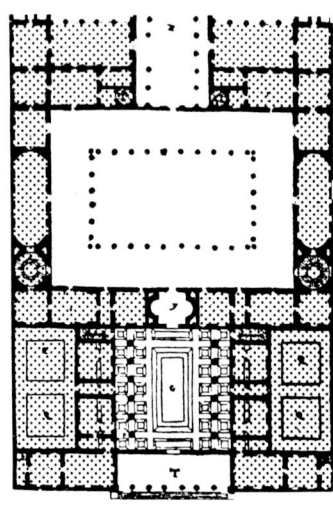
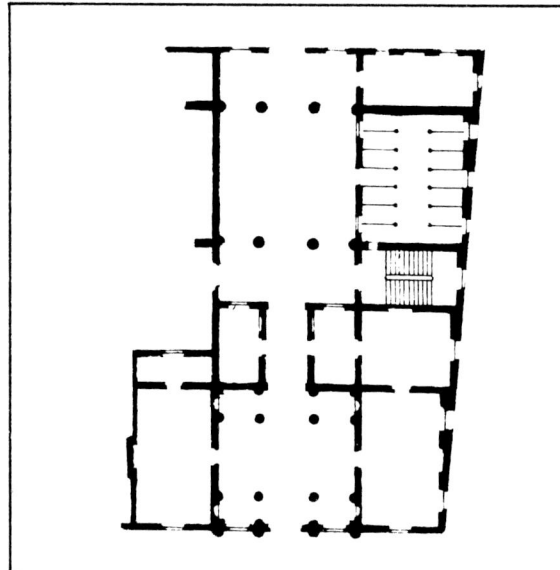

14
Plan of typical Venetian *palazzo*

15
Roman house reconstruction, Palladio

16
Study for the Palazzo Barbaran, Palladio

17
Montagnana, Villa Pisani, plan, Palladio, 1553

18
Geometric scheme of Palladian villas, after Wittkower

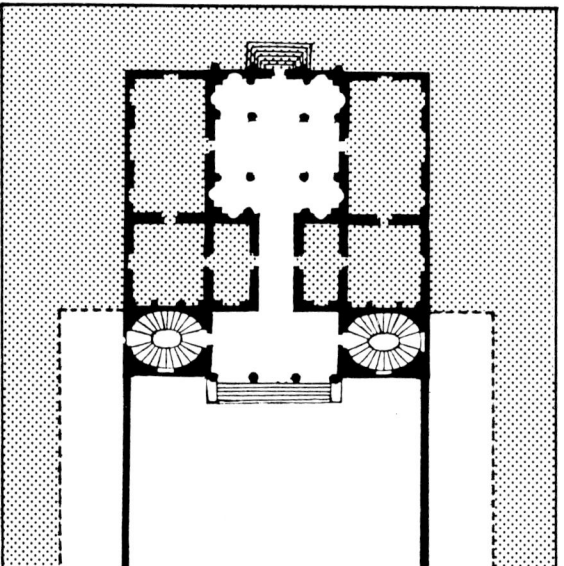
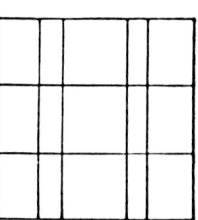

18 Public versus Private

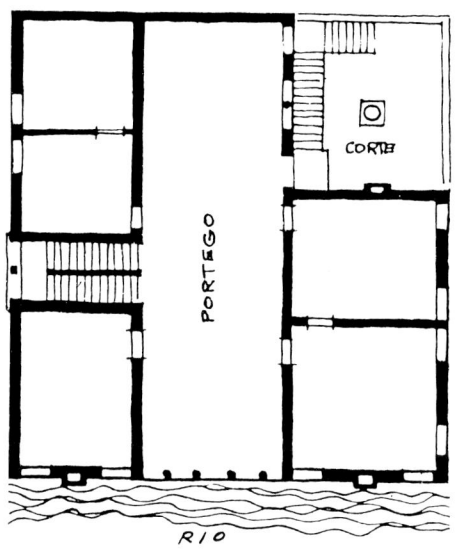

14
Plan of typical Venetian *palazzo*

15
Roman house reconstruction, Palladio

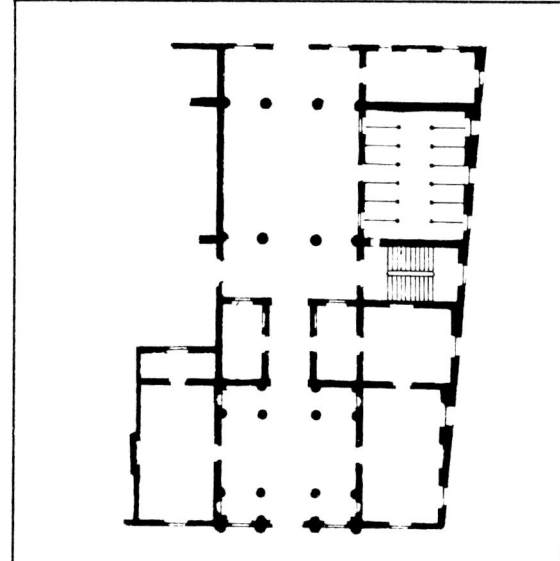

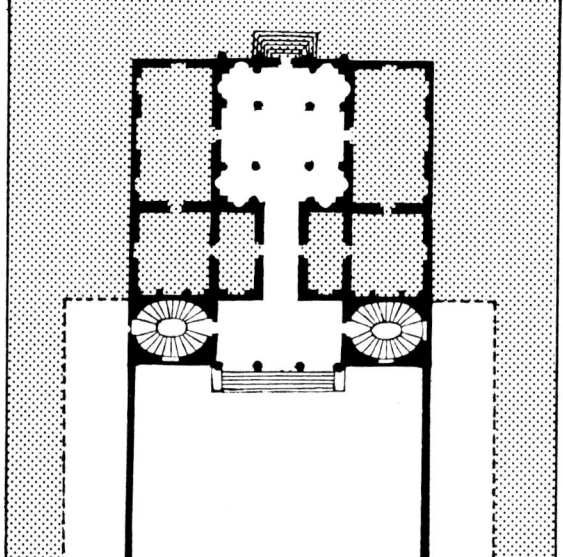

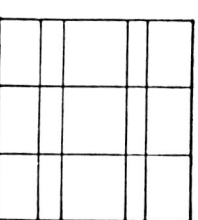

16
Study for the Palazzo Barbaran, Palladio

17
Montagnana, Villa Pisani, plan, Palladio, 1553

18
Geometric scheme of Palladian villas, after Wittkower

organizations of the early Renaissance to the open, extended, deep space developments of the Baroque).

Andrea Palladio was a central figure in the quest, for he summed up early and high Renaissance ideals and prefigured the Baroque. He was able to fuse the ideals of unity and continuity by combining the central and sequential plan types and so became the undisputed master of the totally controlled plan. Since the totally ordered plan is the foundation of French public architecture, and is the antithesis of the French *hôtel* plan, just how it is achieved is of some consequence to this investigation.

One of Palladio's most brilliant inventions and the key to his villas is his fusion of the Roman house type with the Venetian plan type. The essence of this invention can be clearly seen in one of his studies for the plan of the Palazzo Barbaran in Vicenza. Here the Roman sequence of atrium, tablinum, and peristyle have, in effect, been compressed laterally and inserted into the *portego*, or central hall, of a Venetian three-part plan, thus qualifying and giving sequence to the otherwise excessively long and inarticulate Venetian hall. From this plan it is easy to see the derivation of the more complex five-part schema for the villas[2] and, in addition, to see the villas as fragments of Roman houses, where only part of the plan is built and the rest of the spatial sequence is only implied.

The primary grid of this prototypical schema and the system of proportions together control and order both the figural central space and the secondary rooms of the typical Palladian villa plan. In addition, there is a secondary system of gridding which further subdivides the plan and contributes to the relationship of the inside to the outside. While the central space is reflected directly on the facade by the portico or loggia, the windows in the solid side portions of the facade align with the doors of the secondary rooms, which are themselves arranged in series, or *enfilade*. These axial relationships then produce a secondary grid of slots, or zones of space, which unites the rooms and relates them to the exterior. In the Villa Foscari, *La Malcontenta*, the system is carried even further by the frescoes of the walls: a trabeated system of painted columns and beams actually frames not only the real windows and doors, but also painted landscapes and architectural details. Thus each room is gridded phenomenally and literally in a manner similar to the overall building. This control of plan, section, and elevation results in a unity rarely achieved until Palladio.

Indeed, with the typical Palladian plan it is difficult to imagine that a problem ever existed. If, as Wittkower has suggested, "classical aesthetics saw beauty and truth in the simple and typical,"[3] then the Palladian plan was surely an inspiration to the classical-idealist mentality. As such, it differed in four important ways from the plan of the French *hôtel:* in the ordered gridding of the plan, section, and elevation; in the use of only rectangular and functionally generalized rooms; in the insistence on bilateral symmetry; and in the open sequence of space along a central axis. These are also precisely the characteristics so cherished by French architects of Baroque public buildings.

The axial implications of Palladio's interpretation of the Roman plan, and his use of layered space and facades, made it possible to build up more complex compositions using loggias and out-buildings to extend the axes and spaces of the central block deep into the landscape and, at the same time, to frame the central block and tie it to the land. Of his many schemes for both flat and hilltop sites, the unrealized project for the Villa Trissino at Meledo is somehow the most compelling and influential. Its combined implications of central focus and spatial extension must have appealed to Baroque architects in general and certainly influenced the *château* at Versailles and Blenheim Palace.

19 Palladio and the Italian Renaissance

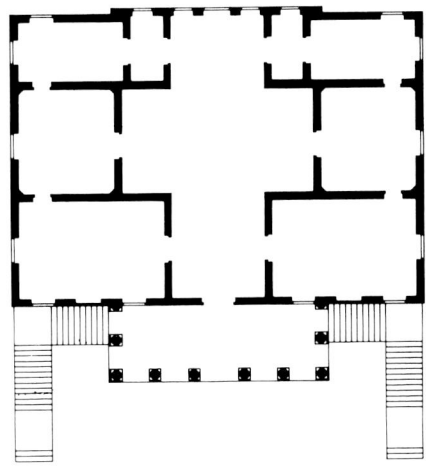

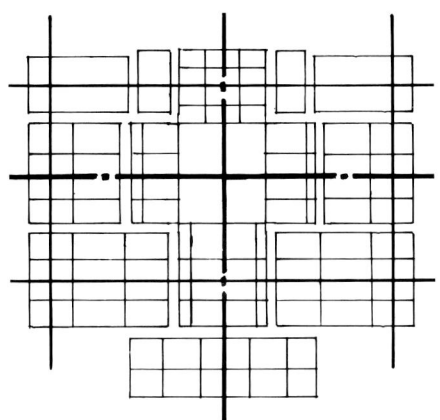

19
Villa Foscari (*La Malcontenta*), plan, Palladio, c. 1550

20
Geometric scheme of Villa Foscari

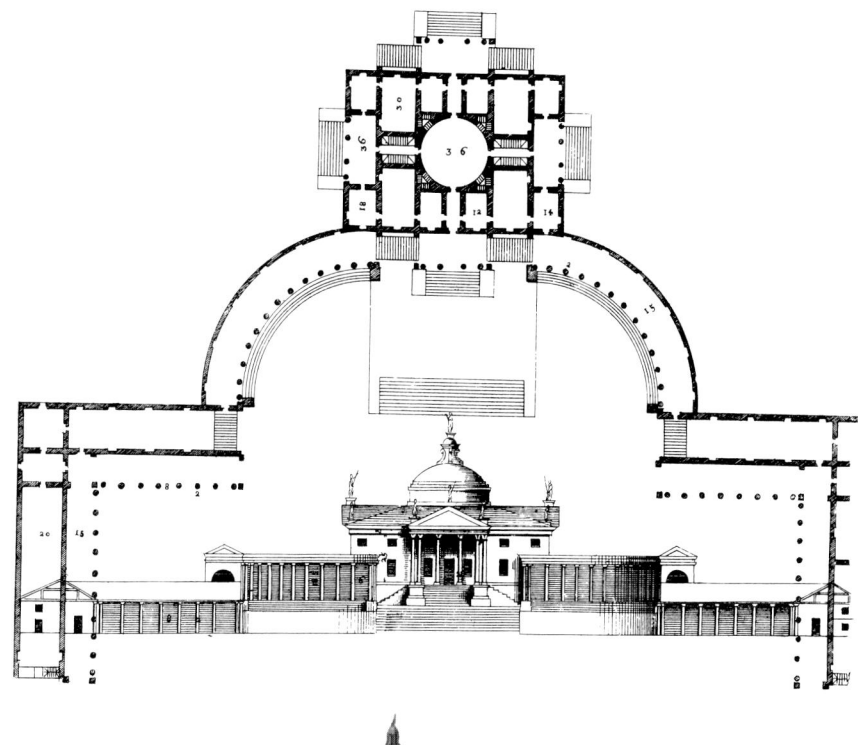

21
Meledo, Villa Trissino, plan, Palladio, c. 1553

22
Meledo, Villa Trissino, model

Versailles and Blenheim: Total Design

Versailles and Blenheim represent the apex of Baroque culture and planning in France and Britain. The *château* and the palace are enormous buildings that appear small only in the context of their elaborately developed and controlled landscapes. Both buildings open to the surroundings on one side, and, conversely, both have a central focus that is the result of a compositional buildup beginning implicitly, if not literally, at the horizon. At Blenheim the center is occupied by the hall; at Versailles, by the bedroom of Louis XIV. It had taken approximately two-and-a-half centuries to go from the fractured city-states of the early Renaissance to the axis-mundi passing through the king's bedroom at Versailles. The concentration of power that was achieved during that time was ominous; and as the symbol of Louis XIV and the seventeenth century, Versailles still represents the epitome of the tyranny of public life, of total architectural and social control. As Hamlin explains:

One might choose the "Levée du Roi" in Versailles as perhaps the most expressive . . . of Baroque scenes. In that square monumental room, crowded behind the white-and-gold balustrade which cuts it in half, stand the favored few of the vast court, to watch in silence as the king gets up from his gorgeous satin-hung bed, aided by the correct court officers, with a ritual which controlled almost every motion.[4]

The pageantry that characterized Baroque culture was supported, at least through the seventeenth century, by French architectural theory. Architects favored rectangular rooms, direct relationship of facade to plan, freestanding buildings, and above all, symmetry. (The unrelenting rigor of this system apparently prompted Mme de Maintenon, during the last years of Louis XIV, to complain that unless something changed she would even be obliged to "die in symmetry."[5]) The plans of both Versailles and Blenheim are generally gridded, and the rooms, arranged in *enfilade*, are contained and unified. "What the French liked," Emil Kaufmann observes, "was . . . to express the ideas of both unification and differentiation distinctly, but without any exaggeration. Any abruptness was to be softened; the harsh exigencies of the Baroque system were to be reconciled to the refined national taste."[6]

Louis Le Vau: Differentiation and Discontinuity

Two notable exceptions to the Baroque emphasis on totally unified order are the Château de Vaux-le-Vicomte and the Collège des Quatre Nations, both the work of Louis Le Vau. Each illustrates a different aspect of an underlying problem: the former is an example of discontinuity in internal planning, the latter of discontinuity in urban design. Le Vau did not attempt to conceal the inner contradictions of the Baroque system, but rather chose to express them by allowing one part to rule over the others, absolutely.[7] He did not soften abruptness, and he so exaggerated differences that a distinct schism developed between the public and private realms. He then exploited the schism.

The main building at Vaux-le-Vicomte is freestanding and bilaterally symmetrical, and the rooms relate regularly to the facade openings. Of primary interest, however, are the central vestibule and the domed oval salon, which protrudes past the rear facade of the building in a convex curve. Conversely, a shallow, curved recession on the entry side of the building contains a projecting central bay that is nonetheless set back from the frontal surface of the block. Thus the building is a rather narrow rectangular block penetrated through its minor axis by a figure or sequence that is out of phase with the rest of the plan. The primary axis of this central sequence connects the exterior spaces of front and back, and only the secondary axis extends laterally in *enfilade* from the oval salon to unite the bank of primary rooms. In contrast to most Palladian villas, the rest of the rooms are not related in *enfilade* but by

23
Versailles, site plan of the *château*. Engraving by Le Pautre.

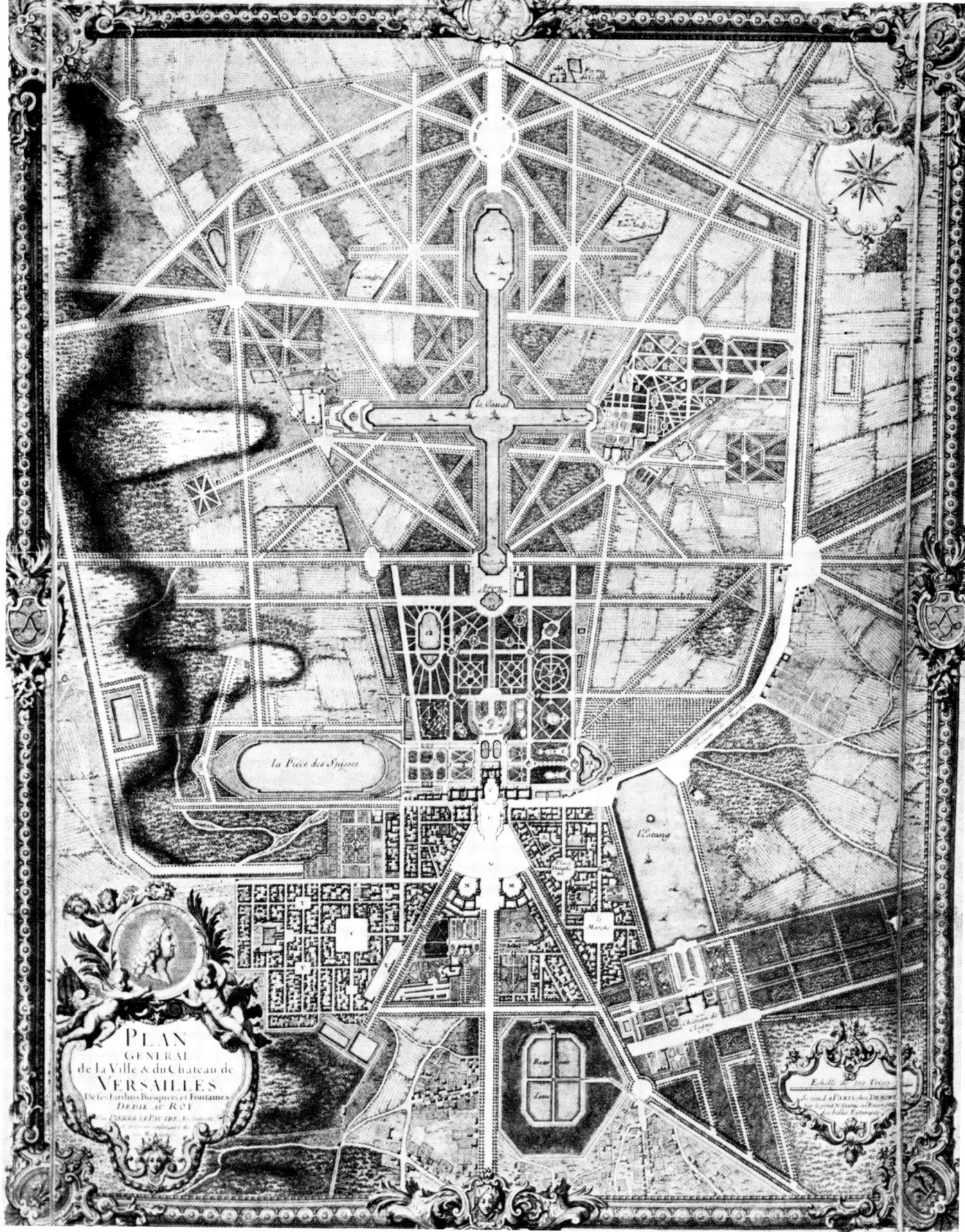

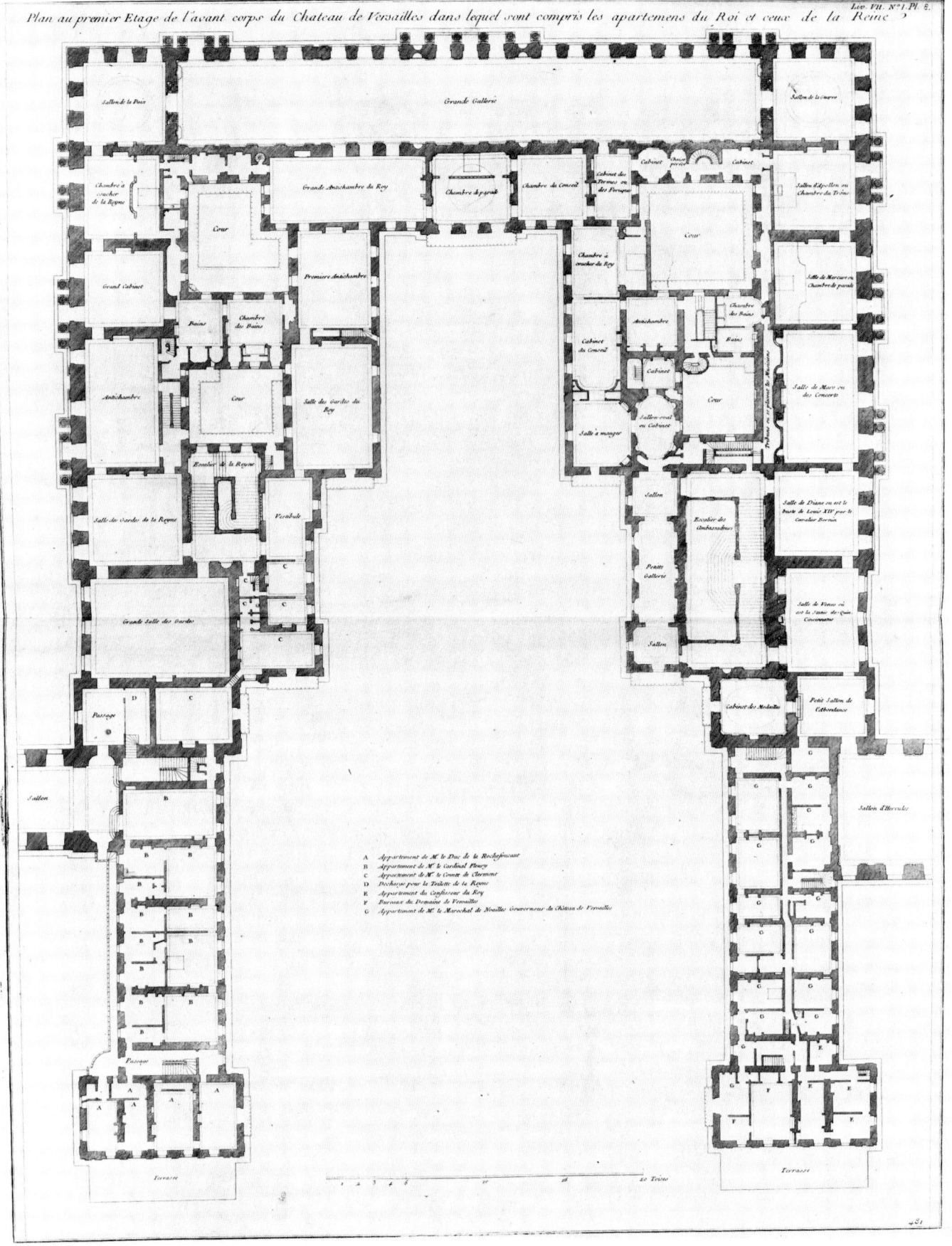

24
Versailles, plan

25
Versailles. Engraving by Perelle.

23 Louis Le Vau

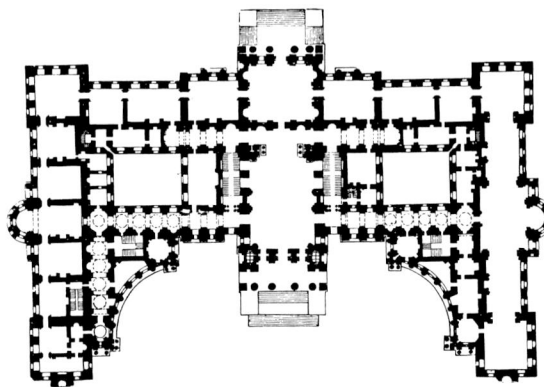

26
Blenheim Palace, plan,
Vanbrugh, 1705

27
Blenheim Palace, aerial
view

a more random series of connections. The result is that these areas of the plan—the private parts of the house—form a kind of residue, or *poché*, distinct from the public rooms. The grand public sequence thus seems a function of the site rather than of the building, and a separation between public and private is thereby provided.

The principle of discontinuity is also employed by Le Vau in the Collège des Quatre Nations. Here the schism is not so much between the internal parts of the plan, but between the monumental civic structure of Paris and the normative residential texture lying behind Le Vau's site. The Collège is located directly across the Seine from the square court of the Louvre and just at the point where the old wall of Philip Augustus met the river at an odd angle. Having an irregular site and only a limited depth within which to work, Le Vau designed a facade that is regular and symmetrical toward the river and reminiscent of Palladio but that also serves as a veneer for a completely disparate organization. The facade frames the domed central block and presents a public face to the river and Louvre beyond, but with its discontinuity from front to back, the plan could not be further from the totally controlled plans of Palladio.

Discontinuity, whether between exterior and interior or between public and private, did not exist for Palladio; he favored unity and continuity. If Louis Le Vau's exploitation of the opposite principles of differentiation and discontinuity were unique among French public buildings, then it must be emphasized that this special whim or talent was, in time, to become almost uniquely French and that this type of designed discontinuity is the core of domestic French architecture—of the French *hôtel*.

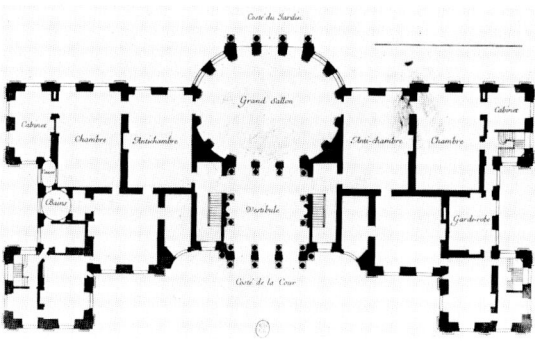

28
Vaux-le-Vicomte, plan, Louis Le Vau, c. 1656–60

29
Vaux-le-Vicomte, spatial sequence

30
Vaux-le-Vicomte, aerial view

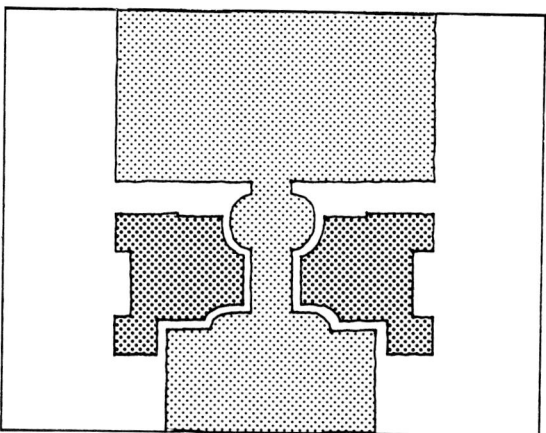

26 Public versus Private

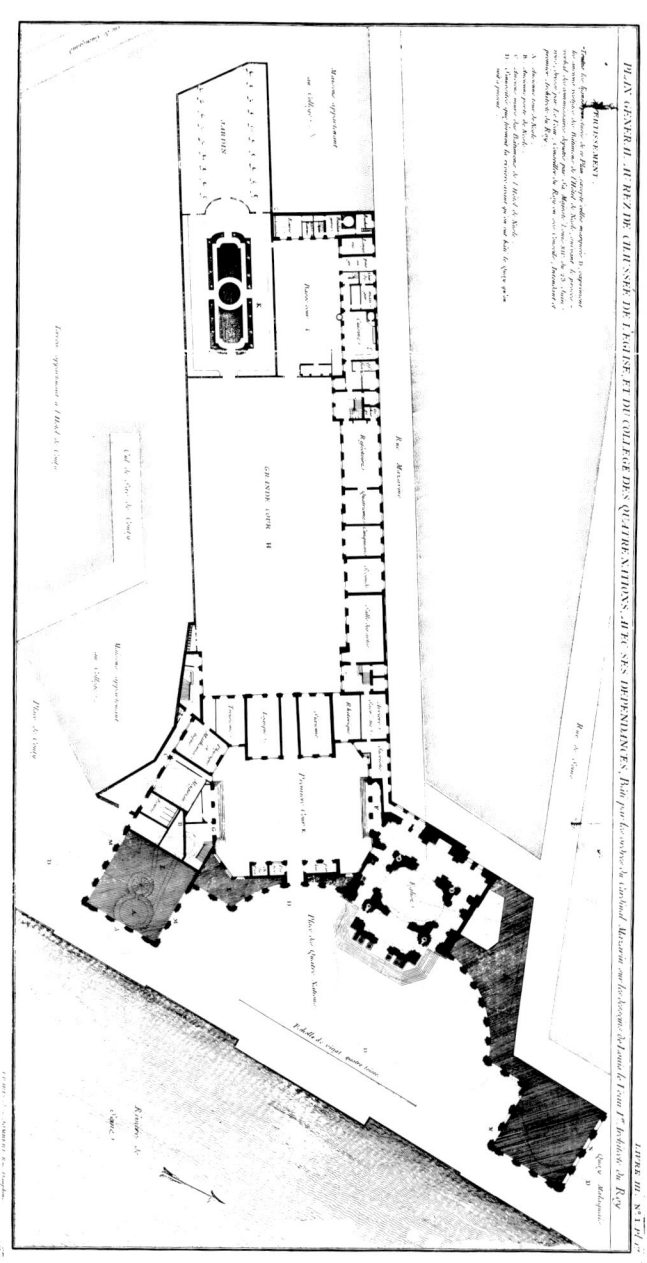

31
Collège des Quatre
Nations. Engraving.

32
Collège des Quatre
Nations, plan, Louis Le
Vau, 1660–68

33
Detail from the Turgot plan showing the Collège des Quatre Nations and its relationship to the urban structure of Paris in 1739

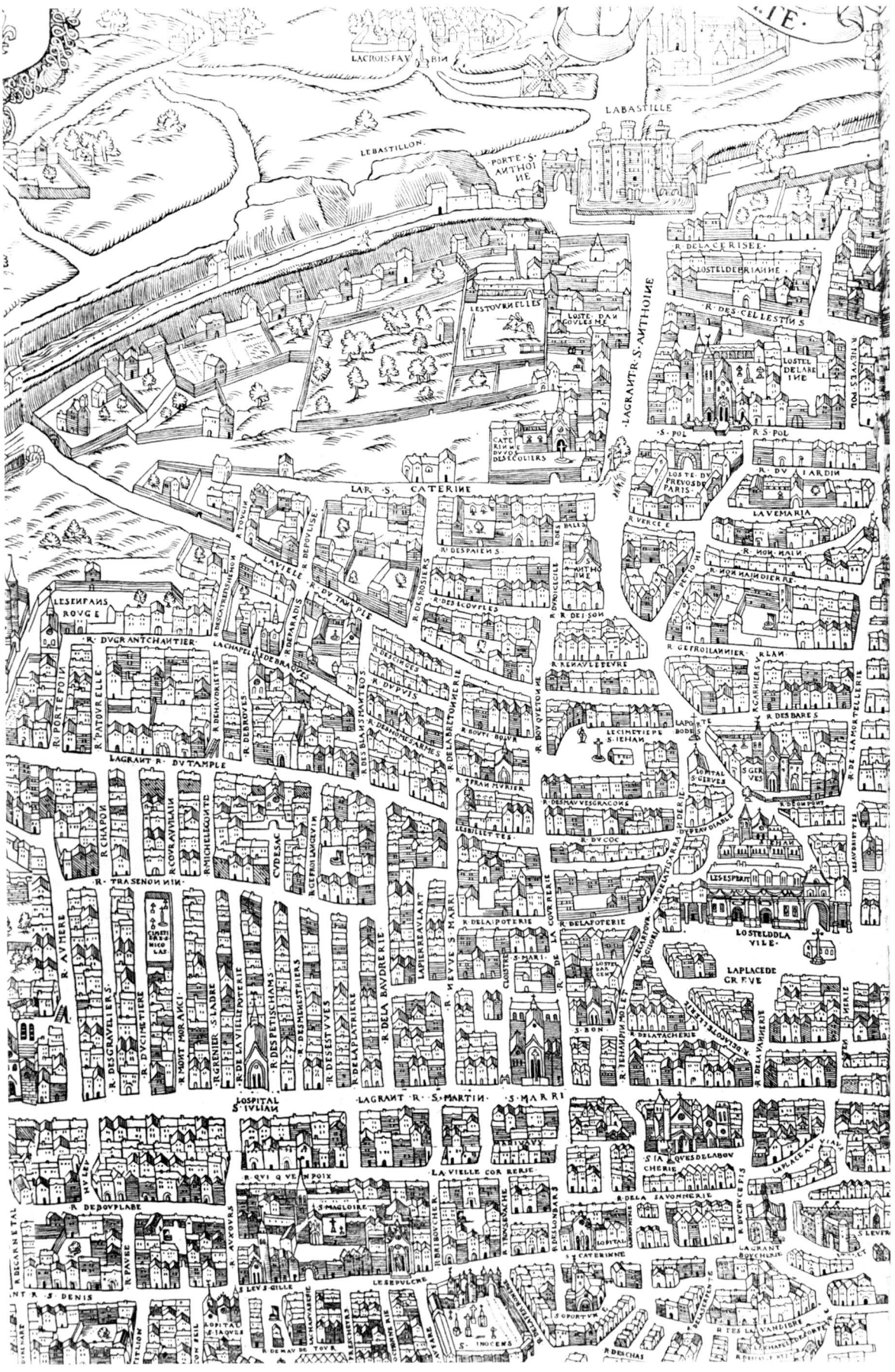

34
Paris, Le Marais, before 1559. Detail from the Truschet and Hoyau plan.

35
Vigevano, Piazza Ducale, Bramante, 1492–94

2 *The Prototypes*

Italian Renaissance Space

The prototypes for the royal squares, *hôtels*, and illustrated architectural books appeared near the middle of the sixteenth century at the end of the reign of François I. They resulted from the second wave of Italian influence, which coincided with Sebastiano Serlio's arrival in France in 1540 or 1541. While each prototype was affected in some way by French taste—the "modo di Francia"—each was fundamentally a crisp product of the Italian Renaissance, and each profoundly influenced subsequent French developments. Their timeliness was also an important factor, for they occurred as Paris was about to become the seat of French government, thereby ensuring the city's long-range development. François I's intention to make Paris the capital of France was continued by successive French kings, and although the Wars of Religion severely curtailed the construction of public buildings during the last half of the sixteenth century, the construction of town houses continued unabated because the upper classes needed to be near the court. Few examples of domestic architecture survive from this period, but it firmly established the new style and the urban destiny of Paris.[1] Two famous views of the city bracket this period and record the changes between François I and Henri IV: the plan called "Aux Trois Personnages" of c. 1540 and the Merian plan of 1614.

The invasion of Italian taste at the end of the fifteenth and the beginning of the sixteenth century may have been marked more by an enthusiasm for Italian Renaissance details and envy of Italian culture than by understanding of either, but the second wave of Italian influence around 1540 was of special significance. During this period, the Italian concept of space—Renaissance space—was introduced into French architecture and urbanism. In Italy the discovery of perspective and the resultant enthusiasm for willfully controlled architectural space had completely transformed architecture. Space was the medium of the age, the principal means of articulating a new view of the universe. In Florence the medieval tower house had been replaced by the courtyard buildings of the Renaissance, and, conceptually, the casual aggregate of the Piazza della Signoria gave way to the restrained will of the Piazza SS. Annunziata. In France an analogous change occurred as the medieval castle was transformed from a highly figural, apparently solid, freestanding fortress into a large courtyard building with attached gardens and as the porousness of the bastide town square was replaced by the regular closure of the Renaissance *place*. The most compelling image of Italian Renaissance urbanism, and the prelude to the French residential squares, was the Piazza Ducale in Vigevano (1492–94).[2]

The Place Ducale at Vitry-le-François

In France the first example of this new urbanism and the prototype for the royal squares of Paris was the Place Ducale of Vitry-le-François.[3] Begun in 1545 by Girolamo Marini, Vitry-le-François was a fortified grid town composed of sixteen square blocks. The Place Ducale occupies the center of town at the intersection of the two principal streets, but because these streets penetrate the square at the center rather than at the edges, the space is clearer and more contained than those of the bastide towns. Except for the cathedral in one corner, the facades of the square are regular and repetitive, and the cornice and roofs form a continuous horizontal line that is crucial to the perception of the space. The houses surrounding the square are all of the same fixed depth—like a thick wall—with the public space of the square on one side and the private space of the block interiors on the other. It is as if an ideal space had been cut out of the urban fabric and was then provided with a unified liner or facade. The platonic regularity of this space was a new concept to France. If the ideal regularity of the urban fabric surrounding the square and the presence of smaller sub-squares tended to diminish the contrast between structure and event, between figural void and background texture, the contrast would be emphasized later in the Place Royale in Paris. The Place Ducale was quickly followed by other squares in new towns such as Navarrenx and Philippeville, but the square of Vitry-le-François was more unified.

Had the Wars of Religion not intervened, Paris would also have had a royal square and a coherent example of Renaissance urbanism half a century earlier than it ultimately did. After Henri II was killed in a jousting tournament on the grounds of the old royal palace, the Hôtel des Tournelles in the Marais, his widow, Catherine de Médicis, had the building destroyed. Four years later, in 1563, a proposal was made to use the abandoned site for a new urban development, a residential square of uniform houses, to be called the Place de Valois. Unfortunately, no graphic records of this project exist,[4] but it is known that Philibert de L'Orme's brother Jean was to have designed the streets and spaces. The site remained derelict until the late sixteenth century, when it was used as a horse market by Henri IV's minister, Sully, before being developed as the Place Royale by Henri IV.

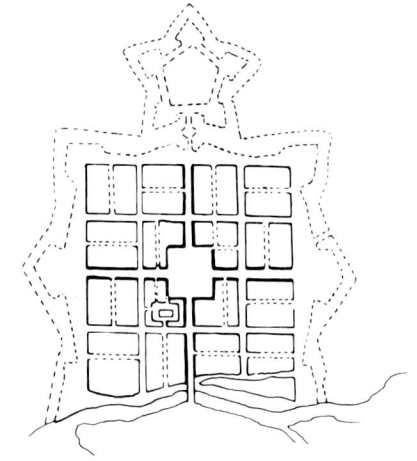

36
Vitry-le-François, plan, Girolamo Marini, begun 1545

37
Vitry-le-François, Place Ducale, aerial view

Le Grand Ferrare

The Italian Renaissance spatial sensibility also figures prominently in the development of the French *hôtel* in the middle of the sixteenth century, but the earliest traces of this new attitude toward space and volume may be seen in the *châteaux* of Bury (1511–24) and Villandry (1532). The traditional French medieval *château* had been a square block with round turrets at the corners—a fortified object-building; the *châteaux* of Bury and Villandry, however, are courtyard buildings with strong horizontal emphasis and relatively simple flat walls—a revolutionary change and the pattern for later *châteaux*. Bury, in fact, is the country ancestor to the "classic" *hôtel* of the late sixteenth century: a U-shaped courtyard building in which the main living rooms occupy a *corps-de-logis* between the forecourt and the formal garden to the rear. The two side wings define the forecourt and contain the secondary rooms on one side and a long gallery on the other, and the fourth side of the court is closed by a low screen wall and the main entry gate. A service court to one side and another garden complete the organization of Bury; thus, only the round turrets at the corners clearly mark the building as a country *château* and not an urban *hôtel*. Town houses of the late fifteenth and early sixteenth centuries were also courtyard buildings, and were in general the urban ancestors to the "classic" *hôtel*,[5] but most were a picturesque mélange of medieval and Renaissance motifs and lacked the spatial clarity of the *châteaux* of Bury and Villandry.

There are thus two models for the French *hôtel*—one urban, the other rural—and later *hôtels* were never able to shed completely the

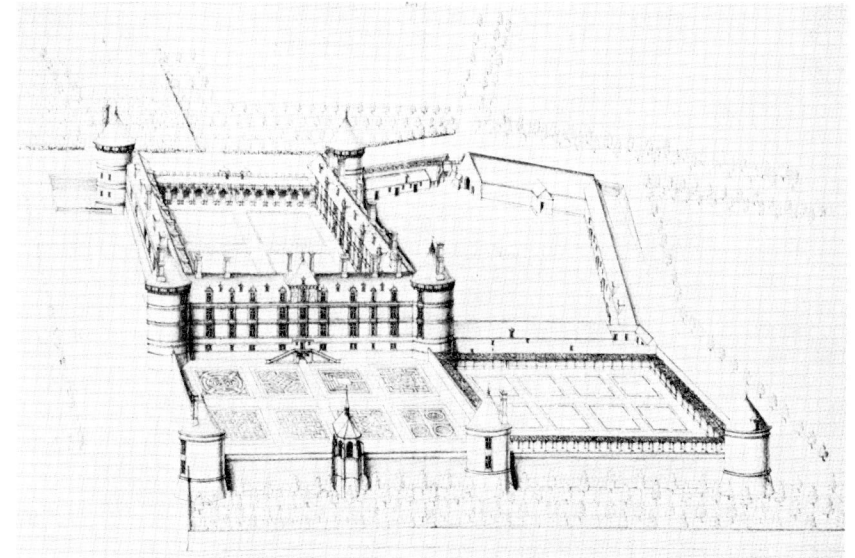

38
Bury, *château*, 1511–24.
Drawing by Du Cerceau.

39
Villandry, *château*, 1532

32 The Prototypes

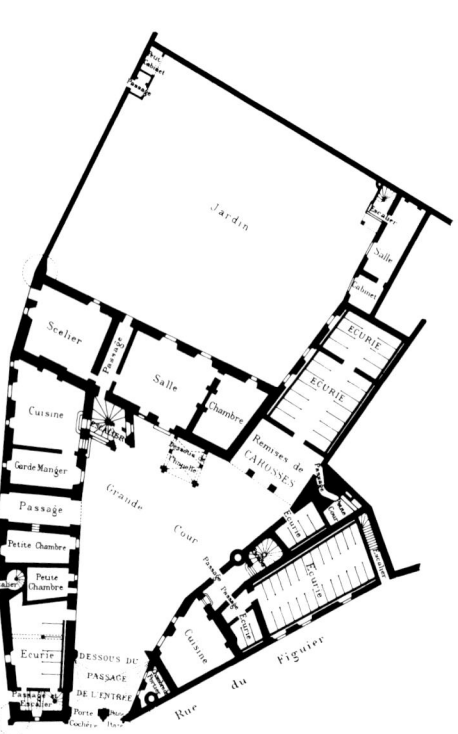

40
Hôtel de Sens, ground floor plan, 1475–1507. The oldest *hôtel* in Paris. This and the Hôtel de Cluny are the only surviving ones from the middle ages.

41
Hôtel de Sens. Drawing by Gaignières.

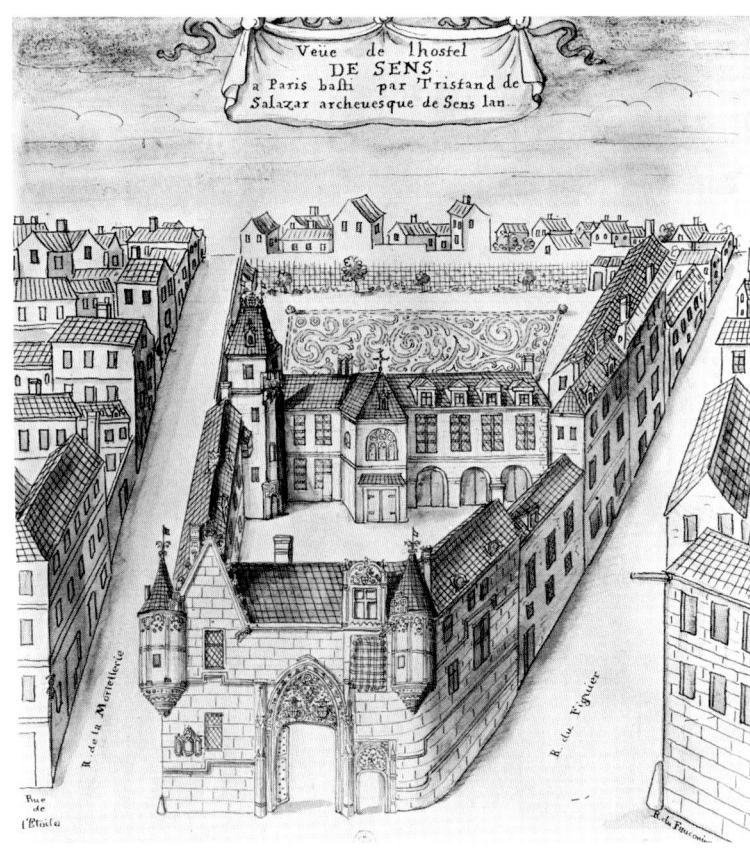

42
Hôtel de Cluny, ground floor plan, 1485–1510.
A. entry
B. concierge
C. portico
D. kitchen
E. court
F. grand stair
G. garden
H. ground floor rooms
I. room overlooking garden
K. open room under the chapel
L. gallery leading to the latrine
M. antique room—probably the stable
T. service court

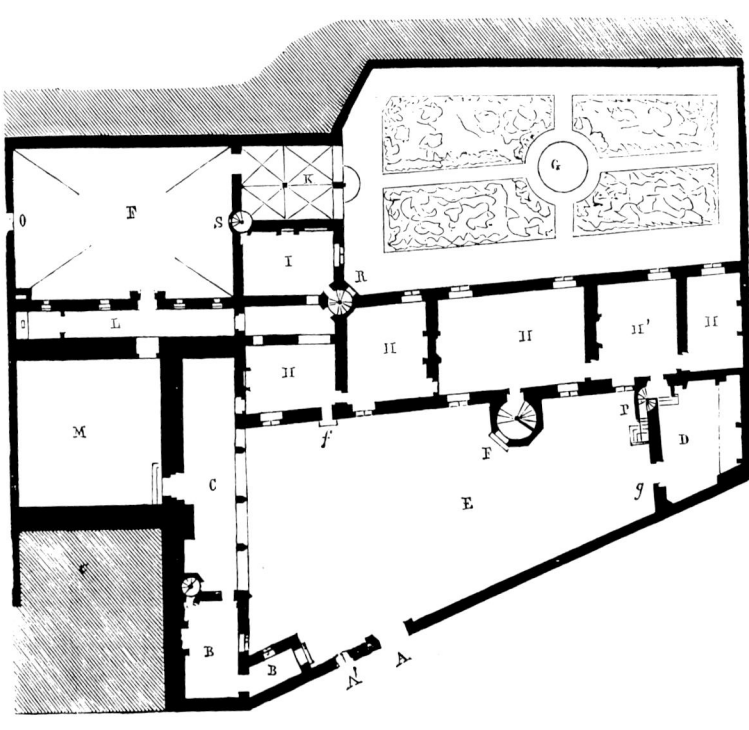

43
Caen, Hôtel de Escoville, court, 1535–38

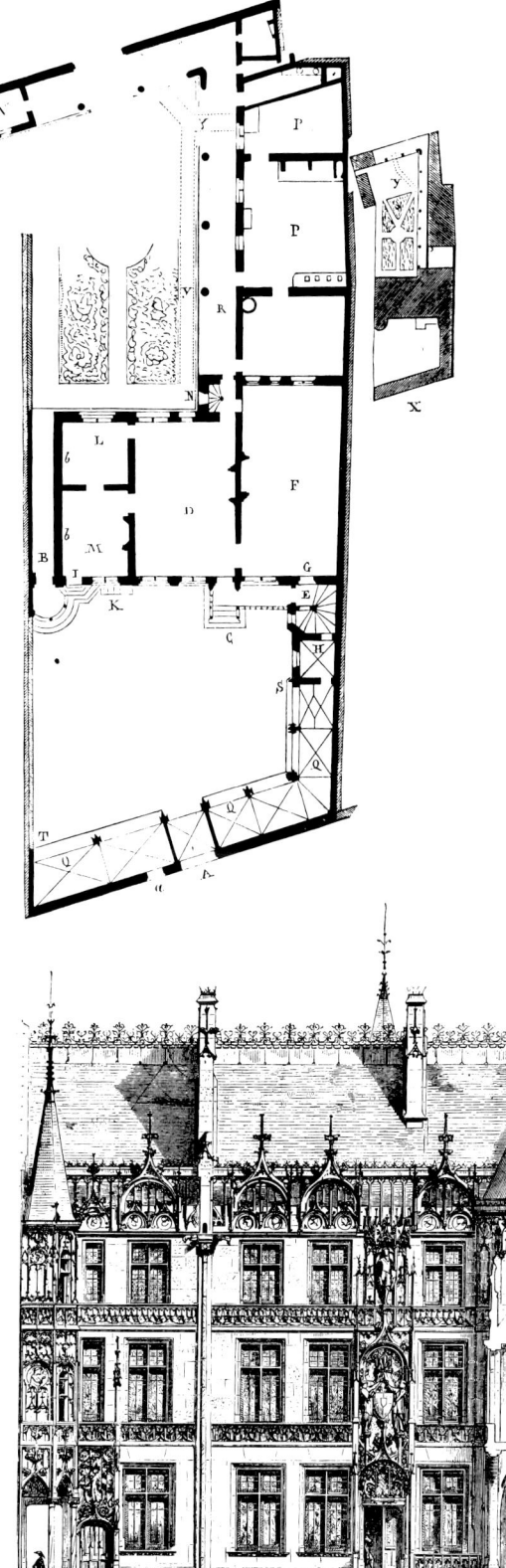

44
Hôtel Le Gendre, ground floor plan, c. 1506. After Viollet-Le-Duc. (The portion to the rear of the garden may have been misrepresented by Viollet-Le-Duc.)

- A. entry into court
- B. passage to garden
- C. principal entrance
- D. *salle*
- E. grand stair
- F. *salle*
- I. secondary entrance
- L. room
- M. room
- N. service stair
- O. service court
- P. kitchen
- Q. portico under a continuous gallery
- R. portico
- X. site plan

45
Hôtel Le Gendre, court elevation

34 The Prototypes

dual sources of their ancestry. It was Serlio who clarified both and provided the most sharply focused example for future development. In fact, his two built houses, Ancy-le-Franc (c. 1546) and Le Grand Ferrare (1544–46), might now be seen as Italian commentaries on the two French types, the *château* and the *hôtel.*

From the outside, Ancy-le-Franc appears to be exactly what it is, a French *château* designed by an Italian. The building is large and block-like with high French roofs, and the corners are articulated as square pavilions, each with an independent roof. From the courtyard, however, the building is almost pure Italian. The tall windows, the dormers, and especially the high pitched roof are all obviously "local," but the control of the wall surface and the clarity and unity of the space could at that time have been produced only by an Italian. Ancy-le-Franc is quite different from Le Grand Ferrare, but the spatial effect of the courtyards of the two buildings must have been similar.

Unlike Ancy-le-Franc, Le Grand Ferrare is clearly an urban house. Built by Serlio in Fontainebleau between 1544 and 1546 for Cardinal Ippolito II d'Este, it established the standard form of the *hôtel* for more than a century.[6] But even though it is that much more lucid than its peers, it is still typologically related to its country cousins, such as Bury. Like Bury, Le Grand Ferrare has all the elements of the typical *hôtel* scheme. The house enclosed three sides of a square court, while the fourth side was closed to the street by a wall containing the public entrance. The main living wing, the *corps-de-logis*, is a single zone of rooms between the court and the garden. The two narrower wings flanking the court contain, respectively, secondary and service

46
Ancy-le-Franc, *château*, plan, Sebastiano Serlio, c. 1546

47
Ancy-le-Franc, *château*, court

48
Ancy-le-Franc, *château*, view

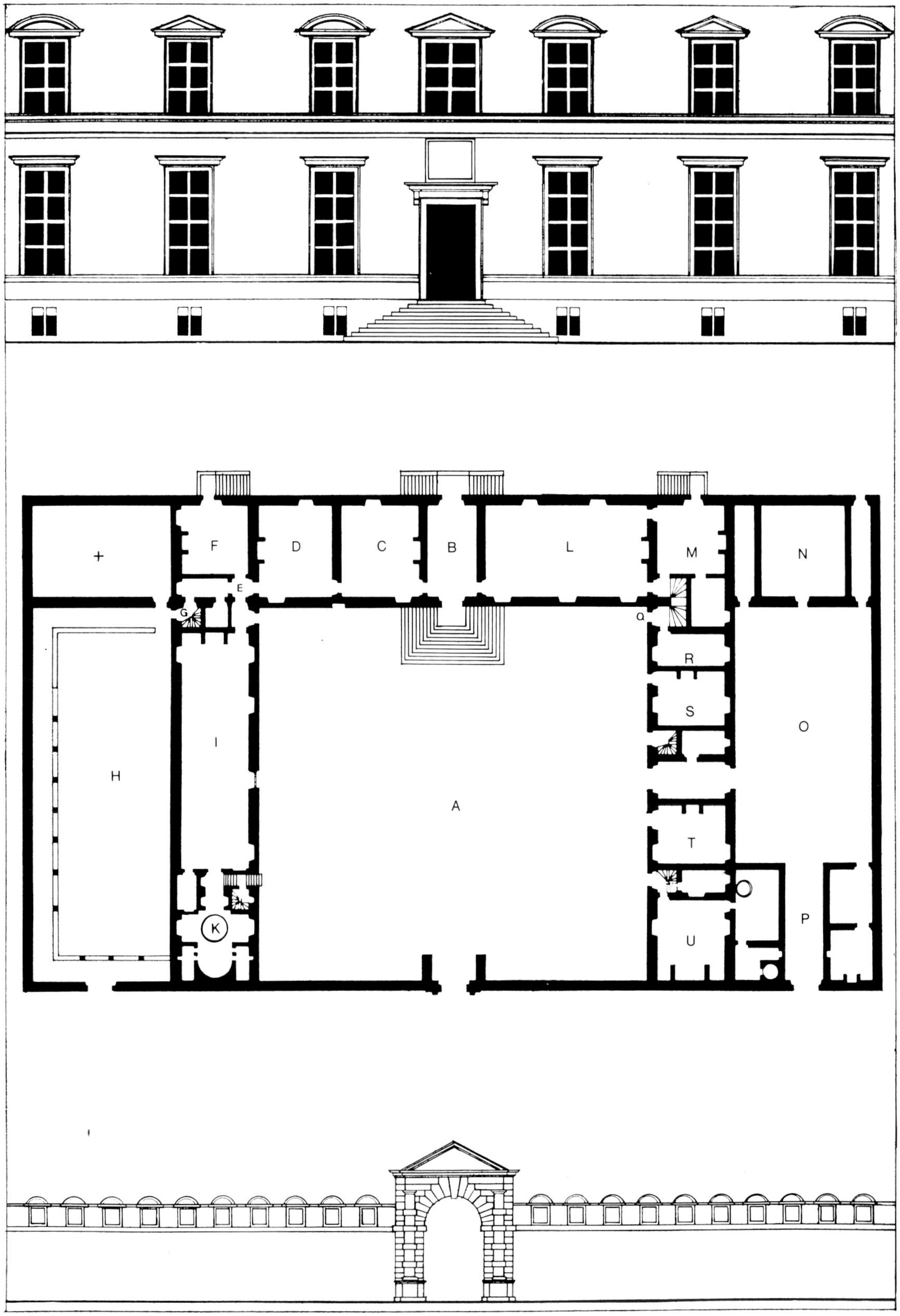

49
Fontainebleau, Le Grand Ferrare (Hôtel de Ferrare), plan, Sebastiano Serlio, 1544–46.
- A. court
- B. vestibule
- C. antichambre
- D. chambre
- E. dégagement
- F. cabinet
- + trellis-covered court
- H. court
- I. galerie
- K. chapel
- L. salle
- M. chambre
- O. service court
- X. service court
- R., S., T. service rooms
- V. kitchen

rooms, and a long gallery and chapel. These wings in turn screen service courts on either side of the plan. The service courts are accessible directly from the street, and the one on the right side, for carriages, is also accessible from the forecourt.

The drawings for Le Grand Ferrare and its several variations in Serlio's unpublished manuscripts for his sixth book,[7] and the axonometric reconstruction by Dinsmoor,[8] indicate a spatial quality similar to Ancy-le-Franc. The walls are simpler and lower than at Ancy-le-Franc, but the space of the forecourt is clearly defined. Ancy-le-Franc is an object-building meant to be seen in the round, whereas Le Grand Ferrare is an urban party-wall building with multiple courtyards that must be experienced sequentially.

The rooms of this *hôtel* are rectangular and are disposed entirely in single flights—like thick walls—around the courtyards. The plan of Le Grand Ferrare thus suggests an equivalence or balance between solid and void, between building and courts, and the building serves as *poché* to the primary sequence of court-vestibule-garden. This sequence, which is so suggestive of the Roman house as it was understood at the time of Palladio and Serlio, was rarely used in French domestic architecture. That may be because the bilaterally symmetrical relationship of these elements about a single axis—a relationship prized above all others in Baroque public buildings—was either not considered appropriate or necessary for private houses, or else was not generally feasible. Whatever the reason, later *hôtels* show a casual but conscious aversion to this kind of direct axial continuity. If the typical *hôtel* is in complete contrast to the Palladian plan, Serlio's Le Grand Ferrare is somewhere in between: slightly relaxed and pragmatically accommo-

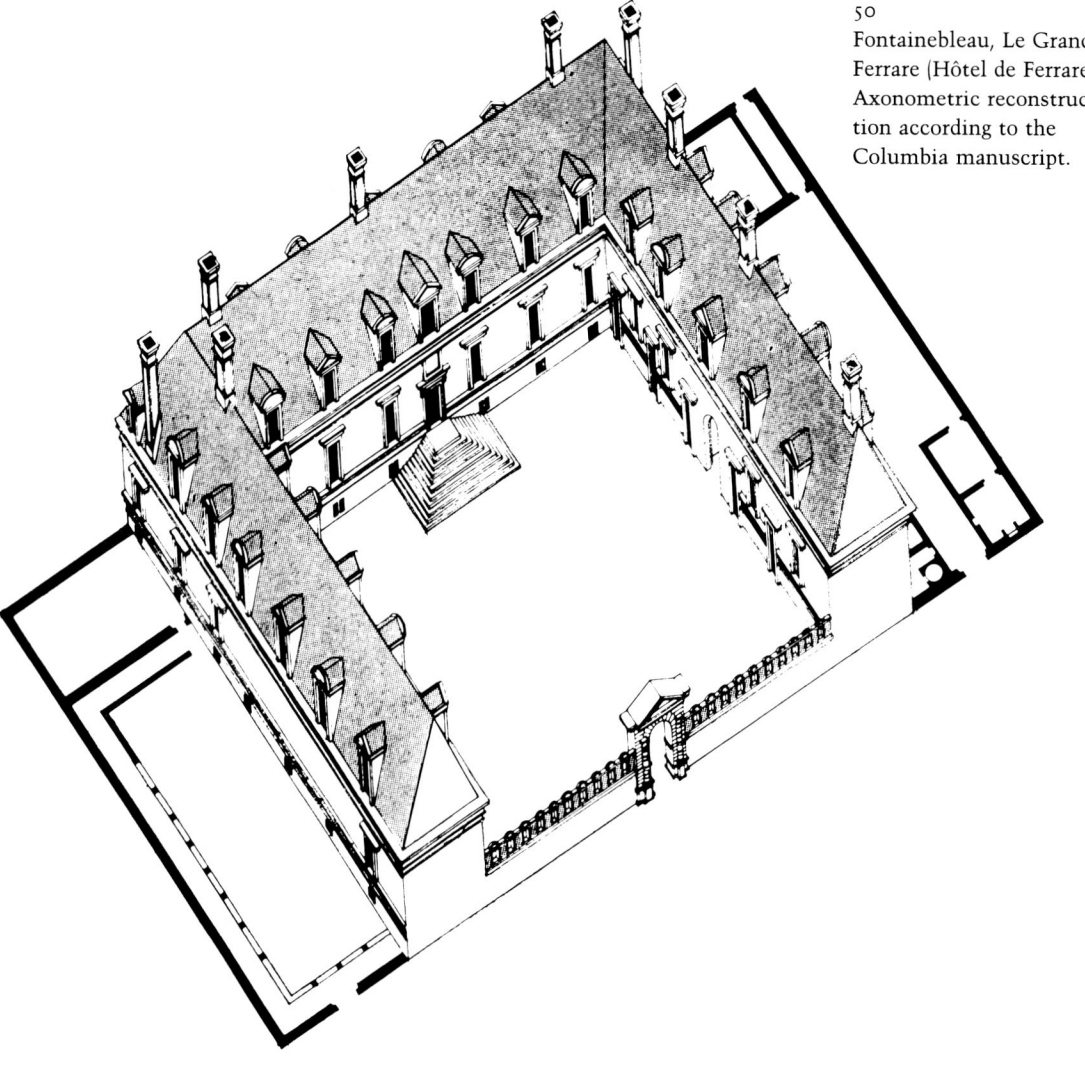

50
Fontainebleau, Le Grand Ferrare (Hôtel de Ferrare). Axonometric reconstruction according to the Columbia manuscript.

dating, but a regularized classical-idealist type nevertheless.

The contrast between the "regularity" of Serlio's prototype and the "irregularity" of other *hôtels* of the time may be seen by comparing Le Grand Ferrare to a *hôtel* constructed in Paris during the same decade for Jacques de Ligneris, President of the Parlement de Paris. The Hôtel de Ligneris, now the Hôtel Carnavalet, is almost contemporary with Le Grand Ferrare (and is the only surviving Paris house from this period), yet it shows none of the same propensities for axial continuity. On the contrary, although the site is regular, the plan is slightly asymmetrical—just enough for it to seem at first glance accidental.

Upon closer observation, however, the plan reveals a subtle but coherent order, as its most noticeable "irregularity" or deviation from the ideal type is the discontinuity between the court and the garden. The dual entrance in the corners of the court and the asymmetrical disposition of rooms in the *corps-de-logis* contribute to this discontinuity, but the main factor is the lack of alignment between court and garden. Because the wings flanking the forecourt are of different widths, the central axis of the court does not align with the central axis of the garden beyond; yet the windows of the *corps-de-logis* are regular and symmetrical to both the court and garden.

This difference in alignment is resolved in the central room of the *corps-de-logis*, where a window marks the center of the court and a panel between windows marks the center of the garden. Thus, the building fabric disengages the public court and the private garden, allowing each to be independent and "locally symmetrical," but it also relates them and resolves the schism between them through the principle of "re-centering." Crucial to this type of organization is the ideal nature of the principal voids, that is, the spatial clarity of the court and the garden. The stability and focus of these spaces—especially the forecourt—allow for variation in the surrounding building mass and thereby for the adaptation of the idealized type to programmatic and contextual circumstance. Although these ideas are understated in the Hôtel Carnavalet, they are present, and therefore the building provides a hint about the direction of future developments and a comment on a timeless architectural argument about the relationship between the ideal and the circumstantial.

The Hôtel Carnavalet (de Ligneris) is also similar to a project that was published nearly ten years later by Du Cerceau.[9] Both the building and the project are the same *hôtel* type, but in contrast to the willful symmetry of Du Cerceau's plan, the plan of the Hôtel Carnavalet appears cavalier. The question is thus inevitable: Is Du Cerceau's plan an idealized improvement of its deformed and accommodating predecessor, or has the predecessor, by being both ideal and real, been rendered limited and dry in its subsequent version? If an argument may now be made that each is useful and that each serves to inform, illuminate, and criticize the other, it is also highly likely that at the time no such agonizing was called for. The insistence on ideal regularity was simply not required for domestic buildings.

The loss of so many late-sixteenth-century Parisian *hôtels* is sad, but what evidence remains suggests that most were variations, either regular or irregular, of the classic, urban, party-wall type formulated by Serlio. Welcome relief from this historical hiatus is the still extant Hôtel d'Angoulême, built in 1584 on a site opposite the Hôtel Carnavalet for Diane de France, daughter of Henri II.[10] It is also unfortunate that, unlike later buildings, the lost buildings of this period were not recorded in publications. Other than Du Cerceau's two volumes of *Bastiments*, which did not record any of these *hôtels*, the only built examples recorded in contemporary illustrated treatises were Le Grand Ferrare in Serlio's unpublished sixth book and Philibert de L'Orme's own house, built about 1557 in the Marais and illustrated in his *L'Architecture* of 1567. Instead, the principal treatises on domestic architecture were more like handbooks, offering a variety of *types* which could be developed as solutions to particular combinations of circumstances.

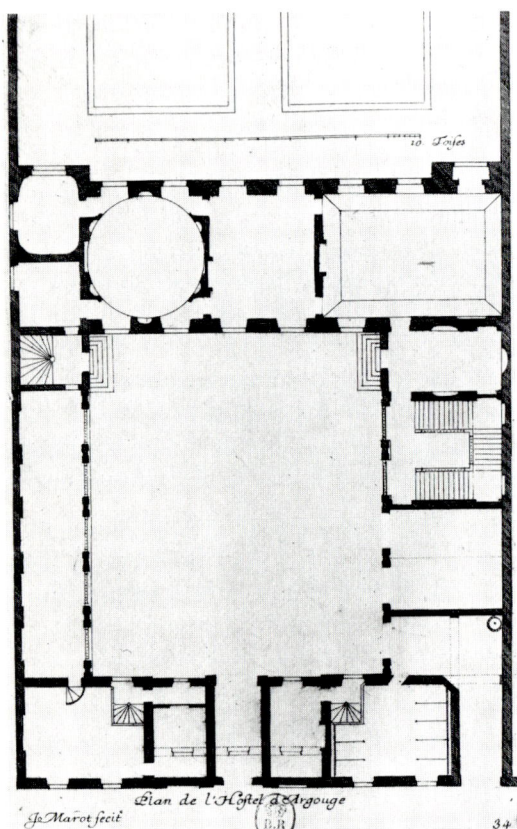

51
Hôtel Carnavalet, plan, begun late 1540s

52
Hôtel Carnavalet, original facade

53
Hôtel Carnavalet, facade as altered by F. Mansart

54
Hôtel Carnavalet, court as altered by F. Mansart and again in the nineteenth century

55
Project for a *hôtel*, plan and elevation, Jacques Androuet Du Cerceau. From the *Livre*.

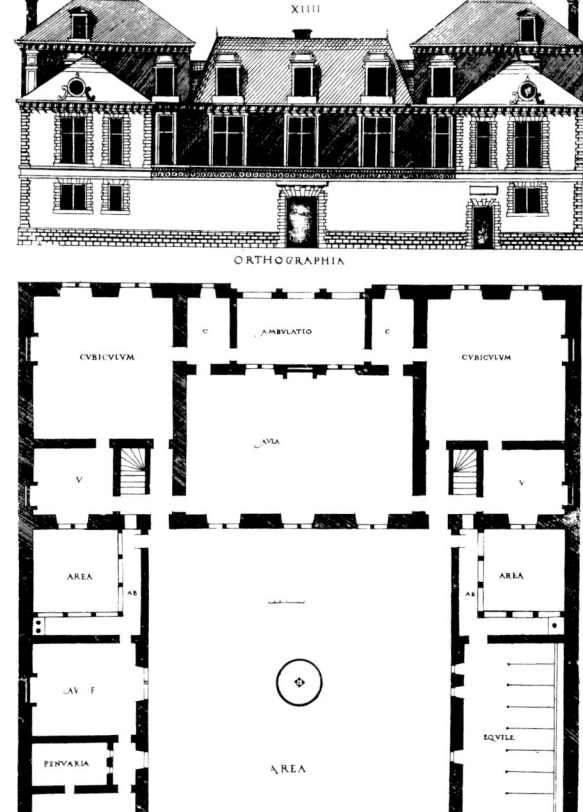

56
Hôtel d'Angoulême (Lamoignon), court, Baptiste Du Cerceau, 1584

Serlio and Du Cerceau

The theoretical work of Serlio published between 1537 and 1584 was indeed revolutionary, especially because Alberti's famous treatise was written in Latin and contained no illustrations until the edition of 1550. Serlio's books were primarily composed of illustrations, and the little accompanying text was in Italian or, later, in Italian and French. The dependence on plates bore out his intention to make a handbook of architectural design that would show ideas in their application. His work became the model for the books of Palladio, Vignola, Du Cerceau, and de L'Orme.

Serlio's important manuscripts for the sixth book were actually the first works in which domestic architecture was dealt with in an architectural treatise. He provided examples of a wide range of sizes and types of dwellings for several different categories of owner—from small houses for the poor to palaces for princes and kings—arranged by country dwellings and city dwellings. In addition, the smaller projects are each illustrated in the "Italian manner" and in the "French manner." Though unpublished at the time, these manuscripts must have been known to at least Du Cerceau since his own work seems to derive from them.

Du Cerceau's first book, the *Livre d'architecture*, published in 1559, concerns the design of town houses and, like Serlio's manuscripts, presents a range of sizes from small, single, one-story blocks to grand houses for the nobility. The largest houses resemble country houses more than town houses and as such exhibit both the characteristics and the problems of adapting a country house to the city. Like the Château de

57
Project for a *hôtel*, perspective, Jacques Androuet Du Cerceau, 1559. From the *Livre*.

Bury, they are composed of a main living block, the *corps-de-logis*, facing a court enclosed by lower galleries on the sides and a screen on the street front. The front corners, the street entrance, the ends of the *corps-de-logis*, and the building entrance are all expressed as pavilions with independent roofs. The result gives the effect of several detached buildings connected by wings, where the plasticity of the building, rather than the spatial effect, dominates. This was the scheme for Du Cerceau's Château de Verneuil (begun in 1568) and later for Salomon de Brosse's Luxembourg Palace (begun in 1615). It would emerge again as the model for the Rococo *hôtels* of the Faubourg St.-Germain.

The smaller houses illustrated by Du Cerceau are similar to the larger ones in their schematic organization, but they are much more regular. The roofs articulate each component, but the overall massing and especially the plan are suavely contained and unified. The court is clearly defined as an outdoor room, and the general emphasis of the composition is horizontal. The *corps-de-logis* of these houses is usually composed of planning units or *appartements* connected by a living room or *salle*. Each *appartement* consists of a *garde-robe*, a *cabinet*, a *chambre*, and sometimes an *antichambre* as well. These planning units first appeared at Chambord in the early part of the century and were the basis for future domestic planning. Although there is little evidence of the social rituals associated with these units, they appear to have been used with great flexibility. Even the dining room, for example, was unspecified until the seventeenth century, and then only occasionally.

The last great architecture book of the classical period was the work by which Du Cerceau is best known: the two volumes of *Les plus excellents bastiments de France*, published in 1576 and 1579. The *Bastiments* illustrates the great sixteenth-century *châteaux* and gardens but contains no *hôtels*.

Despite the disruption caused by the Wars of Religion, the basic form of the urban square, the *hôtel*, and the illustrated architecture book became firmly established in the sixteenth century. When the seventeenth century opened to greater stability under Henri IV, development continued as if no disruption had occurred.

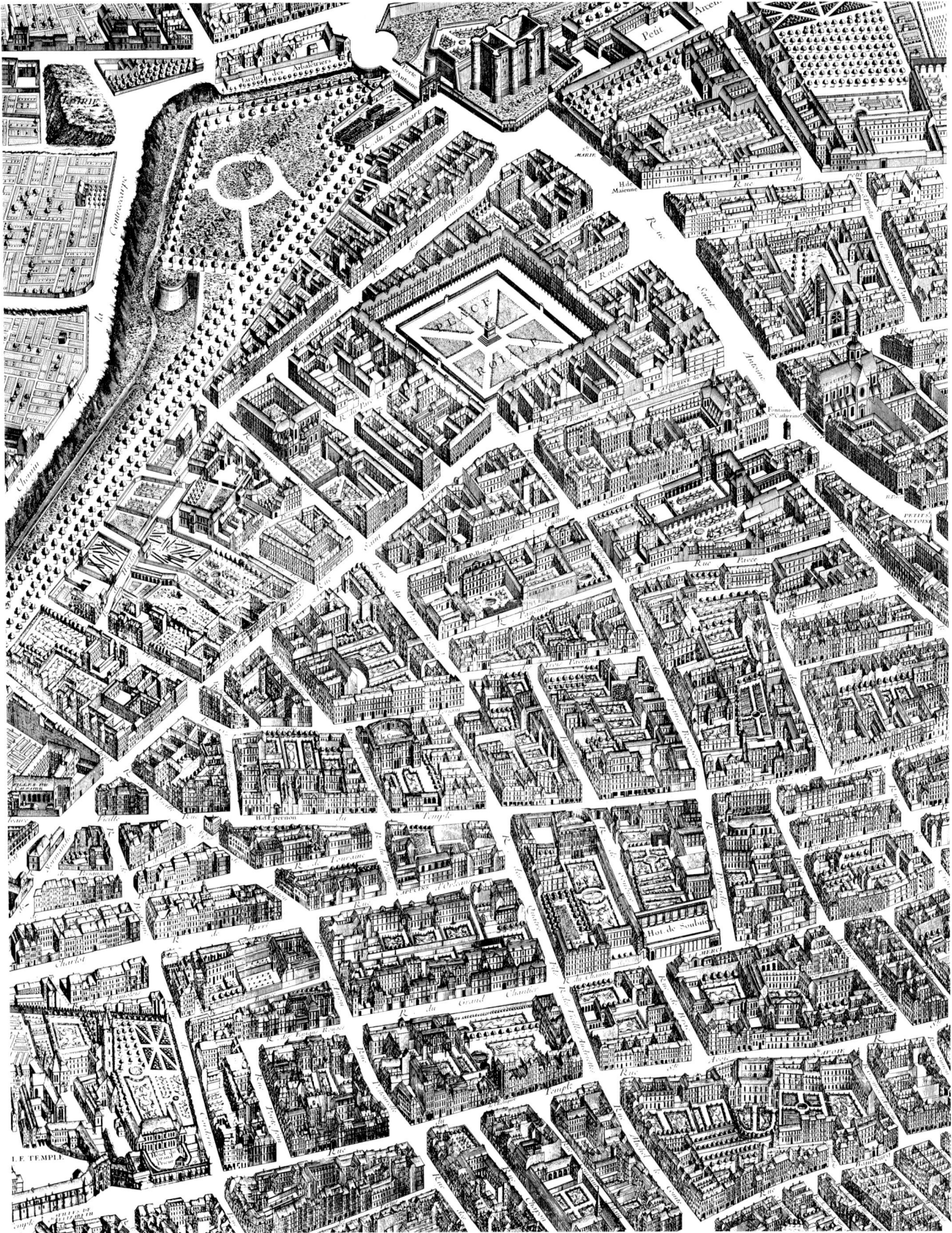

58
Le Marais and the Place Royale (1605–12). From the Turgot plan.

59
Hôtel de Mayenne, Jean or Jacques II Androuet Du Cerceau, 1613. Engraving by Chastillon. The *hôtel* may be seen in the Turgot plan, to the above right of the Place Royale in the rue St.-Antoine.

3   Public Spaces: The Baroque Hôtel

Between the entry of Henri IV into an exhausted Paris in 1594 and the retreat of Louis XIV to Versailles after the death of Mazarin in 1661,[1] Paris was transformed and the classic urban *hôtel* achieved its decisive form. The Place Royale, built during the first decade of the seventeenth century, was the first of the three royal squares of Paris and marked the beginning of the second phase of *hôtel* building. This was a prolific period of construction in which anyone who could afford to build apparently did. It is estimated that in the first half of the century more than 350 *hôtels* were built in Paris,[2] and although the basic characteristics of the urban *hôtel* had been outlined in the previous half century, it was during this era that its formal principles were fully developed. New design manuals appeared in the 1620s, and Jean Marot published the most important of the newer *hôtels* during the second half of the century. The city plans that illustrate Paris at critical moments of this period are the Merian plan of 1614, the Gombust plan of 1652, and the Nicolas de Fer plan of 1697.

One man was essentially responsible for launching this stimulating period of production: Henri IV. With his minister, Sully, Henri IV reestablished the state and the arts after the disruption caused by the Wars of Religion, and he initiated several important town planning projects. This was, in effect, the beginning of modern France, and Henri IV's achievements as a statesman and town planner seem all the more remarkable given the brevity of his reign and the conditions under which he began.

The urban condition of Paris must have been no less deplorable than the state of the French economy when Henri IV arrived in 1594. At that time, the city had virtually no significant public open space. The inner city, including the river banks and bridges, was a dense, impacted medieval network of overhanging buildings and narrow streets; there were only two bridges crossing the Seine; and sanitation was almost nonexistent. The only areas convenient for building without demolition were the swampy Marais, which had remained largely unsettled, and the marshy tip of the Ile de la Cité.

These two areas became the sites of Henri IV's three famous urban squares. The Place Royale (1605–12), originally intended as a manufacturing and residential precinct, was built on the site in the Marais formerly occupied by the old royal palace, the Hôtel des Tournelles. The Place Dauphine (begun in 1607), a residential and commercial venture, was built on the triangular end of the Ile de la Cité between the newly finished Pont Neuf and the royal palace. Finally, the Place de France (designed in 1610), intended as a monumental new entrance to the city, was to have been built on vacant land to the east of Le Temple.

These projects are unique in their clarity, and each illustrates the dual goals of Henri IV. On the one hand, each project was intended to stimulate the economy by providing work for the citizens and by reestablishing a national pool of artists and craftsmen; on the other hand, each was intended as a civic improvement that would benefit the people and provide a visible public dimension to the city. Taken together these two beneficent aims represent a conscious effort to create an organic relationship between the state and the arts and to transform Paris into the capital of France.

44 Public Spaces: The Baroque Hôtel

The Urban Squares of Henri IV

The Place Royale, now the Place des Vosges,[3] was the first example of Renaissance urban space in Paris and the direct descendant of the Piazza Ducale in Vigevano and the Place Ducale in Vitry-le-François. Unlike its predecessors, however, the Place Royale had no monumental public building as its focus, and originally no monument occupied the center of the space. Rather, it was a pure, unified space without conspicuous focus: formally, it was specific and finite; functionally, it was general and flexible. A monumental spatial addition to the city, nevertheless, it was the forerunner of the great English and Spanish squares and is still a suggestive model for the traffic-free residential square.

The site for the project had remained derelict for nearly half a century—since the Wars of Religion interrupted Catherine de Médicis's plans for a residential square—and Henri IV intended it as the nucleus of a manufacturing district that would stimulate the economy. Toward this end, a building for the manufacture of velvet was constructed on the north side in 1604. Evidently, Henri IV originally wanted to form a square surrounded by workers' housing south of the new factory, and a contract was signed in 1605 creating a new square.[4] But in 1606, after the failure of the factory, the east, south, and west sides of the square were developed as houses for the nobility. The abandoned factory building was subsequently destroyed and the north side of the square completed by a row of houses identical to the others. The whole square, 140 × 140 meters, was completed in 1611, a year after the assassination of Henri IV, and it was inaugurated in 1612.[5]

60
Le Marais. Detail from the Jaillot plan.

45 The Urban Squares of Henri IV

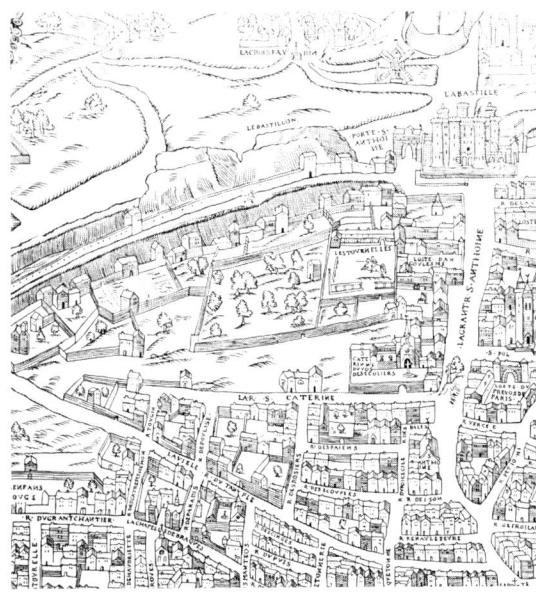

61
Hôtel des Tournelles
(site of the Place Royale),
1551. Detail from the
Truschet and Hoyau
plan.

62
Place Royale. Engraving
by Chastillon.

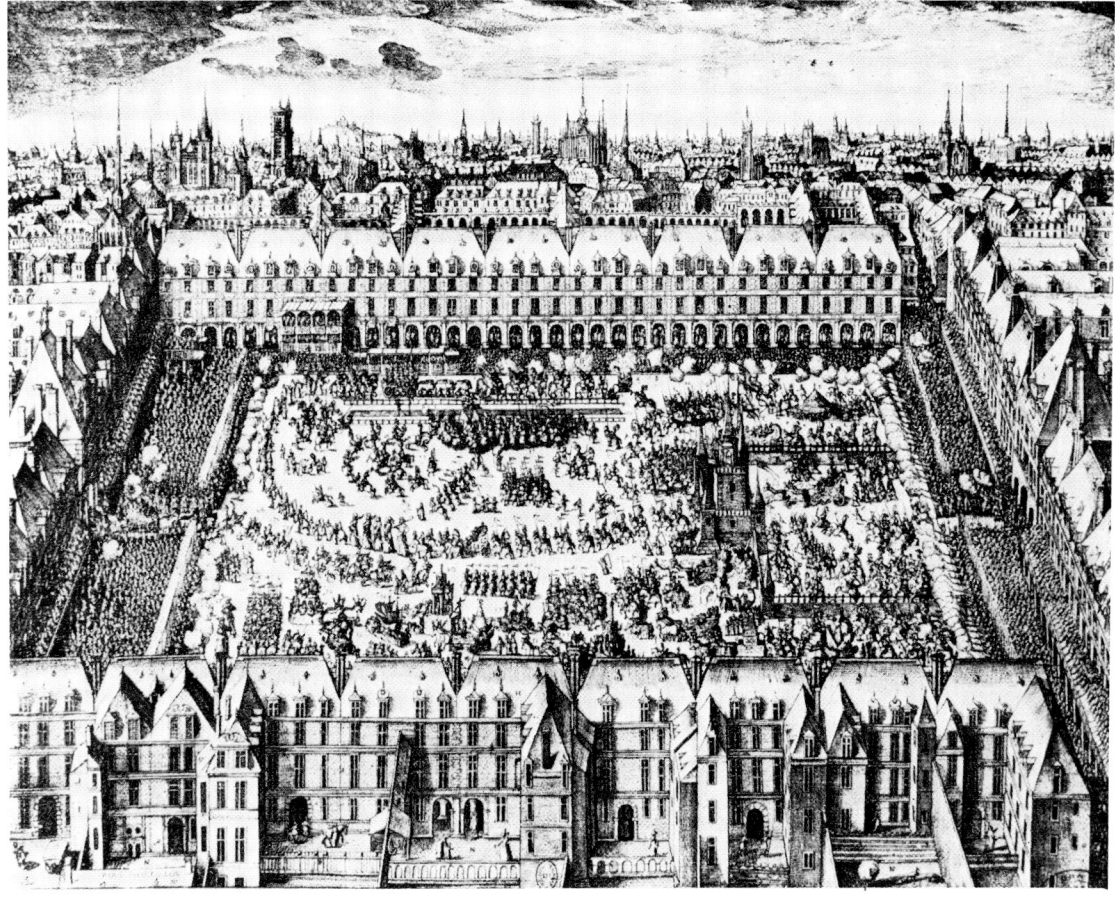

46 *Public Spaces: The Baroque Hôtel*

63
Place Royale. Engraving by Perelle.

When completed, the square was a totally enclosed space except for the street entrance on the northwest corner. There was a minor entrance under the house in the northeast corner,[6] and the principal street entrances to the north and south were under the raised central pavilions, the Pavillon du Roi and the Pavillon de la Reine. The rest of the houses were regular repetitive units of moderate size. Each house of four bays was built individually on a lot rented from the king for a nominal fee, providing the owners built according to the prescribed format, which included a public arcade on the ground floor, articulated but continuous high French roofs, and identical facade designs.

The result was a discreet collaboration between public gesture and private amenity—what Blunt describes as a combination of the regularity of Italy with the Flemish grouping of small, independent houses.[7] For a modest sum, less affluent members of the aristocracy—those who could not afford a large private *hôtel*—could have a private house fronting on a grand public space and could enjoy the idea that they were contributing to that public realm. This balance between public and private, between individual expression and collective identity, reflects a rare but provocative moment of formal and social history.

At once an urban and social stabilizer, the Place Royale was the focus of court and civic activity. It was also a stimulant in that it sponsored the surrounding development of the Marais by the wealthier nobility. Until it was turned into a statue square in 1639 with the addition of the equestrian statue of Louis XIII, the Place Royale served its original functions of *promenoir*, public assembly, and tournament grounds. As a great outdoor room, it served as the living room of the Marais. Formally, it is the most complex of Henri IV's three squares because of the ambiguity of the building fabric beyond the space of the square. Visually, the square appears to be formed by a shallow zone of identical houses, whereas in reality the houses recede from the square to varying depths. These houses then engage the buildings, such as the Hôtel de Sully, which line the surrounding streets, thereby slurring any definable edge between them. Thus, the square's formal role in its immediate context can be compared to that of the *cour d'honneur* of the *hôtels* of the district.

Unlike the Place Dauphine, where the buildings are of consistent depth and the configuration of the space is a result of the configuration of the site, the Place Royale tends to function independently of the irregular block within which it occurs. It is separated from its "outside" face on the surrounding streets by a complex, varied matrix of private buildings and spaces that disengage the inside from the outside and mask any relationship between the two. In the Place Dauphine, "a block" or "a building" may be discerned; in the Place Royale, no "building" can be truly identified. There is an apparent world of contiguous buildings, but this world is only implied by the facades, which define the public realm and distinguish it from the private realm beyond. Thus, the complex, interstitial urban tissue formed by the various houses may be seen as a kind of habitable *poché*, an infinitely variable fabric, which is the residue of formal discontinuity. This idea was developed in the *hôtels* of the seventeenth century, and by the end of the century it was carried to its urban extreme in the Place Louis-le-Grand (Place Vendôme), where a schism between public and private is raised to high art.

Several provincial squares were also built in the early years of the seventeenth century. Though similar to the Place Royale, the squares at Charleville (1608), Henrichemont (1608), Montauban (1616), and Richelieu (c. 1632)[8] are less memorable than Henri IV's Parisian squares. What is remarkable about Henri IV's squares is how three simple geometric forms—square, triangle, and semicircle—were infused with urban, social, and symbolic meaning and were thereby transformed into three of history's most compelling urban images.

The Place Dauphine resulted from Henri IV's decision to complete the unfinished Pont Neuf at the tip of the Ile de la Cité.[9] When the bridge was finished in 1604, the left bank was opened up by the extension of the axis of the bridge as the rue Dauphine. Marie de Médicis then offered the city an equestrian statue of the king, to be erected on the tip of the island between the two halves of the bridge. This evidently sponsored the development of the Place Dauphine, because in 1607 Henri IV began the triangular space, formed by regular repetitive houses, and focused on the point at which the statue was to be erected. This simple combination of elements—bridge, street, statue, and triangular *place*—crystallized into a monumental civic ensemble at a critical location, thereby contributing to the larger order of the city. In this sense it anticipates the great urban schemes of the eighteenth century, such as the Place Louis XV and the squares of Nancy.

The last of Henri IV's town planning projects was the semicircular Place de France,[10] which was designed in 1610 but never finished. In this project political and symbolic content was the overriding consideration because at that time France was still not a completely unified nation,

48 Public Spaces: The Baroque Hôtel

64
Place des Vosges, typical *hôtel*

65
Place des Vosges (Place Royale), aerial view

49 The Urban Squares of Henri IV

66
Site of the Pont Neuf and the Place Dauphine (L'Ile de la Cité). From the Legrand plan showing Paris in 1380.

67
The Pont Neuf and the Place Dauphine. From the Turgot plan.

68
Place Dauphine. Engraving showing the decoration for the entry of Louis XIV into the Place Dauphine, August 26, 1660.

69
Place Dauphine, plan, 1610

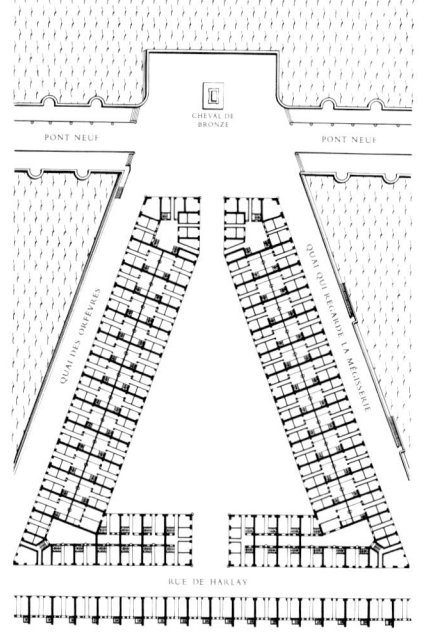

and some areas were particularly independent. The intention was therefore to create a symbol of national unity as well as of civic pride—France as a unified entity of individual elements—and the Place was designed accordingly. It was to be located on vacant land behind Le Temple and adjacent to the wall of Paris between the Porte St.-Antoine and the Porte du Temple. A new gate, the Porte de France, was to open into a large, semicircular space defined by seven public buildings separated by streets radiating from the *place*. Each was to bear the name of a major French province: Picardy, Dauphine, Provence, Languedoc, Guienne, Poitou, Bretagne, and Bourgogne. Beyond the public buildings was an outer ring of streets named for Brie, Bourbonnais, Lyonnais, Beaune, Auvergne, Limousin, and Perigord; and finally the extensions of the radial streets were named for Saintonge, La Marche, Touraine, La Perche, Angoulême, Berri, Orléans, Beaujolais, and Anjou. Only a small part of the scheme was carried out, but this concept of a monumental gateway to the city is known from the engraving by Claude Chastillon. And if, today, the idea of the Place de France seems a bit "quaint" or "naive," we need only consider the power of Jefferson's lawn at the University of Virginia—the idea for which now seems equally "quaint"—in order to feel renewed enthusiasm for the Place de France.

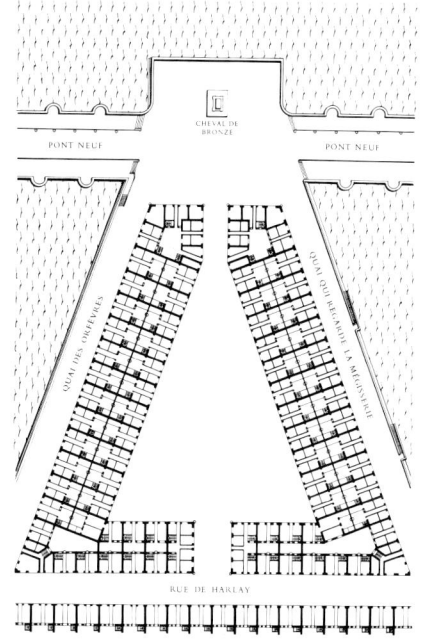

68
Place Dauphine. Engraving showing the decoration for the entry of Louis XIV into the Place Dauphine, August 26, 1660.

69
Place Dauphine, plan, 1610

and some areas were particularly independent. The intention was therefore to create a symbol of national unity as well as of civic pride—France as a unified entity of individual elements—and the Place was designed accordingly. It was to be located on vacant land behind Le Temple and adjacent to the wall of Paris between the Porte St.-Antoine and the Porte du Temple. A new gate, the Porte de France, was to open into a large, semicircular space defined by seven public buildings separated by streets radiating from the *place*. Each was to bear the name of a major French province: Picardy, Dauphine, Provence, Languedoc, Guienne, Poitou, Bretagne, and Bourgogne. Beyond the public buildings was an outer ring of streets named for Brie, Bourbonnais, Lyonnais, Beaune, Auvergne, Limousin, and Perigord; and finally the extensions of the radial streets were named for Saintonge, La Marche, Touraine, La Perche, Angoulême, Berri, Orléans, Beaujolais, and Anjou. Only a small part of the scheme was carried out, but this concept of a monumental gateway to the city is known from the engraving by Claude Chastillon. And if, today, the idea of the Place de France seems a bit "quaint" or "naive," we need only consider the power of Jefferson's lawn at the University of Virginia—the idea for which now seems equally "quaint"—in order to feel renewed enthusiasm for the Place de France.

49 The Urban Squares of Henri IV

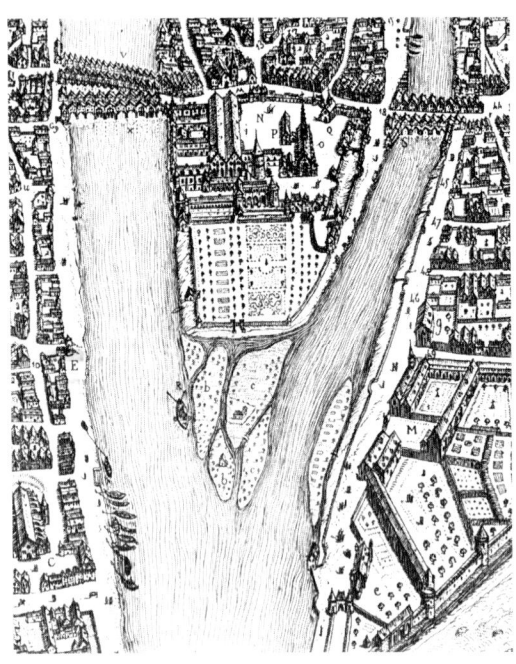

66
Site of the Pont Neuf and the Place Dauphine (L'Ile de la Cité). From the Legrand plan showing Paris in 1380.

67
The Pont Neuf and the Place Dauphine. From the Turgot plan.

51 The Urban Squares of Henri IV

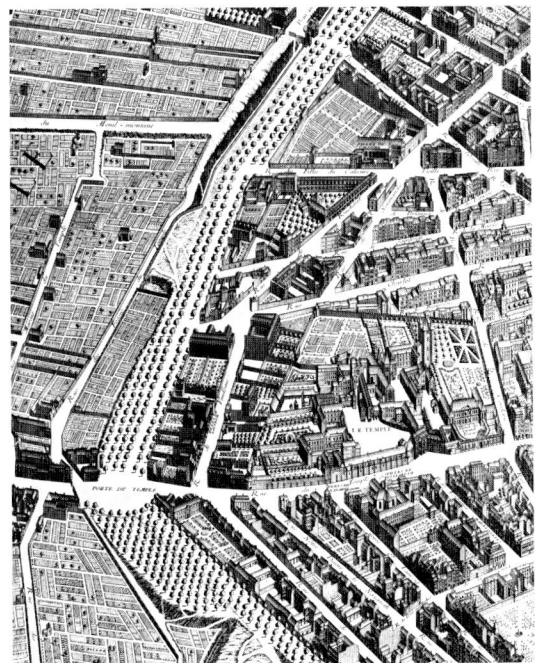

70
Site of the Place de France. From the Turgot plan. The Place de France was planned to go directly behind Le Temple. Rue Charlot and rue de Boucherat (formerly rue-neuve St.-Louis, now rue de Turenne) are the only executed elements of the Place de France scheme.

71
Place de France. Engraving by Chastillon.

The Baroque Hôtel

The urban initiatives of Henri IV and conditions of relative stability in the early years of the seventeenth century helped sponsor an extraordinary increase in the construction of *hôtels*, particularly in the Marais, but also on the Ile St.-Louis and later in the new western quarter around the Palais Royal. The point of departure for these *hôtels* was the classic courtyard type established during the last century; and an examination of one of the first of the new *hôtels*, the Hôtel de Sully (1624–29), reveals little advance over the Hôtel Carnavalet of some seventy years earlier. Perhaps the distress caused by the years of social turmoil had delayed the transformation of the *hôtel*, but the next thirty years, between the Hôtel de Sully and the Hôtel de Beauvais (1652–55), were to do the opposite. During that brief period, all of the formal techniques latent in the earlier *hôtels* were developed in rapid succession: asymmetry, local symmetry, recentering, figural rooms, functionally specific rooms, discontinuity, sequence, and hierarchical levels of *poché* all became highly developed techniques that transformed the Baroque *hôtel* type into a sophisticated instrument of society and of urban architecture.

Two new treatises guided the early works of this period. One was Louis Savot's *Architecture françoise*, first published in 1624. This is an unillustrated text covering a wide range of issues from siting and the basic form of the house to the types of rooms (*anti-salles, salles,* etc.) and a formal description of their sizes and proportions plus locations of doors and fireplaces, etc. In addition, a large portion of the book is devoted to practical considerations of building in Paris, including building regulations and the cost of materials. The companion volume to Savot's treatise is, by contrast, an illustrated handbook in the tradition of Serlio and Du Cerceau: Pierre Le Muet's *Manière de bastir pour toutes sortes de personnes*, published in 1623. Like its predecessors it contains a variety of designs for different categories of owner. Each type is illustrated on several different sites, and the projects range in size from units as small as twelve feet wide and twenty-five feet deep to more elaborate *hôtels* fronting gardens. The first edition contained only projects, but when it was republished in 1647 with an amended title (*Manière de bien bastir...*), a second part was added to illustrate Le Muet's own built work.

It was Le Muet who, in the small text of his treatise, called attention to a new topic in French architecture, *la distribution*, or the functional arrangement of the plan. This quality existed on equal footing with beauty and solidity and was to become increasingly important to French architects. By the eighteenth century it would be elevated to the status of *l'art de la distribution (des plans)*, as distinct from *la décoration (des façades)*. But in the early seventeenth century, developments were slow. Hautecoeur points out that at the Louvre in the sixteenth century, Henri II had only two rooms—a *chambre de parade* and a *chambre à coucher*—in which he slept, ate, worked, and received visitors,[11] and conditions in the early seventeenth century were not much improved. The plan was still relatively primitive, with simple, multipurpose rooms reflecting the modest life under Henri IV.

The project for *hôtel* type 1, site 9, in Le Muet's treatise typifies the larger *hôtels* in the book and illustrates the state of the art during the early years of the century. The basic form of the building is that of the traditional party-wall *hôtel*, where the building defines a forecourt and the public rooms are located away from the street between the court and the garden. The services are extremely modest and are located on the ground floor in the wing flanking the court and the street. A stair and space for carriages occupy the side wing, and a privy is located in the corner of the stair, or at point A. The kitchen, storage room, and stables are in the wing separating the court and the street. In the remainder of the ground floor, the *corps-de-logis*, a central stair separates a *chambre* from the main public reception room, the *salle*, while on the upper floor rooms are strung out continuously around the court. At this time the system of the *appartements* still consisted of, at most, three basic rooms: the *chambre*, usually a bedroom; the *garde-robe*, a dressing/storage room where the valet or chambermaid slept; and the *cabinet*, a small study or sitting room. Le Muet, however, shows few *cabinets*, and the provision of *garde-robes* is casual. In short, the theoretical plans of Le Muet are rudimentary at best.

Not until about 1630 under Louis XIII do we become aware of a marked demand for multiple rooms—a room for each activity—and no real change in everyday habits occurred until about 1640. The *salle à manger*, or dining room, for example, first appears as a functionally specific room in the 1630s. Before, the *antichambre*, or waiting room (in itself a new room type), was also used for dining. The change toward greater specialization and separation of functions during the first half of the century resulted in increasingly complicated plans; however, it would be a mistake to think that these complications involved much advance in convenience—this was left to the eighteenth century. Although some steps were taken toward convenience, the public, or reception, parts of the house were the primary focus of attention during this period. According to Babelon:

Problems of the access of visitors and the sequence of the *appartements* were the only ones to interest high society during the epoque of the *Précieuses*. . . . Functional installations for service and comfort remained unexplored areas because they didn't profoundly touch men and women habituated to cold, to the comings and goings of guests and servants, and a thousand inconveniences which we would find insupportable.[12]

One who apparently was "touched" was the Marquise de Rambouillet. Along with the treatises of Savot and Le Muet, the Marquise is traditionally given credit for affecting the planning of the seventeenth-century *hôtel* by insisting on more practical arrangements of rooms and services. Dissatisfied with her architect's design for her own *hôtel*, La Rambouillet reportedly called for drawing paper and laid out the *hôtel* herself.[13] This famous house was the center of aristocratic intellectual life and the Marquise's circle of the *Précieuses*, but since the *hôtel* does not survive, nor are there any drawings of it, the level of her expertise cannot be judged. More than likely the accounts of her influence are exaggerated, as the advances in internal functional planning during this period were slight. On the other hand, her house made a big impression at the time, so we will look at her innovations in the context of the era they are presumed to have affected. One thing is certain, however—the Marquise was one of a series of great French women who through their

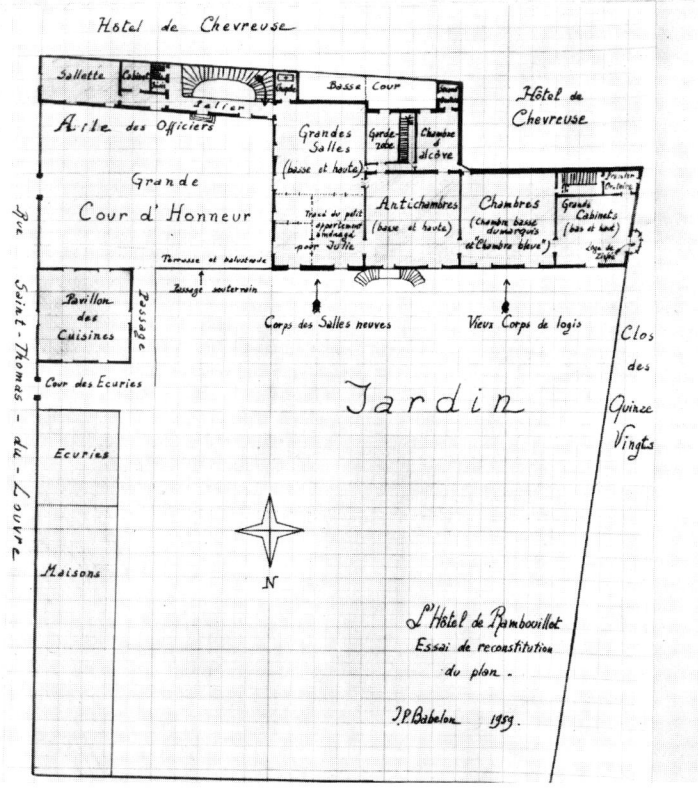

72
Hôtel de Rambouillet, reconstruction by J.-P. Babelon, Marquise de Rambouillet

73
Visite à l'accouchée,
Abraham Bosse

74
L'hiver, Abraham Bosse

personalities and their patronage influenced the development of the *hôtel*. In this sense, the Marquise de Rambouillet was to the seventeenth century what Diane de Poitiers was to the sixteenth and Madame de Pompadour to the eighteenth.

The formal development of the Baroque *hôtel* type begins with the Hôtel de Sully, which along with the Hôtel Chalons–Luxembourg (c. 1615), is the finest surviving *hôtel* from this period. Built between 1624 and 1629 for the financier Mesme Gallet by Jean Du Cerceau, son of Baptiste, it was sold to Henri IV's minister Sully in 1634.[14] The basic form of the Hôtel de Sully is that of the traditional urban *hôtel* of the Marais. The general arrangement is in fact very similar to the Le Muet project described above. Although Le Muet's plan is asymmetrical, it is like a fragment of a symmetrical plan; that is, it is as regular as possible and adheres closely to the classical-idealist tradition of symmetry about a central axis.

By comparison, the plan of the Hôtel de Sully seems at first glance imperfect. The site is irregular, and like the plan of the Hôtel Carnavalet, the most noticeable "irregularity" or deviation from the ideal is the discontinuity between the court in front and the garden behind. This results from the lack of axial alignment between the court and garden, and the central entrance accentuates the condition. In the Hôtel Carnavalet the misalignment was absorbed by the central room; in the Hôtel de Sully it is obscured by the stair, which is shifted so that one flight of the stair aligns with the entrance and the axis of the court. In the Hôtel de Sully as in the Hôtel Carnavalet, themes of local symmetry, recentering, and discontinuity are evident if not overt. But if the plan is still

55 The Baroque Hôtel

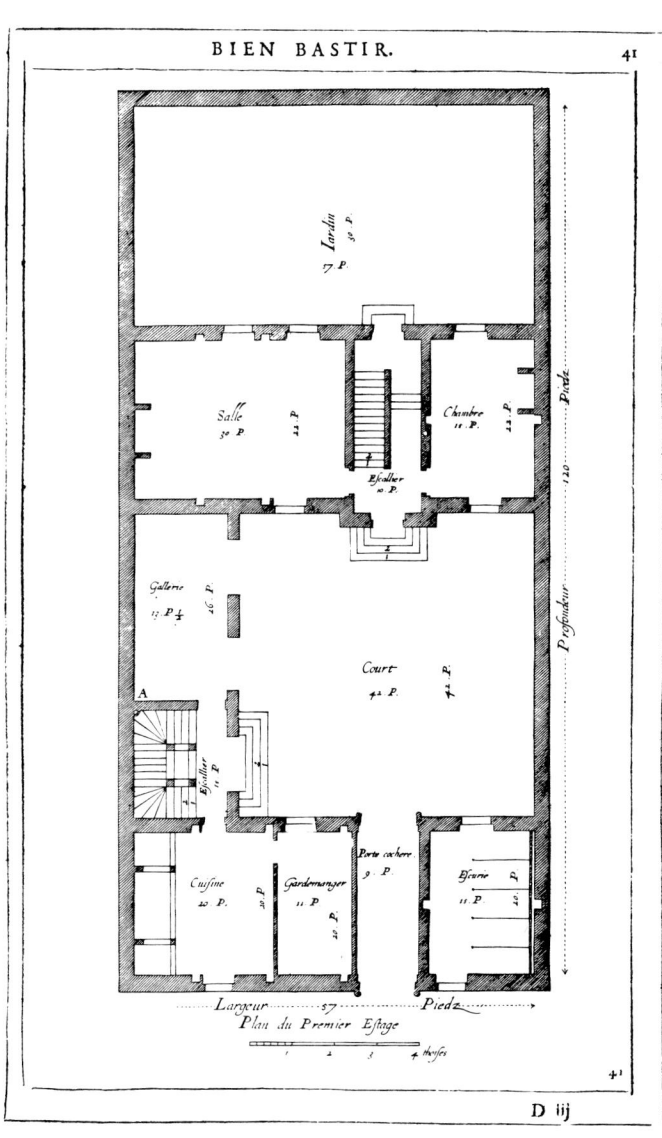

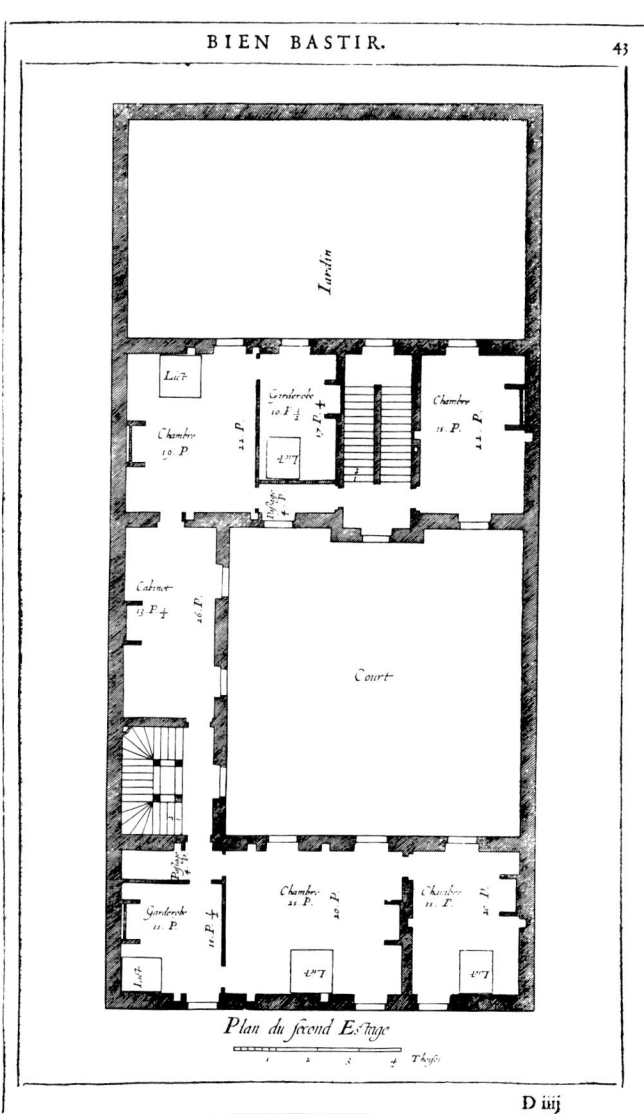

75
Project for a *hôtel* (*Distribution* 1, site 9), ground floor plan, Pierre Le Muet. From *Manière*, 1623.

76
Project for a *hôtel* (*Distribution* 1, site 9), upper floor plan, Pierre Le Muet

77
Hôtel de Sully, ground floor plan, Jean Du Cerceau, 1624–29

78
Hôtel de Sully, facade

79
Hôtel de Sully, court

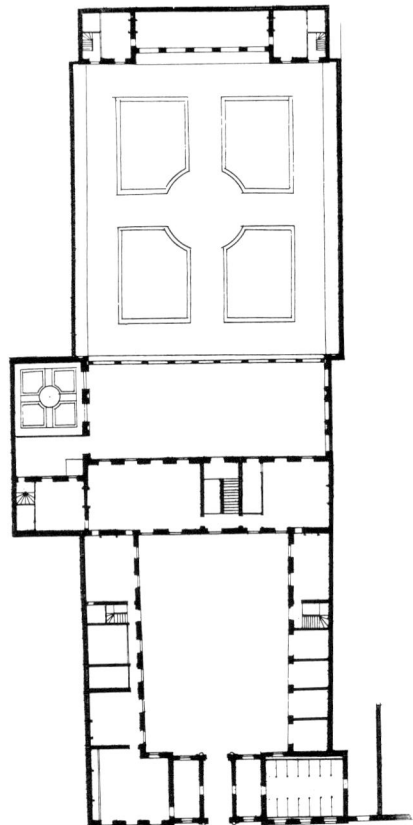
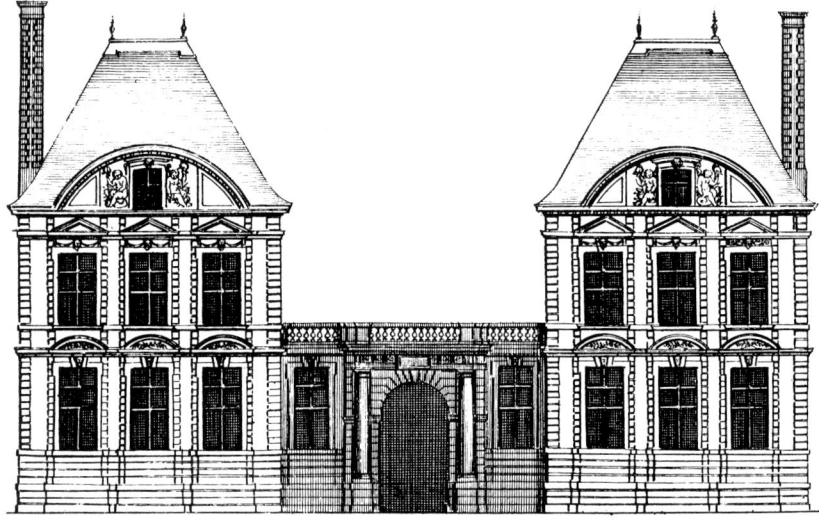

rather unsophisticated, the courtyard and its facades are very powerful indeed.

The long forecourt of the Hôtel de Sully is tapered very slightly in response to the irregular front of the site. The two-story building has a continuous cornice around three of its sides and part of the fourth, and the gap in the fourth, or street, side is closed by a one-story wing containing the *porte-cochère*. Thus, the court has sufficient spatial clarity and closure to have its own identity, and yet it also relates spatially to the public realm of the street. Neither totally public nor totally private, the useful ambivalence of the *cour d'honneur* is assisted by the rigorous neutrality of the wall. Somehow, French walls are stiffer and tauter than Italian walls—perhaps because of the stone and methods of cutting it. But more likely it is because of the greater proportion of window to wall and a strange combination of Italian Renaissance horizontality and French Gothic verticality. For example, in spite of the strength of the cornice in the forecourt of the Hôtel de Sully, the dormers above accentuate the tall, vertical readings of the windows and wall panels. Only the window pediments and the horizontal moldings collaborate with the cornice to restore the wall to a condition of tense, gridded neutrality. And if the aggressiveness of the wall speaks of formality and the public realm, the large French windows allude to potential domestic freedom beyond. As a discreet membrane between public and private, the facade of the forecourt has a doubly unique role in that it is "inside" but still "outside." The great outdoor room defined by these facades is the most important element in the Baroque *hôtel* plan and the most conspicuous element of the urban fabric of the Marais—a mediator between public and private.

Contemporary with the Hôtel de Sully and the theoretical projects of Le Muet was a much larger building, the Hôtel de Liancourt, which is important to future developments. Until this time all *hôtels*, even the Hôtel Carnavalet, had exhibited at least a tacitly coaxial relationship between forecourt and garden. Now, suddenly, the discontinuity latent in the Hôtel Carnavalet is exaggerated into prominence by the asymmetrical plan of the Hôtel de Liancourt, where the forecourt is completely dislocated from the central axis of the garden. This may well have been the result of the building's evolution rather than an intentional design strategy, because in 1623 Jacques Lemercier almost doubled the size of a *hôtel* built by Salomon de Brosse in 1613.[15] The problem of asymmetry was recognized, however, and was dealt with ingeniously.

By the mid-1630s, asymmetry and recentering from front to back were established themes and were exploited whether or not they were demanded by the building's evolution or by the site's irregularities. The Hôtel de Bretonvilliers, for example, had a regular site on the eastern tip of the newly developed Ile St.-Louis.[16] Begun in 1635 by Jean Du Cerceau and continued on an increased scale in 1638 by another architect, probably Louis Le Vau,[17] the Hôtel de Bretonvilliers marks the reemergence of the service court, which, in this case, connects directly to the forecourt rather than the street. The service court forces asymmetry upon the planning, which is only partially adjusted by the long gallery flanking the garden. The remaining portion of the *corps-de-logis* is designed symmetrically about the garden; a blank panel marks the center axis. The forecourt has entrances in the corners and in the center; the central one leads to a vestibule that overlooks the garden. As in Serlio's prototype, Le Grand Ferrare, the rooms are all rectangular and, generally, there is a balance between building and space, or between solid and void.

But the strongly centralized forecourt with its notched corners tends to be perceived as *figure*, alternately controlling and being supported by the *ground* of the building around it. This phenomenon is closely related to the themes of asymmetry and recentering in that both involve the principle of *discontinuity*. The essence of figure-ground relationships is articulation and differentiation rather than unity and integration. Any technique of differentiation will make that part of the organization more identifiable and therefore less continuous with its surrounding fabric. This, then, is the beginning of the art of residue and the core of the argument that the *hôtel* plan is a critique of the classical-idealist plan of Palladio.

The relation between architectural and urban features became more prominent as development in Paris during the 1630s shifted from the Marais to the west end of the city. The new wall of Louis XIII extended the limit of the city to the old wall of Charles V at the western end of the Tuileries gardens, and what became known as the Richelieu quarter was thereby opened up. The nucleus of the urban development of the new quarter was the Palais Cardinal, near the Louvre and adjacent to the rue St.-Honoré, begun in 1632 for Cardinal Richelieu. In addition to building his palace, Richelieu had a portion of the old wall of Charles V destroyed and boldly extended his palace gardens northward across the diagonal path of the wall. The palace, its gardens, and the adjacent rue de Richelieu drastically interrupted the existing city pattern in the area and estab-

58 Public Spaces: The Baroque Hôtel

80
Hôtel Chalons-Luxembourg, entry gate, c. 1608–15

81
Hôtel Chalons-Luxembourg, garden facade

82
Hôtel de Chevreuse, Clément Métezeau, after 1622. Engraving by Marot.

59 The Baroque Hôtel

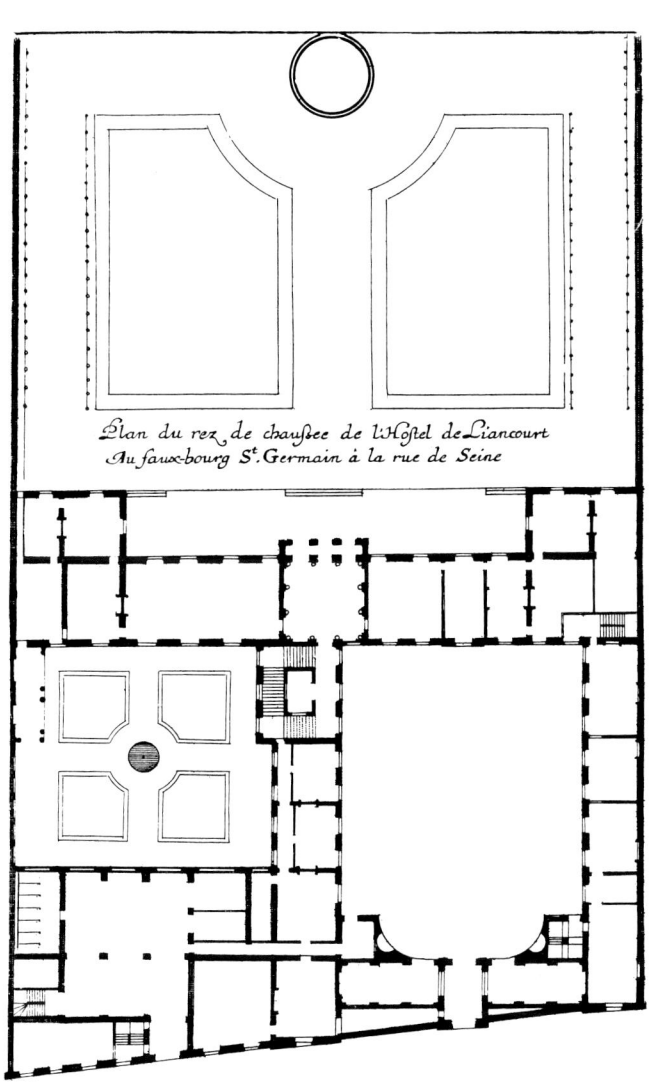

83
Hôtel de Liancourt,
ground floor plan,
Salomon de Brosse and
Jacques Lemercier,
1610–23+

84
Hôtel de Liancourt.
Engraving by Marot.

85
La visite d'une galerie de tableaux, Abraham Bosse (after Cl. Vignon)

86
Hôtel de Bretonvilliers, ground floor plan, Jean Du Cerceau, begun 1635

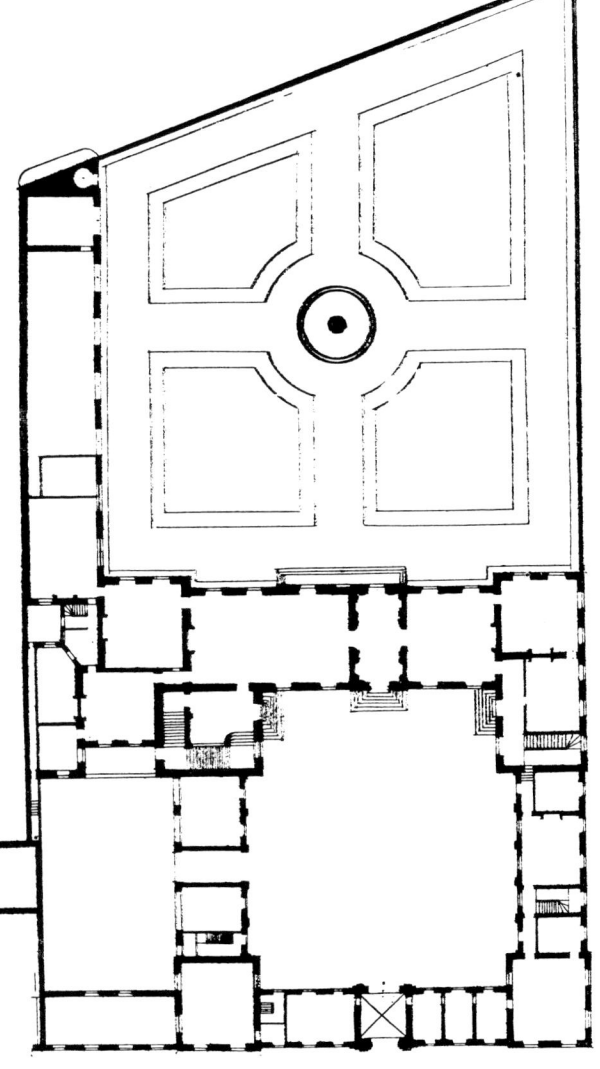

lished a new grid, or rather reinforced a latent one, perpendicular to the axis of the Louvre. This new grid became the dominant one for the development of the Richelieu quarter, while in the older part to the east, the diagonal pattern remained with the rue des Fossés Montmartre following the line of the old wall. This diagonal met the grid of the Palais Cardinal (later Palais Royal)[18] and terminated at the triangular site of the Hôtel de la Vrillière, begun in 1635. Thus the Hôtel de la Vrillière—and later the Place des Victoires—became a joint between two urban sectors. The city pattern before the insertion of the Palais Cardinal and the Hôtel de la Vrillière can be seen in the Merian view of 1620; and the pattern after, but before the Place des Victoires, can be seen in the Gombust plan of 1652. The Turgot plan of 1739 shows the addition of the Place des Victoires and the resolution of the street network.

Built by François Mansart for Louis Phélypeaux de la Vrillière, the Hôtel de la Vrillière is, in its main parts, a version of the Hôtel de Bretonvilliers.[19] The alterations are definitive: the garden wing is on the opposite side of the garden from that of the Hôtel de Bretonvilliers, creating a greater shift of axis between forecourt and garden; the entrance vestibule is more emphatic; and the principal rooms of the *corps-de-logis* are more coherently organized and linked in *enfilade*. But the most important difference between the two buildings is the way in which the Hôtel de la Vrillière relates to the urban context. The site is a large, irregular triangle, and the building is organized orthogonally to the old diagonal urban pattern. The principal street facade is thus perpendicular to the axis of the rue des Fossés Montmartre, an axis extending all the way to the Porte St.-Denis. It is in alignment with this monumental axis that Mansart located the *cour d'honneur* of the *hôtel*, thus establishing a surprisingly powerful relationship between the *hôtel* and the city. While the court is rectangular, its unity and its context increase its figural importance vis-à-vis the irregular surrounding texture. The back side of the *hôtel*, toward the rue des Bons Enfants and the Palais Royal is, by contrast, handled in the most perfunctory and offhand way. Only the garden is positively shaped in order to hide the irregularities created at the rear of the site. This project demonstrates the degree to which a large "field" can be stabilized and controlled by carefully conceived platonic voids and points the way to subsequent formal developments, culminating in the Hôtel de Beauvais.

Most *hôtels* built during the 1630s and 1640s by Le Muet, Mansart, Louis Le Vau, and others[20] were variations of the basic schema of the Baroque type illustrated by the Hôtel de la Vrillière. Generally they had rectangular rooms, and although the sequence of spaces was not yet highly developed, they did reflect the increased specialization alluded to earlier.

For the remainder of this period, the most important formal innovations pertained to internal planning as a continued hierarchical extension of the public realm. Some of the changes may be seen by comparing the built works in Le Muet's enlarged work of 1647 with the prototypes in the earlier edition. For example, even the relatively modest Hôtel Tubeuf indicates more functionally specific rooms than a similar early project; and the Hôtel d'Avaux, still standing in the rue des Archives, is of another order of magnitude entirely. The social rituals of a society increasingly obsessed with hierarchy and public display were having a significant impact on both the size and the *distribution* of the *hôtel*. As the public rooms multiplied so did the service rooms, and therefore servants and servants' rooms. A large *hôtel* could have as many as eighty to over a hundred inhabitants;[21] even the number of horses increased. As all areas of the *hôtel* became larger and more functionally specific, several innovations in planning occurred.[22]

One important innovation was better grouping of the rooms of the *appartement*. There were two systems of grouping: *enfilade*, rooms in a row with doors opening along an axis, and *massée*, or clustered rooms. The Marquise de Rambouillet insisted on the principal rooms being arranged in *enfilade* along the garden side of the *corps-de-logis*, with the large doors along a single axis that opened up a perspective across the whole width of the site. This gave grandeur and continuity to the public sequence of rooms. The *massée* system allowed for more flexibility in circulation and sequence among the public rooms; and in the more private parts of the house, it allowed for useful discontinuity or disengagement, *dégagement*, between service and served rooms.

Both systems, *enfilade* and *massée*, benefited from another innovation: the *corps-de-logis* formed by a double zone of rooms rather than a single zone. This type of *hôtel* was illustrated by Le Muet in 1623 as number 5, site 9, and a version of it, the Hôtel de Jars, was begun in 1648 by François Mansart. The arrangement allowed for more rooms on a narrow site and for greater flexibility of rooms. Consequently, for example, the owner's rooms gradually migrated out of the wings flanking the court, leaving them for services and domestics. Savot, in his treatise of 1624, expressed particular fondness for the practi-

62 Public Spaces: The Baroque Hôtel

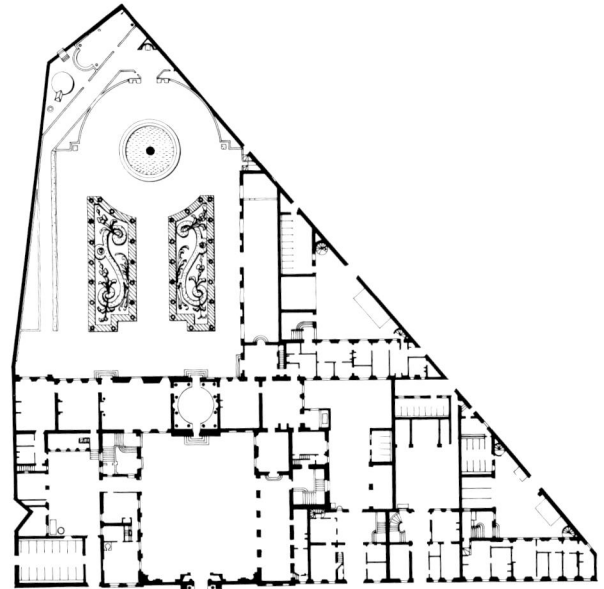

87
Hôtel de la Vrillière, plan, François Mansart, begun 1635

88
Hôtel de la Vrillière. Detail from the Turgot plan.

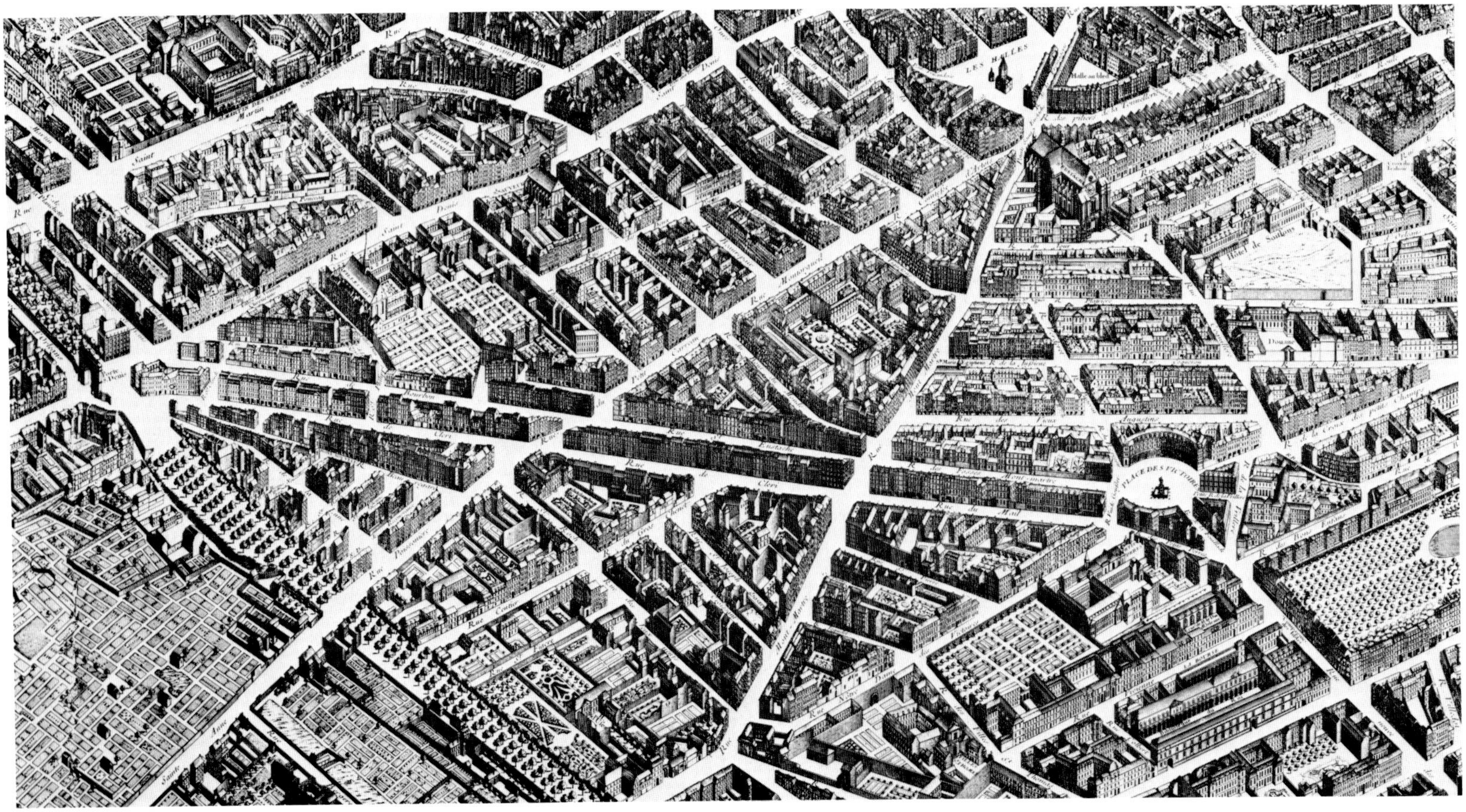

63   The Baroque Hôtel

89
Hôtel de la Vrillière.
Engraving by Marot.

90
Hôtel de la Vrillière.
Engraving by Marot.

91
Hôtel Bautru de Serrant, Louis Le Vau, 1634–37. Engraving by Marot.

92
Hôtel Séguier (Bellegarde), Jean Du Cerceau, 1612–34+. Engraving by Marot.

65 The Baroque Hôtel

93
Hôtel Falcony, Jean Du Cerceau, 1640. Engraving by Marot.

94
Hôtel Duret de Chevry (Mazarin), Jean Thiriot, 1635–41. Engraving by Marot.

66 Public Spaces: The Baroque Hôtel

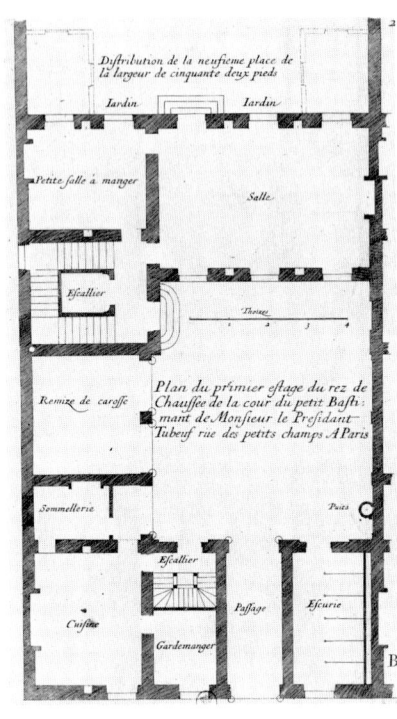
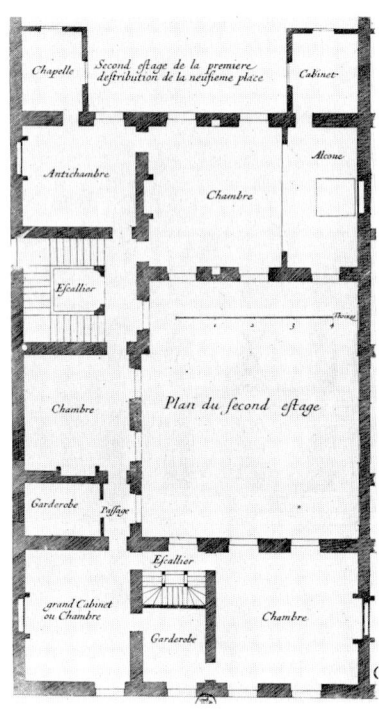

95
Hôtel Tubeuf, ground floor plan, Pierre Le Muet, before 1643

96
Hôtel Tubeuf, upper floor plan

97
Hôtel Tubeuf, section

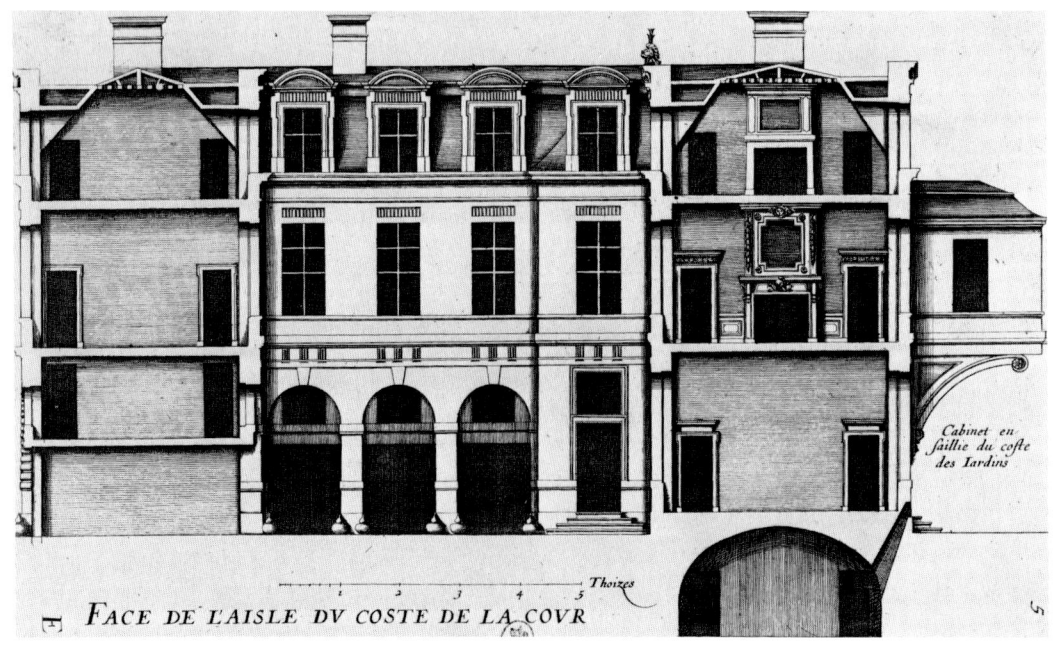

67 The Baroque Hôtel

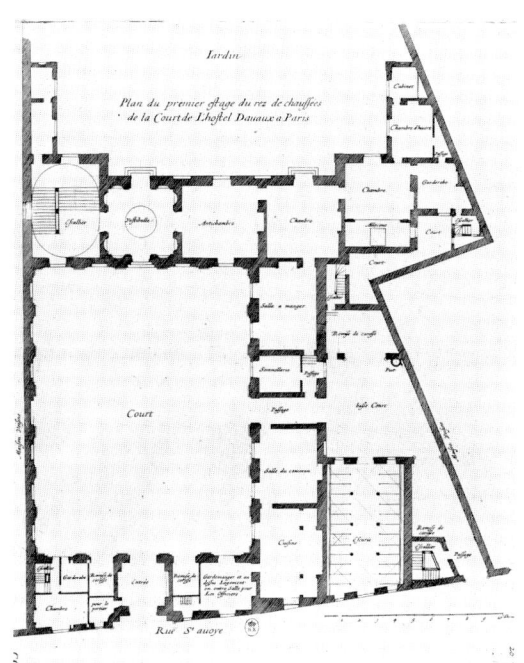

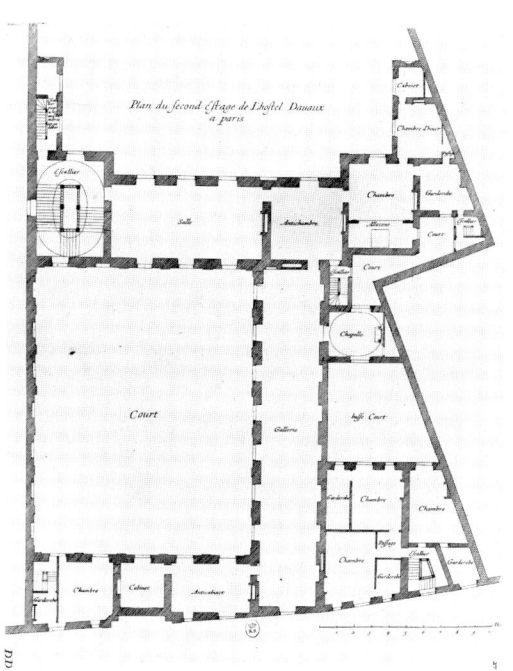

98
Hôtel d'Avaux, ground floor plan, Pierre Le Muet, 1640

99
Hôtel d'Avaux, upper floor plan

100
Hôtel d'Avaux, section

68 Public Spaces: The Baroque Hôtel

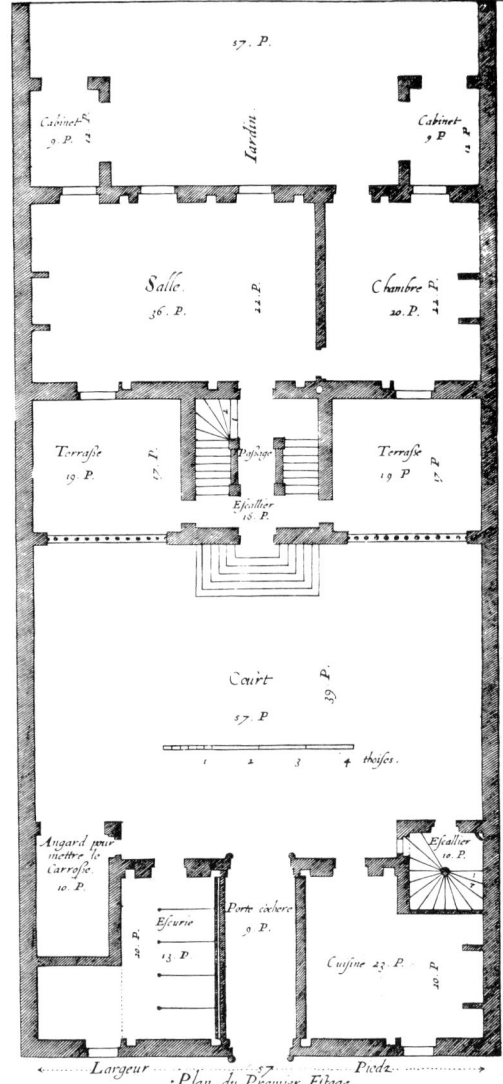

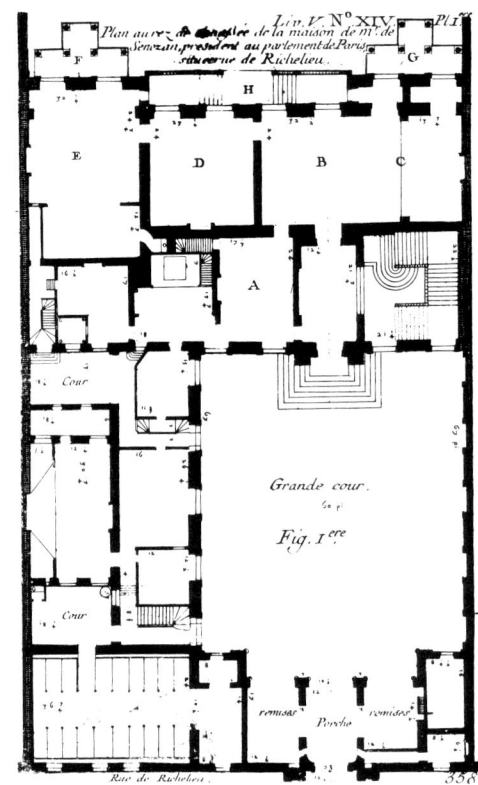

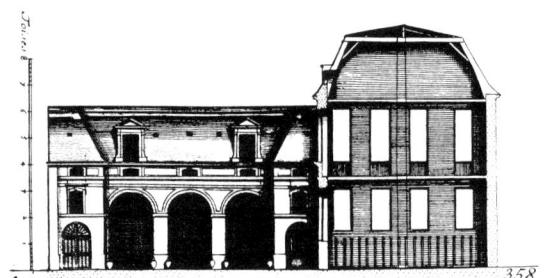

101
Hôtel project 5, site 9, plan, Pierre Le Muet. From Le Muet's *Manière...*, 1623.

102
Hôtel de Jars, plan and facade, François Mansart, begun 1648

cality of the double zone, as it provided cool rooms in the summer and warm rooms in the winter.[23] The double-zone *corps-de-logis* also made possible a major improvement in the form and location of the grand stair. The Marquise de Rambouillet had criticized the stair in the center of the single *corps-de-logis* (as in the Hôtel de Sully) because it occupied the best part of the building and interrupted the *enfilade* of the *appartements*. She insisted instead on the other traditional location, the angle of the court; but this made the entrance awkward and the sequence long. The double zone solved everything by allowing the entrance to be in the middle of the building and the grand stair on the court side, opening off the *vestibule* and leading to the upper floor or *bel étage*. Finally, the double zone gave architects more freedom to resolve axial discrepancies between forecourt and gardens. It became standard practice for most later *hôtels*.

The hierarchy that began to inform the plan also altered the section; floors were differentiated by height, and mezzanines (*entresols*) appeared. In general the *entresols* were used over the service areas to house the servants, but since the large rooms were cold and drafty in the winter, about mid-century architects began to install mezzanines with small rooms. Louis XIV, for example, had a small *appartement de commodité* above his study in the Louvre.[24] But these amenities were few in the seventeenth century.

During the *ancien régime*, and especially in the seventeenth century, when most life was public life, privacy had a completely different meaning from what we understand today.[25] The sequence of reception took precedence over comfort, and display was more important than intimacy. It is therefore useful to understand the hierarchical sequence of reception, in relative terms, from the most public to the most private rooms. The key parts of the *hôtel*, and the pride of its owners, were the *appartements* of the master and mistress of the house. Each spouse had a suite of rooms, and guests were received in one or the other depending on whim or the season of the year—the cooler ground floor rooms in summer, the warmer upper rooms in winter. Generally, however, the *bel étage* was occupied by the women, while the ground floor was for the master of the house.

The newly expanded sequence began with the *cour d'honneur*. Guests left their carriages and servants here and then entered the *vestibule*. This was one of the new room types which opened to the grand stair and the *antichambre*, itself a new room type. Generally square, the *antichambre* was the first reception room, where people waited to be received or where they were received if they were not allowed further. The servants waited here or in the *vestibule*. If there was no designated *salle à manger*, the *antichambre* also served as a dining room for the family. Sometimes the *antichambre* was preceded by a *grande salle* for parties, ballets, and receptions, but over a long period of time, this was reduced in size and significance. Ultimately, it became the *salon*.

After the *antichambre* came the principal reception room, the *chambre* or *chambre de parade*, a vast square room containing a large bed from which visitors were received. No effort was spared in the decoration and furnishing of this room because it was the showpiece of the *appartement*. It derived from rooms in the *châteaux* that had to be maintained for the sovereigns in case they came to visit. The area along the side of the bed, the *ruelle*, was where the mistress of the house received *en lit* her more familiar guests. Babelon described the *ruelle* as a "theater of the chatter boxes" and a forum for the "literary assaults of the *Précieuses*."[26] This intimate space was the precedent for a smaller room adjacent to the grand one. The Marquise de Rambouillet is credited with initiating the change when she remade a *garde-robe* into a *chambre à alcôve*. The idea took hold, and by 1640 the great ladies no longer slept in the *chambre de parade*, which was then reserved for reception, but in the *chambre à alcôve* or *chambre à coucher*. This was, according to Babelon, a "first step . . . toward comfort."[27] In addition, many women were beginning to receive in their *cabinet* or in an *antichambre* transformed into a *salon*.[28]

The *chambre* was served by one or more *garde-robes* for clothes and a personal domestic's lodging, and sometimes there was also an *arrière garde-robe* where the *chaise percée*, or commode, was kept. Bath suites began to appear in larger *hôtels* around mid-seventeenth century—Madame de Beauvais possessed one—but bathing was not yet a high priority.

The last room in the sequence was a small, intimate room with "original" decoration, the *cabinet*. Like a small study, it was used for writing, sleeping, or intimate conversation. The Marquise de Rambouillet's famous "loge de Zirphée," for example, was such a room: half a hexagon with windows on three sides, sitting stools, and consoles with Venetian vases.[29] These *cabinets* became the famous *boudoirs* of the eighteenth century. Occasionally there was also a *serre-papier*, or small study, for keeping papers, and any of a variety of larger rooms such as libraries, chapels, and especially *galeries*.

70 Public Spaces: The Baroque Hôtel

As the public rooms became more specialized, so did the service rooms, which became even further separated from the living spaces. The functions associated with the storage and preparation of food were segregated from the stables and carriages, preferably into the opposite wings of the court, and the servants were lodged in the garrets and *entresols* near their work areas. One or more service courts became necessary because of increased commotion, noise, and odors. As a result of functional segregation, the kitchens were a long way from the dining room, requiring that food be reheated.

Although *privés* were beginning to appear in some houses, it was standard practice to have latrines in the service court. It was here that the master's "chaise" was emptied each day. Modern standards make the contrast between the habits of the nobility and the public splendor of the *ancien régime* difficult to imagine. "Private" customs were inexplicably crude: noble ladies thought nothing of relieving themselves in such places as the loges of theaters and the passageways of Versailles. Hautecoeur recounts Viollet-le-Duc's story of visiting Versailles with a lady who had lived there under Louis XV: when they passed a stench-ridden corridor, she remarked, "Ah, that reminds me of the good old days."[30]

If privacy was neglected during this period, the formal devices that later made it possible were developed in rapid succession, starting with Le Vau's Hôtel Lambert, begun in 1640 for Jean Baptiste Lambert. Here Le Vau used uniquely shaped rooms—round-cornered court, octagon, oval, and round-ended gallery—orchestrated into a hierarchical sequence of public spaces to brilliantly resolve a difficult site on the eastern tip of the Ile St.-Louis. Located on the street that formed

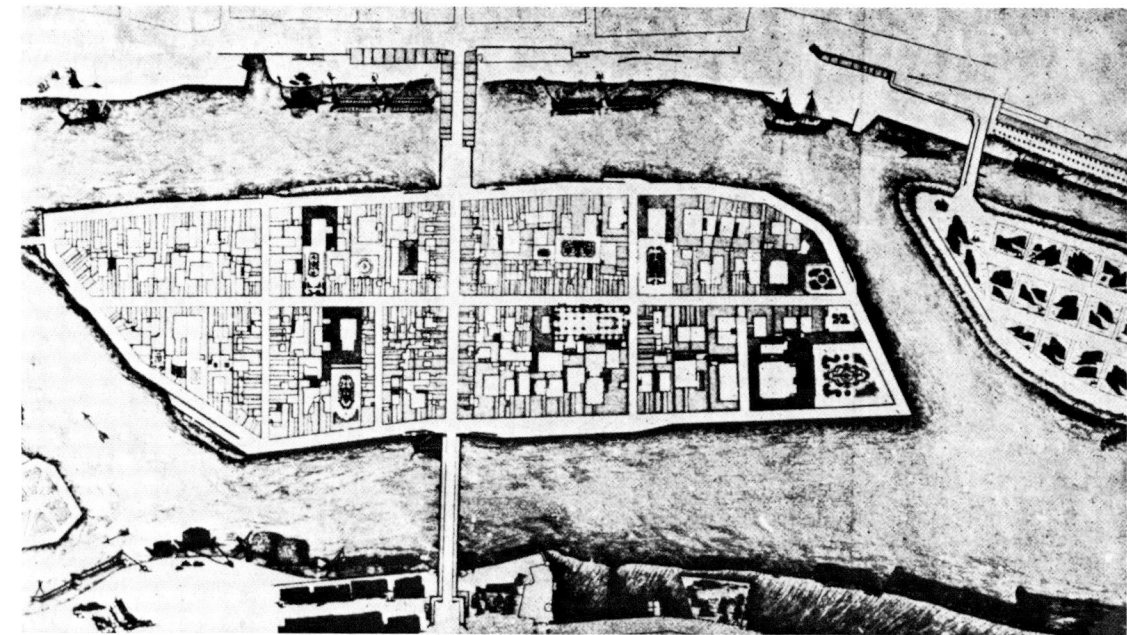

103
L'Ile St.-Louis, plan showing the Hôtel de Bretonvilliers and the Hôtel Lambert on the eastern tip of the island

71 The Baroque Hôtel

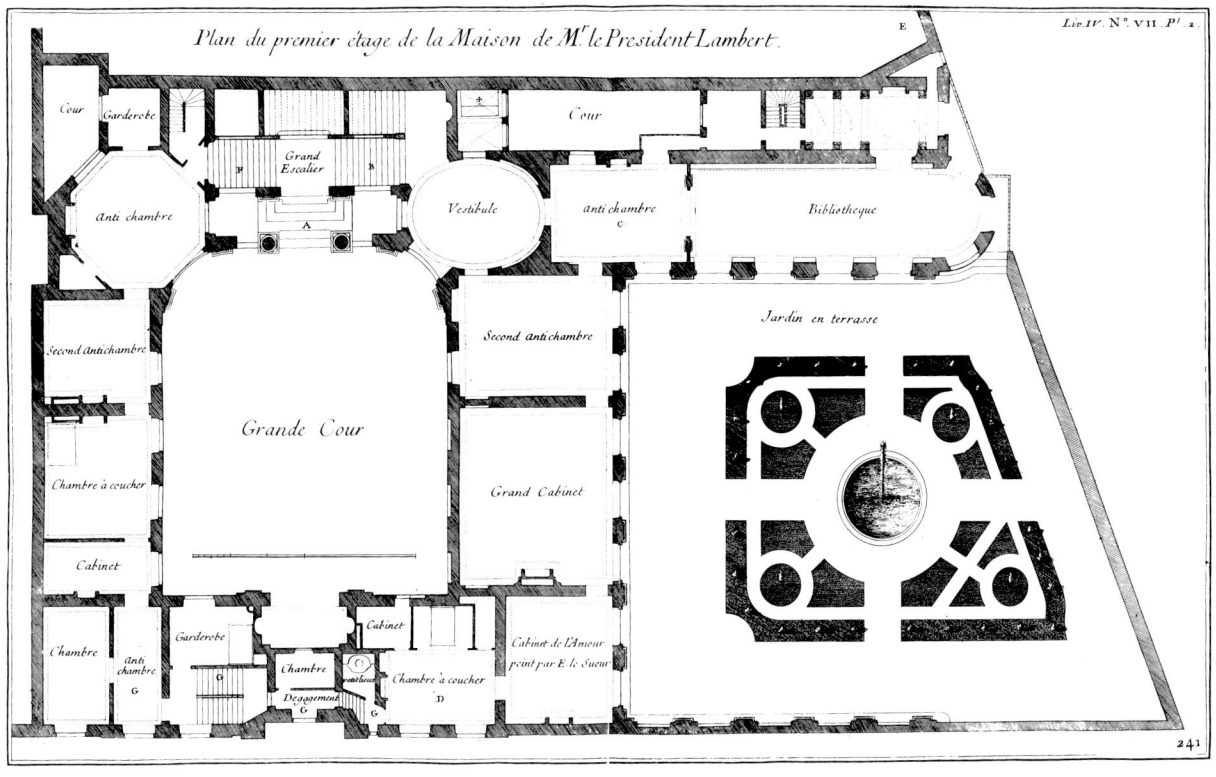

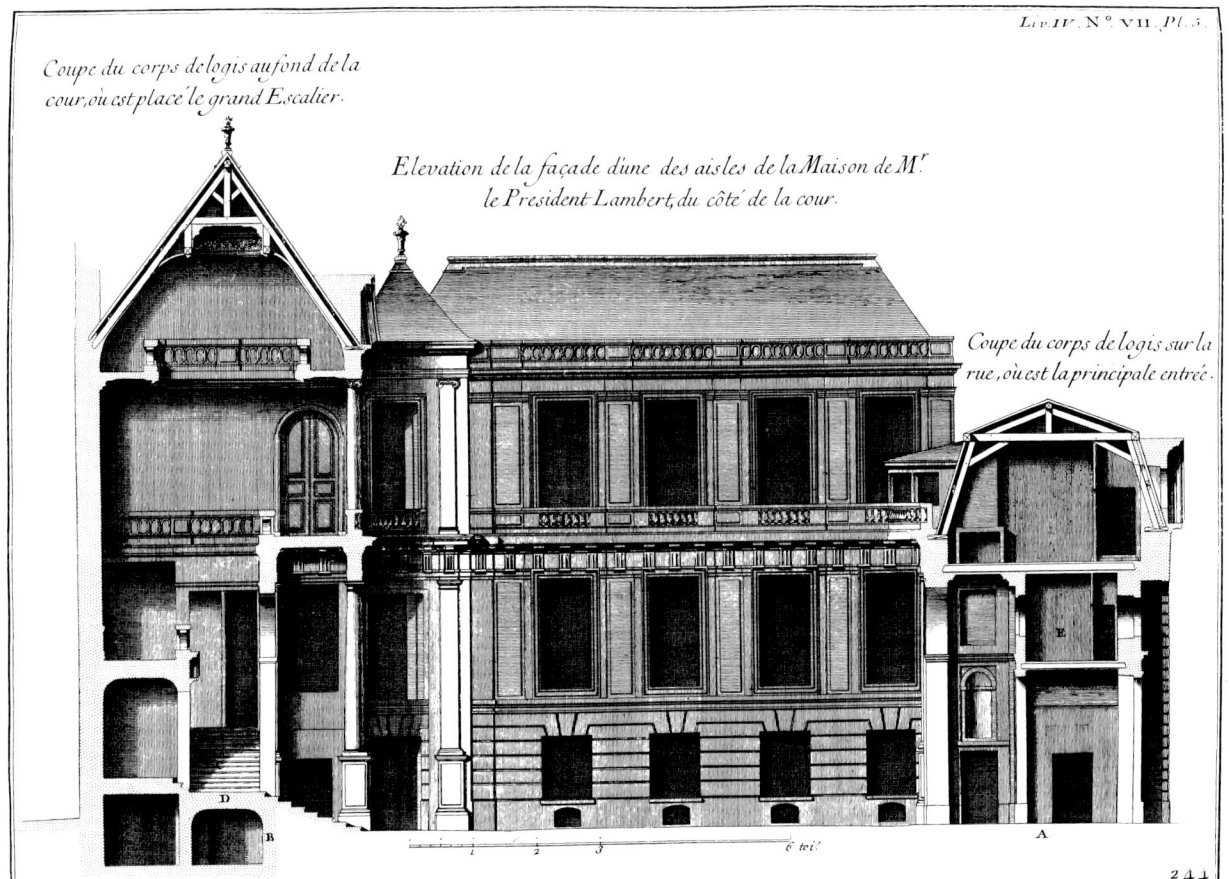

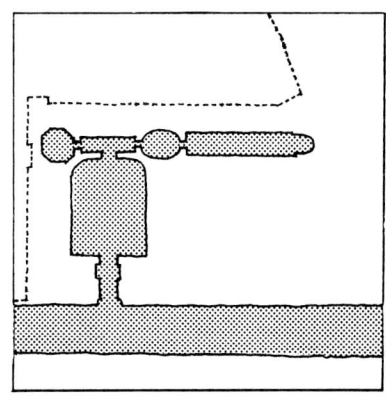

104
Hôtel Lambert, terrace level plan, Louis Le Vau, 1642–44

105
Hôtel Lambert, section

106
Hôtel Lambert, spatial sequence

the central axis of the island, the *hôtel* was across from and parallel to the Hôtel de Bretonvilliers. In fact, Le Vau's *hôtel* can be seen as a sophisticated commentary on its larger neighbor, for the plan type is similar. With the Hôtel Lambert, however, Le Vau turns the axis of the forecourt perpendicular to that of the garden so that entrance from the main street terminates across the court with the grand stair. Then the stair leads up to a zone of vestibules and a long gallery that is parallel to the street, overlooks the raised garden, and ends in a bow window looking up the Seine. The principal public rooms are located in the wing separating the court and garden, the secondary rooms are in the opposite wing, and the service rooms are over the entrance on the street side.

Here, as in Vaux-le-Vicomte, the public sequence of space is more a function of the site than of the internal disposition of the plan, and the episodes of this sequence collectively form an articulate figure distinct from the rest of the house. The particular shapes of the rooms as well as their size, location, light quality, and so on contribute to the closure and identity of this figure against the ground of the rest of the building. Only upon closer observation do other figures or sets of rooms begin to emerge.

Clearly, the Hôtel Lambert is a turning point in *hôtel* design. The use of varied, figurally shaped rooms was the last addition to the set of compositional techniques that had been evolving for many years and that were soon to give French architects complete hegemony over the art of the plan. Themes of symmetry/asymmetry, recentering, local symmetry, hierarchical figure-ground relationships, and the hierarchical exploitation of residue or *poché* all exploited the principle of dis-

107
Hôtel Lambert, court

108
Hôtel Lambert, gallery, Louis Le Vau and Lebrun, c. 1650

continuity. Although these themes were nurtured within the classical system, they made the French *hôtel* into the strongest counter argument to that system and therefore a highly sophisticated instrument of urbanism.

The most spectacular virtuoso demonstration of the principles of the Baroque *hôtel* is Antoine Le Pautre's Hôtel de Beauvais, constructed for Catherine Henriette Bellier between 1654 and 1657 in the rue St.-Antoine near the Place Royale.[31] The site fronts on two streets, not at right angles to each other, and has a highly irregular configuration with no parallel sides. The site was actually composed of three lots occupied by medieval houses, and Le Pautre incorporated part of their foundations into his own design.[32] The site's limited area precluded a private garden, so Le Pautre placed the double-zone *corps-de-logis* on the street side of the *cour d'honneur*. On the ground floor, shops facing the street are separated by a *porte-cochère* that connects the street to a round vestibule and then to the court. The rear of the plan contains stables, services, and a passageway to the rear street. The grand stair leads up from the ground floor to another vestibule on the second floor, which in turn leads to the public rooms overlooking the street. Secondary rooms, a gallery, and a chapel flank the courtyard and are separated by a hanging garden from an *appartement* facing the back street. The remainder of the plan is filled with ingeniously contrived smaller rooms and private circulation.

In urban design terms, the building fills the highly irregular site, as if poured into it, and maintains the continuity of the street to form a kind of urban *poché*, out of which the central figure of the courtyard appears to be carved.[33] On the ground floor, this figure is related to the

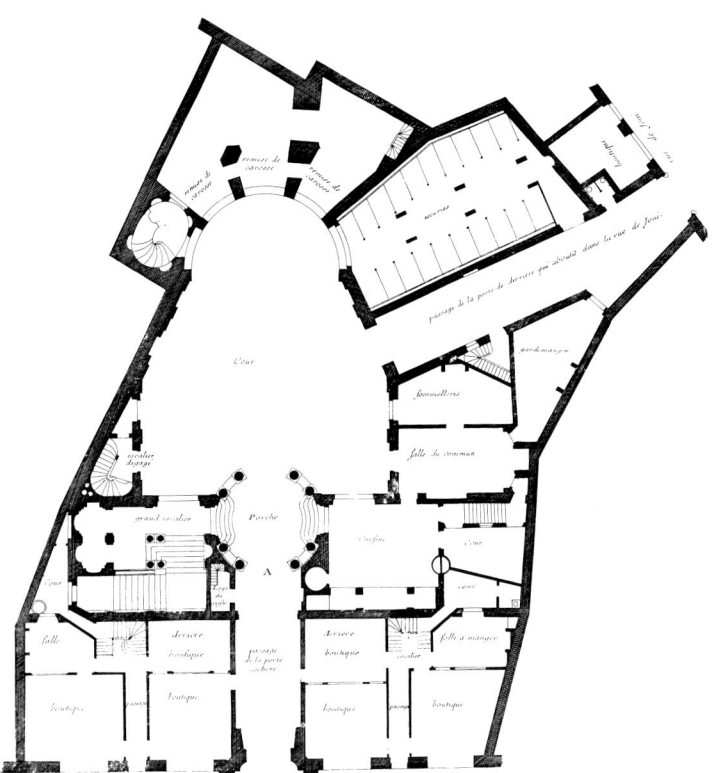

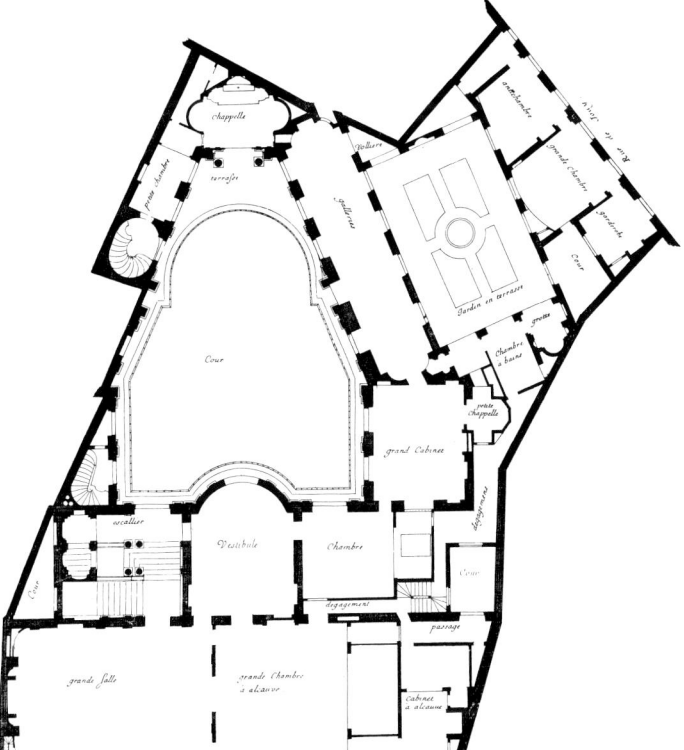

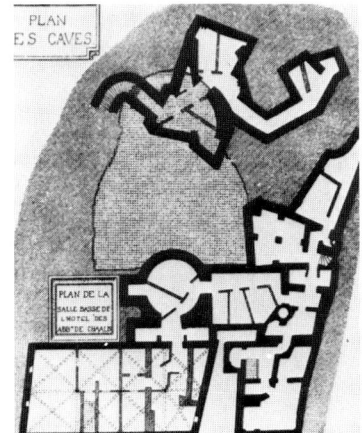

109
Hôtel de Beauvais, ground floor plan, Antoine Le Pautre, 1652–55

110
Hôtel de Beauvais, upper floor plan

111
Hôtel de Beauvais, plan of medieval foundations, by M. Du Seigneur

74 Public Spaces: The Baroque Hôtel

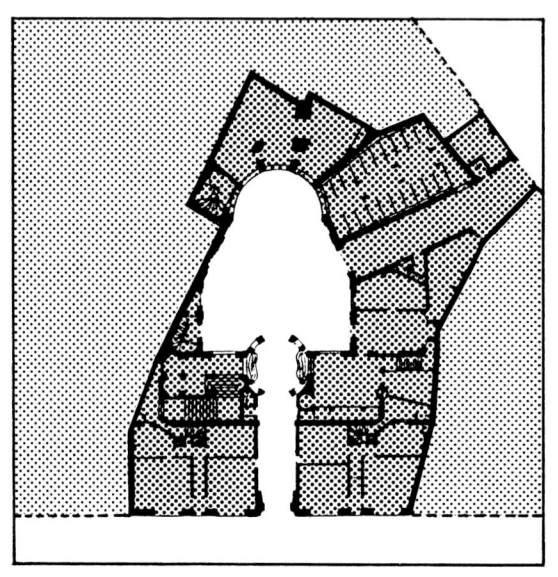

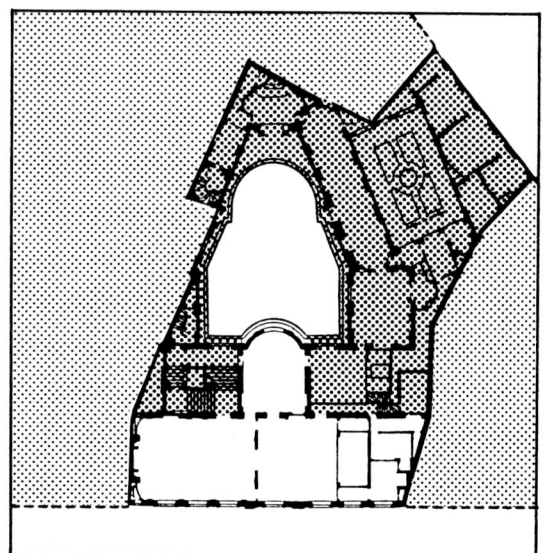

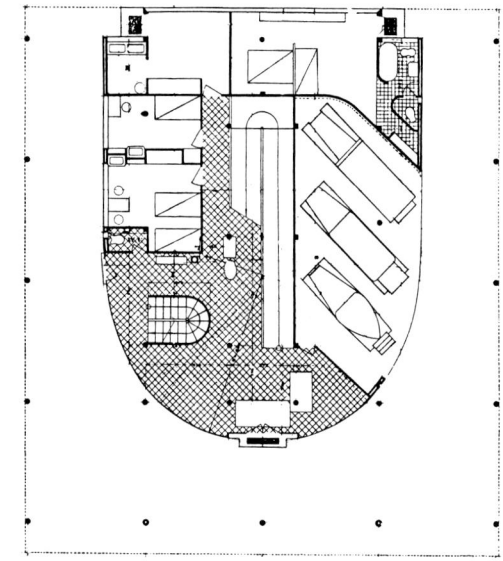

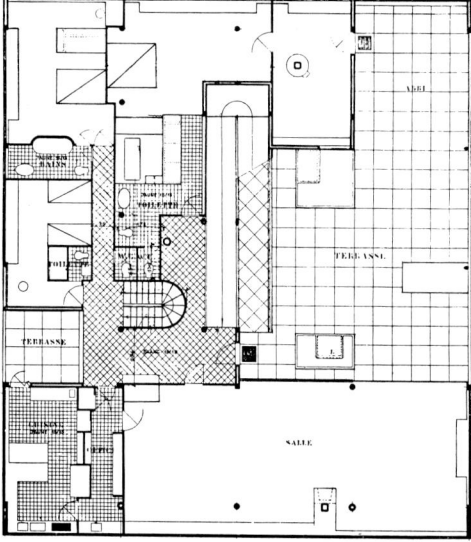

112
Hôtel de Beauvais, central figure on ground floor

113
Hôtel de Beauvais, central figure on upper floor

114
Villa Savoye, ground floor plan, Le Corbusier, 1928–31

115
Villa Savoye, upper floor plan

public space of the street by the *porte-cochère* and vestibule; on the second floor, by the vestibule and the zone containing the *grande salle*. The closure, specificity, and identity—the symmetry—of this event permits the freedom of the perimeter. Quite simply, the regular symmetrical shape of the courtyard conceals the varied rooms disposed around it and also, therefore, the irregularities of the site. This kind of organization, platonic and controlled on the inside and irregular and accommodating on the perimeter, is extremely evocative and is reminiscent of freestanding composite buildings, such as the typical monastic plan, and of urban "field" buildings, such as the Friday Mosque at Isfahan. And it is the inverse of the Villa Savoye, where the tautness and regularity of the perimeter control the disposition of the plan.

In the Hôtel de Beauvais, local symmetry and figural space combine to form a kind of designed discontinuity that gives the building its unique qualities. Indeed, the whole plan can be seen as a hierarchy of locally symmetrical figures, each supported by analogous levels of *poché*. Secondary and then tertiary rooms are collaged into the plan in concentric but asymmetric layers, and the organization of rooms varies between floors. The freedom of the plan produces no fewer than four separate grids plus an astonishing variety of room sizes and configurations, not to mention the extended and elaborate sequence, or *promenade*. But it is the notion of successive levels of figure-ground relationships that is the primary lesson of the Baroque *hôtel* type. Rather than insisting upon total design, as in Baroque public buildings, the architects of the *hôtels* utilize the principle of discontinuity to demonstrate that independence and identity of the part can be achieved without sacrificing the unity of the whole. In this respect the Hôtel de Beauvais, like most French *hôtels*, may be seen as a collision of the ideal and the circumstantial, a collision which in turn may very well have become something of an ideal in itself—an ideal of demonstrable virtuosity.

In many ways the Hôtel de Beauvais is the culmination of the great period of seventeenth-century *hôtel* building. Though many notable *hôtels* were built in the 1650s and early 1660s, such as the Hôtel Guénégaud (1653) by François Mansart, the Hôtel Salé (1656) by Bullier, the Hôtel Amelot de Bisseuil (1657–60) by Pierre Cottard, and the Hôtels Lauzun (1656–57) and de Lionne (begun 1662) by Le Vau, none was as flamboyant or as innovative as the Hôtel de Beauvais. The death of Mazarin in 1661 and the beginning of the rule of Louis XIV marked a significant change in French culture and architecture. The focus during this spectacular period was on public buildings rather than *hôtels* and on Versailles rather than Paris. Culturally, it was the opposite of the last forty years of the sixteenth century, the period of the Wars of Religion, but its effect on the development of the *hôtel* was as disruptive to private building as the previous period had been to public building.

116
Cistercian Monastery, plan

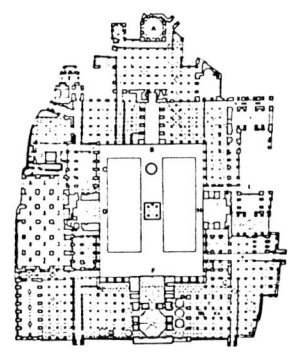

117
Isfahan, Friday Mosque, plan

76 Public Spaces: The Baroque Hôtel

118
Hôtel de Beauvais, facade, Antoine Le Pautre. Engraving by Marot.

119
Hôtel de Beauvais, court

120
Hôtel de Beauvais, court

121
Hôtel Amelot de Bisseuil, Pierre Cottard, 1657–60

122
Hôtel Amelot de Bisseuil. Engraving by Marot.

Marot

Jean Marot published the *hôtels* of this period in two volumes: the *Recueil* or "Petit Marot" (c. 1660–70) and *L'Architecture* or "Grand Marot" (c. 1670). Unlike the first books of Du Cerceau and Le Muet, Marot's books contain no theoretical projects, only *hôtels* that were actually built. And, unlike the treatises of Blondel and d'Aviler, which were to follow shortly, Marot's books contain no theoretical text. Rather, they document the work of a period when domestic architecture developed unfettered by overt theory, a period when tradition and convention provided a framework conducive to exceptional architectural invention and experimentation.

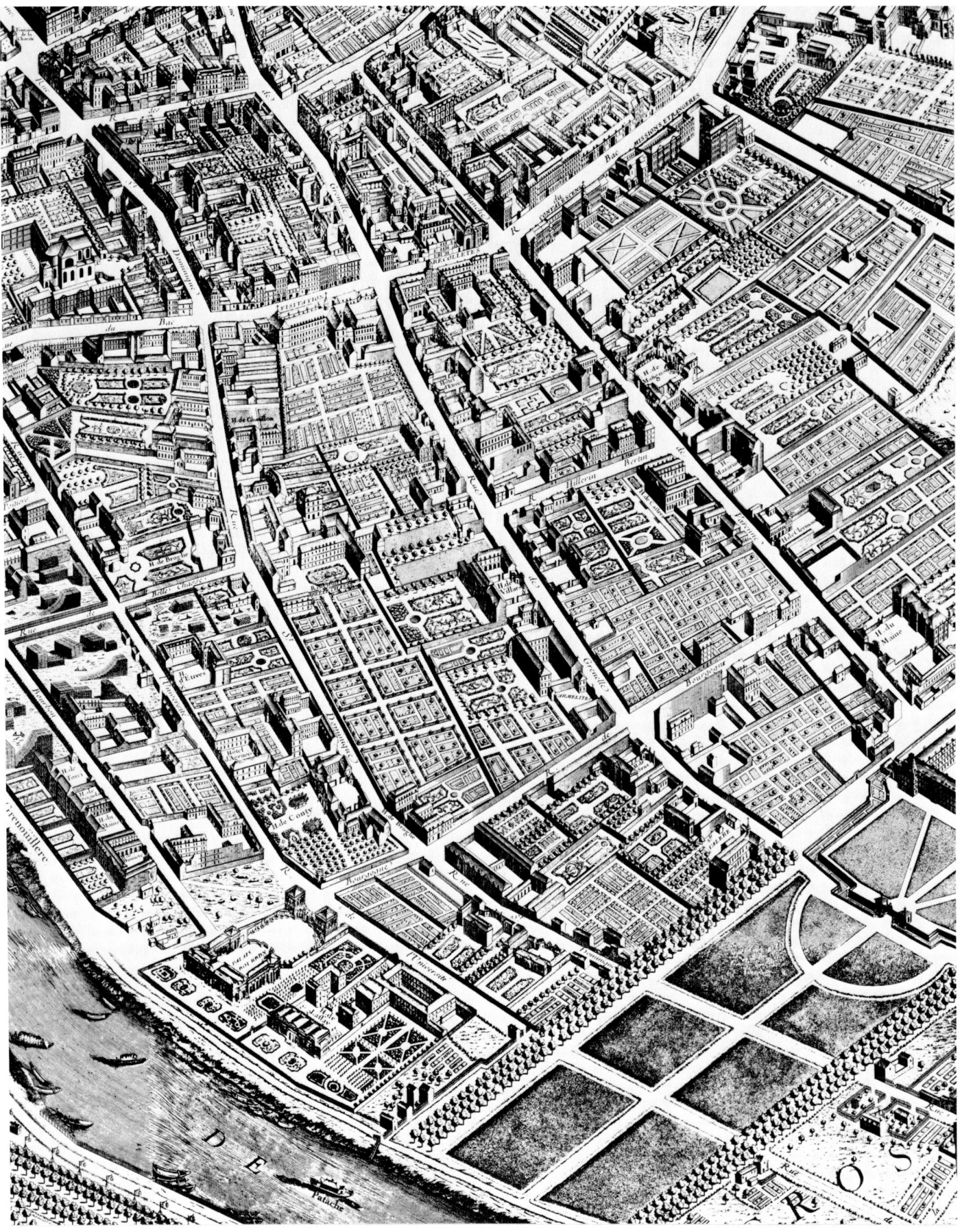

123
Faubourg St.-Germain. From the Turgot plan.

124
Hôtel de Matignon, Jean Courtonne. From the Turgot plan.

4 *Display and Retreat: The Rococo Hôtel*

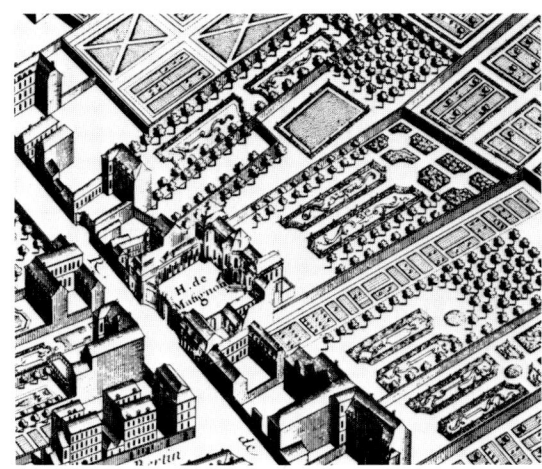

The Rococo *hôtel* is a transitional type that developed, roughly, between the construction of the final version of the Place Louis-le-Grand in 1699 and the publication of Blondel's *Architecture françoise* in 1752. Culturally, this was a time of transition, from the public dominance and formality of the Baroque to new individual freedoms and a greater emphasis on private life in the last half of the eighteenth century. Architecturally, the transformation was manifested in the Rococo *hôtel* type in two ways: as a transition from the party-wall urban *hôtel* of the Baroque period to the freestanding suburban *hôtel* of the Neoclassic period and as advances in internal planning. But the setting for the development of the Rococo *hôtel* is that blind spot in domestic architecture, the gap in *hôtel* building which began with the abandonment of Paris for Versailles by the young Louis XIV after he assumed the rule in 1661.

Two decades of collaboration, 1661–83, between Louis XIV and his advisor Colbert were characterized by successful wars, centralization of power, and the beginning of a series of important public projects. Among these were the Collège des Quatre Nations (1662), the Champs-Elysées (1667), the east front of the Louvre (1667), Le Vau's project for Versailles (1669), the *boulevards* of Paris (1670), and the Invalides (1670). In 1671 the Academy of Architecture was founded. Under the direction of Colbert, art was dominated by Lebrun and architecture by J. H. Mansart. The court at Versailles became the envy of Europe, and all art was subordinated to the will of the king, a symbol of his absolute authority and a tribute to his grandeur. The social rituals of court society became firmly established at Versailles; and although there would soon be a reaction to the rigorous formality under Louis XIV, the etiquette and ceremony that developed during this period would continue as dominant social influences on architecture throughout the *ancien régime*.[1]

Colbert's death in 1683, however, marked the start of a period of decline in which war, extreme financial difficulties, and a changing sensibility all took their toll. Louis XIV became increasingly egomaniacal and autocratic as Louvois, Colbert's successor, catered injudiciously to his whims and caprices. The king's personality had a direct influence on his building program; despite the many economic difficulties of the time, in the mid-1680s he commissioned three important projects, all by J. H. Mansart—the Grand Trianon (1687), the Place des Victoires (1685), and the Place Louis-le-Grand (1685). The two urban projects are of special importance historically, socially, and architecturally, as they form the joint between two disparate periods and two distinct cultures. Formally, they reflect the aspirations and problems of both, but they are not so much an articulation of the two as a collision between them.

The cultural differences emerge in a brief comparison of the Place des Victoires and the Place Louis-le-Grand, constructed at the end of the century, to the Place Dauphine and the Place Royale, built at the beginning. All four were royal squares; all were residential squares; and all were pure geometric forms. But whereas the Place Dauphine and the Place Royale of Henri IV were sound business ventures intended as amenities for the people of Paris, the Place des Victoires and the Place Louis-le-Grand were beset with economic problems and were intended primarily as grand gestures to flatter the king. Their different intentions resulted in equally diverse concep-

80   Display and Retreat: The Rococo Hôtel

tions. Neither of the earlier squares contained a statue and both were formed by identical adjacent houses; thus the focus was not strongly central but peripheral. In the case of the Place Royale, the equilibrium of the space is also reinforced by the closure and stability of its square shape. In addition, both of the early squares were located adjacent to, but not on, major circulation routes, thus ensuring a certain protected calm while providing the benefits of proximity.

If all of this contributed to the original quality of these spaces and if these characteristics provided a kind of natural immunity to future urban changes, then something approaching the opposite may be said of the Place des Victoires and the Place Louis-le-Grand. Both of these were statue squares in which the central figure of the king determined the proportions of the space and was its focal point. The surrounding facades were regular and repetitive. Where emphasis occurred, as in the pedimented projections of the Place Louis-le-Grand, it served to articulate the space of the square itself rather than a house behind. The facades in both cases were designed independently of the houses and in fact masked their random widths. The shapes of the two squares also reinforced their centrality, and their locations in the urban context were problematic right from their inception, especially that of the Place des Victoires.

The Maréchal de la Feuillade developed the Place des Victoires on a site near the northeast corner of the Palais Royal gardens, just in front of the Hôtel de la Vrillière.[2] As originally conceived by Mansart, the *place* was almost a complete circle in plan and was obviously intended to upstage the Hôtel de la Vrillière as the termination of the diagonal rue des Fossés Montmartre. In this form,

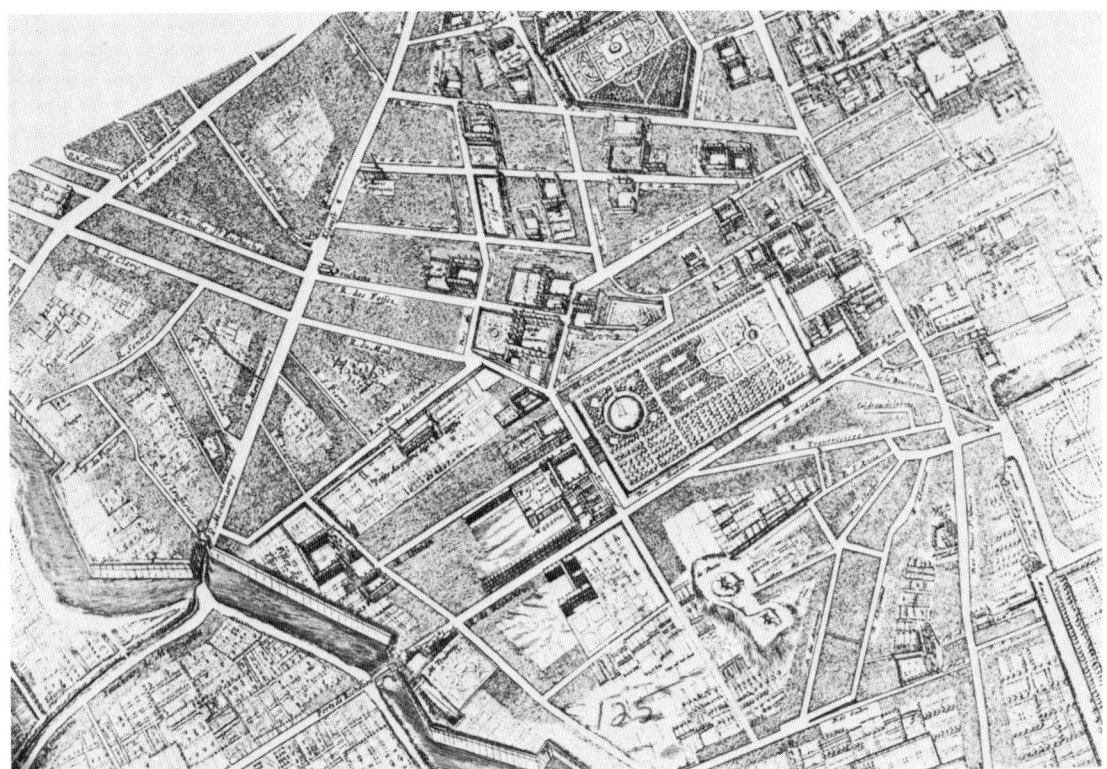

125
Detail from the Gombust plan of 1652 showing the Palais Royal, the Hôtel de la Vrillière, and the future site of the Place des Victoires

126
Detail from the Turgot plan of 1734–39 showing the Place des Victoires

81   *Display and Retreat: The Rococo Hôtel*

127
Place des Victoires, plan signed by Mansart

128
Place des Victoires, Jules Hardouin Mansart, begun 1685. From the Turgot plan.

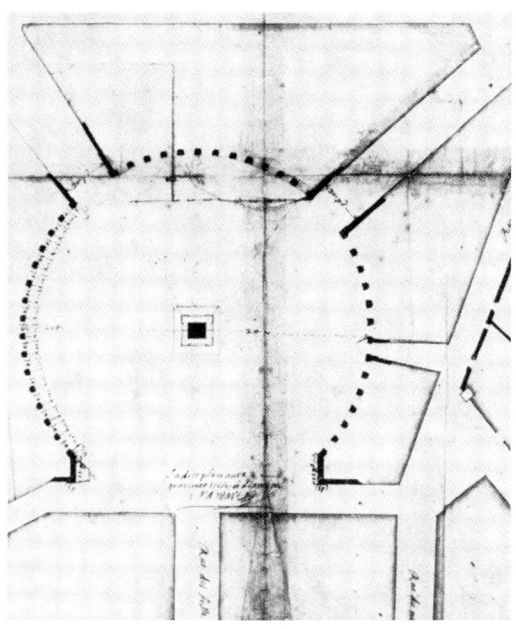

129
Place des Victoires. Engraving by Nolin.

it would have been pierced by only five streets, two of them being the extensions of the rue Neuve des Petits Champs and the rue de la Croix des Petits Champs. The Place des Victoires would thus have served as a knuckle or hinge between the two city grids and would have given the Hôtel de la Vrillière a less conspicuous urban role. The statue in the original scheme logically faced the rue des Fossés Montmartre.

Unfortunately, however, the square was not built as planned. The rue de Fossés Montmartre was allowed to continue past the square to the Hôtel de la Vrillière, and the statue was placed facing the *hôtel* rather than the street. Those simple changes totally destroyed the intent of the square and doomed it to permanent use as a traffic circle. Another street, the rue Etienne Marcel, was cut through in 1883, further compromising the enclosure of the space. It was an ironic end, since not all the houses were completed in time for the inauguration of the square by Louis XIV in 1686 and the remaining open spaces had to be filled with painted canvas facades.[3]

The faked completion of the Place des Victoires may be seen as fatuous, unnecessary flattery or as formally suggestive, but at the very least it symbolizes a social and architectural schism, one that is expressed even more clearly by the historical development of the Place Louis-le-Grand.[4]

The Place Louis-le-Grand

As the nucleus of the St.-Honoré district, the Place Louis-le-Grand was located above the Tuileries gardens between two important streets, the rue St.-Honoré and the extended rue Neuve des Petits Champs. The idea for the *place* apparently originated with Louvois and Mansart; it was intended to be the equivalent in the western part of Paris of the Place Royale. The new royal square was to be an intellectual and administrative center, a statue square bounded by the royal library, the mint, the academies, and the chancellery. Toward this end, in 1685 the king acquired the property, which consisted of the Hôtel de Vendôme and its grounds as well as the adjoining gardens of the Couvent des Capucines.

The king then decreed that the facades of the new square be built according to designs approved by His Majesty. He reasoned that construction of the facades by the owners themselves would involve considerable expense, and if each owner were to build according to his fantasies, some facades would be built less well and all would vary according to individual tastes and sensibilities. Louis XIV therefore proposed to build uniform facades himself, sell off the lots behind, and reimburse the treasury with the profits. Posters of advertisement explained that lots of any width could be acquired as long as they were at least two bays wide. In 1686 construction of the facades designed by J. H. Mansart began.[5]

The completed freestanding facades are illustrated in a view of the square of Aveline, and the plan is shown in context as the Place des Conquêtes on the 1697 plan of Paris by Nicolas de Fer. The square in this form was 152 by 177 meters, enclosed on three sides by uniform arcaded facades, and open to the rue St.-Honoré "like a theater toward the stage."[6] The opening in the north side was on axis with Mansart's facade for the church of the Couvent des Capucines and was closed by a triumphal arch. But by 1698, twelve years after the beginning of construction, no buildings had been constructed behind the facades.

In January 1699 J. H. Mansart was made superintendent of buildings as well as Premier Architecte, and on the first of April he signed a drawing of the plan and elevation of his design for a new octagonal square. This project was approved by the authorities on April 4, and on April 7 the king made a royal declaration changing the form of the square and ceding the property, excluding a plot reserved for Mansart, to the city of Paris. The city was then to demolish the existing facades, construct the new ones, and sell the terrain behind. According to the king, the reason for the change of plans was that the old facades were unsuitable for residences. In May 1699 the existing facades were demolished and the new ones begun.[7] This second version is illustrated in a view by Perelle and given in context on the 1728 plan by Delagrive and the Turgot plan of 1739.

As finally built, the Place Louis-le-Grand was a rectangle, 140 by 124 meters, with diagonal corners; the center was occupied by an equestrian statue of the king; and the perimeter was broken only in the middle of the north and south sides. These openings connected the square to the rue Neuve des Petits Champs and the rue St.-Honoré, and the vistas were terminated by the facades of the convents of the Capucines to the north and the Feuillants to the south. It was not until

83   The Place Louis-le-Grand

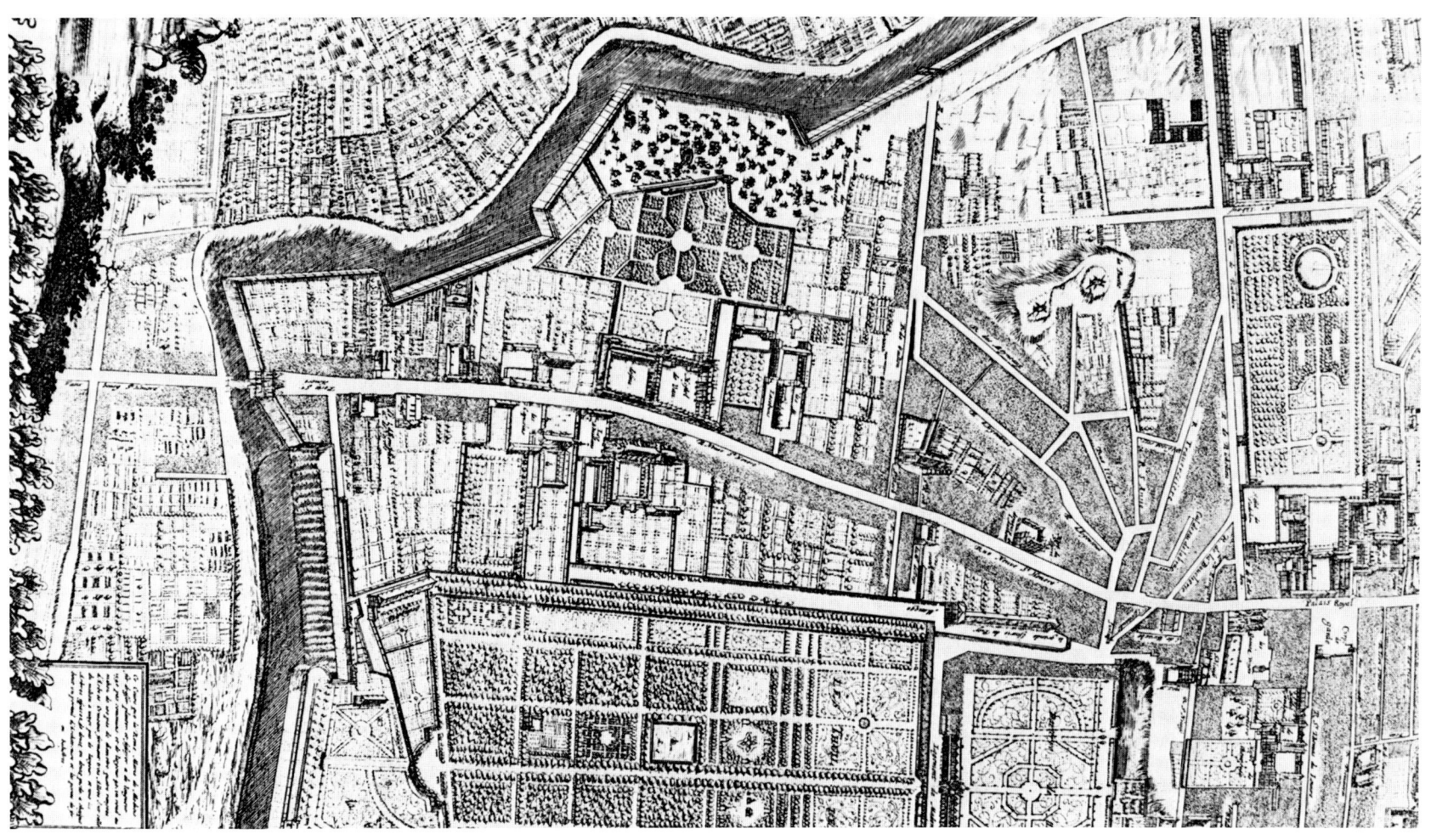

130
Detail from the Gombust plan of 1652 showing the Hôtel de Vendôme (site of the Place Louis-le-Grand, later Place Vendôme)

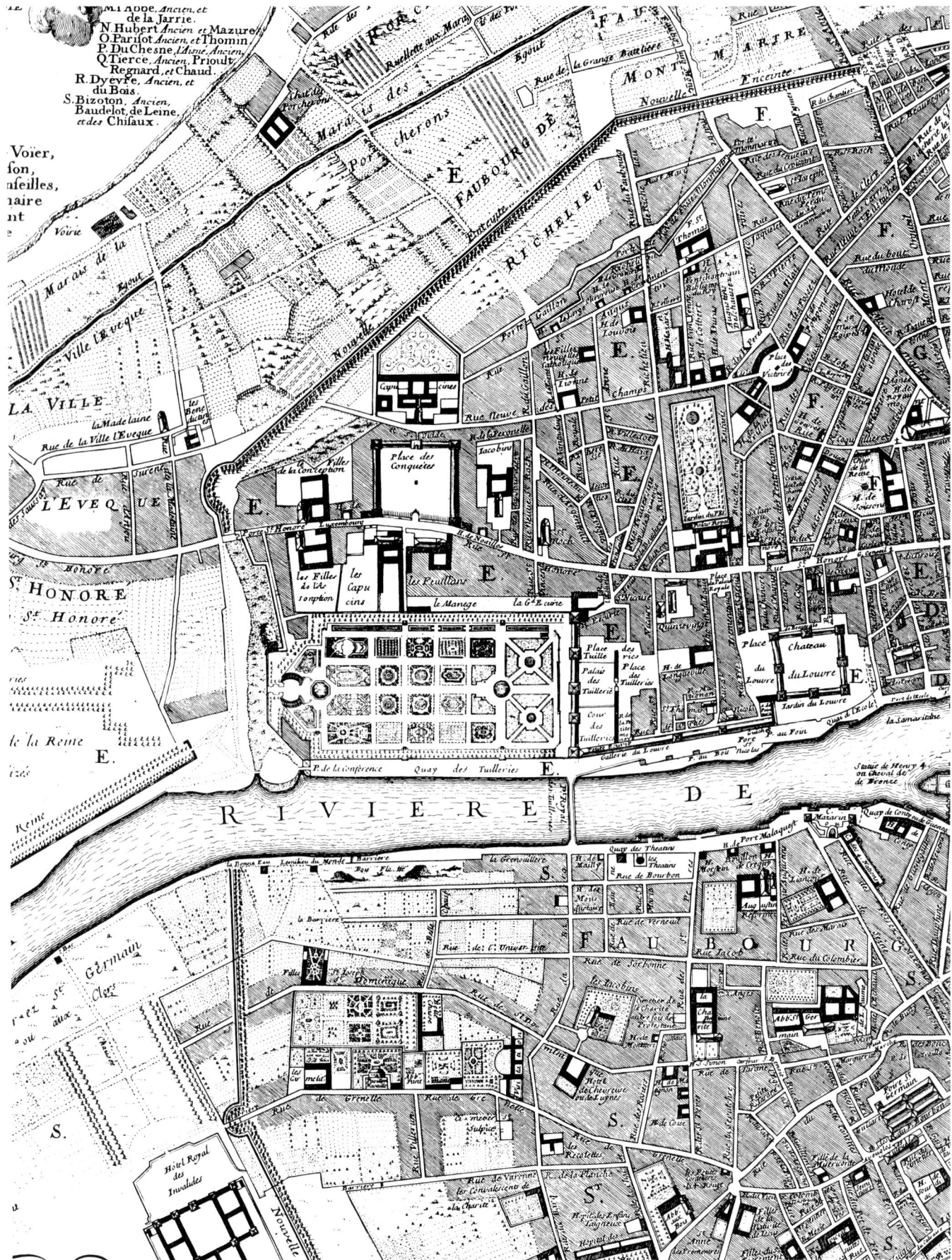

131 Detail from the Nicolas de Fer plan of 1697 showing the first version of the Place Louis-le-Grand (then Place des Conquêtes)

85 The Place Louis-le-Grand

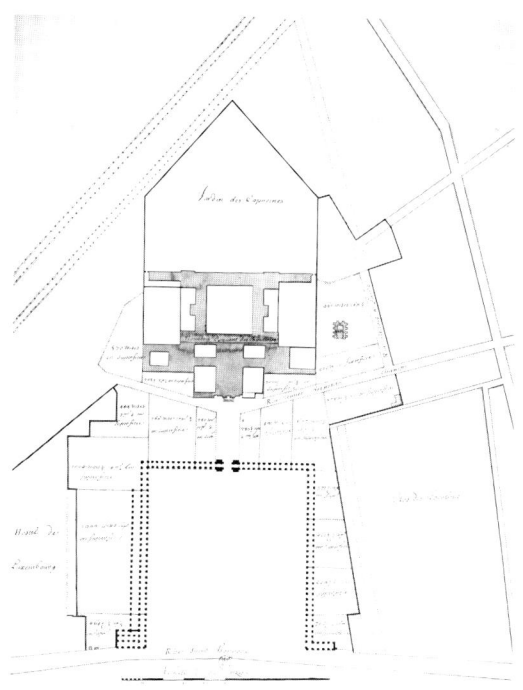

132
Place Louis-le-Grand, plan of the first version (then Place des Conquêtes), Jules Hardouin Mansart, begun 1685

133
Place Louis-le-Grand, first version. Engraving by Aveline.

134
Place Louis-le-Grand, inauguration of the first version. Engraving.

86   *Display and Retreat: The Rococo Hôtel*

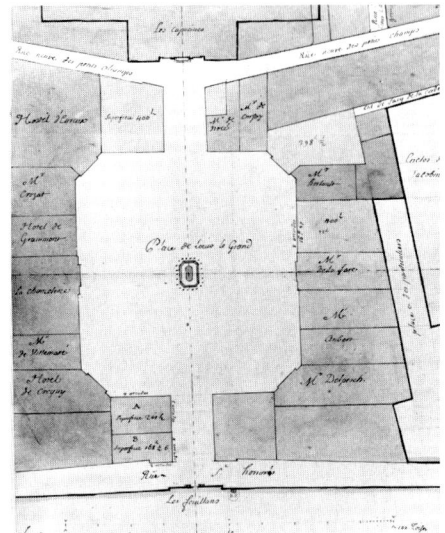

135
Place Louis-le-Grand (now Place Vendôme), plan of the second version, Jules Hardouin Mansart, begun 1699

136
Place Louis-le-Grand, second version. Engraving by Perelle.

137
Place Louis-le-Grand, comparative plan of first and second versions

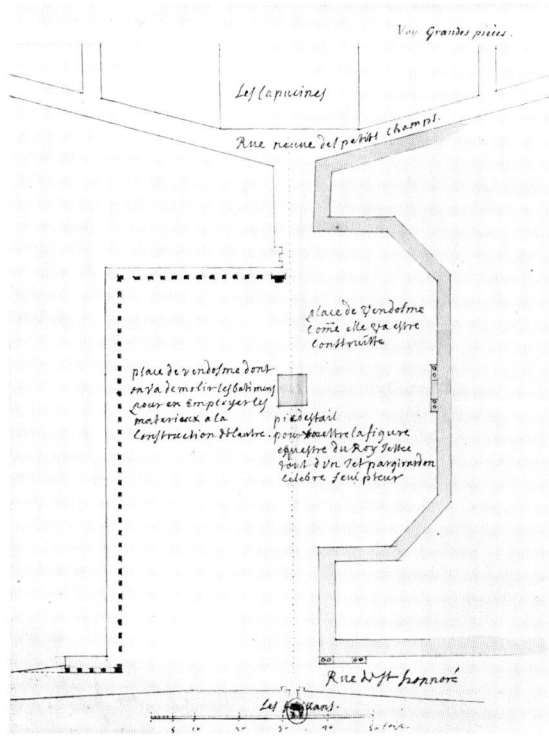

after the French Revolution that the statue was replaced by the Vendôme column and that the existing openings were extended as the rue Castiglione and the rue de la Paix, thus ruining the proportions and tranquility of the square.

Money was scarce in the first years of the eighteenth century, but a series of wealthy financiers began to buy up the lots surrounding the new *place*. Mansart's new plan, with its increased perimeter, allowed for more lots, and he himself had one of the cut-off corners. His contemporary Pierre Bullet, an architect, and a group of friends bought up several sites in order to propose houses to the *nouveaux riches* of Paris.[8] Construction of the square and all the houses was finally completed around 1720, almost thirty-five years after the project was begun.

The varying lot widths and irregular sites masked by Mansart's facades represent more than an expedient solution to a problem, although they were certainly that. "The motley and varied buildings which arose behind [the] uniform facades," Howard Saalman notes, "lent themselves . . . to a gradual adaptation that could proceed without touching the facades in front."[9] The remark, disparaging in its context, skirts an important point: in the Place Louis-le-Grand, the combination of regular stability in the public realm and irregular variety in the private realm represents an urban concept of great potential. It is an urban analogy to the Hôtel de Beauvais: the square itself is a stable, symmetrical city "room" hiding, and allowing, the peripheral domestic freedoms beyond. That it conceals the variety around it is its strength, not its weakness, for the requirements of the *res publica* are rarely coincidental with those of the *res privata* and insistence on integration of the two is as untenable as the complete hegemony of one. The Place Louis-le-Grand exploited the principle of discontinuity to the advantage of both the public and private realms.

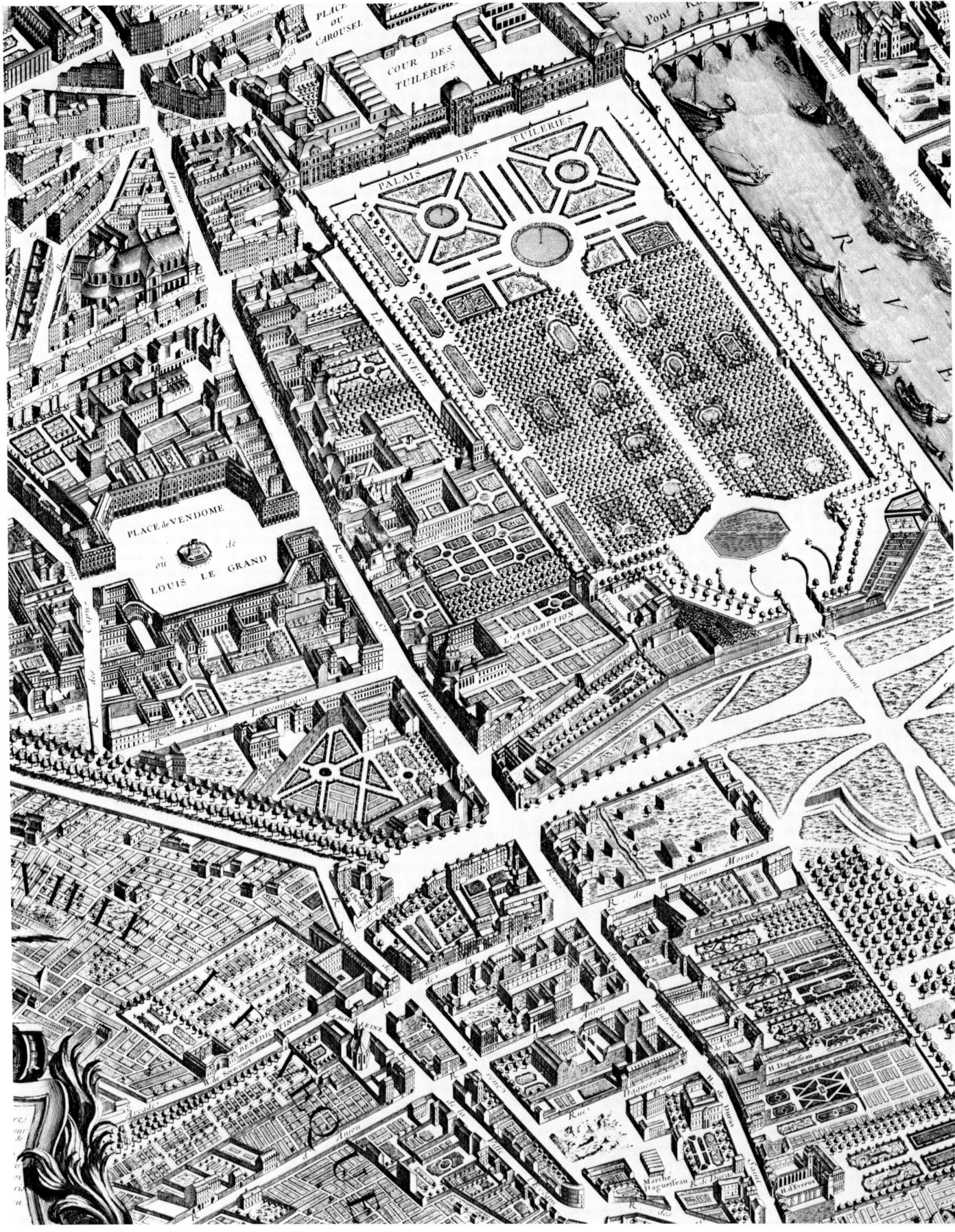

138
Detail from the Turgot plan showing the Place Louis-le-Grand, the Tuileries, and the rue St.-Honoré

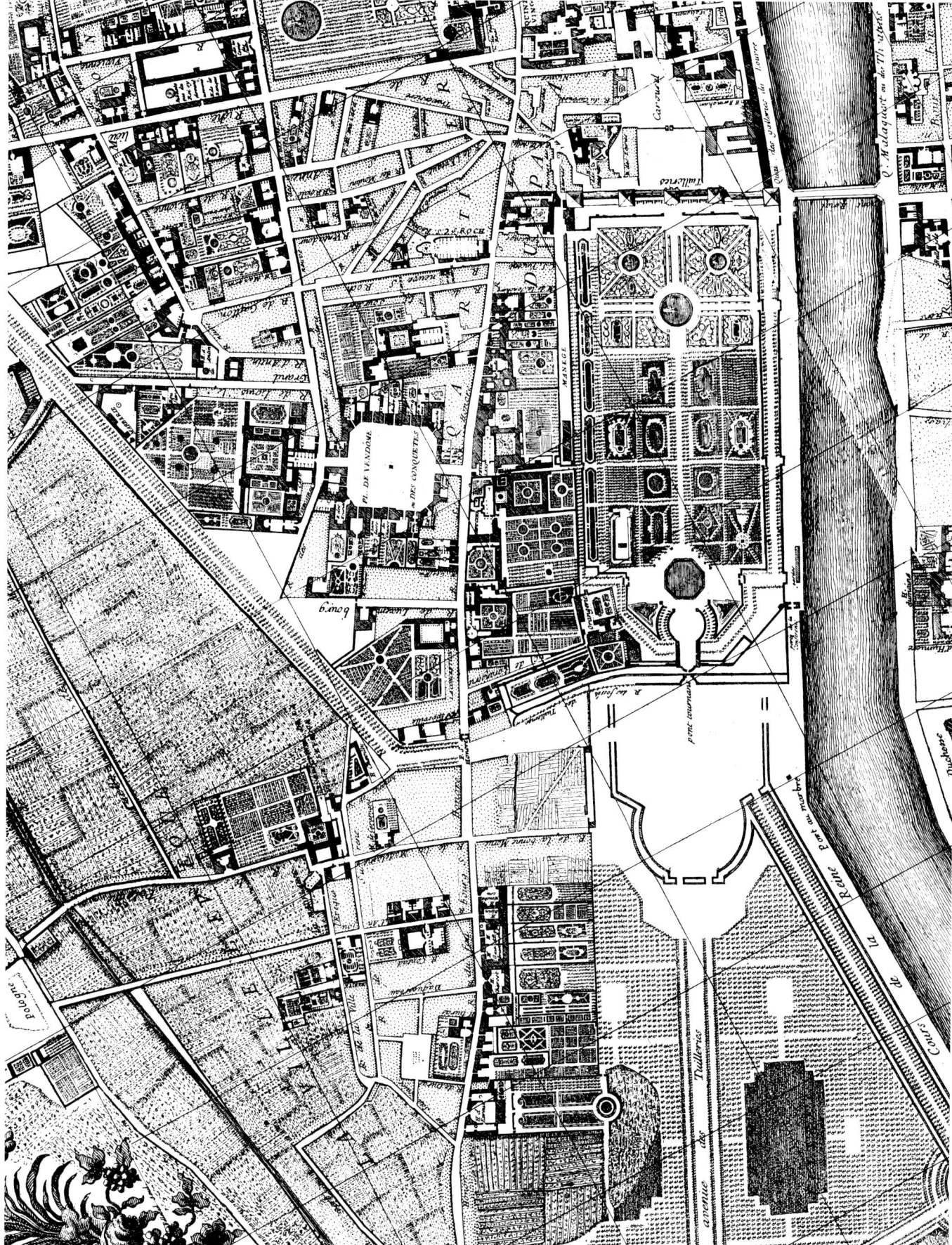

139
Detail from the Delagrive plan of 1728 showing the Place Louis-le-Grand

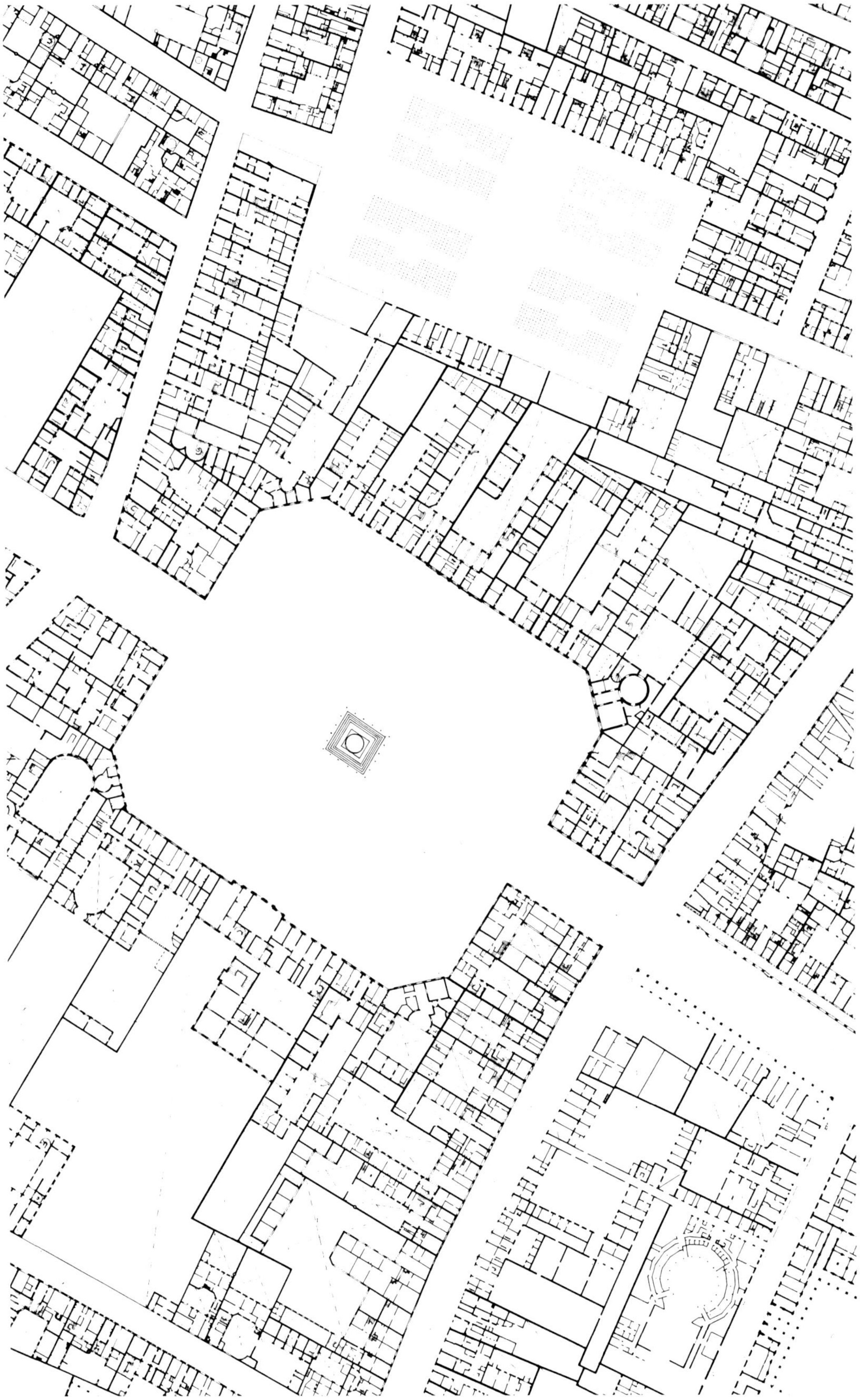

90   Display and Retreat: The Rococo Hôtel

140
Place Vendôme, aerial view

141
Place Vendôme, ground floor plan in the early nineteenth century. Reconstruction after the Vasserot plan by Bruno Fortier, et al.

The Rococo Hôtel

The uneasy alliance between public and private requirements under Louis XIV prefigured a radical transformation of French life under Louis XV. Talbot Hamlin describes the growth of a new sensibility:

> The Rococo period of the eighteenth century was as private as the Baroque was public; it made of personal privacy, of secrecy, of intrigue, of personal experience almost the highest aims of life, dressing them gaily and luxuriously, but in ways designed to emphasize their quality. Rococo architecture became, in a very real sense, an architecture of intrigue, as Baroque had been an architecture of pageantry.
>
> For some time before the death of Louis XIV [in 1715], a revolution against the ponderous ceremonials of court life had been brewing... people began again to demand private lives. By the end of Louis XIV's reign this longing for personal lives and personal privacy had become universal. A complete revolution in social life occurred. People were suddenly interested in individuals and individual relationships, in intimate conversation. Wit began to take the place of eloquence.[10]

This new age brought what was, in effect, a reversal of the building pattern of the previous forty years, when Versailles commanded the attention of the court. In the last years of the seventeenth century a gradual return to Paris began, and the beginning of construction of the second version of the Place Louis-le-Grand in 1699 marked the resumption of *hôtel* construction. From the Place Louis-le-Grand, the renewed building activity spread to the new quarter of the rue St.-Honoré, and the Faubourg St.-Germain rapidly developed into a lush garden suburb. As new *hôtels* proliferated, construction of public buildings ceased; royal patronage was replaced by private patronage. But the private patrons were no longer just the nobility, for "growing trade and international commerce was making luxury possible for people who had never known it before," and that new "wealthy bourgeoisie... demanded amenities which only the court and the nobles had enjoyed a century earlier."[11]

When *hôtel* construction resumed, it did so at the same point of development at which it had been interrupted. This is evident in some of the first *hôtels* erected around the Place Louis-le-Grand, including Pierre Bullet's Hôtel Crozat and Hôtel d'Evreux. Located in the northwest corner of the square, the *hôtels* were built for the wealthy financier Crozat, the elder (1702), and his son-in-law the Comte d'Evreux (1707). The *parti* of the houses is essentially identical, but reversed: a round-ended court with a double-zone *corps-de-logis* at the square end. Since the Hôtel Crozat had the more regular site and more frontage on the *place*, the main rooms were located on this side. Access is through the *porte-cochère* to the court, which opens axially to the garden beyond. The Hôtel d'Evreux has an irregular site and occupies only four of the five bays on the angle of the *place*, consequently the scheme is reversed from the Hôtel Crozat and the *corps-de-logis* is placed on the garden side. The circular end of the court is then entered diagonally from the *place* through the central bay of the corner, and an ingeniously contrived circular vestibule makes the connection.

Although the two *hôtels* were designed individually, and were published that way by Blondel,[12] adjustments to the Hôtel Crozat in 1724 created an integrated whole. The results are revealing. The garden facades, for example, were designed to present one unified facade to the rear. The party wall between the *hôtels* is not straight, but part of the Hôtel d'Evreux was given over to the Hôtel Crozat, so that on the second floor, the keyhole figure formed by an oval vestibule connected to a rectangular terrace riveted the two plans together spatially—and enabled Monsieur Crozat to maintain surveillance of his daughter and son-in-law. Since both houses were paid for by Monsieur Crozat, perhaps surveillance was thought by his son-in-law to be a small price to pay for a fine house on the Place Louis-le-Grand.

Together the Hôtels Crozat and d'Evreux provide a surprisingly consistent display of the principle of discontinuity, from urban design through detailed architectural planning. Like most seventeenth-century *hôtels*, they were urban or contextual buildings. That is, like the Hôtel de Beauvais, they were party-wall buildings, which contributed to the formation of the traditional street or public space by providing a continuous urban fabric. On the most general level, they can be seen as a kind of urban *poché*, with the streets and squares as the figural elements of the city. The *hôtels* were not, however, just private events contained behind a facade, as in medieval or early Renaissance houses; but because of social rituals, they were both public and private and can be seen as primary *poché* to the semi-public space of the *porte-cochère* and *cour d'honneur*. Inside are similar relations: vestibules, stairs, and the main public rooms are supported by the secondary *poché* of the private part of the house, which in turn is backed up by the tertiary *poché* of the service elements. This system of hierarchical levels of *poché* and designed discontinuity not only allows the identity and closure of each of the spaces, sometimes down to the smallest of dress-

92 Display and Retreat: The Rococo Hôtel

142
Hôtels Crozat and d'Evreux, ground floor plan, Pierre Bullet, begun 1702 and 1707

143
Hôtels Crozat and d'Evreux, upper floor plan

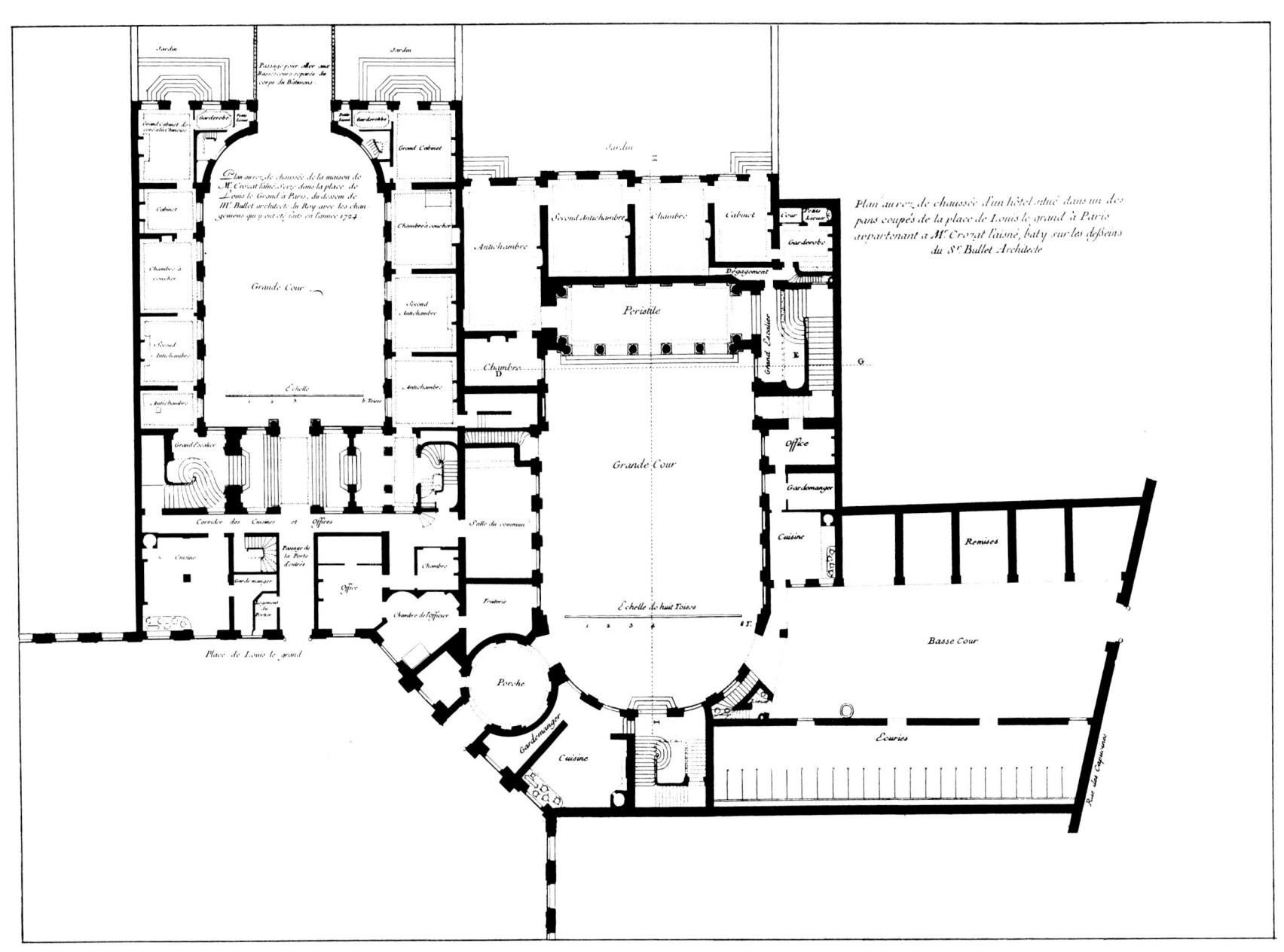

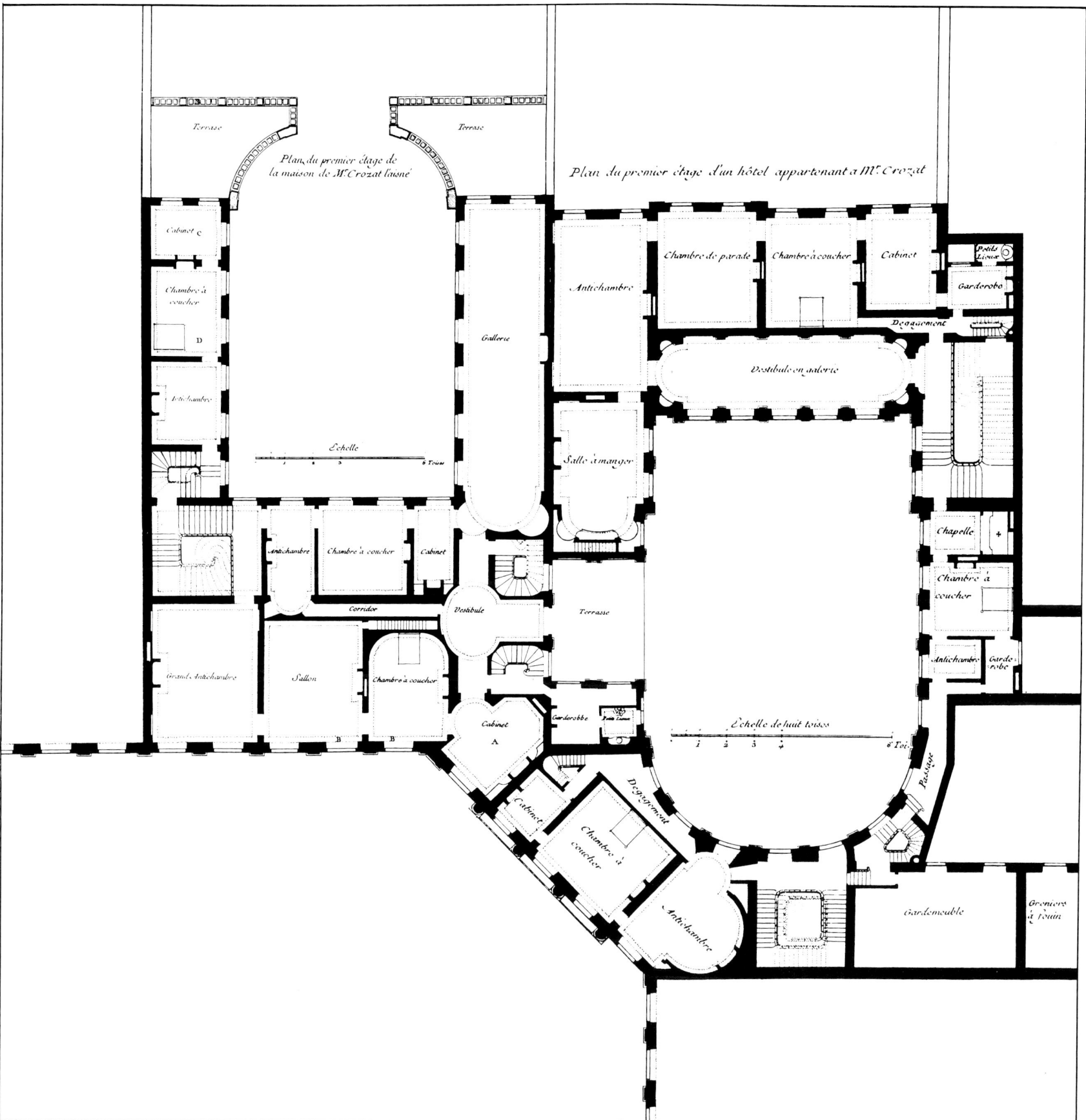

94 Display and Retreat: The Rococo Hôtel

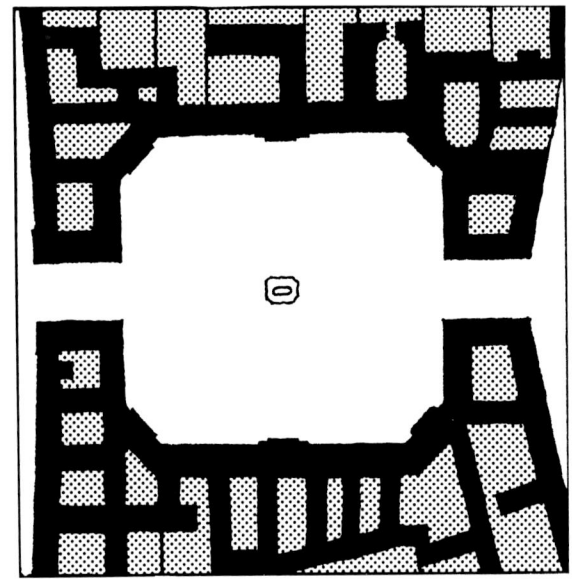

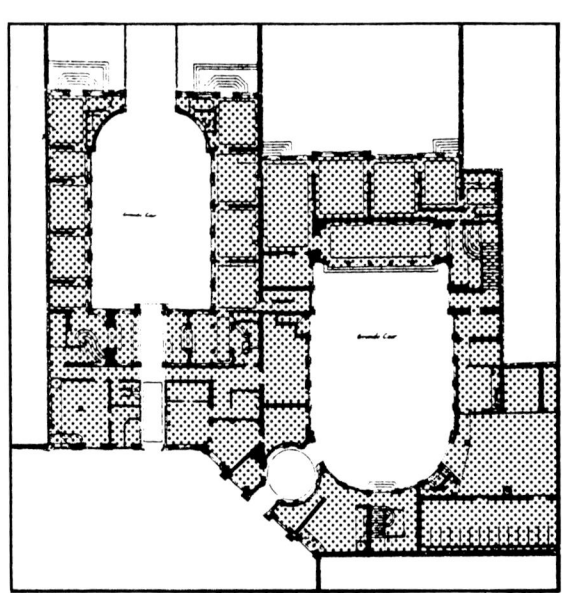

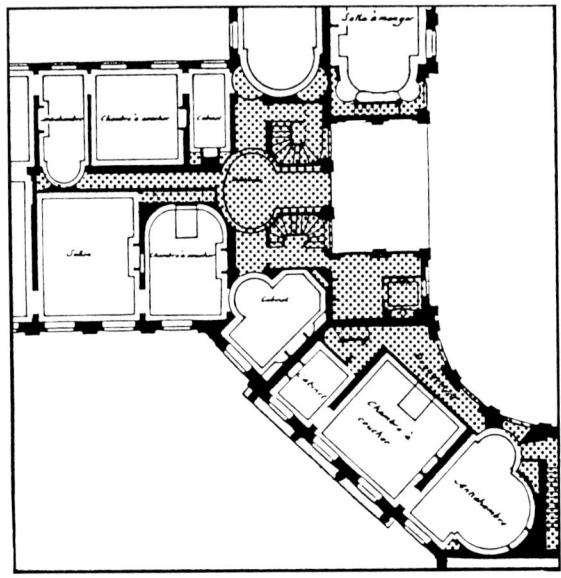

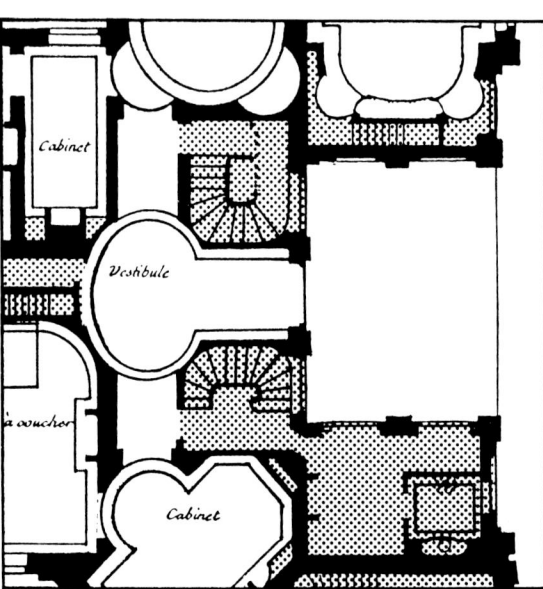

144
Urban *poché*, Place Vendôme

145
Primary *poché*, Hôtels Crozat and d'Evreux

146
Secondary *poché*, Hôtels Crozat and d'Evreux

147
Tertiary *poché*, Hôtels Crozat and d'Evreux

ing rooms, but also wastes very little space with literal *poché*, or thick walls, to resolve awkward joints.

Both *hôtels* have rooms in a remarkable variety of sizes and configurations, and the rooms are generally grouped in sets of three or four connected in *enfilade*. The primary sets, or *appartements*, are located behind principal facades and are connected to the grand stair. The interstitial area, the secondary *poché*, is then ingeniously organized with private circulation, vestibules, and so on. It is in such an area that Monsieur Crozat's keyhole is located. A similar, but more casual, connection is made on the second floor of the Hôtel d'Evreux, between the suite of rooms in the corner of the Place Louis-le-Grand and the bedroom suite located behind the grand stair, across the court from Monsieur Crozat's terrace. The leftover area created by the shape of the court and the shapes of the rooms is filled with service stairs and private passages between suites of rooms. Thus, a third level of *poché* may be observed—that of space between rooms, which accommodates closets, fireplaces, niches, and servants' passages (*dégagements*). This is an architecture of residue.

All the principles of the Baroque *hôtel*—local symmetry, recentering, figural space, architectural promenade, designed discontinuity, and hierarchical levels of *poché*—were solidified near the end of the seventeenth century by the establishment architects J. H. Mansart and Pierre Bullet. But by early in the eighteenth century, most of the older generation of architects had died—Le Nôtre in 1700, Perrault in 1703, and Mansart himself in 1708—and *hôtel* types would subsequently change radically. The tradition of planning, the principles, would nonetheless continue

148
Hôtel d'Evreux, court

96 Display and Retreat: The Rococo Hôtel

to develop as a distinctly French system—*l'art de la distribution*.

As increased emphasis on the individual encouraged, even required, a new type of *hôtel*—one better suited to the needs and aspirations of the emerging society—the relative expanse of the St.-Honoré and St.-Germain districts facilitated its development in a way that the impacted older parts of Paris could not have. This new type of *hôtel*, the Rococo, both evolved from the Baroque type of the previous century and hinted at the freestanding Neoclassical *hôtels* of the late eighteenth century. As a version of the *château* type, it has two principal characteristics: a tendency to articulate the main block of the *hôtel* as a pavilion in a garden and increased particularization of interior planning, including the articulation of public and private areas.

Both characteristics were developed quickly by a younger generation of architects using the models and principles perfected by Mansart and Bullet. These principles can be seen not only in the Hôtels Crozat and d'Evreux, but also in one of J. H. Mansart's last works, a private house designed between 1699 and 1708.[13] This project is like a sophisticated version of François Mansart's Hôtel de Jars in its great variety of rooms, the more elegantly resolved recentering from front to back, and the more coherent circulation. Even more interesting, however, is the planning of the upper floor, where an *appartement de commodité* appears alongside the *appartement de parade* and explicit corridor circulation in the service wing bypasses the individual rooms.

J. H. Mansart had also used a more literal double-loaded corridor scheme in the Château Neuf at Meudon in order to separate and give privacy to several guest suites.[14] This seemingly innocuous

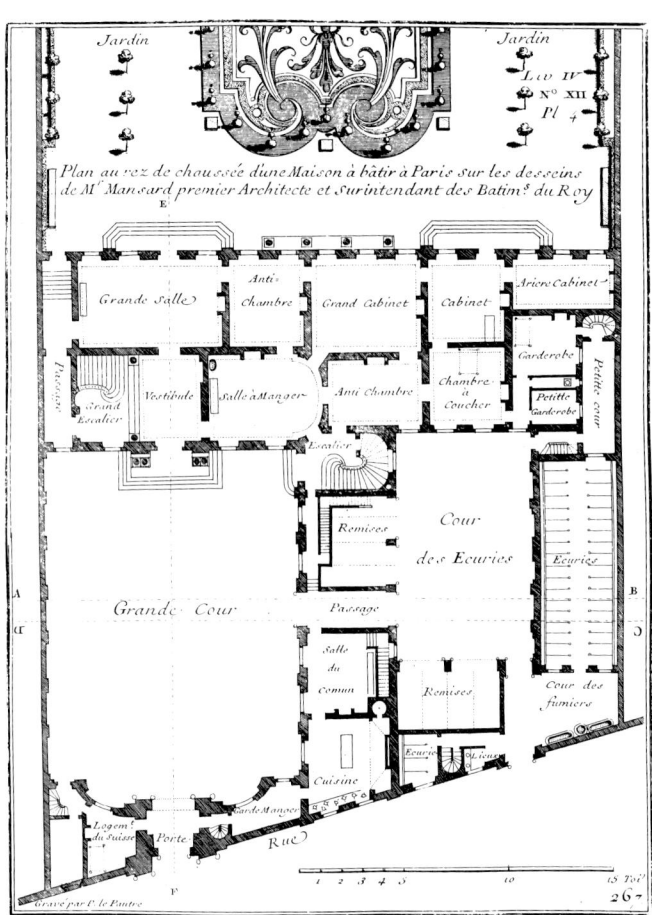

149
Project for a *hôtel*, ground floor plan, Jules Hardouin Mansart, between 1699 and 1708

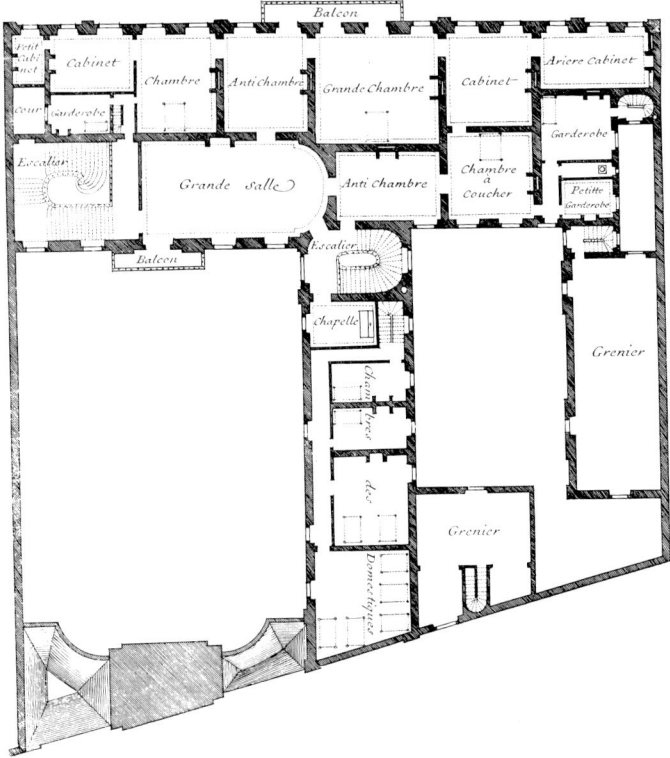

150
Project for a *hôtel*, upper floor plan, Jules Hardouin Mansart, between 1699 and 1708

innovation was actually of fundamental importance vis-à-vis a changing attitude toward personal privacy, and, ultimately, as a technique of modern planning.[15] The related ideas of independent bypassing circulation and *commodité* were to become central preoccupations of his successors. The Hôtel de Varanjeville (1704) by Maurice Gabriel, for example, though primitive by comparison to Mansart's *hôtels*, employs a similar technique in the upper floor containing the private quarters. Here, the circulatory armature bypasses the sets of rooms and connects them to the stair, and only the individual apartments are internally connected room to room. The plan thus has a strangely diagrammatic quality that suggests the work of a talented but slightly reactionary Bauhaus student in the 1920s rather than a progressive but mediocre French designer in the early 1700s.

During the first decade of the eighteenth century, the basic form of the *hôtel* remained essentially unchanged. Lassurance (Pierre Cailleteau, the elder) and Germain Boffrand, Mansart's two principal assistants, maintained the practice of the *hôtel* as urban *poché* by keeping the continuity of building fabric at least around three sides of the court. This can be seen in Lassurance's Hôtel d'Auvergne (1708) and in the unique, one-story Hôtel de Béthune (1708), where a limited site is resolved by turning the garden and the *corps-de-logis* perpendicular to the forecourt. Likewise, Boffrand's Hôtel d'Argenson (1704–5) completely encloses the round-ended court, as does Bullet's Hôtel d'Evreux. Located on a narrow party-wall site between the rue des Bons Enfants and the gardens of the Palais Royal, the Hôtel d'Argenson was fundamentally a symmetrical scheme with the central axis open through

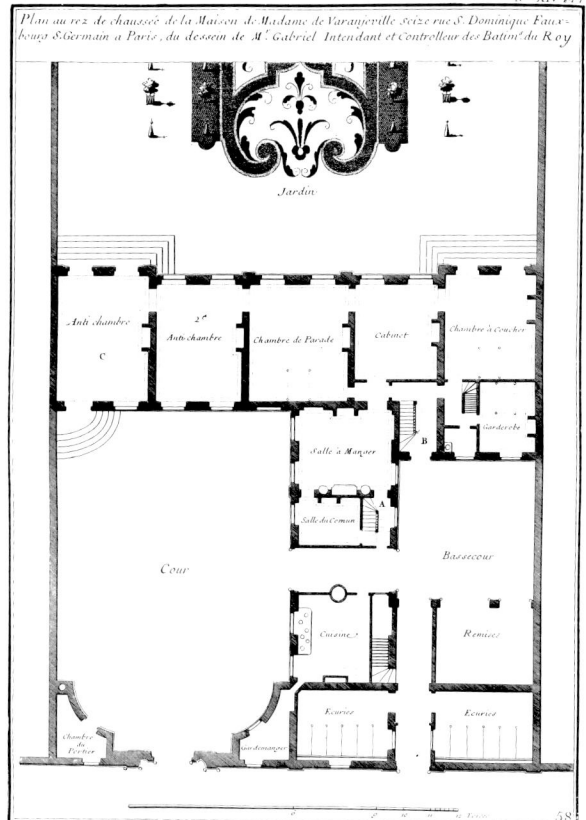

151
Hôtel de Varanjeville, ground floor plan, Maurice Gabriel, 1704

152
Hôtel de Varanjeville, upper floor plan

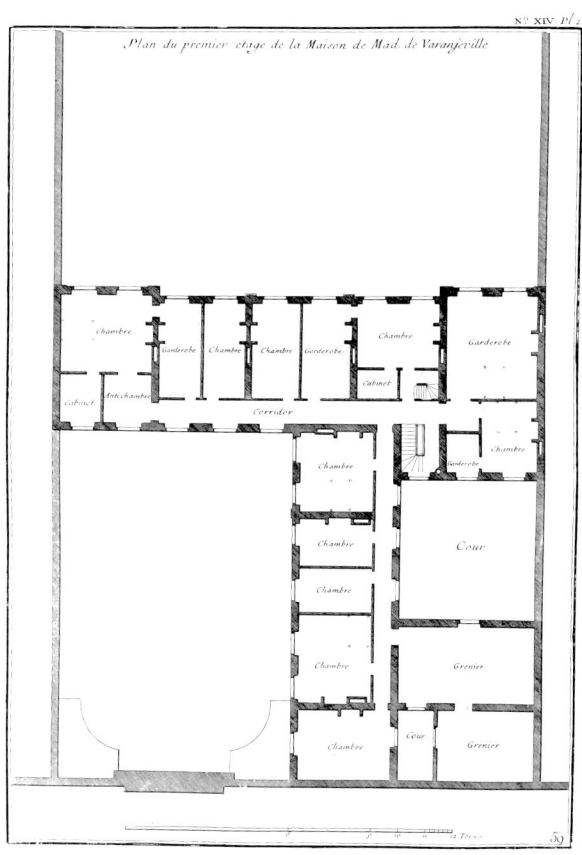

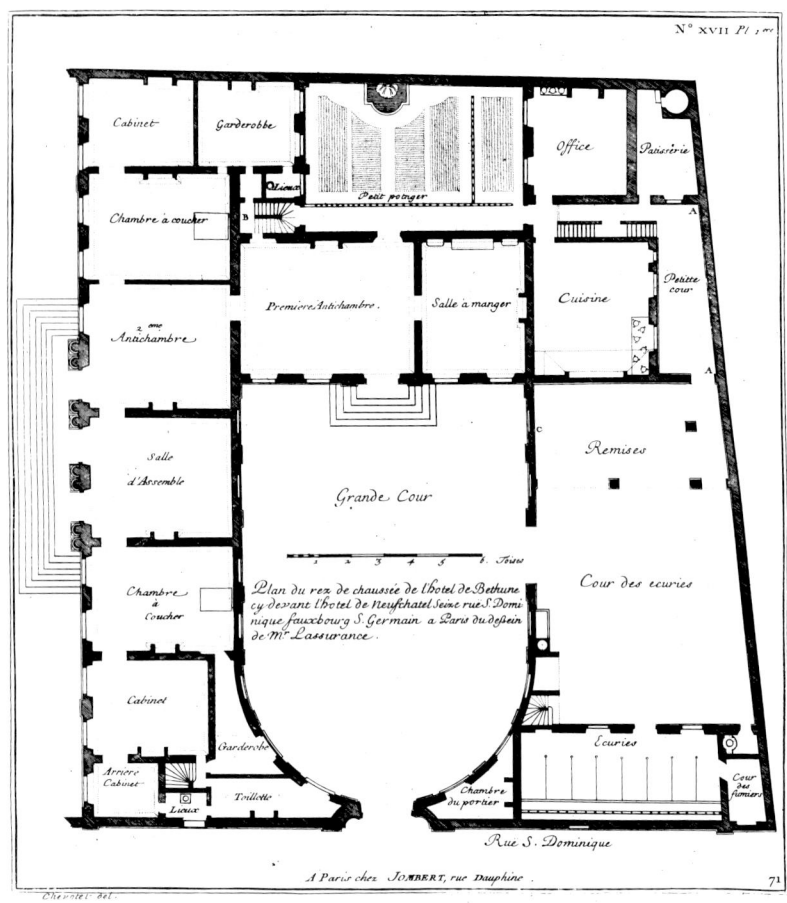
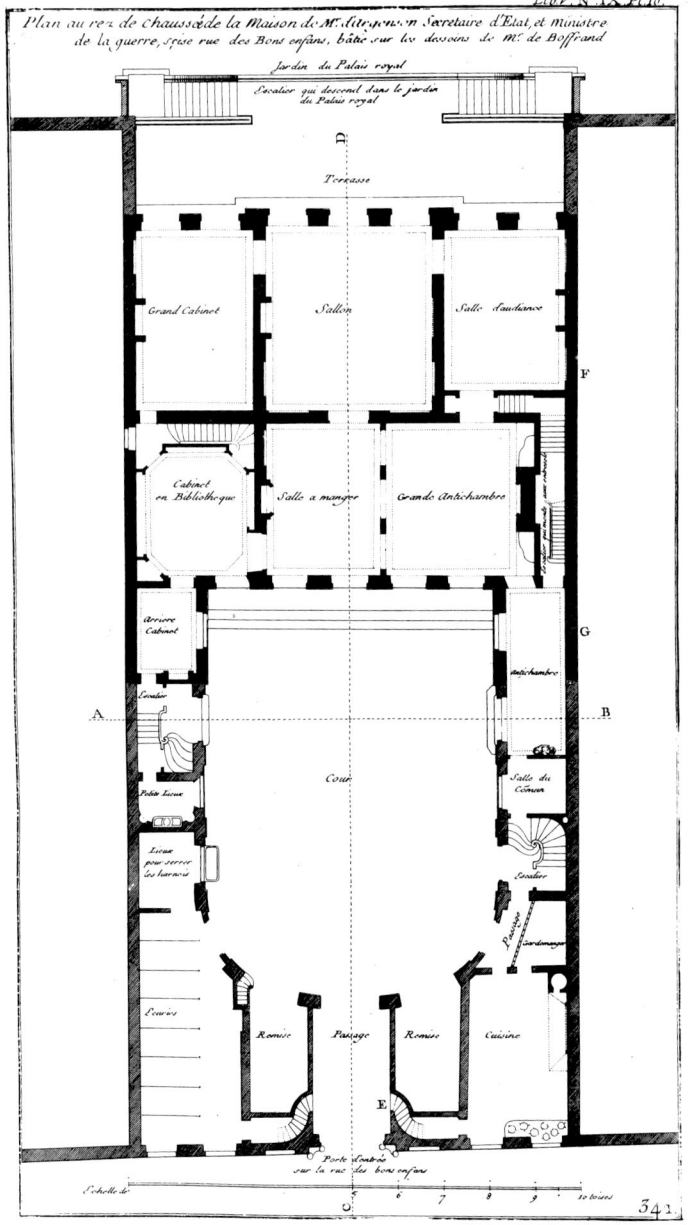

153
Hôtel de Béthune, plan, Lassurance, 1708

154
Hôtel d'Argenson, ground floor plan, Germain Boffrand, 1704–5

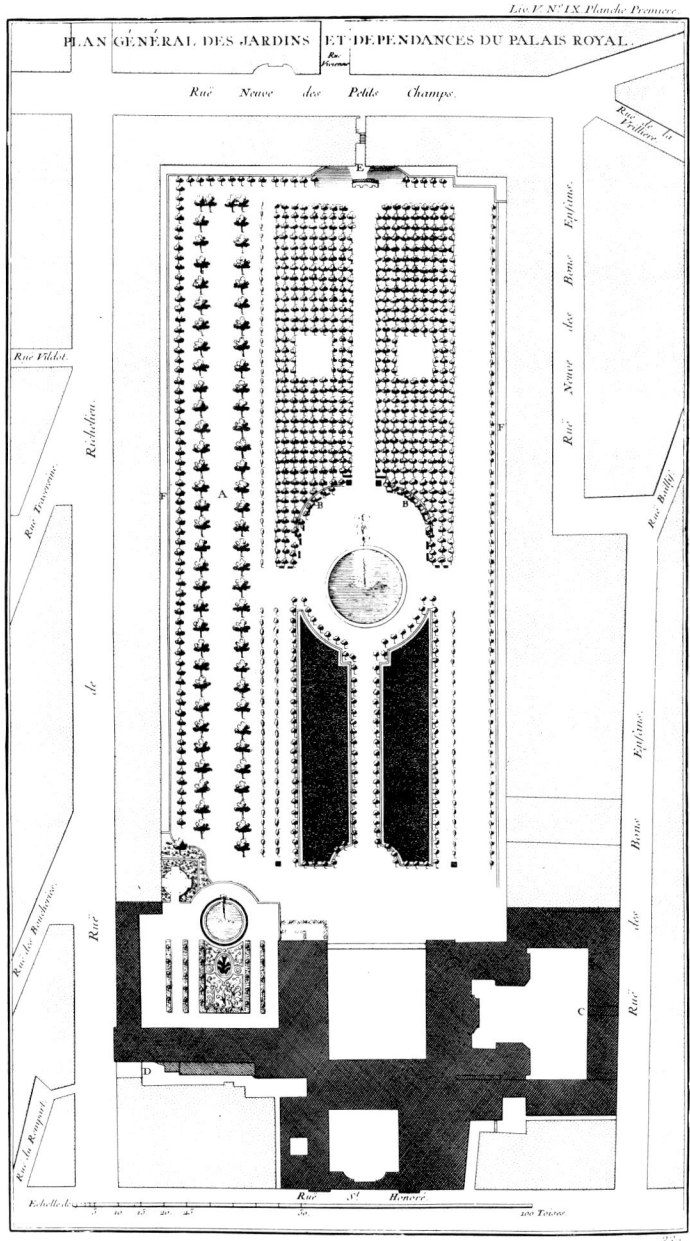

155
Palais Royal, state before 1780. The Hôtel d'Argenson was located on the site indicated in the rue des Bons Enfants.

the building. Since there was no room for a private garden, and no need for one because the building overlooked the royal gardens, only a small, raised terrace was provided off the *corps-de-logis*. This scheme of borrowed grandeur worked quite well until the 1780s, but when Victor Louis's galleries closed off the vista of the royal gardens, Boffrand's building was severely compromised.

Another *hôtel* by the same architect is far more famous and is indicative of impending change, both on the inside and the outside. The Hôtel d'Amelot was built by Boffrand in 1712 as a speculative venture,[16] and it appears at first glance to be a more flamboyant version of the Hôtel d'Argenson. The site is regular, the building is nominally symmetrical, and the plan evokes the Hôtels Beauvais and Lambert. In contrast to the Hôtel d'Argenson, however, the central axis of the plan is blocked, forcing a counterclockwise progression through the sequence of figural rooms. This idea was to become virtually standard in the *hôtels* of the last half of the century, as was the variety and specificity of the rooms. But the oval court, upon which the rest of the organization depends and which in plan is so convincing, is, unfortunately, less coherent in three dimensions. The mass of the building is fractured around the space and even ceases at the two service courts; the definition is continued only by a screen wall. A lower mass completes the composition at the street and forms the entry gate. Thus, although the building mass extends from party wall to party wall, and although in plan the space of the oval court appears to control the organization, in reality the plastic qualities of the solids are dominant. Here, figural solid competes with figural void.

156
Faubourg St.-Germain.
From the Jaillot plan.

101 The Rococo Hôtel

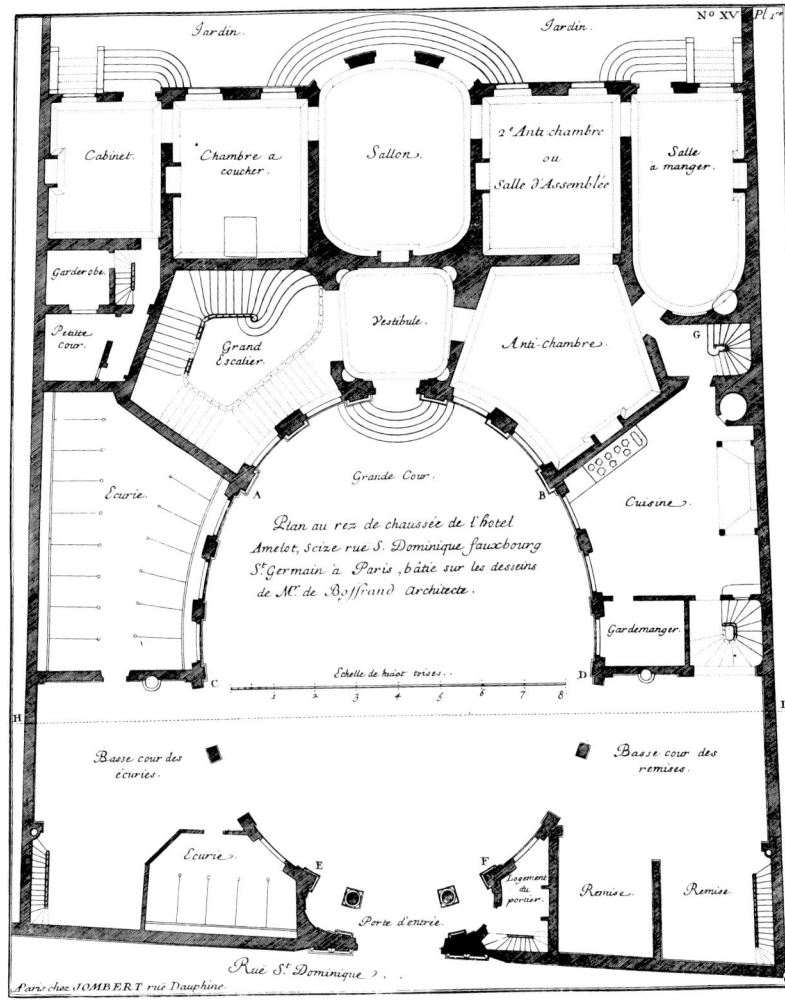

157
Hôtel d'Amelot, ground floor plan, Germain Boffrand, 1712

158
Hôtel d'Amelot, court

The separation, isolation, and articulation of the *corps-de-logis* is progressively clarified in the more normative plans of Robert de Cotte's Hôtel d'Estrées (1713),[17] Armand-Claude Mollet's Hôtel d'Humières (1715), and Jean Courtonne's Hôtel de Matignon (1722–24). In these *hôtels*, the wide main block is articulated from the side wall as well as from the street, so that from either side, court or garden, it reads as a pavilion. Like mini-*châteaux*, these buildings were manifestations of the independence and individuality characteristic of the period. Though forced by social pressure to be near the court, the nobility had reluctantly traded country houses for urban villas—but a pavilion in a controlled, private garden offered the best of both worlds. And one is compelled to believe that Salomon de Brosse's Luxembourg Palace (begun 1615), hovering as it did at the edge of the Faubourg St.-Germain, between the city and the gardens, also hovered in the imaginations of the nobility, a grand ideal, attainable in miniature.

Symmetry and regularity governed the exteriors of the buildings of this period, but the converse may be said of its interiors; as exteriors became simpler, interiors became more complex. The plan yielded to flexibility, convenience, and the practical proliferation of secondary rooms. Bathrooms begin to appear in the house, and the *appartement de commodité* appears alongside the *appartement de parade*, thereby turning the *hôtel particulier* into the primitive ancestor of the *machine à habiter*. The plan of the Rococo *hôtel* marked the beginning of modern functional planning,[18] and the idea of a regular envelope masking an idiosyncratic plan was to become the typical French method of planning during the eighteenth century.

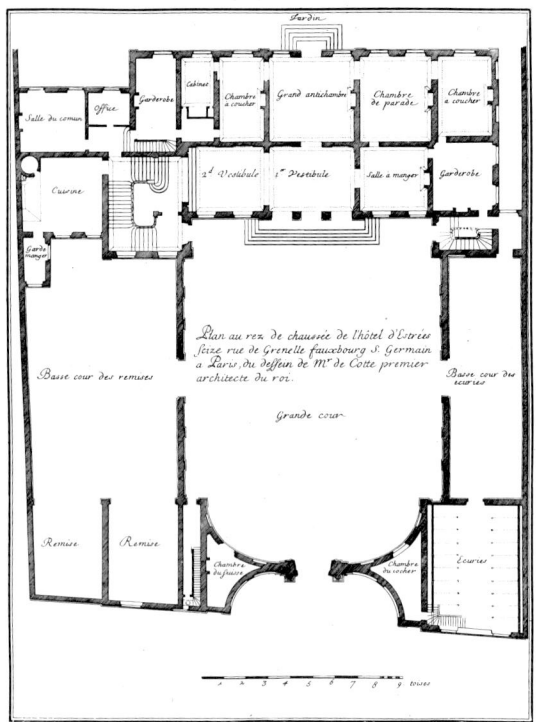

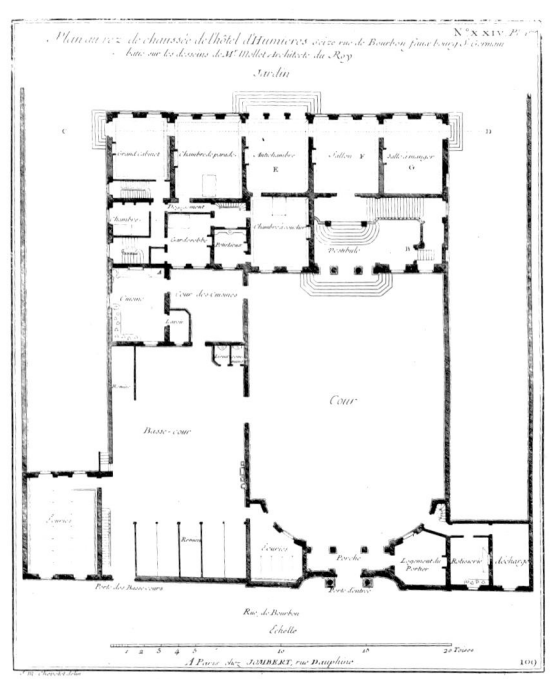

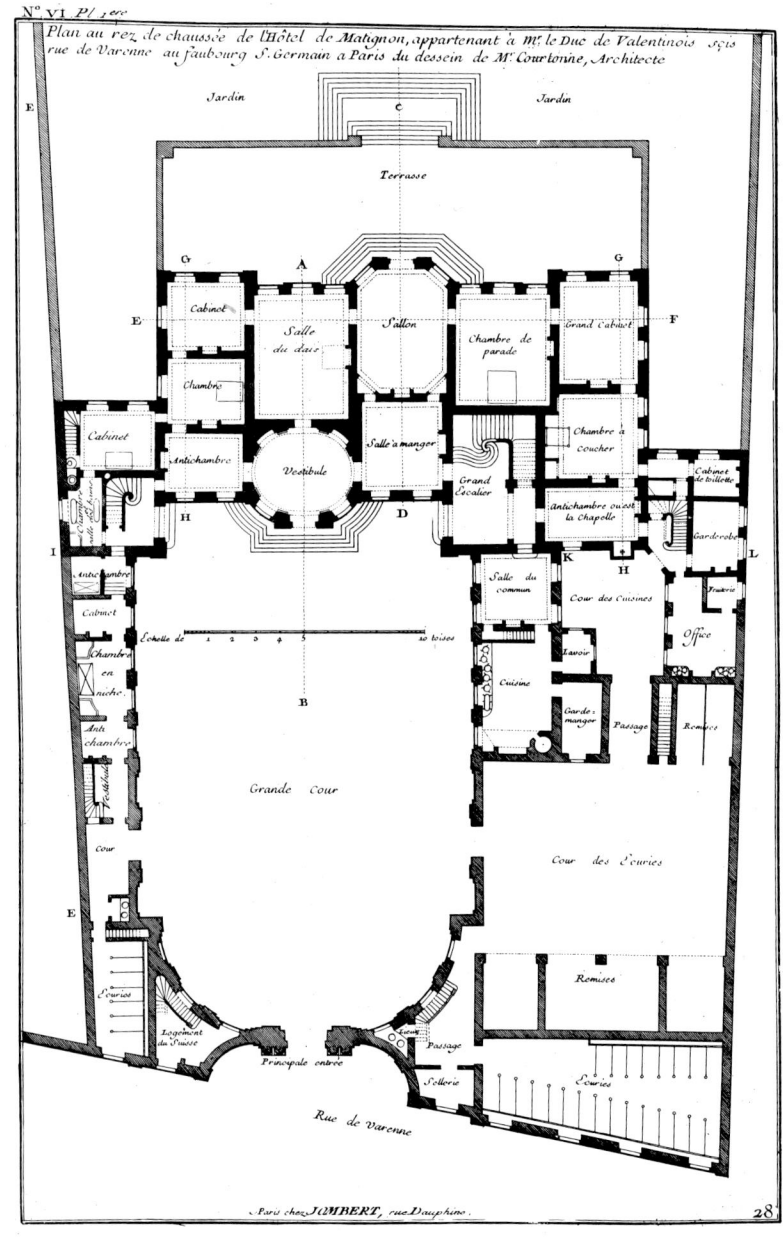

159 Hôtel d'Estrées, ground floor plan, Robert de Cotte, 1713

160 Hôtel d'Humières, ground floor plan, Armand-Claude Mollet, 1715

103 The Rococo Hôtel

161
Hôtel de Matignon, ground floor plan, Jean Courtonne, 1722–24

162
Hôtel de Matignon, garden facade

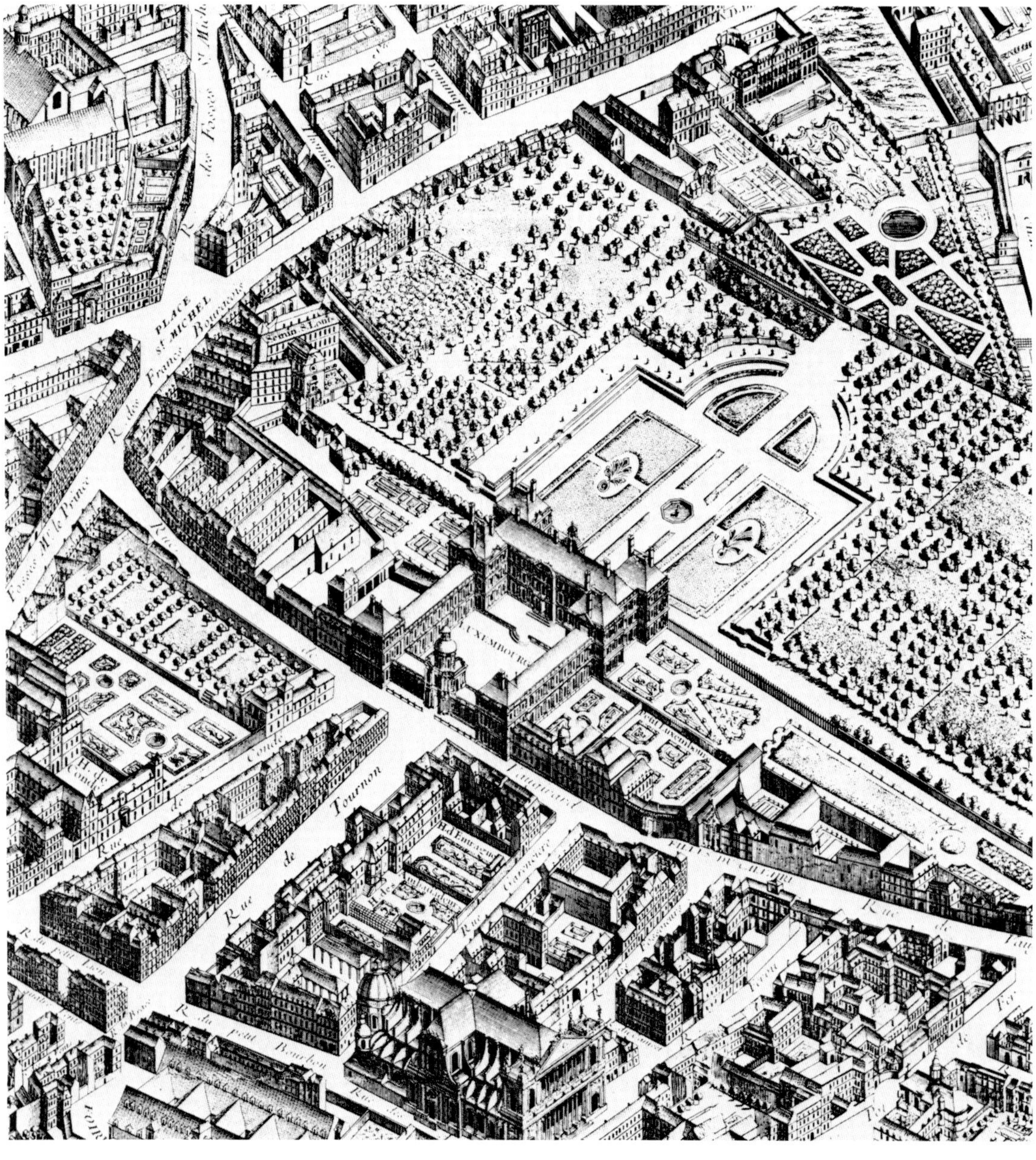

104   *Display and Retreat: The Rococo Hôtel*

163
Luxembourg Palace, Salomon de Brosse, begun 1615. From the Turgot plan.

164
Luxembourg Palace, plan

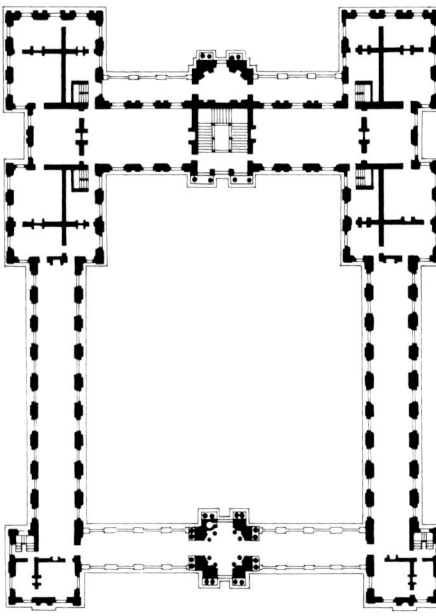

Domestic architecture also became fertile ground for theoreticians, and the resumption of extensive private building was accompanied by a spate of treatises. It is not clear whether these treatises actually altered and promoted the development of the *hôtel* or were simply handbooks codifying events after the fact. Although an examination of the buildings suggests the latter, the truth may lie between; either way, they now serve as useful milestones that bring order to an increasingly complex subject.

Other than Jean Marot's publications of actual buildings, the first treatise on domestic architecture after those of Savot and Le Muet was C.-A. d'Aviler's *Cours d'architecture*, which first appeared in 1691.[19] This superb book does seem to be a codification of the state of the art, and it was clearly the model for J.-F. Blondel's treatise of 1737. The first volume of d'Aviler's *Cours* is like a very elegant seventeenth-century "Graphic Standards," covering everything from sample site and garden layouts to garden details, *hôtel* layouts, window frames, hardware, paving, and so on. The second volume is a dictionary of terms pertaining to the "art of building," in which d'Aviler explains all the terms that appear in the first volume.[20] This is, of course, a great contrast to Savot's spartan formal description in 1624, and reflects the degree to which everything began to be articulated, rationalized, and codified under Louis XIV. The progression to greater complexity and specificity was to continue in art, in society, and in the French language itself.

The most important difference between d'Aviler's treatise and the practices of the 1640s is that he calls not only for an *appartement de parade* ("that of the grand rooms on the *bel étage*"), but also for an *appartement de commodité* ("that which is less grand and more used") and an *appartement des bains* ("a suite of rooms ordinarily on the ground floor, which includes a *salle*, a *chambre*, a *garde-robe*, a *salle de bain*, and the *étuve* . . . and is richly decorated").[21] It is part of his rationalizing his formal predilections as functional necessities, a tendency amply illustrated when he explains that the corners of the *chambre à coucher* are rounded to facilitate the *dégagement* off one corner and to provide a place for the *chaise de commodité* in the *garde-robe* off the other.[22]

D'Aviler's *Cours* was republished in many editions in the eighteenth century, but the edition of 1710 was the most popular manual of the period. This edition, by A. Le Blond, contained thirteen new pages on *la distribution*, illustrations of four new *hôtels*, and a new section on stairs. The differences between this and the first edition were in the expanded sequence and more precise description of the *appartements* and the service rooms. Le Blond begins his addition, appropriately entitled *De la nouvelle manière de distribuir les plans*, by stating: "Buildings are different one from another . . . and one cannot give absolute rules for the layout of plans. One can only make general observations about arrangements of rooms."[23] He then describes the overall disposition of the plan in several versions and explains the sequence and order of the rooms of an early eighteenth-century *appartement (de parade)*, the particular use of each, and the *dégagements* required for each.[24] Although Le Blond's prescription for the *hôtel* was even more rationalized than its seventeenth-century counterpart, it still did not extend significantly into areas of comfort and convenience; but this was soon to change.

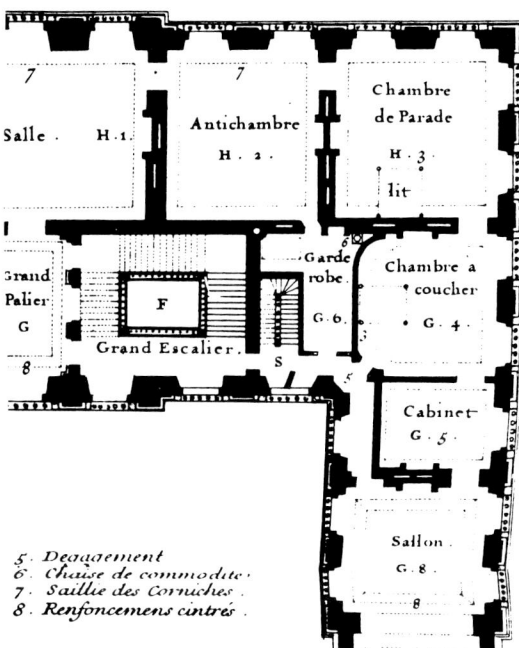

165
Design for a *hôtel*, plan detail, C.-A. d'Aviler, 1691

When Louis XIV died in 1715, the focus of court life shifted to the Palais Royal for the eight years of the regency of his nephew, the Duc d'Orléans. A debaucher and an incompetent leader,[25] the Duc d'Orléans was nevertheless an educated connoisseur who made the Palais Royal the stage for a whole new cast of characters that included Oppenordt, Cartaud, and the painter Watteau. During this period of regal relaxation, interior design took on new meaning and, not coincidentally, issues of convenience became more important.

This new aspect of *la distribution* received early attention in the work of Armand-Claude Mollet. His Hôtel d'Humières (1715) provided bathrooms near the bedrooms and an array of secondary rooms in the main block, but his Hôtel d'Evreux is a more characteristic example of the new planning techniques.[26] Built in 1718 on the rue St.-Honoré, the *hôtel* was the most prominent of a long row of noble *hôtels*. It was built for the Comte d'Evreux, subsequently passed to Madame de Pompadour, and is now the Palais de l'Elysée. The scheme is typical of Rococo *hôtels*—a generally symmetrical plan with an articulated *corps-de-logis* between the court and the garden. But in a unique departure, although most of the ground floor is occupied by grand public rooms arranged in counterclockwise sequence, the area to the left of the entrance is filled with small bedrooms, service rooms, and passages. This system of private rooms extends out of the main block and along a small flower garden as another private *appartement*.

The asymmetrical development of the plan behind a regular facade and its juxtaposition of public and private elements are even more prominent in the Palais Bourbon (1722–29). The plan of

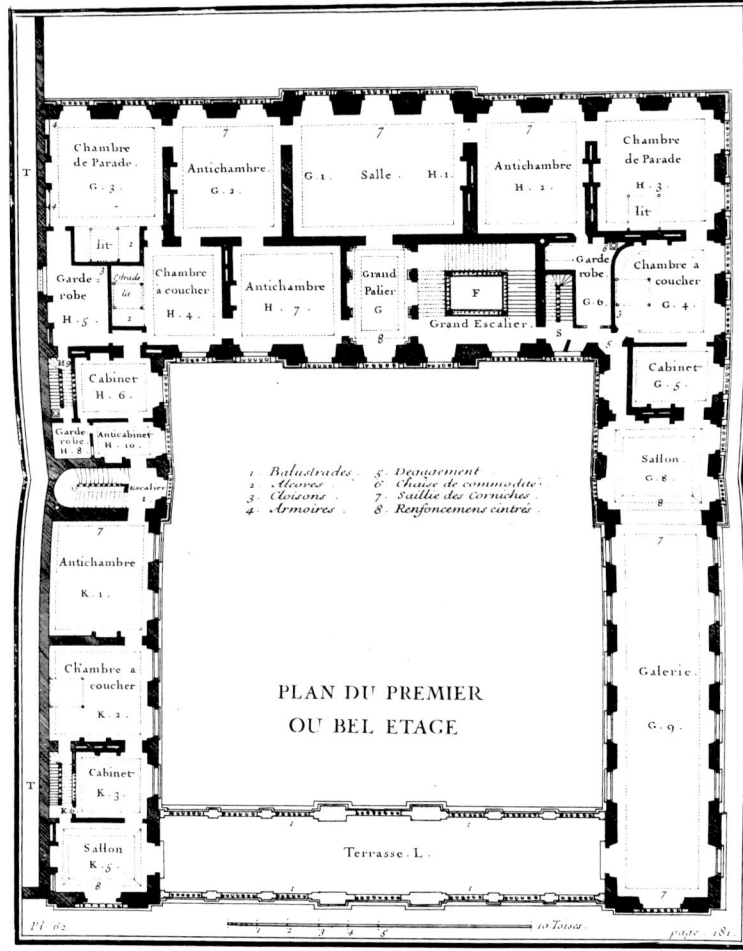

166
Design for a *hôtel*, upper floor plan, C.-A. d'Aviler, 1691. From d'Aviler's *Cours*. This plan illustrates the classic *distribution* of the main floor, the *bel étage*, of a *hôtel* near the turn of the century. There are five *appartements*: two ceremonial and three private. The two ceremonial *appartements* (G1-3 and H1-3) are arranged in *enfilade* along the garden side. The *appartement* to the right (H1-3) is linked in *enfilade* to a large private *appartement* (G4-9), and that to the left (G1-3) is linked *en suite* to a smaller private *appartement* (H4-10)—both on the court side. Rooms H6-10 may also be used as a small separate *appartement* linked to the last *appartement* (K1-5).

107 The Rococo Hôtel

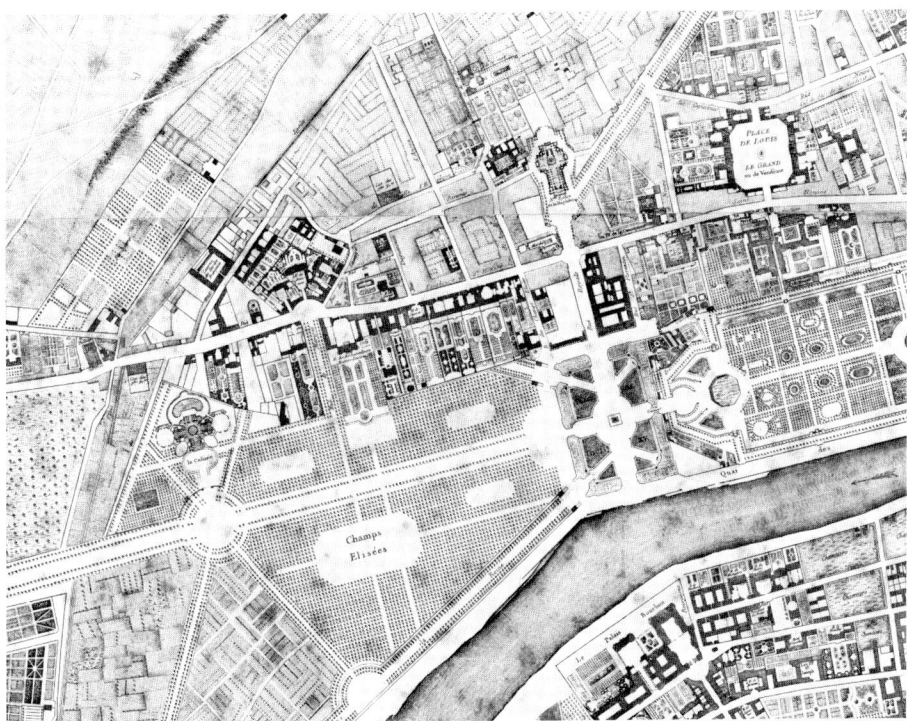

167
Rue St.-Honoré, plan.
From the Jaillot plan.

168
Hôtel d'Evreux, ground
floor plan, Armand-
Claude Mollet, 1718

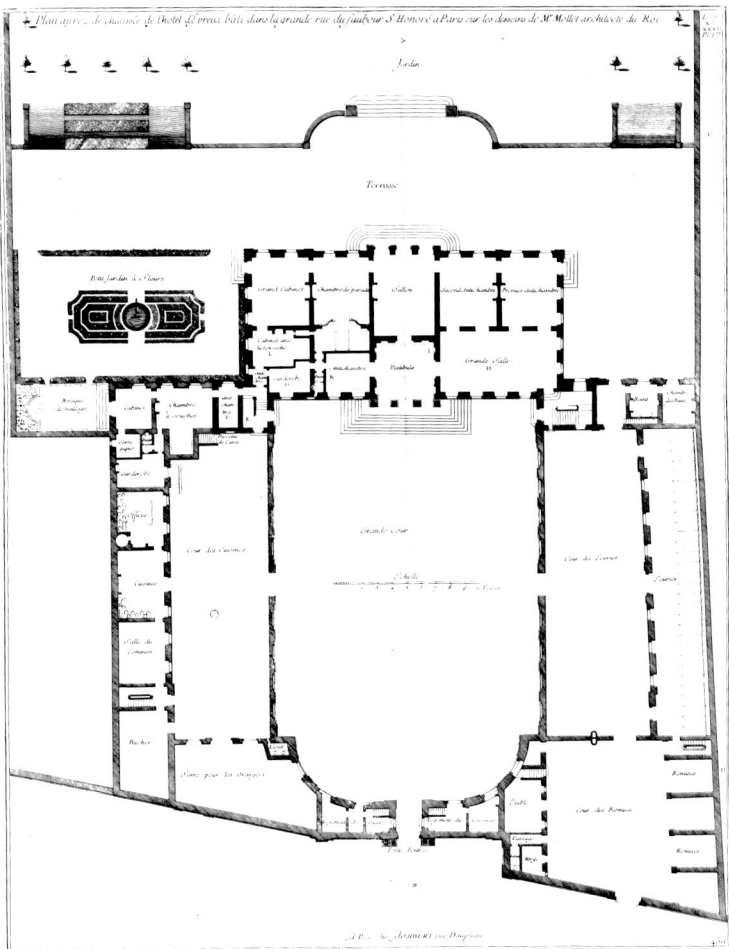

108 Display and Retreat: The Rococo Hôtel

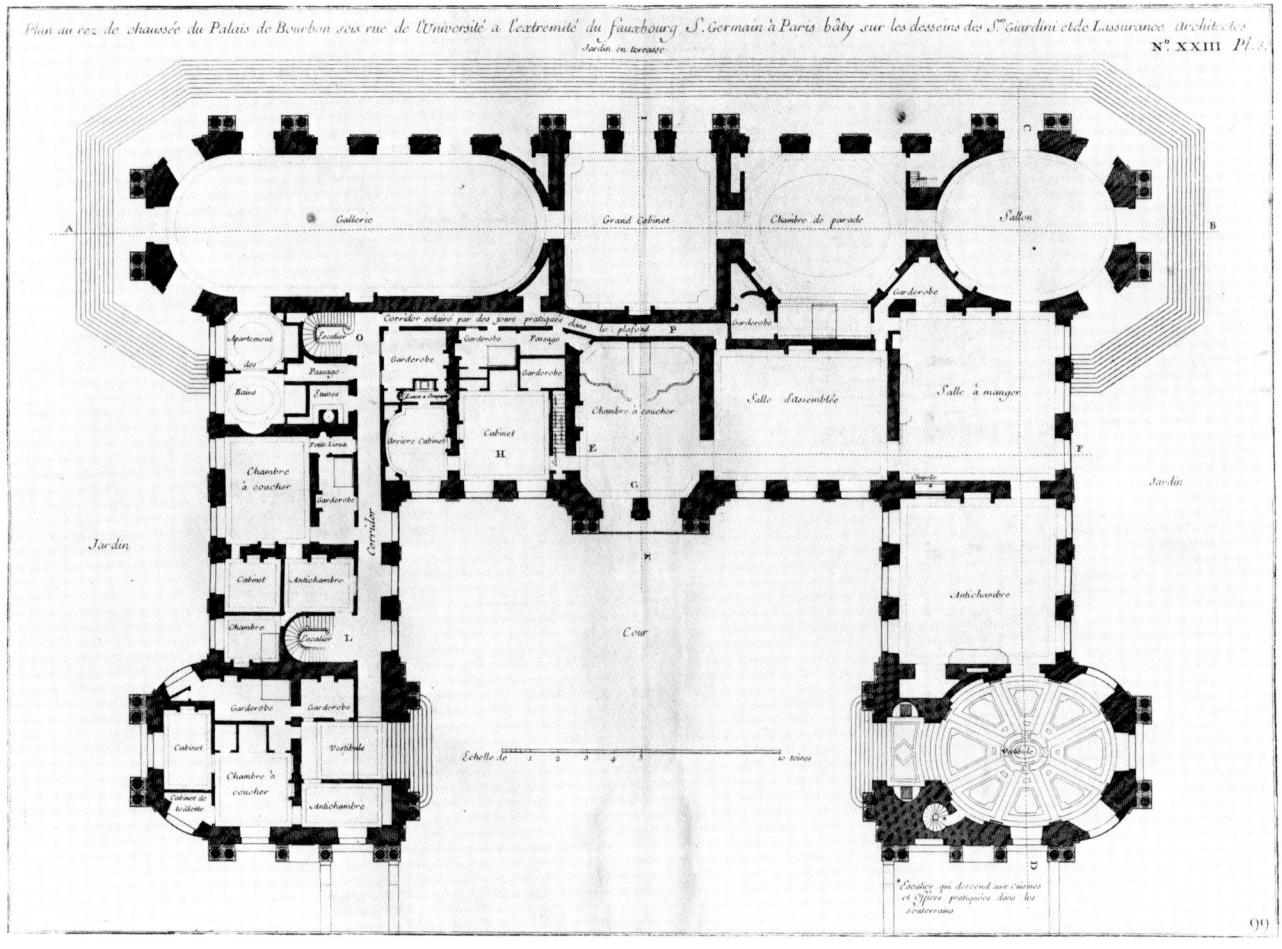

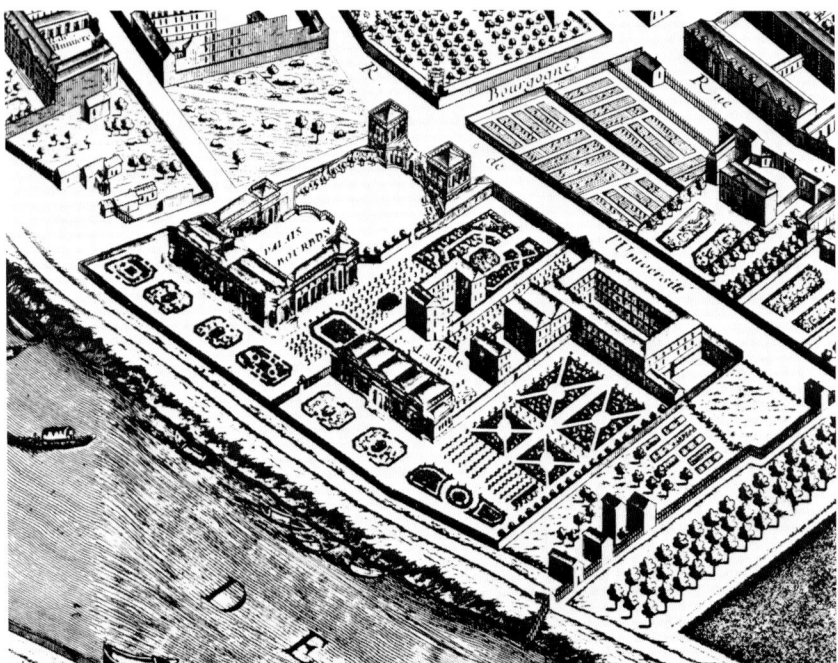

169
Palais Bourbon, ground floor plan, 1722–29

170
Palais Bourbon and the Hôtel de Lassay. Detail from the Turgot plan.

the Palais Bourbon can be seen as equivalent to the Place Louis-le-Grand in that it is the expression of two distinct cultures. It is almost as if an earlier Baroque building had been adapted by a Rococo architect to simultaneously accommodate both public and private modes—adjacent, but independent. Since the *palais* was built by several architects of different generations, this was very nearly the case. That its original owner was the Duchesse de Bourbon-Condé, daughter of Louis XIV and Madame de Montespan, may partially account for the uniqueness of the Palais Bourbon, which seems to span two ages and reflect the requirements of both.

Begun in 1722 by the Italian architect Giardini, the building was continued after his death that same year by Lassurance. Lassurance himself died before the facades were complete, and the work was completed by Aubert and Gabriel between 1724 and 1729. The articulate plan configuration and the sober facades are by Giardini and Lassurance, respectively; but within this regular, symmetrical shell the planning was developed by Aubert and Gabriel.

The most remarkable characteristics of the Palais Bourbon come from the unexpected presence of two internal worlds, which Richard Etlin describes as a bipolar system of display and retreat.[27] A hierarchical sequence of grand public rooms begins in the right-hand wing, circles counterclockwise across the front, and culminates in the enormous gallery; adjacent to this in the left-hand wing are the relatively small living quarters—the *appartements de commodité* and the *appartement des bains.* This section contains a mezzanine as well and is connected to the *appartement de parade* by a top-lit passage that bypasses the duchess's apartment. The duchess's bedchamber occupies the center of the court side of the plan, thereby blocking the central axis of the organization and forcing the honorific circulation to the periphery. There is very little communication between the public and private parts of the palace, as the principal connections are through the duchess's bedchamber and, interestingly, through the *appartement des bains* off the end of the gallery. The residual areas of the plan are all ingeniously utilized as dressing rooms, storage, stairs, and passages, even in the public part of the plan. Blondel and Patte considered this building to be the beginning of the modern residence.[28]

After the French Revolution, the Palais Bourbon was extensively remodeled. Between 1795 and 1797 the semicircular Hall of the Council of Five Hundred was arranged by the architect Gisors in the *corps-de-logis* of the building, with the semicircular side of the room toward the river. The podium of what eventually became the Chamber of Deputies, the French parliament, thus stood in what had been the duchess's bedchamber. Since her bedchamber had occupied the focal position in the center of the plan—the *axis mundi*—as had her father's bed at Versailles, French government was assured of a certain symbolic historical continuity. In 1806 Poyet added the Corinthian portico that "adjusted" the river facade to be a perpendicular terminus to the Madeleine/Place Louis XV axis. The building is still the seat of the French parliament.[29]

The Palais Bourbon represents a high point of internal planning during this period, and, with the Hôtel de Biron (1728–31), also by Gabriel and Aubert, it signaled the end of the prolific phase of *hôtel* building. The Hôtel de Rouillé (1732) by Jean-François Blondel and Jean-Silvain Cartaud's Hôtel de Janvry (1732–33) were among the last aristocratic *hôtels* built. But while few large *hôtels* were built in Paris for the next thirty years, construction of middle-class houses increased,[30] accompanied by an architectural turn toward interior decoration.[31]

Since the beginning of the eighteenth century, Paris had been the artistic and financial center of France, and during the regency it was the political center as well. For a time after the court's return to Versailles in 1722 and Louis XV's coming of age in 1723, the artistic center remained in Paris; but with the king's marriage in 1725, the focus again shifted to Versailles, and the urban *hôtel* diminished in importance. Country houses again became fashionable; and while middle-class Paris set about the construction of city houses, the rich bourgeoisie and the aristocracy were busy in the countryside erecting *maisons de plaisance, pavillons,* and *folies.* Thus, the beautiful plan of Paris by the Abbé Delagrive (1728) and a spectacular aerial view, the so-called Turgot plan (1734–39), capture the city at an essentially complete stage of its development.

The *hôtels* of this subphase were published by Jean Mariette, assisted by the young Jacques-François Blondel, as *L'Architecture françoise,* beginning in 1727. More or less contemporary with Mariette's handbook of built work were two theoretical treatises dealing with the form and layout of the *hôtel.*[32] C.-E. Briseux's *Architecture moderne,* published in 1728, is like a combination of the early seventeenth-century treatises of Savot and Le Muet, updated to the early eighteenth century: the first volume is the text, which deals with the practical aspects of building and with the *distributions* of projects; the second volume illustrates a wide range of projects from

110   Display and Retreat: The Rococo Hôtel

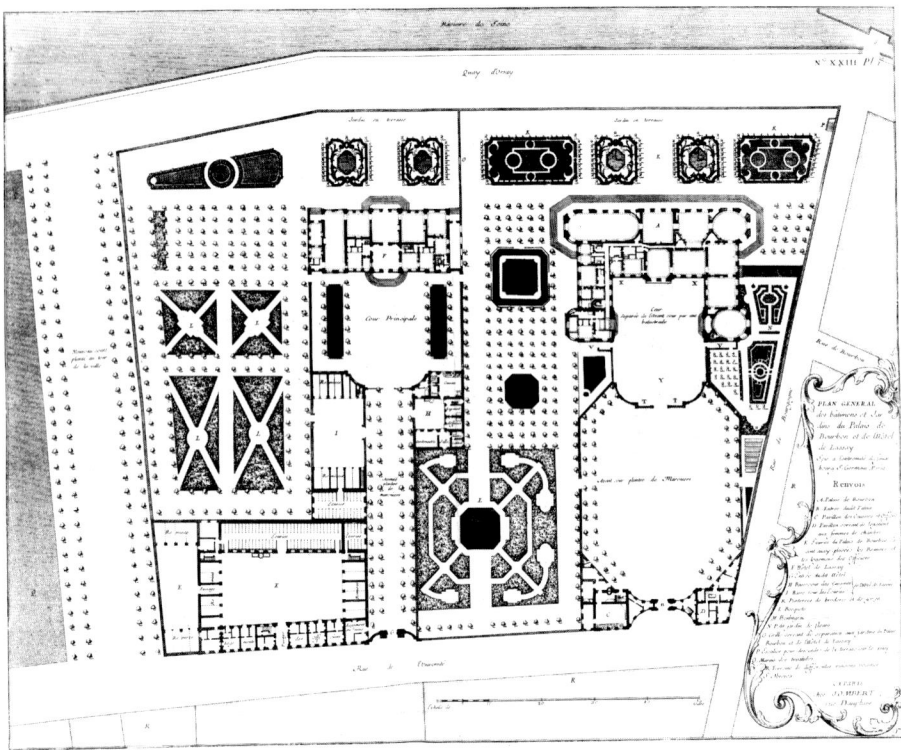

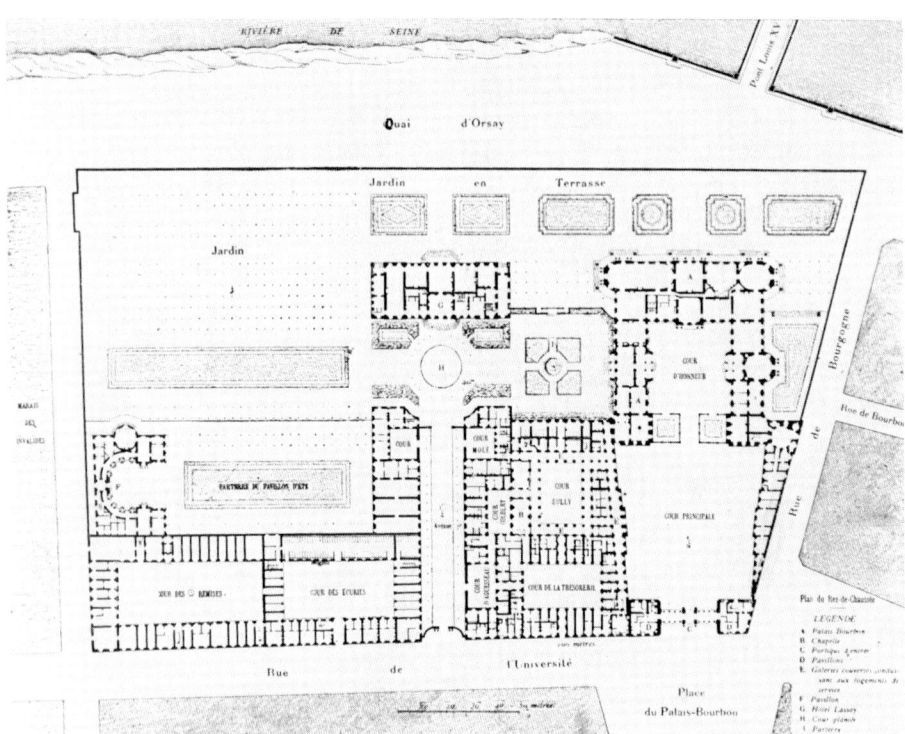

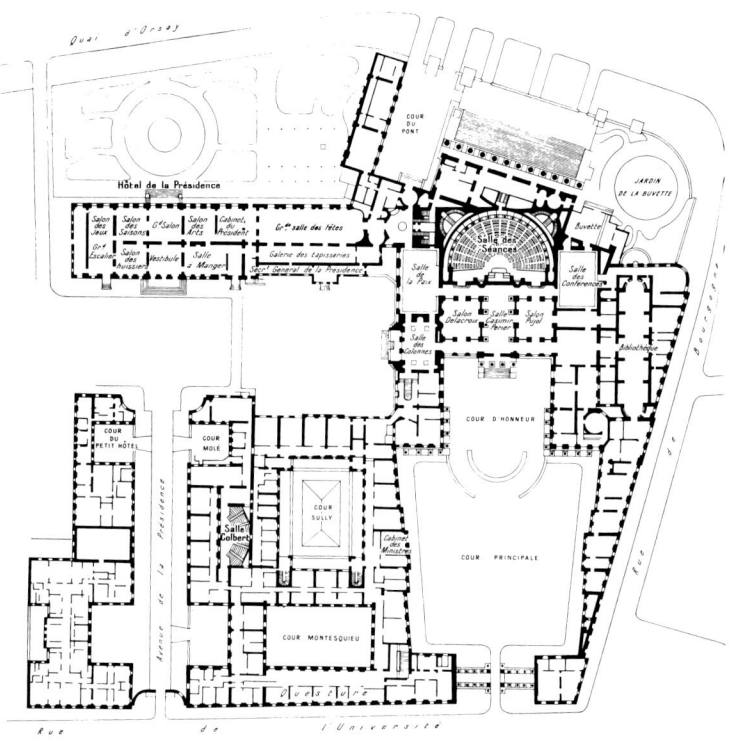

171
Palais Bourbon and the Hôtel de Lassay, site plan, 1722–65

172
Palais Bourbon, site plan in 1789

173
Palais Bourbon, site plan

111 The Rococo Hôtel

174
Palais Bourbon, Hall of the Council of Five Hundred, Jacques-Pierre de Gisors, 1795–97

175
Palais Bourbon, Chamber of Deputies

176
Palais Bourbon, aerial view

very small houses to large *hôtels*. On the whole, Briseux's work is rather dry and academic, and the projects do not seem particularly advanced compared to the planning of the Palais Bourbon.

Jean Courtonne's *Traité de perspective . . . , avec les remarques sur l'architecture . . .* , published in 1725, is more interesting, however. As the title indicates, most of the book concerns perspective, but his "remarks," however brief, are pithy. Courtonne reflects, for instance, that symmetry is necessary only when the parts can be seen at the same time; for that reason, all the external parts must be perfectly symmetrical. In the interior, however, each part should be regular in itself, but the total should consist of a variety of rooms. He points out that this does not require each room to have a different contour,[33] because a *distribution parfaite* consists of an organic relationship of all the parts, not in different shapes for each room.[34] The contrasting demands of symmetry and variety, perhaps, inform Courtonne's assertion that "it is difficult if not impossible to have a *rapport parfaite* between inside and out if the architect is not the absolute master of his subject."[35]

Despite the lesson of Courtonne's suave Hôtel de Matignon, a sophisticated new mode of life made such a *rapport parfaite* exceptionally difficult. His admonitions against the use of figural rooms also went unheeded. It was the age of the interior decorator and the mania for flamboyant curves; but when new *hôtels* were built, the propensity for curvilinear forms pushed the art of the plan to ever more dazzling levels of sophistication. No site seemed too difficult or idiosyncratic to be resolved by astounding constellations of rooms and intricately developed areas of *poché*. Two *hôtels* by one of Jacques-François Blondel's

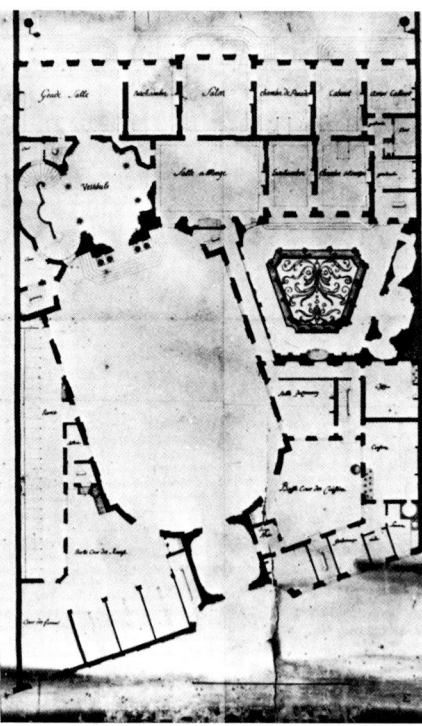

177
Project for a *hôtel*, third Grand Prix de Rome, ground floor plan, Louis Mouret, 1727

178
Hôtel de Soubise, Salon de la Princesse, Germain Boffrand, 1736–39

113   The Rococo Hôtel

179
Hôtels Rohan (1705–8) and Soubise (1705–9), ground floor plan, Pierre-Alexis Delamair. The oval salon in the Hôtel Soubise was added by Germain Boffrand, 1736–39.

180
Hôtel de Villeroy, ground floor plan, Jean-Baptiste Leroux, 1746

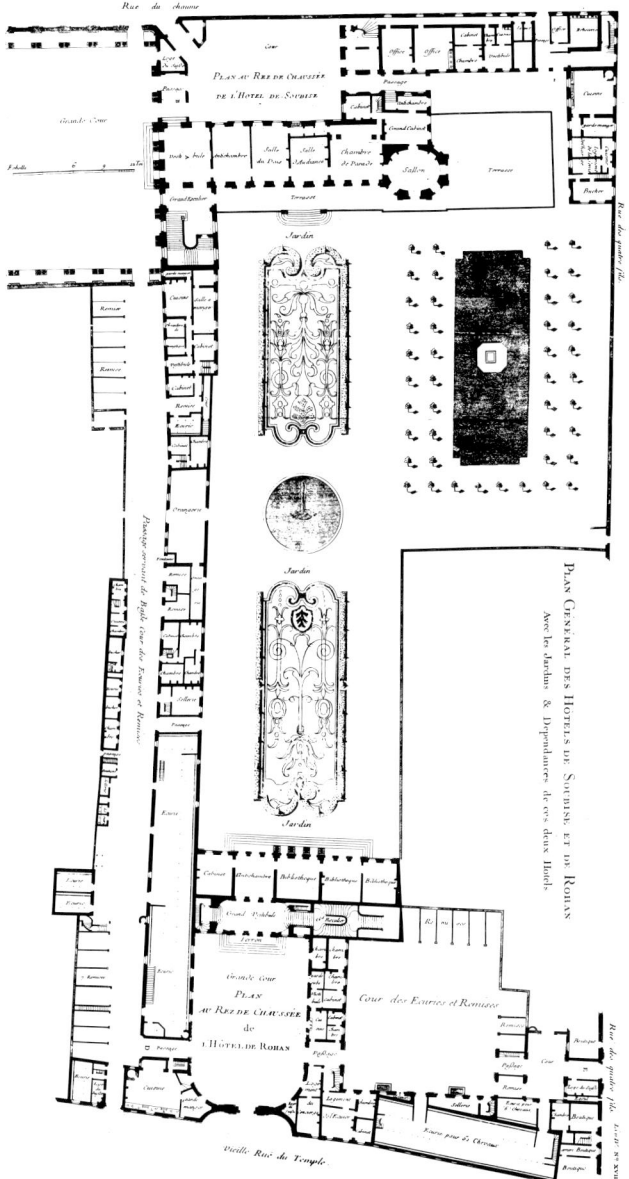
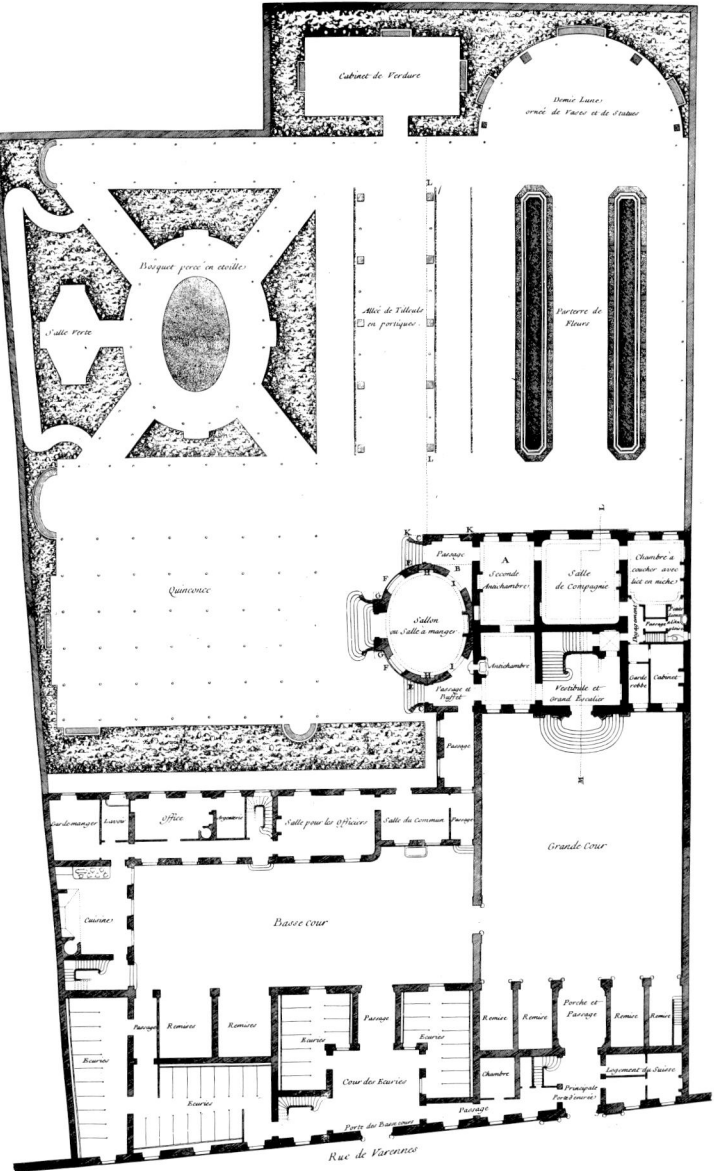

114 Display and Retreat: The Rococo Hôtel

favorite architects, François Franque, illustrate the point. The Hôtel de Villefranche at Avignon (c. 1740) and the abbot's residence at Villers-Cotterets (1765) return to the earlier party-wall plan type but also share the contemporary fascination with complicated interior planning.

That fascination may also be seen in the plans for a house in Bayonne by Juste-Aurèle Meissonier. Though primarily a decorator, Meissonier, like his contemporary Gilles Marie Oppenordt, exerted great influence through his designs. By the mid-eighteenth century, however, both were scorned as representative of the decadent tendencies of Rococo architecture and decoration, and they even elicited the unbridled twentieth-century wrath of Blomfield, who railed that, by Oppenordt's death in 1742, "Meissonier was already outstripping him in vulgarity" and "was an even worse offender."[36] Meissonier's design for a grotto does seem an extravagant fantasy, but his plans for the house in Bayonne are more architectonic and quite ingenious—enough to prompt W. H. Ward to describe it as "one of the best achievements of the Rococo school."[37] The trapezoidal site is open on three sides, and the facades of the three open sides have regularly spaced windows. In plan, four principal rooms, each of a different size and configuration, are organized around a central hall served by a grand stair and a service stair. Meissonier cleverly develops the residual space between the general form of the facade and the particular shapes of the rooms with niches, deep window recesses, and panels, thereby exploiting the lack of congruence between interior and exterior geometries. On the second floor, he uses similar devices not only on the outside walls, but also between rooms so that the interior partitions are like hollow walls con-

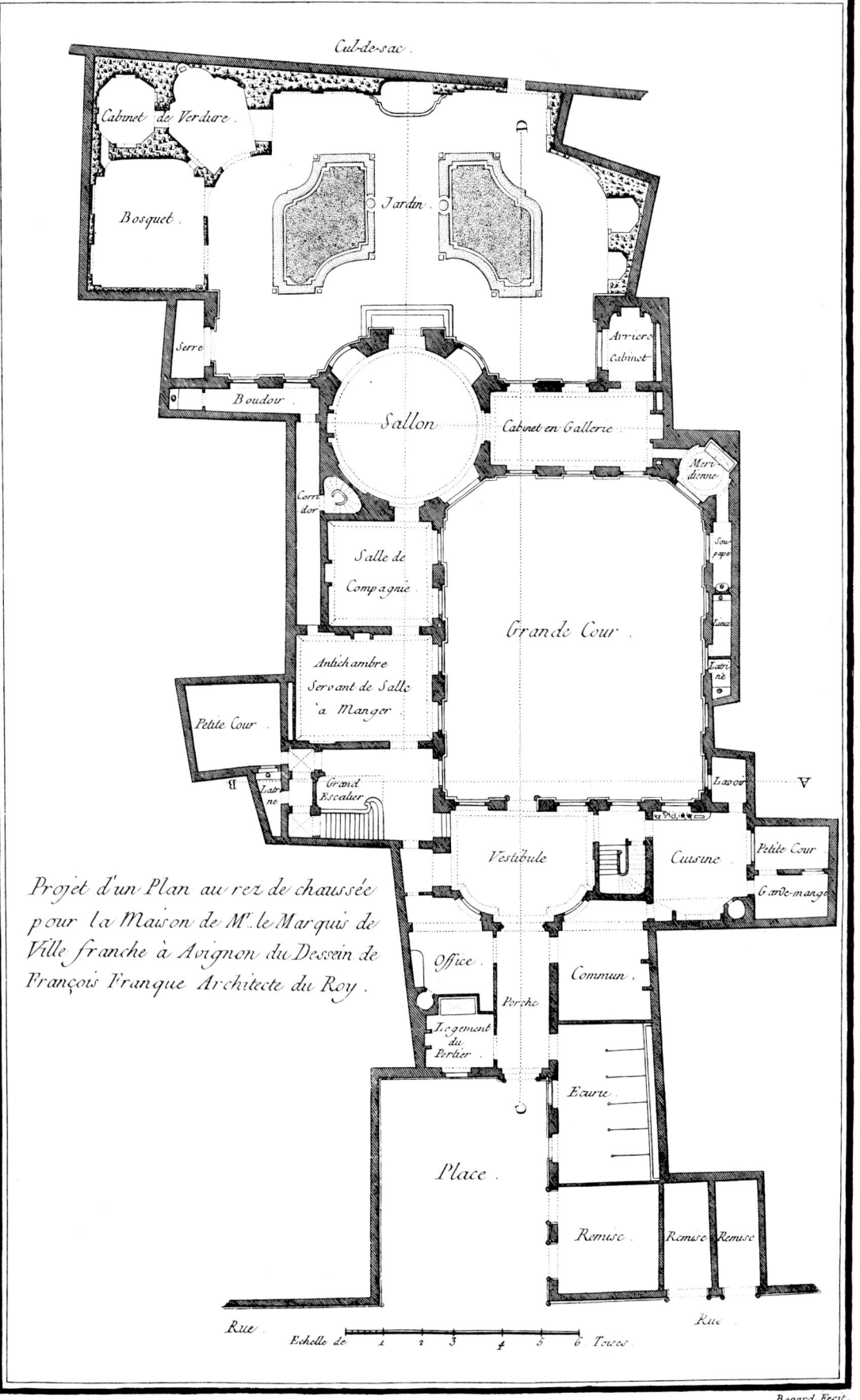

181
Avignon, Hôtel de Villefranche, ground floor plan, François Franque, c. 1740

taining vestibules, bed niches, toilets, and the like. The development of this system of *poché* is the most extensive of all the *hôtels* to date, and despite the Neoclassical reaction to Meissonier and the Rococo, the idea was to be developed still further in the Neoclassical *hôtels* during the last half of the century.

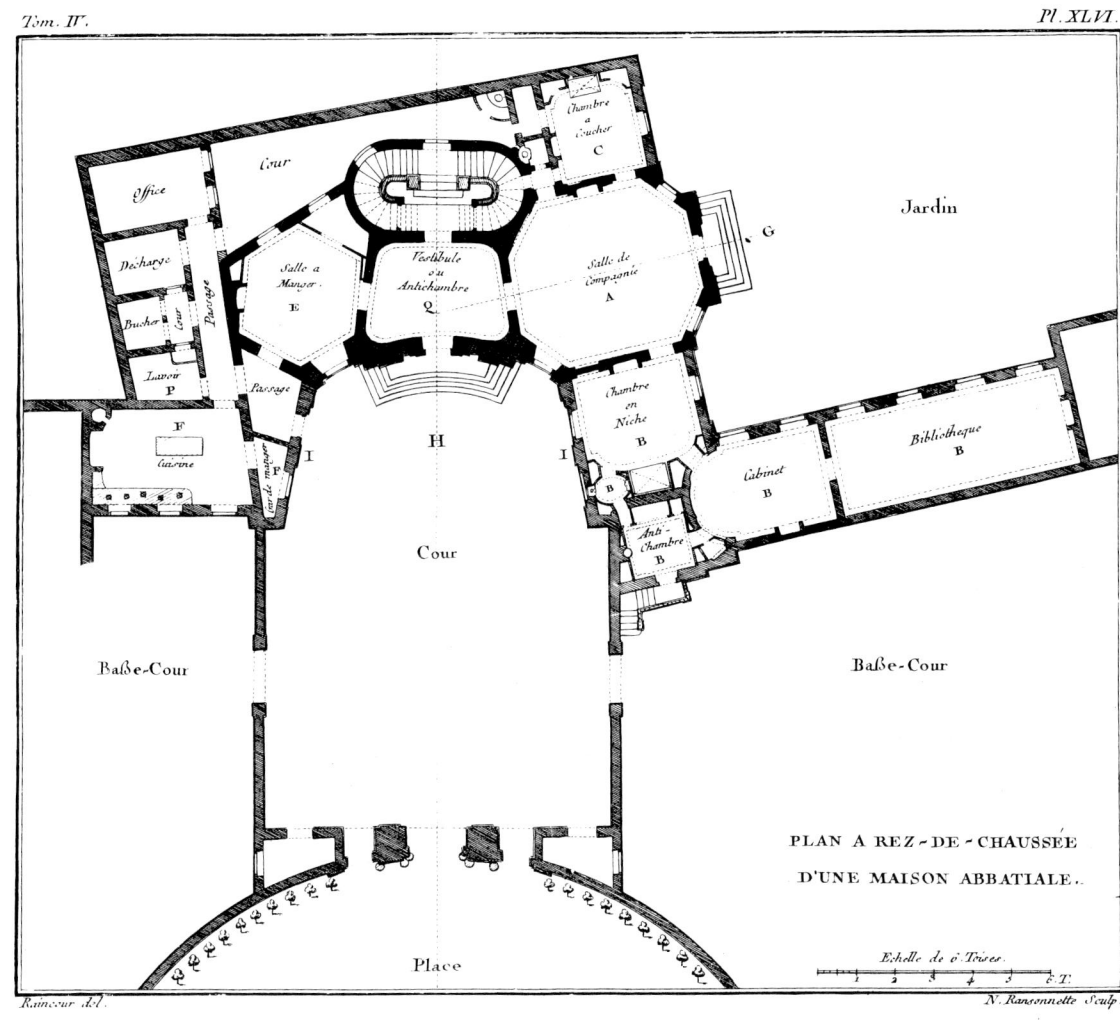

182
Villers-Cotterets, abbot's residence, ground floor plan, François Franque, 1765

116 Display and Retreat: The Rococo Hôtel

183
Design for a grotto, Juste-Aurèle Meissonier

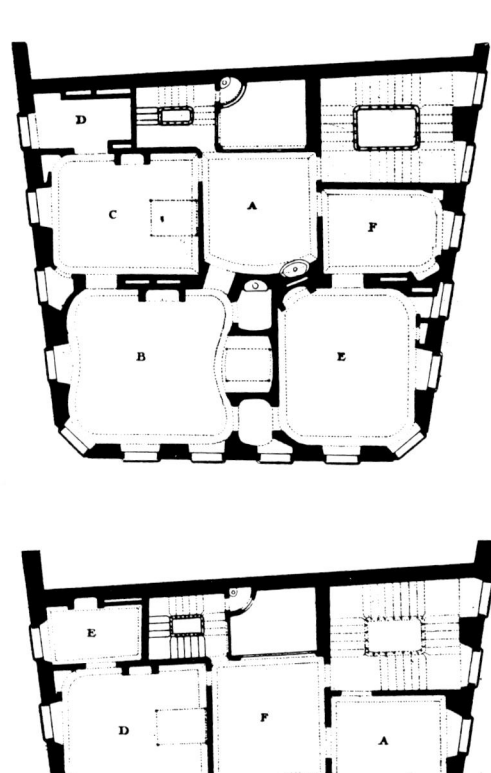

184
Bayonne, Maison de Brethaus, first floor plan, Juste-Aurèle Meissonier.
A. antichambre
B. salon
C. chambre d'assemblée
D. chambre à coucher
E. cabinet
F. salle à manger

185
Bayonne, Maison de Brethaus, second floor plan.
A. antichambre
B. chambre de parade
C. chambre à coucher
D. cabinet
E. grand cabinet
F. antichambre

186
Project for a country house, plans, Charles-Etienne Briseux. From *L'Art de bâtir...*, 1743.

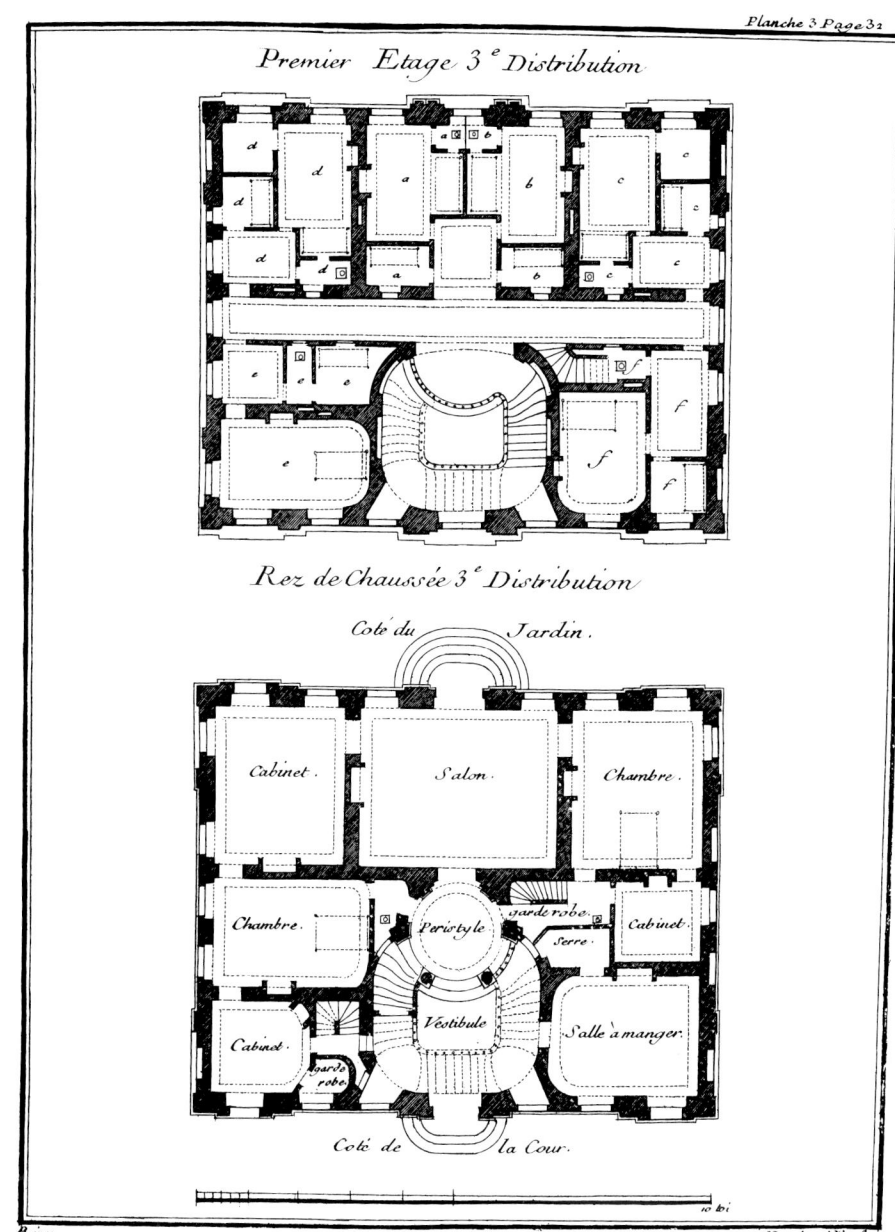

118 Display and Retreat: The Rococo Hôtel

Blondel and Briseux

Two manuals, J.-F. Blondel's *De la distribution des maisons de plaisance et la décoration des édifices en général* (1737 and 1738) and C.-E. Briseux's *L'Art de bâtir des maisons de campagne* (1743), outline the system of the *hôtel* near the middle of the century and set the scene from which the Neoclassical *hôtel* emerged in the 1760s.[38] Three types of *appartements* are identified. The *appartement de parade*, though smaller, was still required for display and was where business associates were impressively received in the morning. There was also an *appartement de société*, where family and friends could be received in a somewhat more relaxed setting. Now obligatory was the *appartement de commodité*, reserved for the master and mistress of the house to retire to in the winter, in case of indisposition, or to attend to domestic affairs.

A specific dining room was commonly provided and was indicated on plans by the presence of buffets. These rooms were often polygonal, oval, or round ended. Smoking rooms and billiards rooms appeared too, but the architectural profession was most occupied with service and convenience. Briseux advocated the use of corridors and passageways, while Blondel preferred *dégagements* and stairs; but in practice, architects explored every system of service in an effort to assure convenience.

Figural rooms were promoted for convenience as well as fashion because they facilitated the *dégagements* by providing residual areas in the plan. They were not without their own form of inconvenience, however. Hautecoeur recounts the reservations expressed by Patte in 1769:

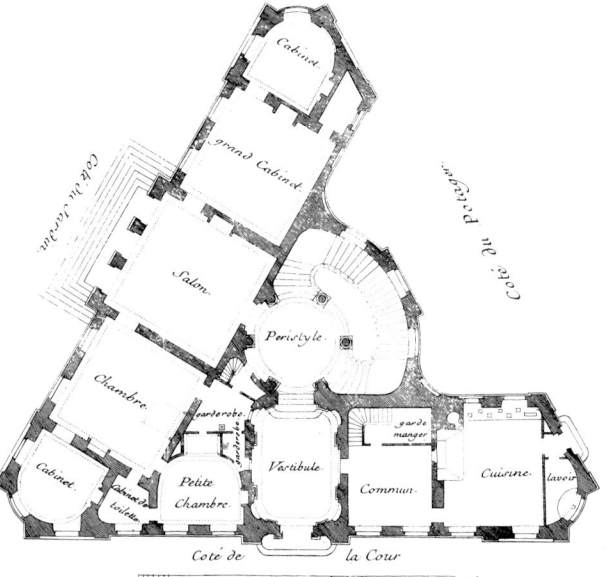

187
Project for a country house, ground floor plan, Charles-Etienne Briseux. From *L'Art de bâtir*..., 1743.

188
Project for a country house, upper floor plan, Charles-Etienne Briseux. From *L'Art de bâtir*..., 1743.

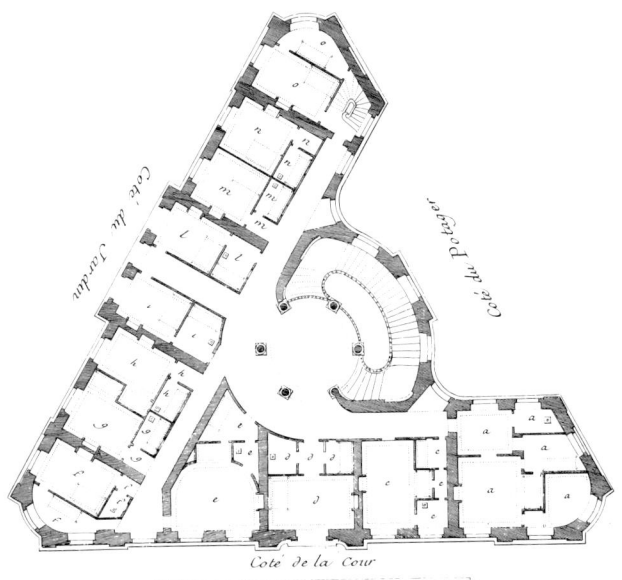

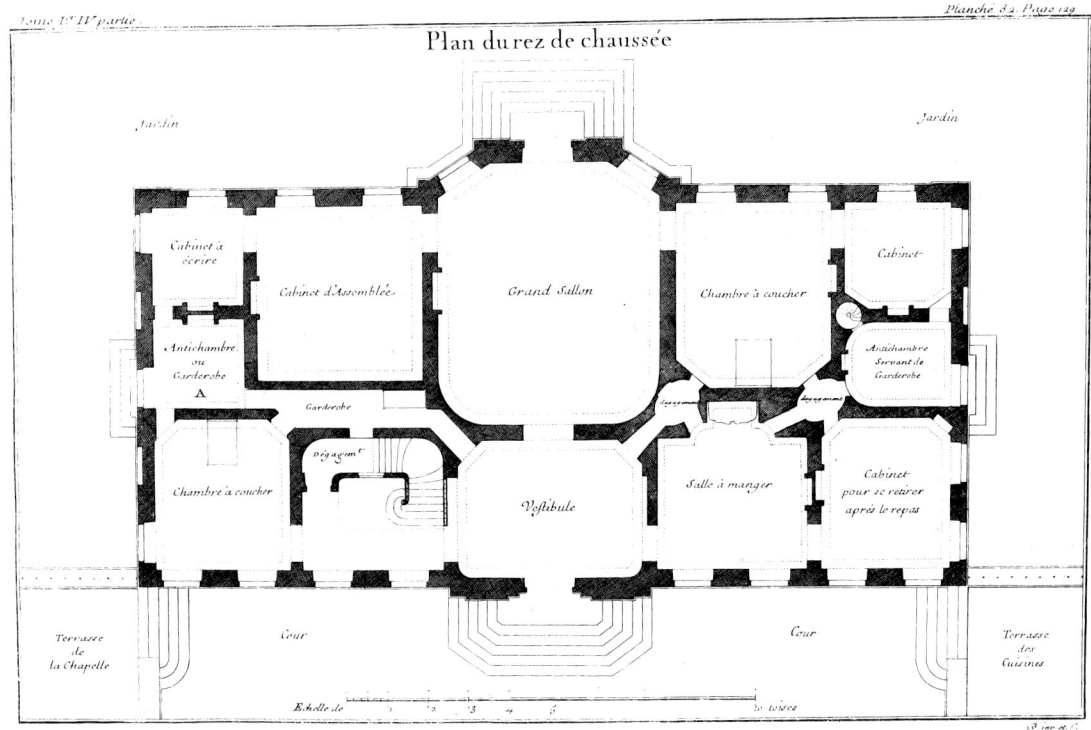

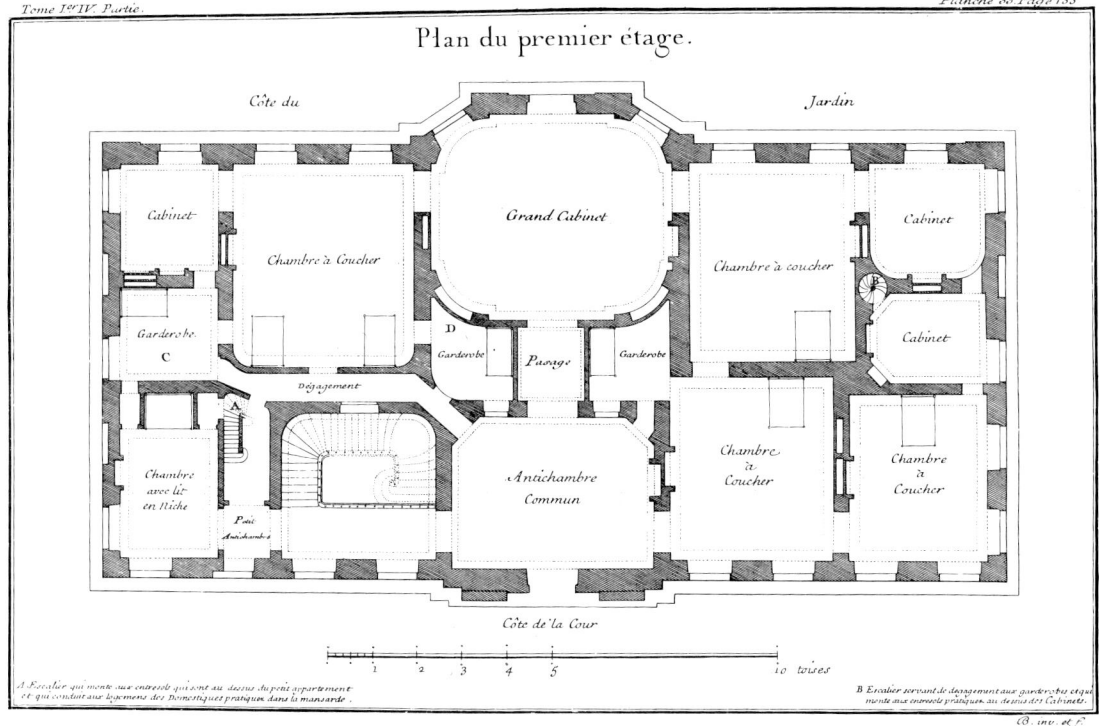

The art of *la distribution* which had been perfected over a period of forty years in France was structurally more of a problem than one would think due to the number of forms which put most plans in turmoil under the pretext of rendering the *appartements* more convenient. The result was a multitude of different structural conditions at each floor such that one could hardly guess how one *appartement* could be placed over the other.[39]

Blondel's *Distribution* is clearly modeled after d'Aviler's *Cours* and gives a beautiful cross section of the state of the art. Like its predecessor, it covers a range of topics from site plans to details of various rooms, including baths and toilets. By comparison, Briseux's *L'Art de bâtir* is rather dry; unlike Blondel he does not show site plans and details, only isolated blocks with highly rationalized plans. But, as compendiums of Rococo architecture, both of these treatises display the architectural characteristics that paradoxically link the Rococo and its imminent replacement, Neoclassicism.

The generally severe reaction to the excesses of the Rococo that began in the 1750s marked another significant change in French architecture and culture. By this time, most of the architects of the previous period were already dead—Courtonne (1739); Aubert (1741); Oppenordt, Jacques Gabriel, and Mollet (1742); Meissonier (1750); Boffrand (1754); and Cartaud (1758)—and critics such as Cochin launched strident attacks on Meissonier and others.[40] Finally, Blondel's publication of the works of this generation, as well as of the preceding one, in his *Architecture françoise* between 1752 and 1756[41] marked the passing of the period of the Rococo *hôtel* and, to a certain extent, prefigured the rise of Neoclassicism through its reaffirmation of classical models and its rejection of the *style rocaille*.

189
Project for a country house, ground floor plan, Jacques-François Blondel. From *De la distribution . . .*, 1737 and 1738.

190
Project for a country house, upper floor plan, Jacques-François Blondel. From *De la distribution . . .*, 1737 and 1738.

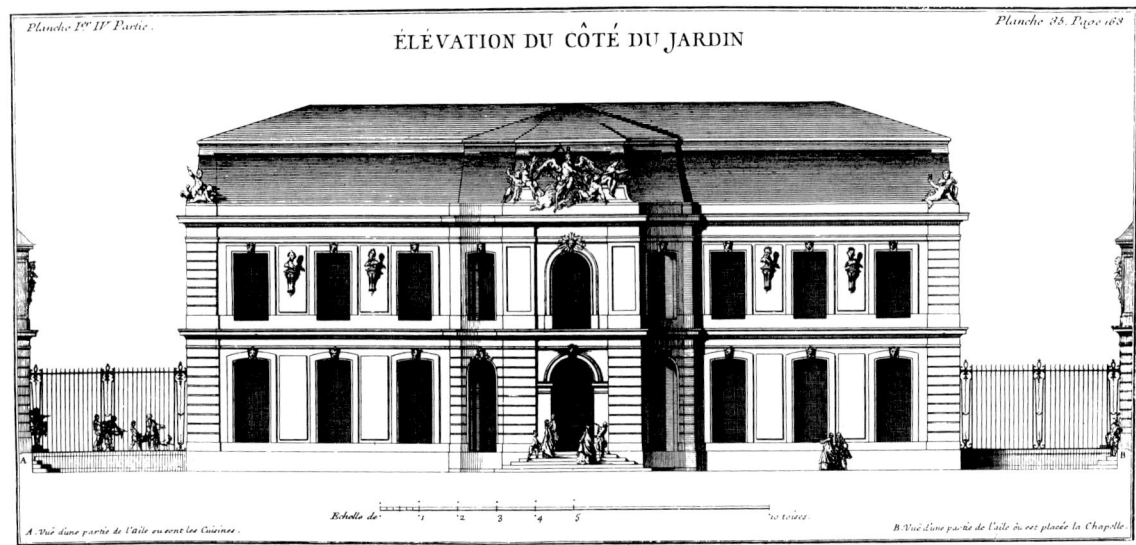

191
Project for a country house, garden elevation, Jacques-François Blondel. From *De la distribution* . . . , 1737 and 1738.

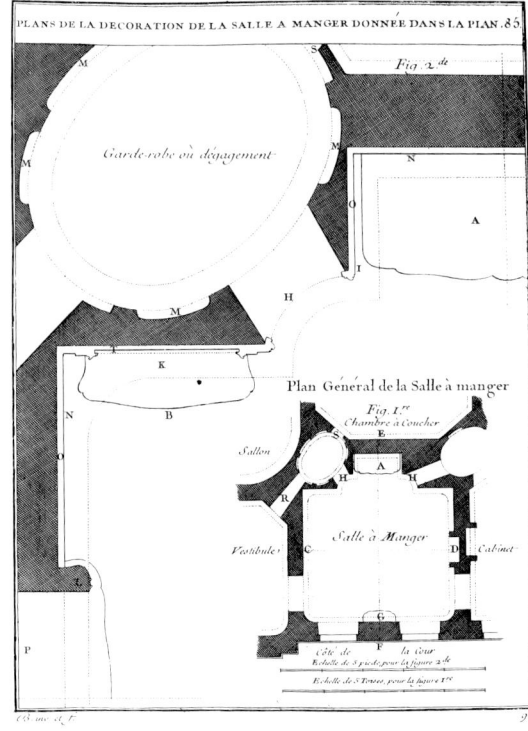

192
Project for a country house, detail plans of the dining room, Jacques-François Blondel. From *De la distribution* . . . , 1737 and 1738.

A. marble buffet table
B. sofa
C. mirror
D. fireplace
G. marble table
H. curved doors
I. niche
K. mirror
M. recesses to simulate symmetrical doors and provide storage
N. projection of the cornice
O. thickness of the paneling
P. foyer
R. service passage
S. door to bedroom

193
Project for a country house, elevation of the dining room, Jacques-François Blondel. From *De la distribution...*, 1737 and 1738.

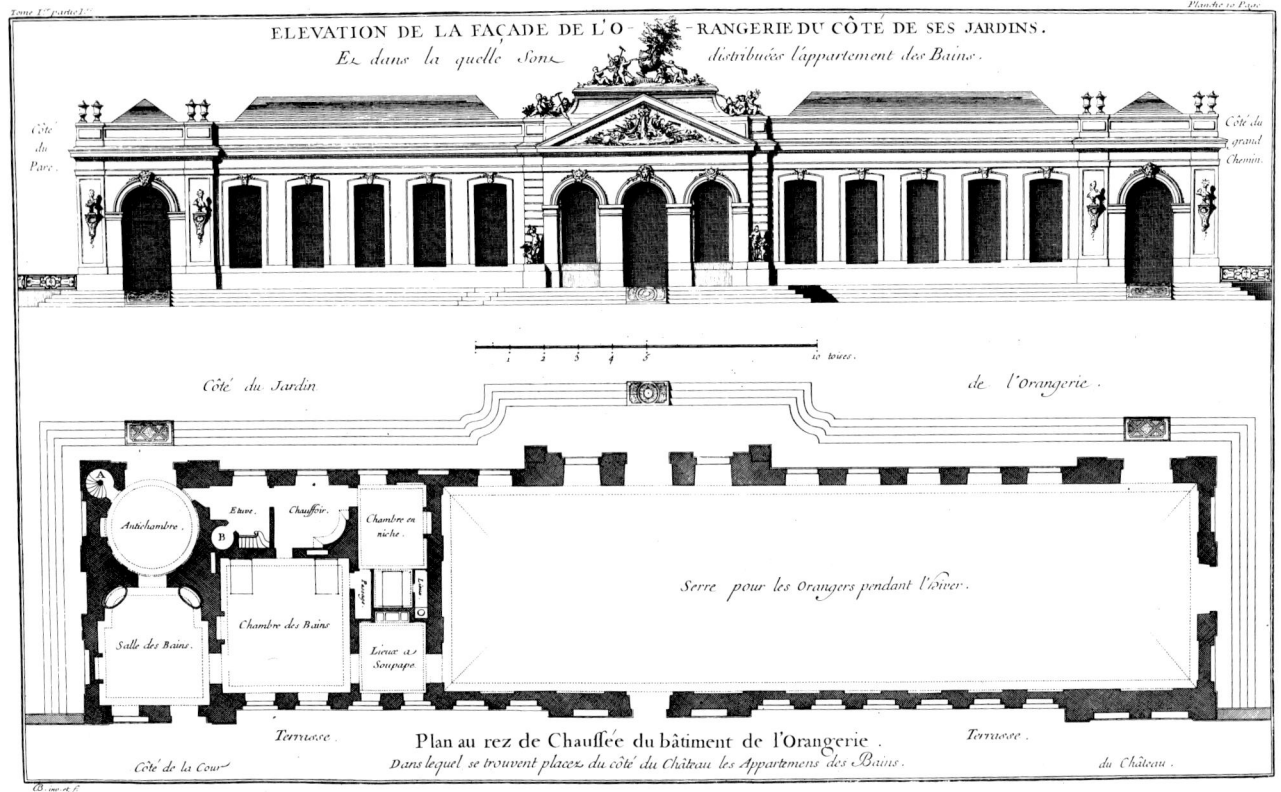

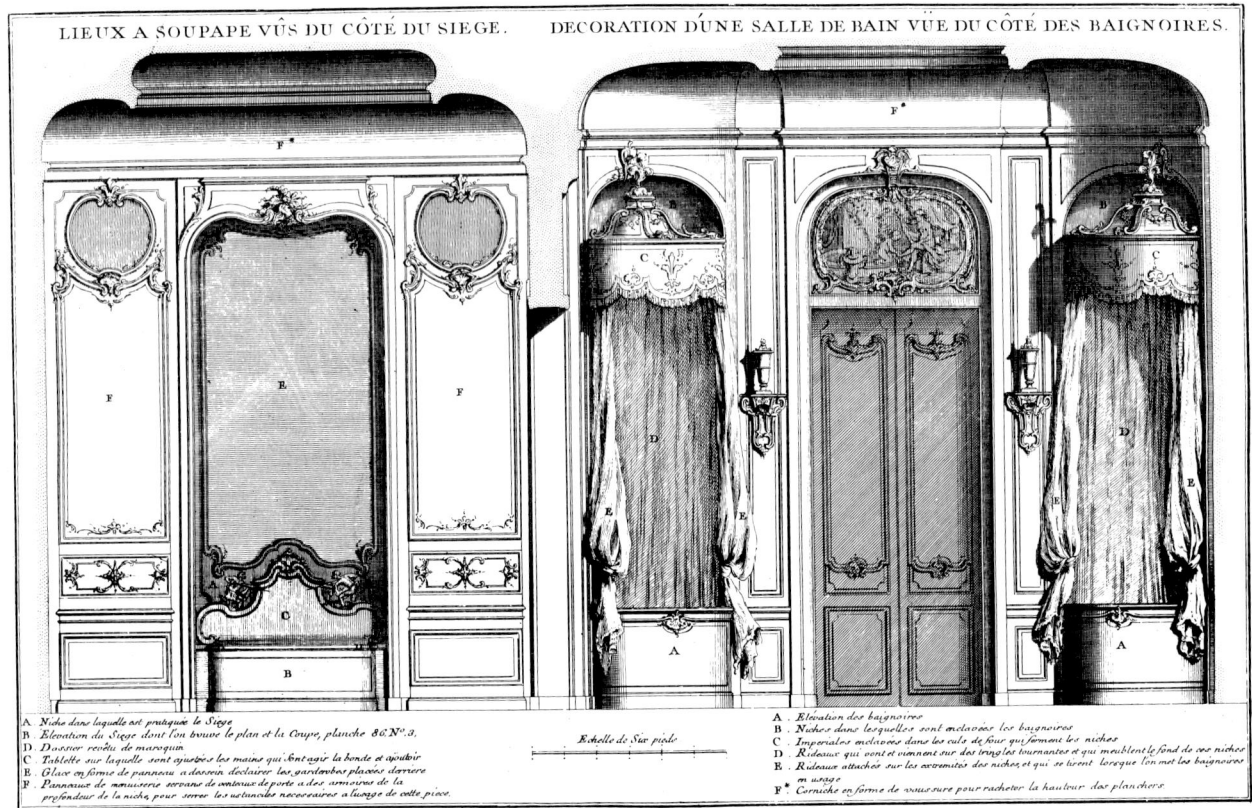

194
An *orangerie* with an *appartement des bains*, plan and elevation, Jacques-François Blondel. From *De la distribution . . .*, 1737 and 1738.

195
Elevation of a *salle des bains* and a *lieux à soupape*, Jacques-François Blondel. From *De la distribution . . .*, 1737 and 1738.

196
Detail plans of a *lieux à soupape* (flush toilet), Jacques-François Blondel. From *De la distribution . . .*, 1737 and 1738.
A. marble top
B. seat below
D. handle for raising seat cover
E. wood seat cover painted to match the marble
F. opening valve
G. water valve for flushing
H. handle for controlling adjustable water pipe (M) and vertical water jet (Q)

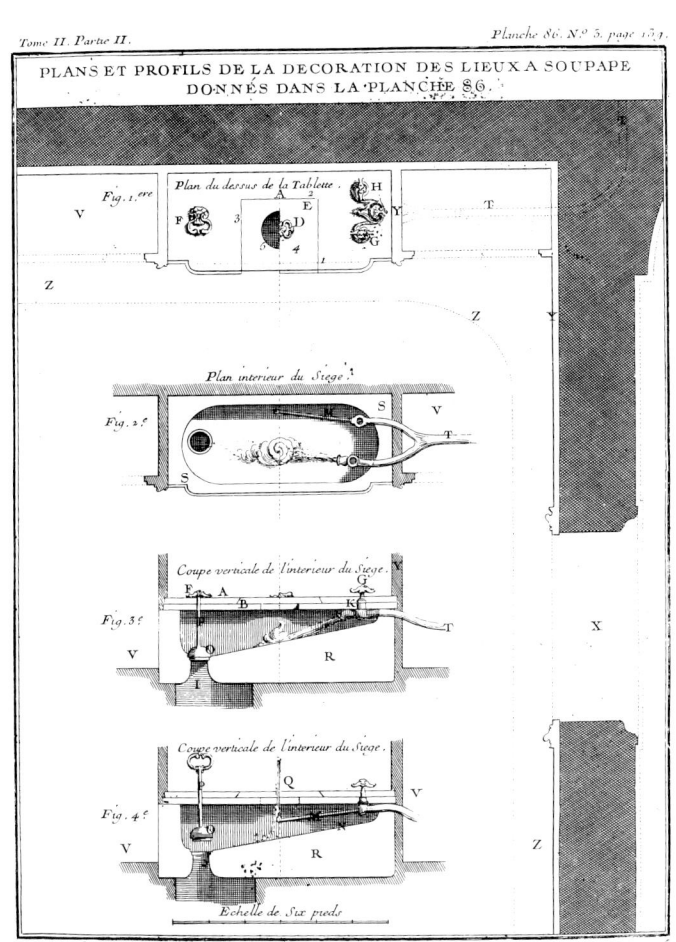
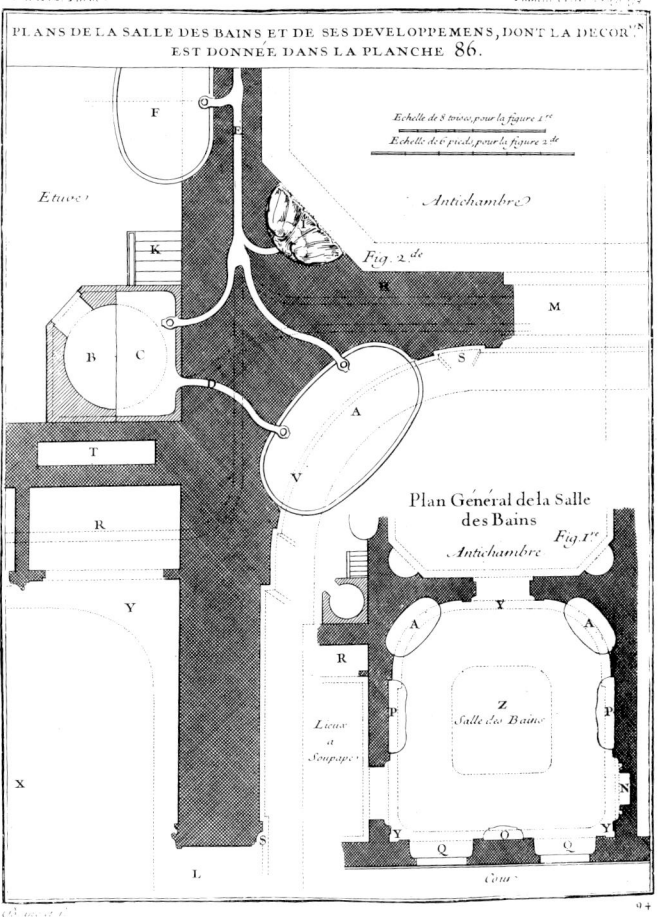

197
Detail plans of a *salle des bains*, Jacques-François Blondel. From *De la distribution...*, 1737 and 1738.
A. bathtubs
B. furnace
C. boiler
D. hot water pipe
E. cold water supply
F. water tank
H. water pipes to other bathtub
I. basin for washing hands
L. door opposite chimney (N), which terminates the *enfilade* of the *appartement des bains*. (The *chambre à coucher* is on the opposite side of the *lieux à soupape*.)

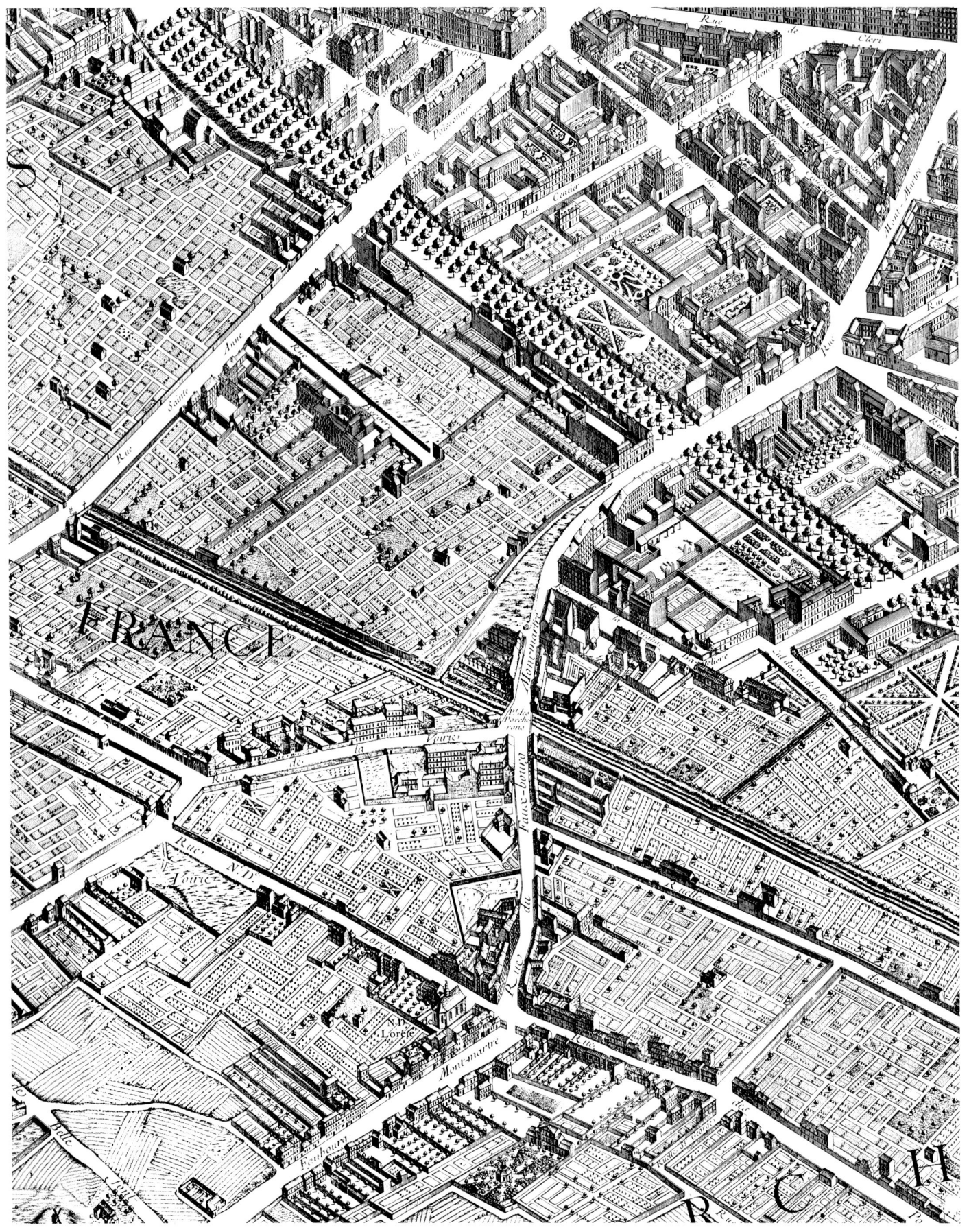

198
Detail from the Turgot plan showing the undeveloped area beyond the *boulevards*

199
Hôtel Guimard, elevation, 1770–72

5 Private Icons: The Neoclassical Hôtel

The development of the Neoclassical *hôtel* type during the second half of the eighteenth century completes the long transformation of the French *hôtel* and heralds a revolutionary change in thought, society, and urbanism. The transformation from the party-wall urban *hôtel* of the Baroque period to the transitional Rococo *hôtel*, to the freestanding suburban *hôtel* of the Neoclassical period reveals the evolution of a modern conception of urban space, just as the internal transformation from simple, functionally nonspecific rooms under Henri IV to the intricate specifications of eighteenth-century *distribution* describes the rise of modern functional planning. But as the *hôtel* became even more rationalized and precise—more "modern"—the boundaries between the aristocracy and the bourgeoisie became increasingly blurred. Indeed, in the later eighteenth century, financiers, actresses, and even architects could own a *hôtel*, whereas in the early seventeenth century the term was exclusively reserved for residences of the aristocracy. In fact, as the limits of the social ladder expanded, so did the number of *hôtels* and, consequently, the number of architects. As a suburban villa, then, the Neoclassical *hôtel* is only a short step away from the modern, single-family suburban house.

The competition for the Place Louis XV (now Place de la Concorde) in 1748 marks the beginning of this fourth period of *hôtel* building, and the publication of the Neoclassical *hôtels* by Krafft and Ransonnette in *Plans . . . des plus belles . . . hôtels* (n.d., 1802?) symbolically marks its close. Construction of *hôtels* continued into the nineteenth century, but the development of the *hôtel* was essentially complete by the French Revolution. As many of the Neoclassical *hôtels* were finished by 1778, the Jaillot plan of that year is to late-eighteenth-century Paris what the Delagrive plan is to the Paris of the early eighteenth century. The Maire plan of 1808 is still more complete; it shows all of the Neoclassical *hôtels*, and provides a legend to public buildings, *hôtels*, and the like.

As the evolution of the French *hôtel* shows, tradition and practice provided a system within which invention took place. Even the theoretical treatises on domestic architecture were not so much theories of the new as codifications of current practice. Reading them in succession makes it clear that they built upon each other in a way that blurs their differences and reveals their consistencies. In public architecture as well, continuity reigned: classical rules, as they were understood at the time, and the concepts of *convenance* (the correct relation of parts to each other and to their purpose) and *bienséance* (appropriateness or correct form of building to purpose and social rank) had governed all French architectural activity.[1] Architects, Talbot Hamlin notes, "designed directly within the current tradition almost unconscious of any possibility of choice or change."[2] But around the middle of the eighteenth century, all that began to change. A social and intellectual revolution was in the wind.

It would be difficult to overstate the change in art and culture that began during the 1750s. More than just a severe reaction to the stylistic excesses of the Rococo, it differed, as Hugh Honour states, "from most stylistic changes in the history of art by its self-awareness."[3] He means, of course, not simply awareness of a new approach, but awareness of its revolutionary nature; and he quotes d'Alembert (1759) to make the point: "A most remarkable change in our ideas is taking place, one of such rapidity that it seems to promise a greater change still to come. It will be for the future to decide the aim, the nature and the limits of this revolution."[4]

Developments in archaeology and philosophy questioned the reliability of old rules and inaugurated new visions of both the past and the future. Winckelmann ushered in modern scientific archaeology when he differentiated Greek from Roman work, and the new interest in the Greek temple was to be of great importance to architecture. In fact, many architects as well as archaeologists published studies of ancient Greek buildings during this period. Equally important was the discovery and excavation of Herculaneum (1738) and Pompeii (1748), for this ancient world of modest houses and ordinary people stirred the romantic imagination of the rising French middle class. This fresh view of the past, plus the romantic Romanism of Piranesi and his demand for *tabula rasa*, contributed to a wholly new idea of history—to the self-conscious *use* of history as well as the scientific *study* of history. Considered the beginning of art history, these developments also brought with them (or were the products of) the amateur and dilettante—for instance, the leader of the *antiquaires*, the Comte de Caylus, a collector, art historian, and lecturer to the Academy.

The new historical attitude found another voice in the *philosophes*, who launched a frontal attack on the Rococo in the name of rationalism and reason.[5] Their onslaughts against religion, superstition, social inequity, and superficiality were accompanied by a new intellectual agenda based on rigorous rationality. A prime example was Diderot and d'Alembert's *Encyclopédie* (1751–77),[6] which articulated, categorized, and rationalized all aspects of life into one system. The Catholic religion, justice, and the monarchy itself, the pillars of the *ancien régime*, were all called into question by this revolutionary new vision.

As a rational, social art, architecture could hardly remain unaffected by these developments. One effect was the extension of the principles of *la distribution*, the rational or practical arrangement of the plan, to the very fabric of the building. A more abstract expression of rationalism addressed the era's enthusiasm for all things Greek and the parallel nostalgia for the grand simplicity of the age of Louis XIV: the case for the purity of first sources. Its theoretical basis was outlined in Marc-Antoine Laugier's famous *Essai sur l'architecture* (1753), in which he argued for a return to fundamental principles and functional elements. To him, the primitive hut was the ancestor of the Greek temple and the prototype of architecture. He therefore restricted his definition of architecture to the elements of the hut: columns, architrave, pediment, and walls. His insistence on purity of form and on simplicity exerted a profound influence on the new generation of architects, and his presentation of the primitive hut gave architecture one of its most compellingly poetic icons.

But if Laugier called attention to an innocent ancestor of the "noble Greek," it was Rousseau who indicted the corruption of civilized society and brought naturalism and the idea of the "noble savage" center stage. This completed the equation. In Joseph Rykwert's phrase, "Laugier's little hut had been built on Rousseau's riverbank."[7]

It was not just that tastes and sensibilities were changing; nor that a social, political, and intellectual change was taking place. Rather, man's understanding of the world, and the architectural and urban expression of his relationship to it, was profoundly altered during this period. The medieval view of the world held that man is imperfect and that the universe is unknown and unknowable; the Renaissance view was the opposite: man is at the center of a potentially knowable, if not known, universe. With the Enlightenment came a significant shift in this set of relationships, as man stepped out of the center to take a position of equality with other bodies in a rationally ordered natural world.

Since the beginning of the Renaissance, space—enclosed architectural and urban space—had been the principal physical expression of man's relationship to the cosmos.[8] Near the middle of the eighteenth century, the new view of that relationship resulted in a complete inversion of the previous system: rationalized solids set in continuous open space became the ideal urban system. Initiating a radical change in the principal medium of urbanism—one that would find its ultimate expression in the twentieth century—this inversion also represented a fundamental change in humanism. Man's anthropocentric relationship to figural space during the Renaissance was replaced by an anthropocentric relationship to figural, or iconic, solids during the Enlightenment. Before, man had been the subject of space; subsequently, he became another object among many in an increasingly egalitarian landscape.

Laugier's primitive hut is, of course, doubly significant, coming as it did at the apex of this change in focus. This provocative image may be seen in two radically different ways: as a shelter, a haven, a house—in short, as a *space*; and as a logical set of architectural elements—as a *tem-*

ple. The first view probably represents the dominant attitude before 1750, the second view that after 1750. The argument is that of ideal void versus ideal solid, and the change is essentially one of emphasis: from the model of the forum to the model of the acropolis.⁹

The clearest expression of the new ideal was the classical temple or pavilion in a romantic, open landscape; and the most important urban and architectural examples were the Place Louis XV (begun 1757) and the Petit Trianon at Versailles (1762–68), both by Ange-Jacques Gabriel. The Place Louis XV is the last royal square built in Paris and the urban event that preceded the fourth period of *hôtel* construction; the Petit Trianon is the first clear manifestation of the new *hôtel* type.

200
Frontispiece of Laugier's
Essai sur l'architecture
(second edition), 1755.
Engraving by Eisen.

The Place Louis XV

Between 1730 and 1763 little new construction occurred in Paris, but in many provincial towns important urban projects were initiated. Notable among them were the town squares at Rennes (1721–44) and Bordeaux (1735–55) by Jacques Gabriel.[10] Although the model for these squares was the Place Louis-le-Grand in Paris, Bordeaux's Place Royale, especially, involved a new interpretation: the new square was not an isolated or independent urban event, but was designed to connect and relate the space of the Garonne River to the existing street network of the old city. The U-shaped space—like half of the Place Louis-le-Grand—opened to the river, and its closed back side was penetrated by two streets whose axes centered on a statue of Louis XV. Baroque principles of sequence and axial connection are the main distinction between the royal squares of the era of Louis XIV and those of Louis XV, and in this respect the Place Royale at Bordeaux was the prelude to the great royal squares of the 1750s.

After the Peace of Aix-la-Chapelle and before the Seven Years' War—between 1748 and 1756—Louis XV was at the peak of his popularity and royal squares were the rage. In addition to those of Rennes and Bordeaux, one was planned at Rouen (designed in 1750 by Le Carpentier but never built); another at Rheims (designed in 1755 by Legendre and begun in 1758); and a third, the most famous, at Nancy (designed by Emmanuel Héré and built between 1752 and 1755).[11] All were conceived as enclosed urban spaces in the traditional sense. Each was to sacrifice some spatial definition due to axial penetration of the streets, but what closure they lost was more than compensated for by the quality of sequence that was attained. And with loosened spatial boundaries, certain buildings could be read more clearly as important objects in the sequence. As urban form, these squares fall somewhere between the closed squares of the seventeenth century and the *places percées* of the nineteenth century; there is a balance between discrete space and discrete buildings. This delicate balance was not long maintained, so by the time of the Place Louis XV, the object would dominate the space.

The changing attitude toward space and urban form at mid-century is reflected in Laugier's critique of the royal squares of Paris:

Our squares all lack that certain air of grandeur which would suit them so well. The Place Royale, the most spacious of all, could be beautiful if the iron grill round the center, resembling a garden enclosure, were broken up, if the squat porticoes which run all the way round and are worth less than the worst cloisters of a monastery were bricked up, if the great pavilions which conceal the two main entrances were demolished, if the four corners were opened up by great streets—with all this done it would look like a square. As it is, it can only be taken for a courtyard the center of which has been turned into a garden. The Places des Victoires, although the smallest, is however the most beautiful because of the many wide streets leading to it. The Place Louis-le-Grand is . . . like an isolated courtyard to which no street leads directly and which is so well enclosed on all sides that, standing in the center, one would be led to believe that there is no way of getting out.

Laugier then offers a formula for perfection:

For a square to be beautiful it should be a communal center from which people can make their way into different quarters and where, coming from different quarters they can get together; for that reason several streets must lead to it like the roads of a forest to a *carrefour*. Porticoes are the right decoration for squares and if joined to these there are buildings of different height and shape, the decoration will be perfect. Symmetry is necessary but also a certain disorder that varies and heightens the spectacle.[12]

Even if the Place Royale were considered somewhat dowdy by mid-eighteenth-century taste, the Place Louis-le-Grand would not have been, and therefore Laugier's preference for the Place des Victoires reveals a more fundamental objection than style. For Laugier, the city—like buildings—should be composed of rational, articulate elements; and although his emphasis on circulation was not new in itself, when coupled with his preference for articulate buildings, it implied a radically new urban system.

In 1748 the city of Paris, like the provincial towns, decided to erect a statue of Louis XV and to place it in a royal square, another in the series of Place Dauphine (Henri IV), Place Royale (Louis XIII), and Places des Victoires and Louis-le-Grand (Louis XIV). The city was to provide the statue, and the king was to determine the placement; to this end, an equestrian statue was commissioned from the sculptor Bouchardon, and a competition was held for the design of the square. The cost of the project and the choice of site were left open to the competitors, and since the competition was not restricted to members of the Academy, some ninety submissions were received. Nineteen of these, including the project ultimately realized by Ange-Jacques Gabriel, are illustrated on the famous composite plan of Paris published in 1765 by Pierre Patte.[13]

According to Lavedan, the king selected the project by Gabriel de l'Estrade (marked by the let-

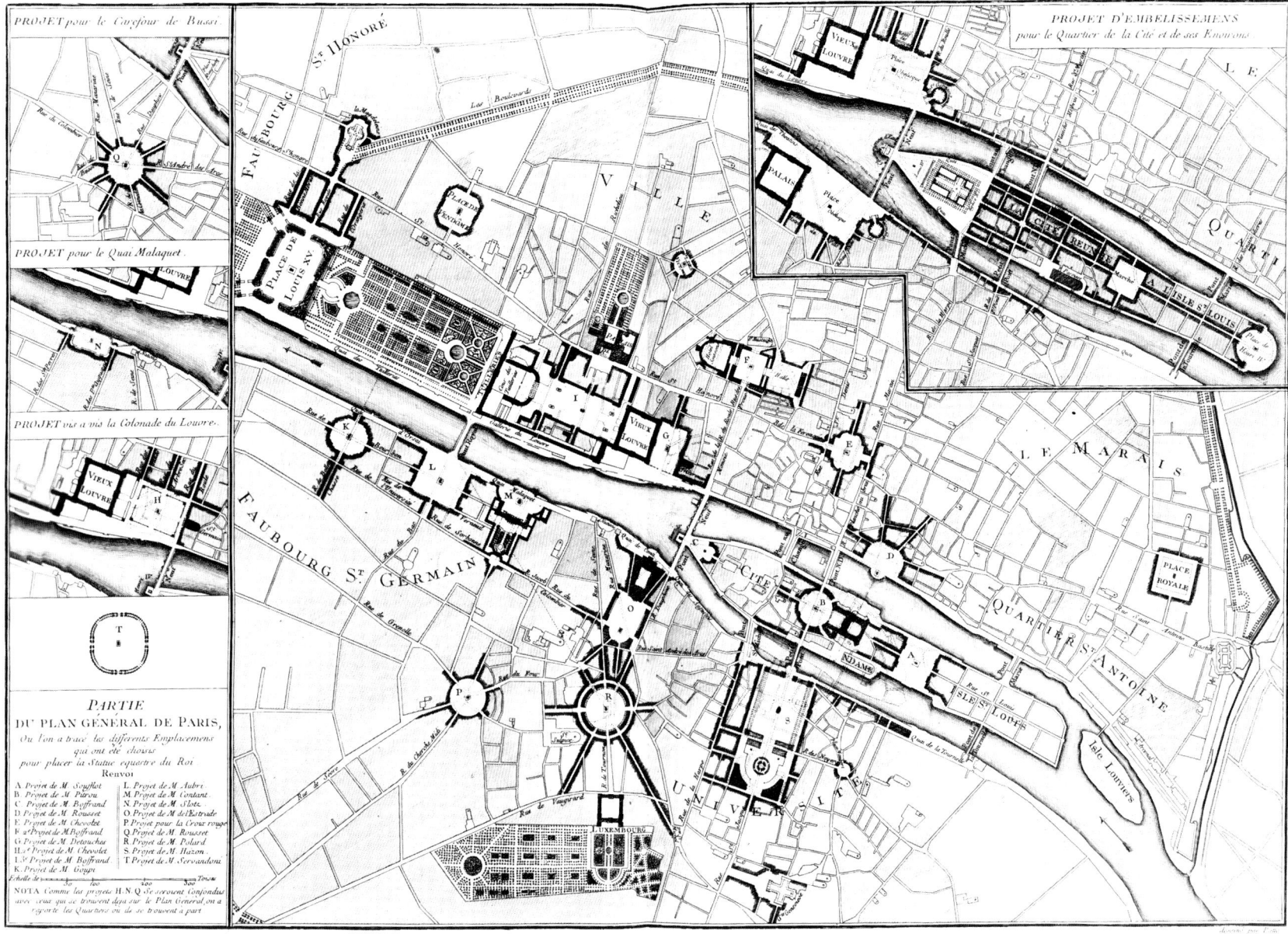

201
Plan of selected competition projects for the Place Louis XV, Pierre Patte, 1767

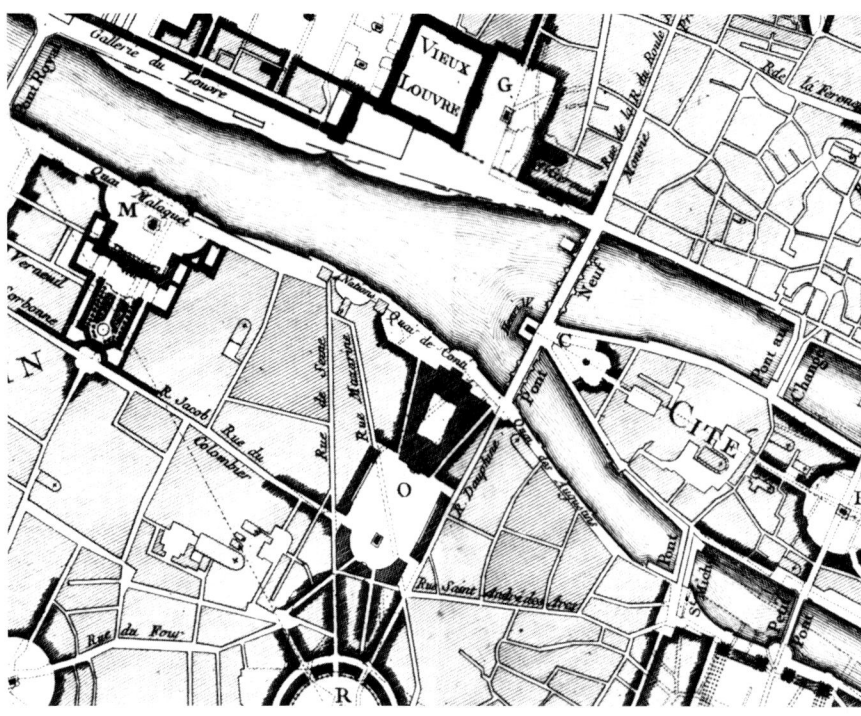

202
Project for the Place Louis XV. From Patte's plan.

203
Site for the Place Louis XV (Place de la Concorde). From the Turgot plan.

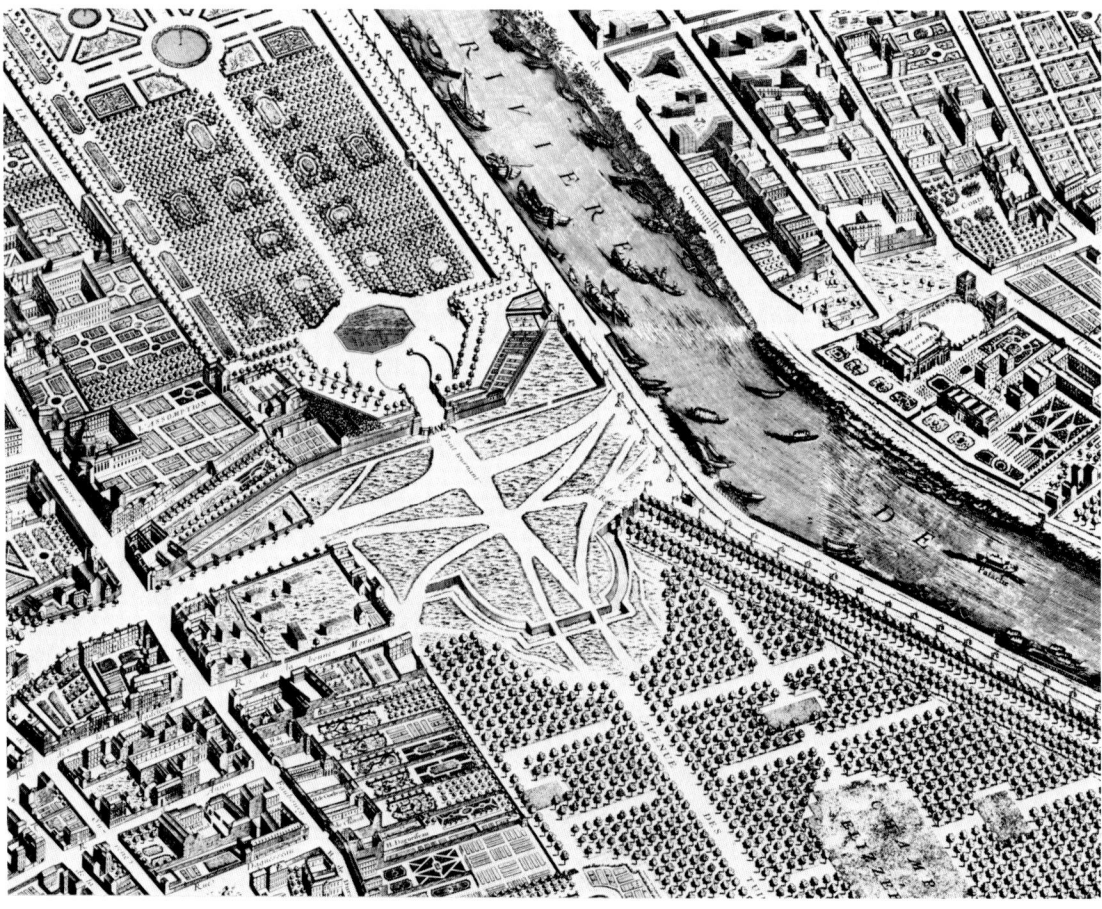

ter "o" on Patte's plan) as the winner.¹⁴ Located on the left bank, on the site of the Hôtel de Conti, l'Estrade's project provided for a new city hall with two fronts, one facing the river and one facing the new Place Royale. Negotiations for acquisition of the site began, but were called off six months later because of the high price asked by the Prince de Conti. Afraid of the enormous expense of acquisition, demolition, and construction, the king renounced his choice and offered as a substitute a site he already owned.¹⁵ This site had long been undeveloped and can be clearly seen on the Turgot plan between the Tuileries and the Champs-Elysées. The city finally accepted the king's offer in 1750, prompting more sharp observations from Laugier:

Statues are the most common ornament of our squares. It is a most reasonable and well-conceived idea to prefer squares to any other location for erecting a monument to the immortal memory of our good kings, but it would be absurd to establish as a principle that every statue must have a square. In our days we have seen thoughtless people make the rash proposal to pull down eight or nine hundred houses to make room for a statue of Louis XV. The king in his usual noble way of thinking opposed so cruel a devastation of his capital and preferred having his statue less well placed to dislodging ten thousand citizens by force. Accordingly the plan was changed, but the idea of a square has not been dropped. It is still thought that the king's statue cannot do without this costly appendage. There is some talk, I am told, of laying out a square on the large plot of land between the Pont Tourant and the Champs-Elysées. I do not doubt that with a great deal of expense one could succeed in creating something beautiful, but it will always be true to say that it is a square in the middle of fields and this thought is enough to hold this project up to ridicule.¹⁶

Despite Laugier's admonitions, the Place Louis XV was constructed on the very site he described.

In 1753 a second competition for the design of the new *place* was announced, but this time the competition was limited to members of the Academy, and only nineteen projects were submitted. None of those were judged acceptable by Marigny, the new Directeur des Bâtiments, and in his report to the king he pointed out the fundamental incompatibility between a *place*, an enclosed public square, and that particular site. Three projects had merit, however—those of Boffrand, Gabriel, and Contant d'Ivry—so the king gave Gabriel, the Premier Architecte du Roi, the commission with instructions to incorporate the best ideas from each of the three schemes into one design that would define the *place* without destroying the view of the Tuileries, the Champs-Elysées, and the Palais Bourbon across the Seine.

No drawings of the original schemes survive, but Marigny summarized them in his report. Gabriel's entry in the competition provided for buildings on both the north and the south sides of the square framing a central axis toward the Palais Bourbon. Although it defined the square better than the others, it ruined the views. Boffrand's project was the inverse and the king's favorite: open on three sides with three buildings and two streets on the north side, it was thought to be too vast and ill defined. Contant's project reduced the size of the *place*, however, by surrounding the central area with a balustrade and deep ditch.

Gabriel's first attempt to combine the best features of each project was approved in 1753, though it appears to be a combination of only Boffrand's and Contant's schemes. His final scheme, approved in 1755, combines features of all three original schemes by reviving his own proposal for one central axis, that of the rue Royale. This last project was more than a single square: it was a scenographic ensemble of three elements—a square, a monumental street, and a church, the Madeleine. In the opposite direction the axis formed by these elements was terminated by the Palais Bourbon. Two important events in the years between the two projects may have influenced the final design: one was the death of Boffrand in 1754, which left Gabriel free to return to one central axis; the other was the publication in 1753 of the elegant sequence of public spaces at Nancy.

Construction of Gabriel's square was a long process. The equestrian statue was erected in 1763, but by Louis XV's death in 1774, only the facades of the twin palaces on the north side had been built. Construction of the rue Royale came later still, and the bridge—the last built by the old monarchy—was begun in 1787 and completed using stone from the Bastille. In 1806 Poyet added a classical portico to the Palais Bourbon's river facade, adjusting its angle to terminate the Madeleine-Concorde axis. The Madeleine itself was finally completed under Louis-Philippe in the nineteenth century.

Of all the events in the long development of this sector, however, the addition of the bridge (now the Pont de la Concorde) on the Madeleine-Bourbon axis had the greatest effect on the future character of the square. Until then the Place Louis XV was admittedly not a proper urban square, but it *was* an elegant garden set-piece, a transition between the Tuileries to the east and the Champs-Elysées and the Cours de la Reine to the west. After the addition of the bridge, the north-south axis was no longer just a visual axis

132 *Private Icons: The Neoclassical Hôtel*

204
Nancy, Place Royale, plan, Emmanuel Héré, 1752–55

205
Place Louis XV, final plan, Ange-Jacques Gabriel, begun 1753

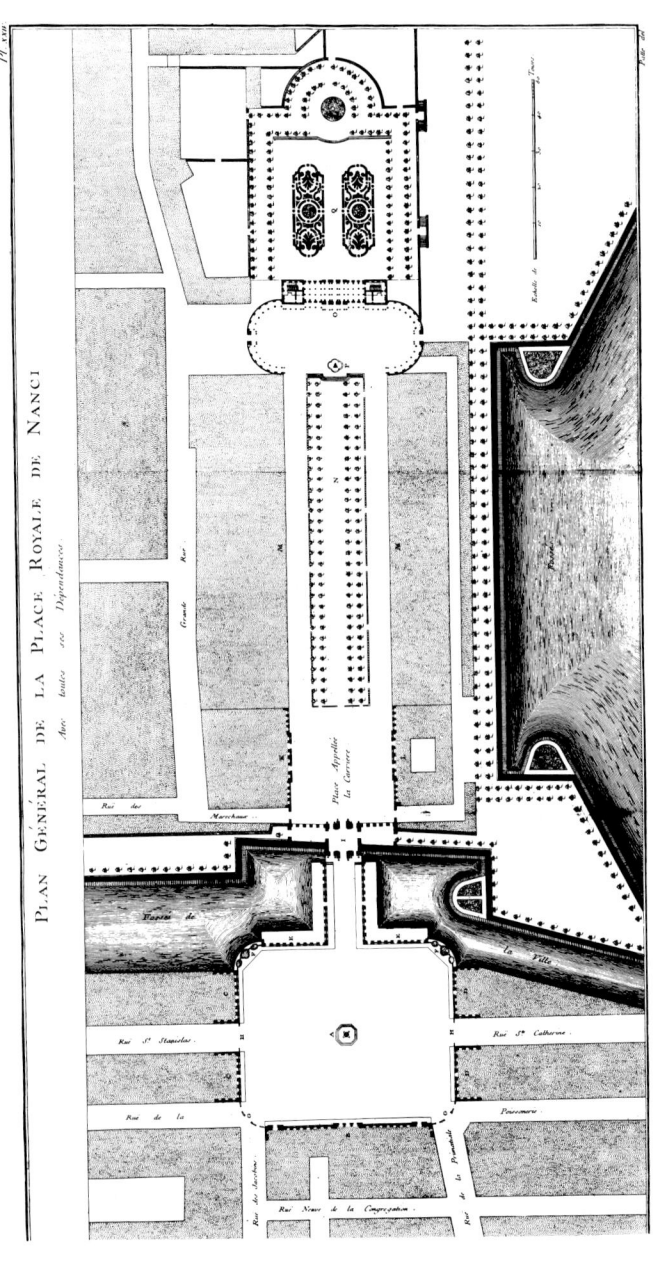
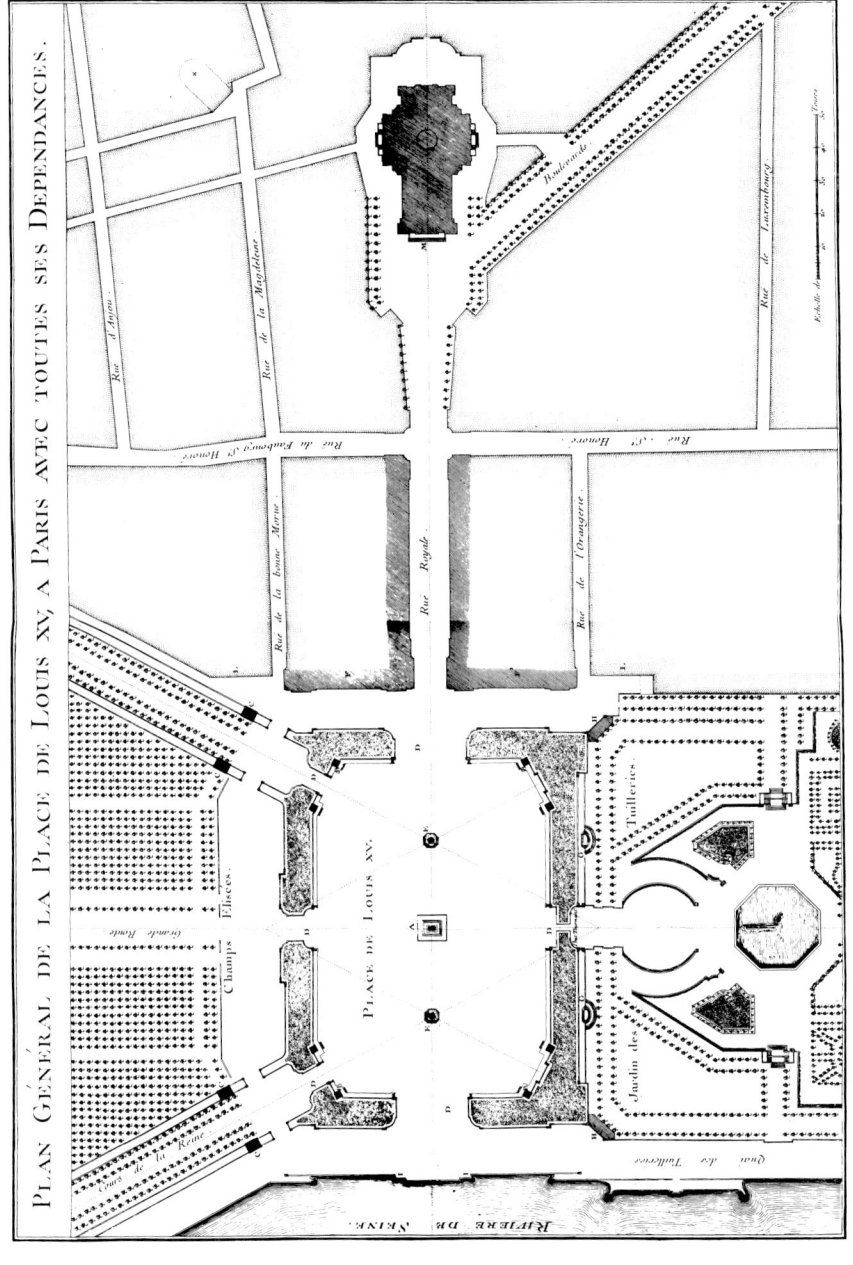

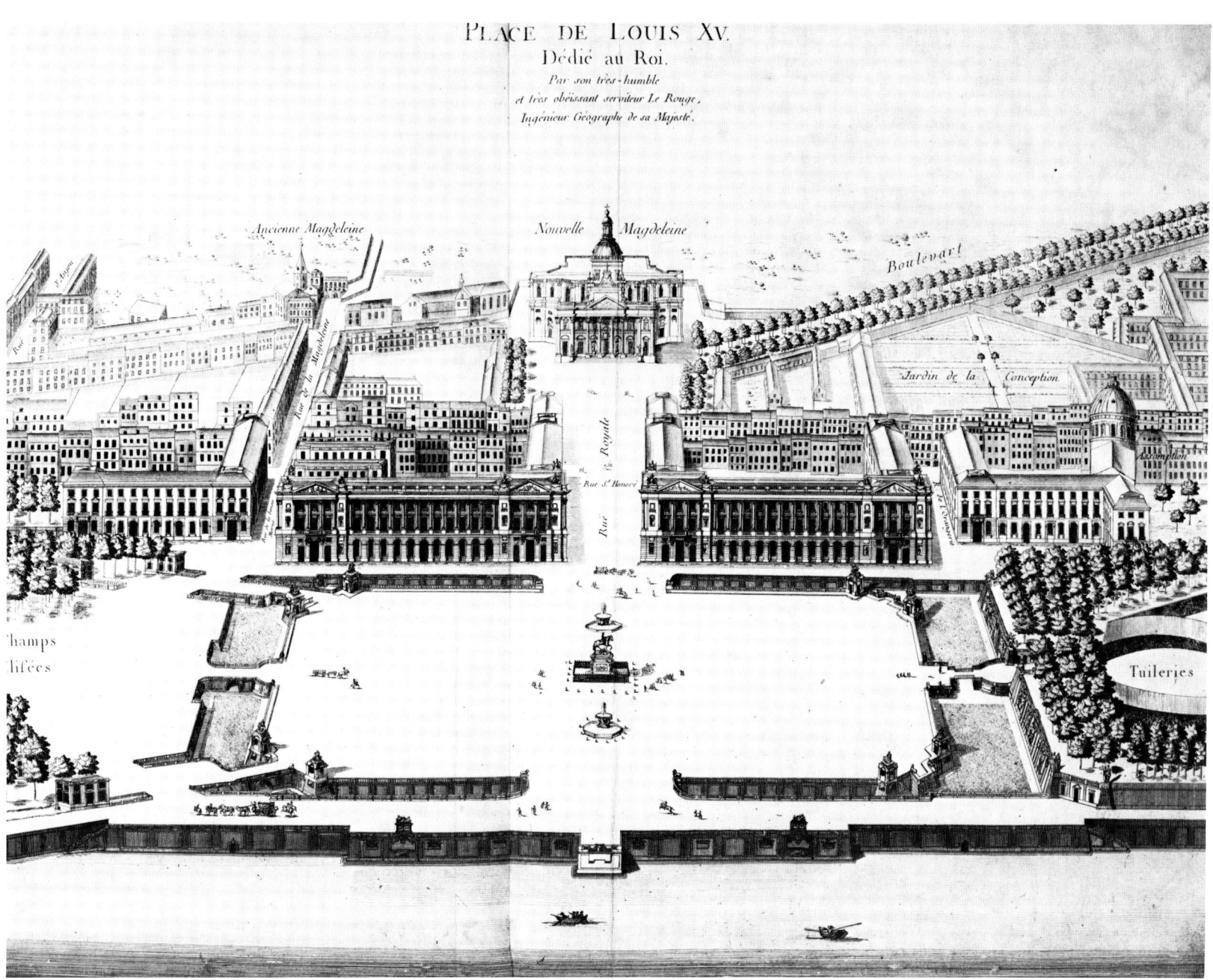

206
Place Louis XV. Engraving by G. L. Le Rouge.

134 Private Icons: The Neoclassical Hôtel

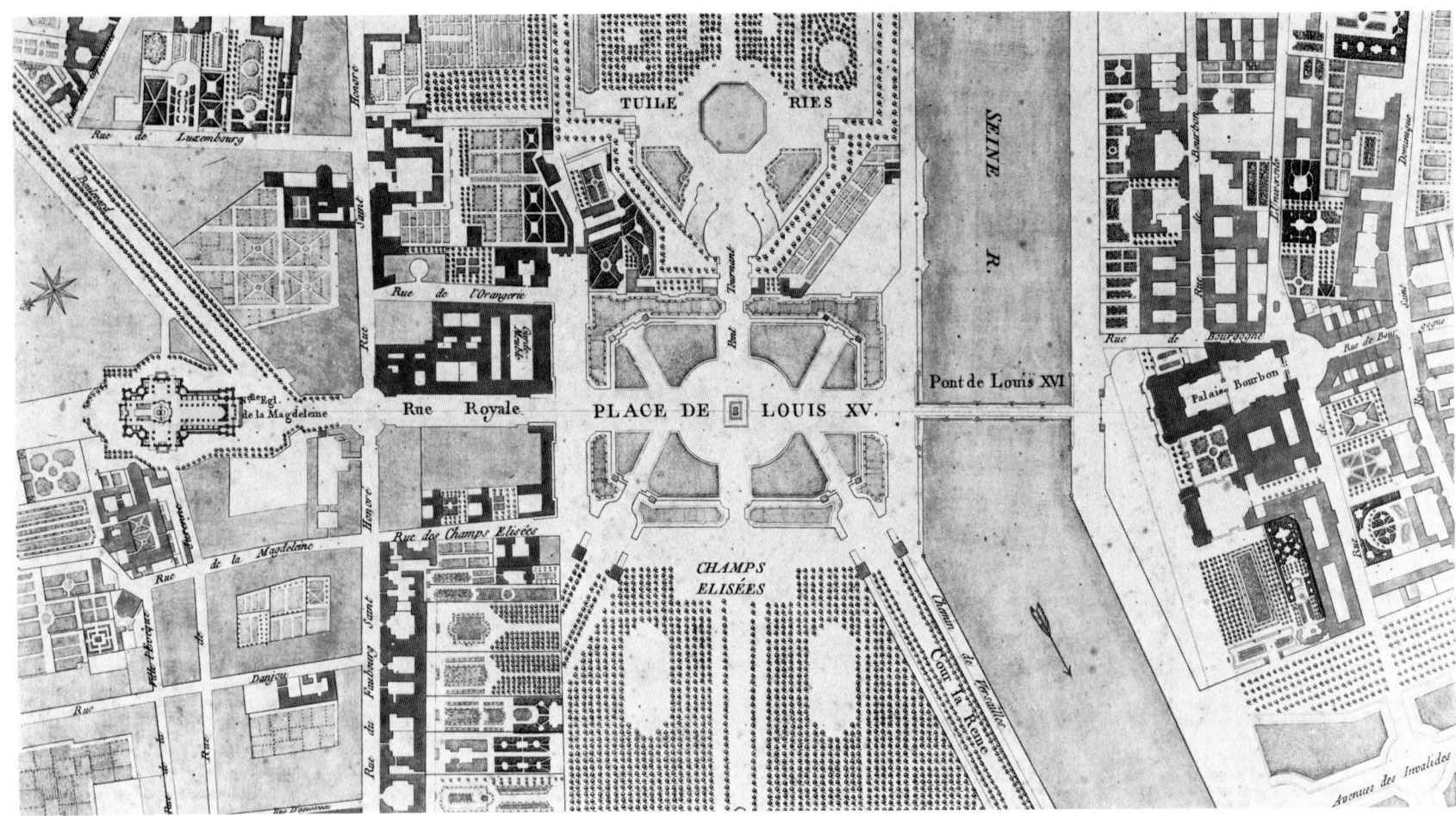

207
Place Louis XV, context
plan showing proposed
new bridge, before 1795.
Engraving by Perrier after
Le Sage.

135　The Place Louis XV

208
Place Louis XV. Engraving by Née after L.-N. de Lespinasse.

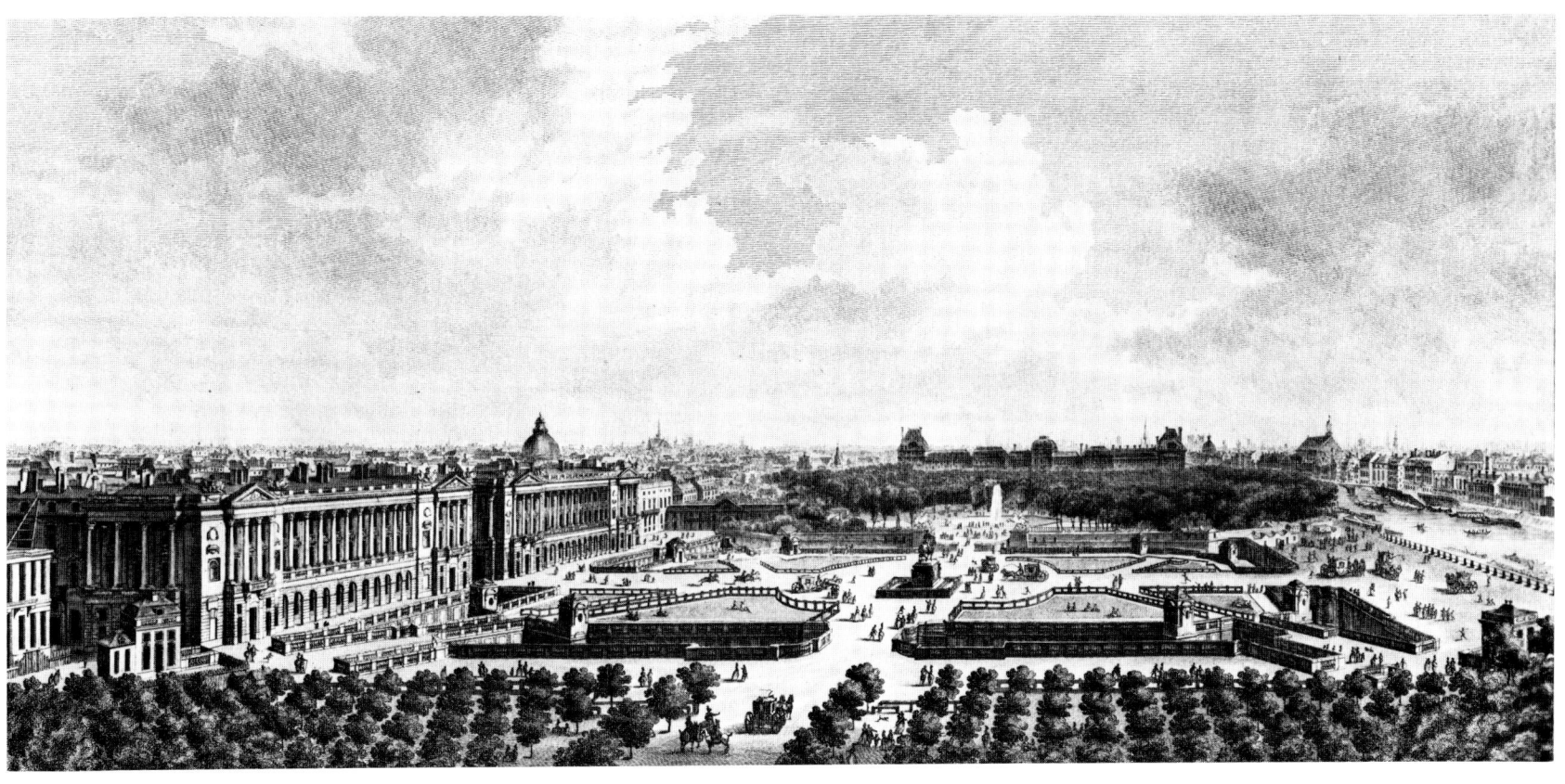

but became an axis of circulation as well. The fate of the *place* as a traffic circle was assured. The filling of the ditches, the *fossés*, by the architect Hittorf was an inevitable consequence.

The Place Louis XV cannot be explained as simply a product of practical considerations, for the city eventually bought the site of the Hôtel de Conti after all (for the Hôtel des Monnaies) and could have erected an enclosed urban square on that particular site. Although an enclosed public space would not have expressed fully the new sensibilities, the Place Louis XV was not a conscious, willful expression of the new ideal either—no one from Laugier to Patte seemed happy with its design. On the other hand, it did reflect the era's changed spatial conception, however inadvertently. Thus the Place Louis XV marks, symbolically at least, the demise of space in western urbanism. What began in France at Vitry-le-François, ended here. There were attempts during the nineteenth century to mechanize and rationalize the classical models of squares and especially streets, and the development of squares continued in Spain, England, and America. But these experiments notwithstanding, the inversion of the urban system that had begun in the 1750s would achieve its ultimate fulfillment in the twentieth century—and the *ville radieuse*.

The Neoclassical Hôtel

Just as the Place Royale initiated the cycle of Baroque *hôtels* that were built in the eastern, Marais, section of Paris and the Place Louis-le-Grand initiated the cycle of Rococo *hôtels* built in the western *faubourgs* of St.-Honoré and St.-Germain, the Place Louis XV was the catalyst for the cycle of Neoclassical *hôtels* built north of the *grands boulevards* on previously undeveloped land. The *boulevards* had long marked the limits of the city; building was forbidden beyond them. When their landscaping matured in the 1750s, the *boulevards* became fashionable for the *promenade à la mode*; and when private building resumed at the end of the Seven Years' War (1763), the areas north of the *boulevards* began to develop rapidly. The model for the Neoclassical *hôtels* in this area, and the most influential building of the period, was Gabriel's Petit Trianon, built at Versailles between 1762 and 1768 for Madame de Pompadour.

The Petit Trianon was indeed a pivotal building, for it completed the tendency of the Rococo *hôtels* toward freestanding pavilions. The Baroque *hôtel* type, organized asymmetrically around a platonic void, was now turned inside-out so that a regularized, freestanding, platonic solid concealed an asymmetrical plan. Each facade of the Petit Trianon is slightly different, but all are symmetrical and three have a central emphasis reminiscent of Palladian villas. The plan, however, is the antithesis of Palladio: only on the west side do the rooms match the facade, with the dining room centered behind the implied portico; and the major central room in a Palladian plan is here replaced by a central solid containing the bathroom and other services. Thus the French talent for creating, and then exploiting, a rift between public image and private accommodation, between inside and outside, endured even when the spatial system was inverted.

To appreciate the extent of this inversion, one need only compare the Petit Trianon with its neighbor, the Grand Trianon, built eighty years earlier. If the mass of the Petit Trianon is assertive, equally so are the voids described by the Grand Trianon; and if the space surrounding the Petit Trianon renders the solid visible, then, conversely, it is the solid of the Grand Trianon that renders the space visible. It is as if the forecourt of the Grand Trianon had been inverted to form its successor.

All that remained to make the Petit Trianon a consistent manifesto of the new sensibilities was for Richard Mique to destroy the geometric gardens of Le Nôtre and replace them in 1778 with a naturalistic English garden furnished with pavilions and temples in a variety of styles. The only remnant of Le Nôtre's formal landscape is on the west side, where a terraced parterre serves as foreground for a perspective of lawns and fountains extending toward the Grand Trianon and terminated by the Concert Pavilion. To the north and east, however, is Mique's romantic park, not wild and untamed, but arranged according to "new but ill-defined principles" so that a man of sensibilities might "find matter for mild ecstasies and lachrymose effusions."[17]

In the Petit Trianon, idea was more important than reality. Even domestic services were designed to support the ideal—to assist in the contemplation of "noble Greeks" and "noble savages." The dining room, for example, was equipped with a mechanical device intended to

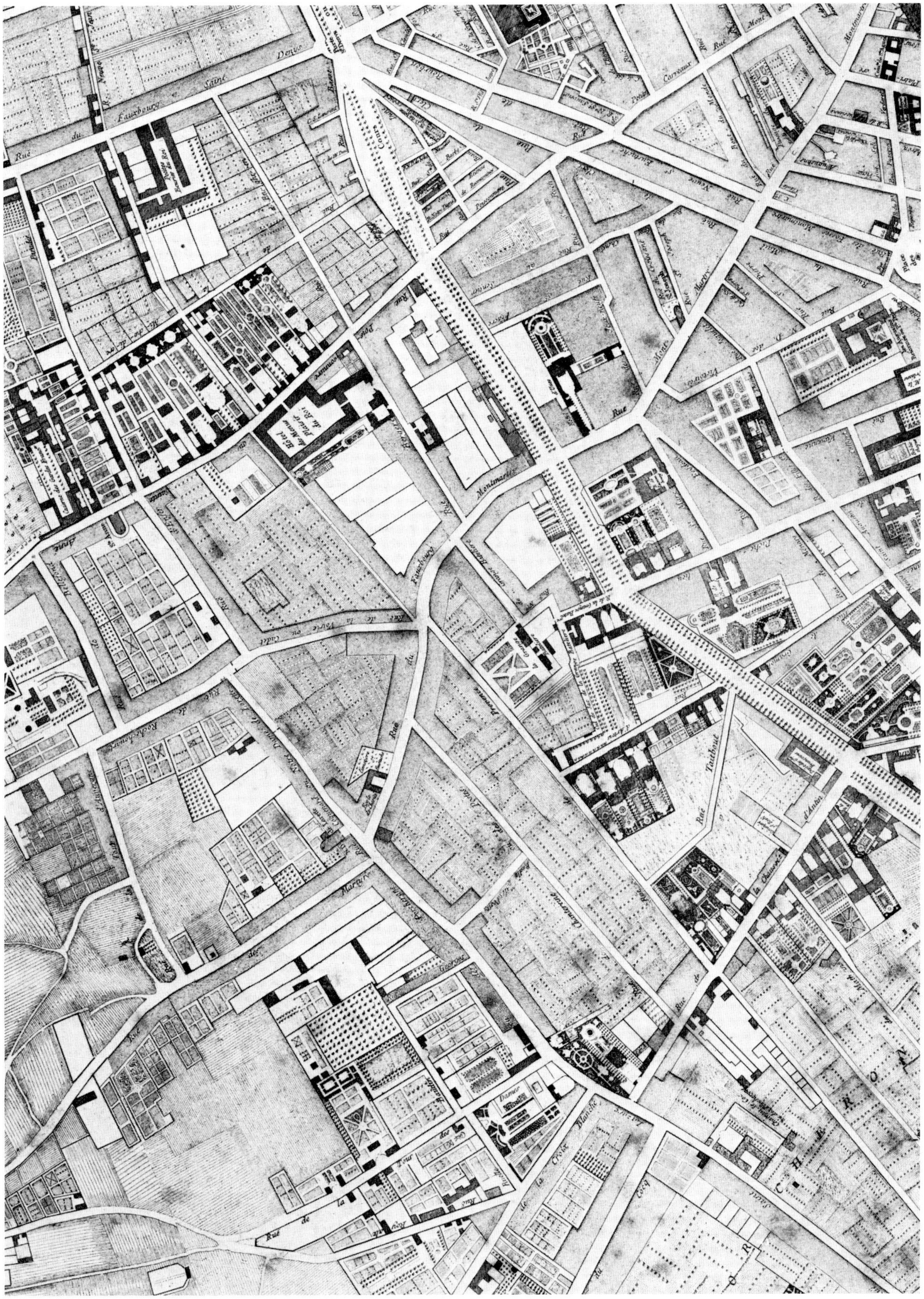

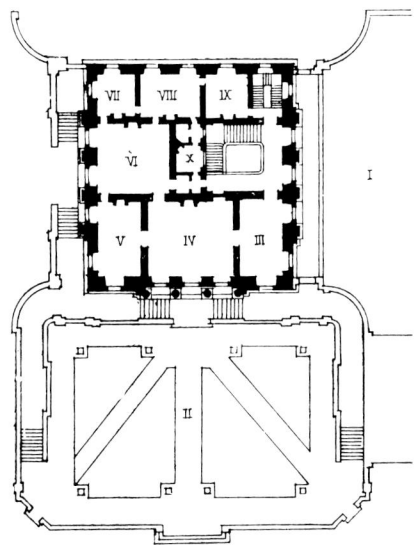

209
Detail from the Jaillot plan showing the undeveloped area beyond the *boulevards*

210
Versailles, Petit Trianon, ground floor, plan, Ange-Jacques Gabriel, begun 1762.

I. entry court
II. parterre toward the Pavillon français
III. *antichambre*
IV. large dining room
V. small dining room
VI. *salon de compagnie*
VII. boudoir (*petit cabinet de Louis XV*)
VIII. chambre à coucher (*cabinet de Louis XV*)
IX. *antichambre*
X. service

211
Versailles, Petit Trianon, south facade

212
Versailles, Grand Trianon, aerial view, Jules Hardouin Mansart, begun 1685

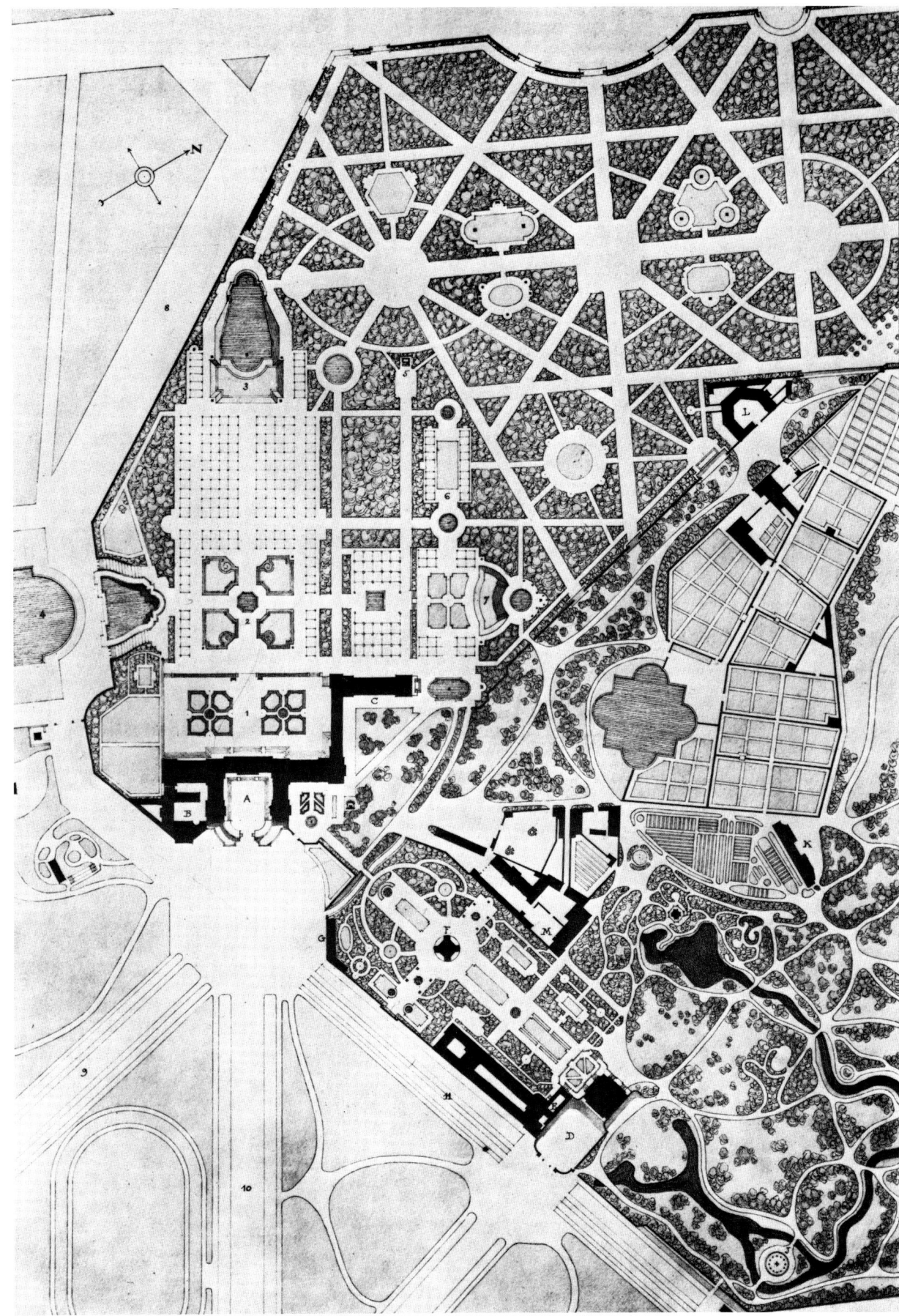

213
Versailles, site plan of Grand Trianon and Petit Trianon

keep the reality of servants out of sight in the basement: the dining table had a center section that would descend into the basement after each course, to be reset and raised again. In the interim, the position was filled by a metal rose.

The Petit Trianon is a sophisticated instrument of contemplation: a not-so-primitive version of Laugier's hut. It is also the restrained forerunner of two related, but very different, attitudes that prevailed in the late eighteenth century. One of these grew out of the triumph of the *philosophes*. Moralizing in tone, rational in approach, and Spartan in its abstract simplicity, this unyielding formal and social idealism was better suited to monumental public buildings—buildings that conveyed a more important "message"—than to private houses. Not surprisingly, it generated more projects than buildings. This attitude is best represented by the late (abstract) work of Ledoux and Boullée. The other attitude was no less self-conscious, but it was much less interested in timeless truths; the circumstantial was as important as the ideal. For the *antiquaires*, history and new knowledge of other cultures provided a multitude of ideas or images that could easily be assimilated by traditional French planning. This attitude may be found in the built work of Ledoux and in the work of Lequeu.

The two strands yielded, on the one hand, the revolutionary but evocative geometry of Ledoux and Boullée, and, on the other, the romantic ruins of the dilettantes. Presumably both the *philosophes* and the *antiquaires* found promise in the reasoned romanticism of Gabriel's little building, because though the lyrical idea of juxtaposing reason and nature could not tolerate too much dilution by circumstantial reality, neither could circumstantial reality be totally excluded. The

214
Design for the Tomb of Newton, Etienne-Louis Boullée, 1734

215
"Column" house and garden for Racine de Monville, Désert de Retz, François Barbier, 1774–84. Engraving.

ideal and the real had to coexist, and the opposing tendencies of abstraction and circumstance remained to be debated.

Public buildings might be ideal statements of pure principle, but the Parisian upper class was not about to sacrifice newly acquired comfort for idea, or reality for abstraction. Thus the increased emphasis on both the ideal and the empirical in the late eighteenth century is most clearly reflected in the Neoclassical *hôtel*, where both "idea" and "program" had to be accommodated. In general, the exteriors of these *hôtels* were varied, but restrained; interior planning became more particularized. As buildings became smaller and smaller, the planning became even more ingenious—the symmetry of the exterior contrasted with an interior freedom that would have been inconceivable to Palladio. Though the freestanding *hôtel* was not the only type built during this period, it was the dominant one. For the remainder of the century, the ideal continued to be the pavilion in the garden.

Claude-Nicolas Ledoux, perhaps more than any other late-eighteenth-century French architect, reflected and expressed the conflicting tendencies of abstraction and reality. He was the most fashionable architect of his day, and, unlike Boullée, he built prolifically. Ironically, however, it is the unbuilt theoretical projects done at the end of his career and first championed in our time by Emil Kaufmann[18] that are almost entirely responsible for his recent popularity. These last projects, with their emphasis on abstraction and pure geometries, were almost always freestanding, symmetrical buildings with regular, gridded plans. The plans were like decentralized, or polycentric, variations on Palladian themes. That is, compositionally they embodied the antithesis of the Baroque principles of hierarchy and dependency. But if their composition spoke of a new egalitarianism, their plasticity and evocative power deflected attention from their own ultimately authoritarian resistance to empirical reality Ledoux's built work capitalized on empirical reality, however; it was the opposite of his theoretical projects and was the embodiment of the typical Neoclassical *hôtel*.[19] The contrast can be seen by examining one of his most extravagant built works.

The Hôtel Thélusson, built between 1778 and 1783 for the slightly strange widow of a wealthy Swiss banker,[20] was one of the most famous of its day, probably as much because of the uniqueness of Ledoux's conception as of its grandeur. It occupied a large site in northern Paris and consisted of three buildings closely set in an informal garden: the dense central block of Madame Thélusson's own house, flanked by two smaller pavilions for her sons. The plan of the main floor of the houses has an abstract quality in the blocks and their composition that is very close to Ledoux's late theoretical works and to his nearby houses for M. Hosten of 1792. The garden plan and the section reveal a lyrical blending of architecture and landscape, however, provoking an image of classical fragments in a romantic landscape—an appearance and a meaning completely different from the abstract purity of his theoretical blocks. Here also is the inspiration of Piranesi: the entry arch, contrived to appear as a ruin, has the proportions of a half-buried triumphal arch.

Some of the romantic quality may have been inspired by the client's desire for a "retreat" rather than a *hôtel*, but other aspects can only be the product of Ledoux's inventive genius. For example, the whole building has, in effect, been turned around on the site so that what would normally have been the garden front—the face with the oval protrusion—faces the main entry, and what would normally have been the forecourt—the semicircular carriage court—terminates the site. Such a cavalier affront to the rules of *convenance* did not go unnoticed at the time, but the house was such an attraction in Paris that tickets were required for admission to see it.[21] The unlikely *parti* was ingeniously resolved by bringing two carriage ways from the entry arch, around a sunken garden, and through the main building to the carriage court behind. From the vestibule under the salon, a grand stair rose to the main floor overlooking the semicircular court, and from there led to a central sequence of three figural rooms: a square, an octagon, and finally an oval, which projected past the surface of the facade and overlooked the garden, the grotto, and the entry arch. The oval protrusion of the salon was connected to the grotto by a mound of natural rock so that from the outside, the exposed oval appeared as an antique temple in ruins. As indulgent and sentimental as the Hôtel de Thélusson seems, it was no more so than Ledoux's "abstract" work; and as inventive as it was, it may still be less satisfying than his smaller, more restrained *hôtels*.

It is not simply that Ledoux's personality had two sides, nor that he reflected opposing French tendencies, but that his work is in many ways a microcosm of French domestic architecture from about 1550 to 1800. His *hôtels*, for example, display a progression that parallels the overall development of the French *hôtels* to such a degree that it seems almost contrived. It is as if Ledoux gradually worked his way through the history

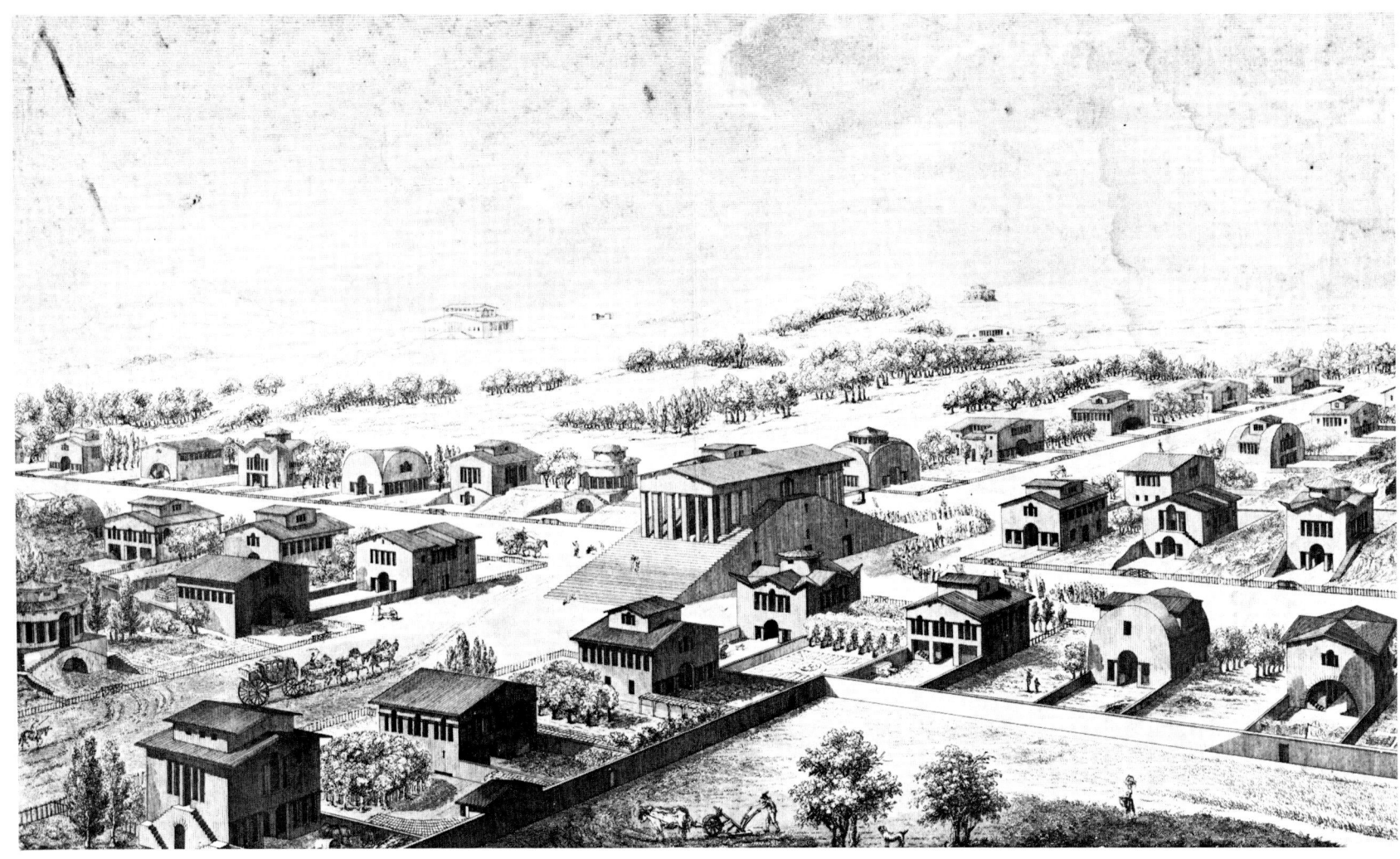

216
Village of Maupertuis,
Claude-Nicolas Ledoux.
Engraving by Ledoux.

143   The Neoclassical Hôtel

217
House of the Agricultural Guards, Claude-Nicolas Ledoux. Engraving by Ledoux.

218
Hunting lodge, Claude-Nicolas Ledoux. Engraving by Ledoux.

144   Private Icons: The Neoclassical Hôtel

219
Entry to a gymnasium,
Giovanni Battista
Piranesi

220
Hôtel de Thélusson,
Claude-Nicolas Ledoux,
1778–83. Engraving by
Ledoux.

221
Antique temple,
Giovanni Battista
Piranesi

222
Hôtel de Thélusson,
Claude-Nicolas Ledoux.
Engraving by Ledoux.

146 Private Icons: The Neoclassical Hôtel

223
Hôtel de Thélusson,
ground floor plan

224
Hôtel de Thélusson,
upper floor plan

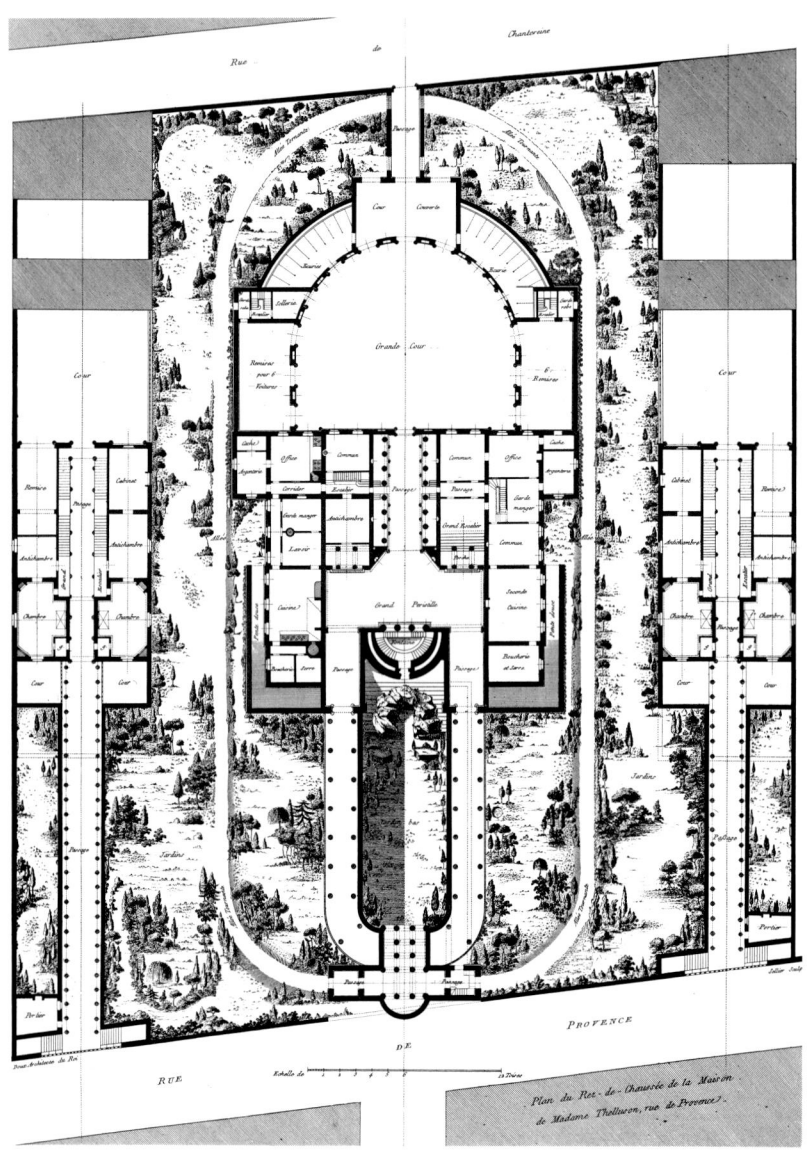
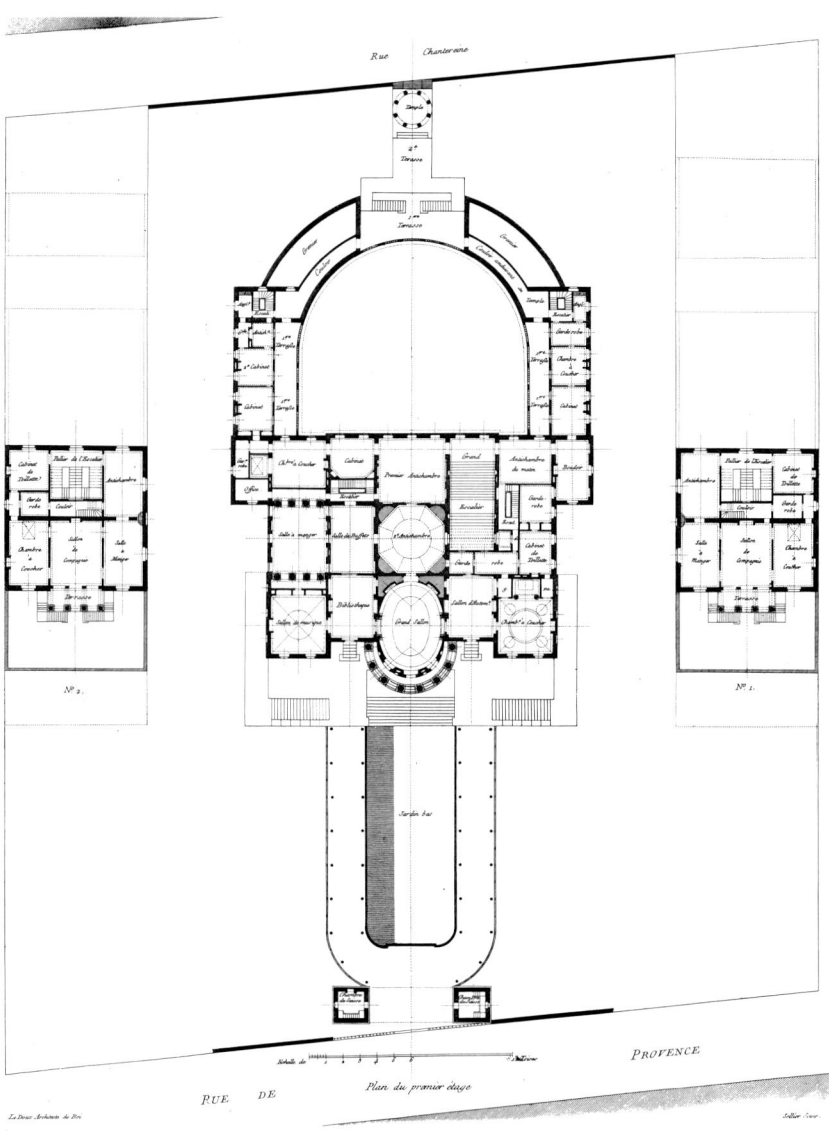

The Neoclassical Hôtel

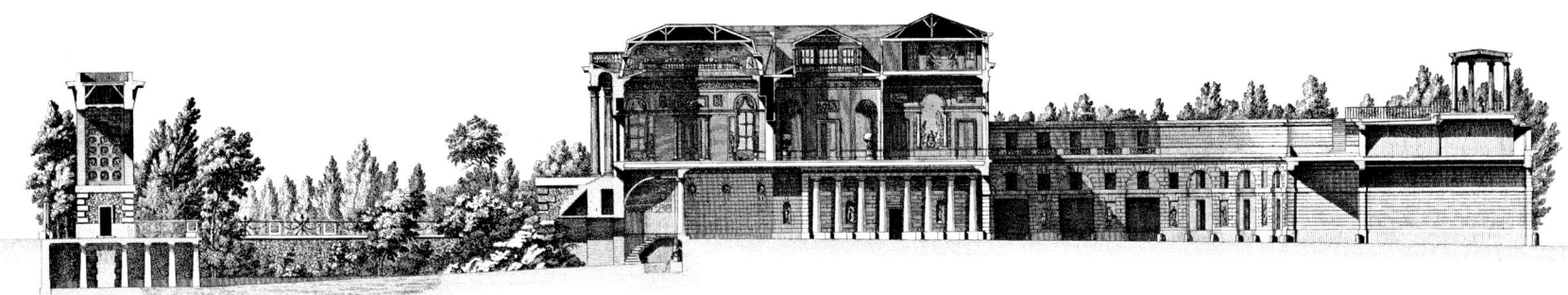

225
Hôtel de Thélusson,
section

226
Hôtel de Thélusson,
garden. Engraving.

148 Private Icons: The Neoclassical Hôtel

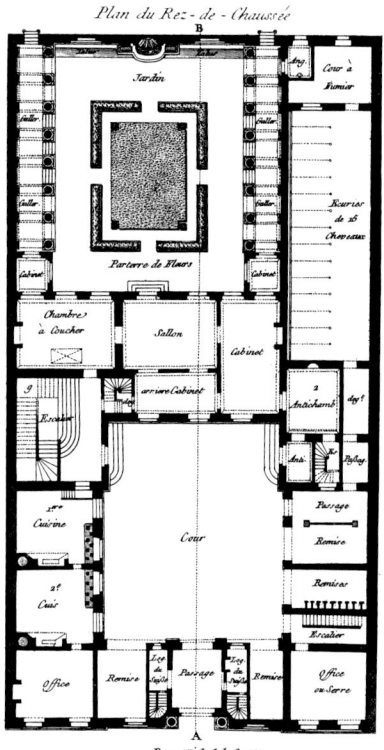

of the *hôtel*. No doubt this was because of the conservative influence of his teacher, Jacques-François Blondel, as well as the fact that two of his earliest *hôtels* were transformations of existing buildings.[22]

Among Ledoux's earliest projects, the Hôtel d'Hallwyl (c. 1764–66) in eastern Paris is the traditional urban *hôtel* type with forecourt, *corps-de-logis*, and private garden behind. The plans might almost have come straight from Le Muet; only the crisp classical detailing of the elevations, the garden colonnade, and the extraordinary *trompe l'oeil* designed for the garden place the building in the eighteenth century.

The unbuilt project for the Hôtel d'Evry (late 1780s?) was to be, like the Hôtel d'Hallwyl, an urban party-wall building organized around an open court, on a small, irregular site between the Palais Royal and the Place Louis-le-Grand in the re-entrant juncture of two streets. Here the model is that of Le Pautre's Hôtel de Beauvais; the building has a court but no garden, and the interior organization is a function of the street rather than the property boundary. The court is centered on the street, its configuration masking the odd angles of the site, while the primary, secondary, and tertiary spaces of the house are each uniquely shaped and arranged in sequence around the court. All of the residual areas are used for rooms or *dégagements*, so very little adjustment of wall thickness is required at the edges of the site. This project is rarely published, though it does appear in Ledoux's own book. Although it is the infill Baroque *hôtel* type, it is rendered as a Neoclassical pavilion in a natural landscape.

The Hôtel d'Uzès (1764–69) for the Duc d'Uzès, a military officer and patron, was a transformation of a *hôtel* on the northern edge of the

227
Hôtel d'Hallwyl, elevation and section, Claude-Nicolas Ledoux, c. 1764–66. The upper colonnade was to be painted on the wall of the adjacent building (see figure 230).

228
Hôtel d'Hallwyl, ground floor plan

149   The Neoclassical Hôtel

229
Hôtel d'Hallwyl, court

230
Hôtel d'Hallwyl, section

231
Hôtel d'Evry, ground floor plan, Claude-Nicolas Ledoux, 1772–80(?)

232
Hôtel d'Evry, upper floor plan

233
Hôtel d'Evry, facade

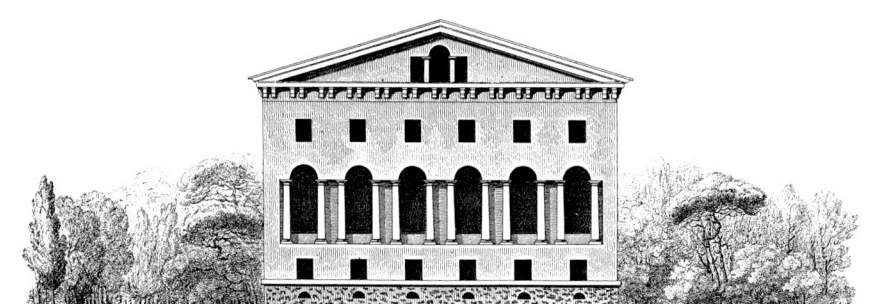

151 The Neoclassical Hôtel

234
Hôtel d'Uzès, entrance gate, Claude-Nicolas Ledoux, 1764–69. Engraving by Ledoux.

235
Hôtel d'Uzès, court

236
Hôtel d'Uzès, plan

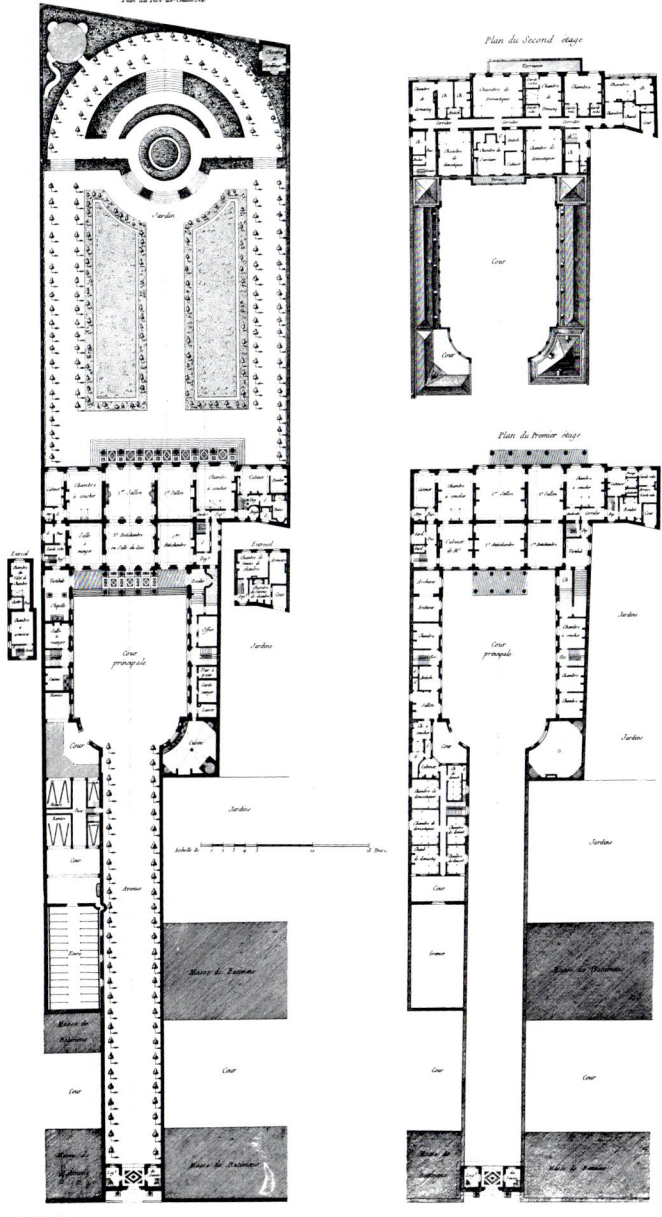

152 Private Icons: The Neoclassical Hôtel

city. Like the Rococo *hôtels* of western Paris, it had a forecourt, double-zone *corps-de-logis,* and garden. The site was asymmetrical, and, typically, the facades responded to the central axes of court and garden, but with no internal adjustment between them. In Rococo fashion, the service wings were lower than the main block so that especially when it was seen from the long approach avenue, the building had the effect of a country building, a *château.*[23] A pair of freestanding triumphal columns with military decoration flanked the entry gate, and this ensemble, combined with the columnar frontispiece at the end of the entry drive, made a very powerful approach to a private house—one which violated Blondel's sense of *convenance.* The military theme was continued with greater delicacy on the interior of the house and was, in contrast, much admired by Blondel.[24]

The increased public assertion of private buildings, and the tendency for decoration and detail to reflect the character of the owner, were characteristic of late-eighteenth-century *hôtels.* Architects found fresh inspiration in the personalities of their clients, which led to great diversity in the simple format of the Neoclassical *hôtel.* It also added a new dimension to *l'art de la distribution,* as may be seen in the Hôtel de Montmorency.

The Hôtel de Montmorency (1769–70) was the first of Ledoux's *hôtels* to be designed as a compact Neoclassical plan, although technically it was a party-wall building with only three exposed sides. It was also the first of Ledoux's "nine square" plans. What is important, however, other than the flamboyant sophistication of the plan, is that the fundamental concept of the building, *la distribution,* is very much a function of the na-

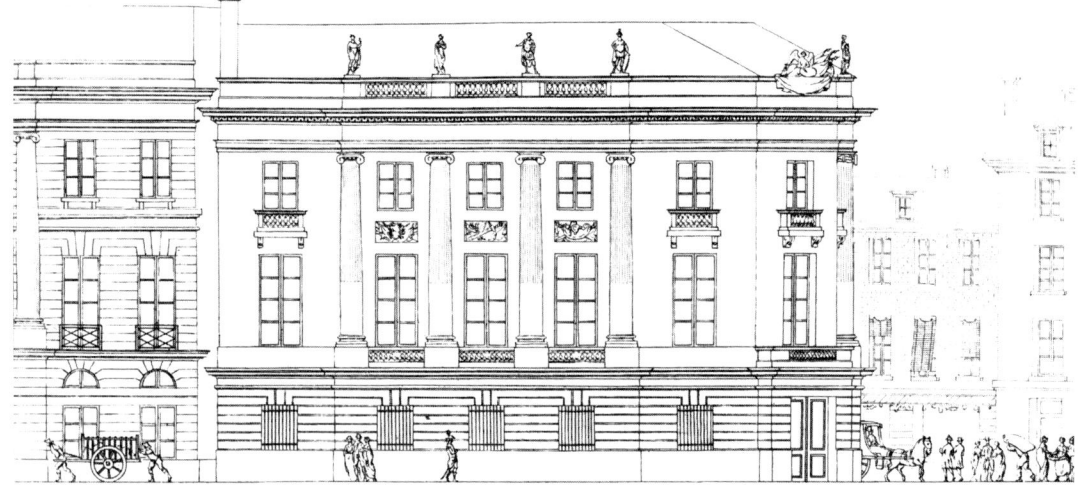

237
Hôtel de Montmorency, section and elevation, Claude-Nicolas Ledoux, 1769–70

153 The Neoclassical Hôtel

238
Hôtel de Montmorency, plans, section, and elevations

ture of the client. The patrons, husband and wife, were each independent members of the house of Montmorency.[25] Thus the diagonal public sequence divides the house into two equal halves: the princess's bedroom is located on the main floor behind the columnar frontispiece facing the boulevard, and the prince's bedroom is in a similar location facing the side street so as to give equal expression and equal facilities to each. The public entrance to the *appartements* of the prince and princess were from the corner *salon*, but each also had a private access to the *dégagements* of their respective suites via small stairs ingeniously hidden in the residual areas of the plan.

In 1770–71 Ledoux built an elegant, freestanding pavilion for Madame du Barry in the park of the Château of Louveciennes; but his masterpiece of the period, and the only building to rival the planning of the Hôtel de Montmorency and the evocative quality of the later Hôtel de Thélusson was the Hôtel Guimard (1770–72), also known as the Temple of Terpsichore.

Mlle Guimard was the first dancer of the opera and was apparently equally well known as a lover; the site for her house was provided by one gentleman friend, the house itself by another, and her own financial support by still another.[26] Her house was located near the Hôtel de Montmorency in the rue de la Chaussée d'Antin; and though it was sandwiched between two other *hôtels* on a narrow site, the main block enjoyed space all around it, more like a villa than an urban *hôtel*. The street was screened from the forecourt by a block containing a theater above the service rooms and entry. A small garden, equal in depth to the house, was provided to the rear.

The facade of the main block had a high central portion—like a triumphal arch—out of which

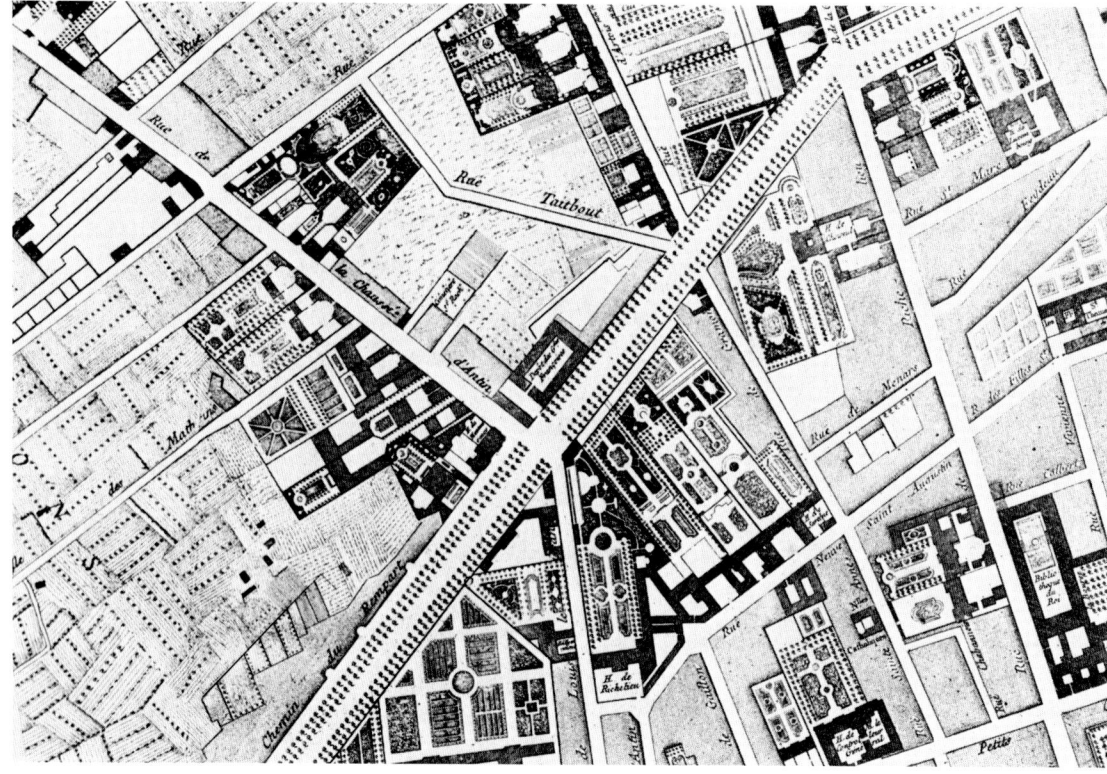

239
Chausée d'Antin. Detail from the Jaillot plan.

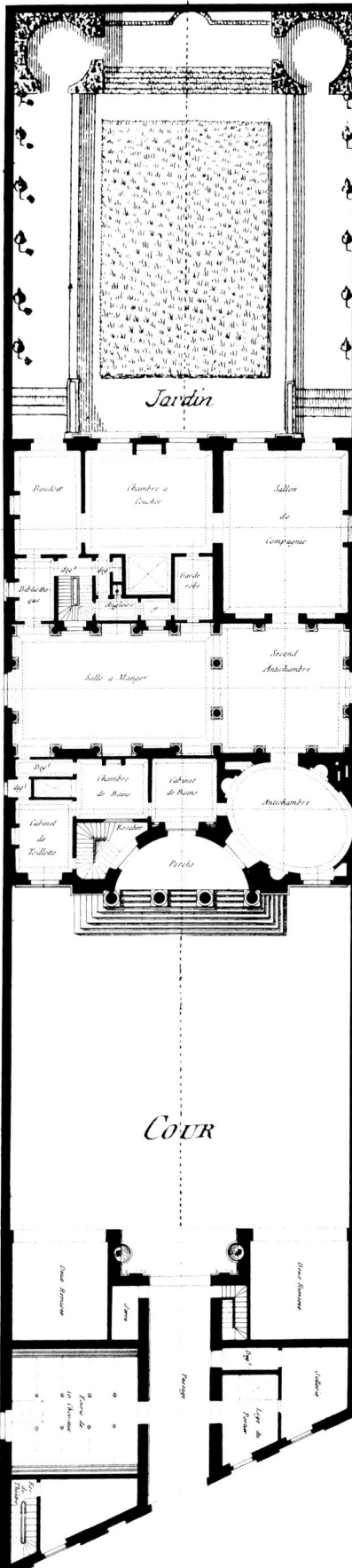
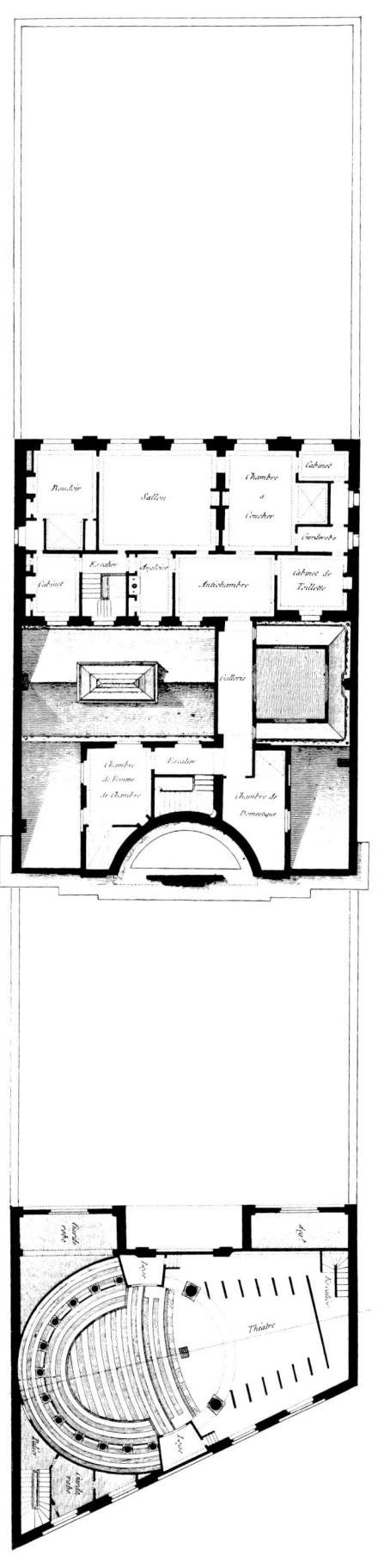

240
Hôtel Guimard, ground floor plan, Claude-Nicolas Ledoux, 1770–72

241
Hôtel Guimard, upper floor plan

156   Private Icons: The Neoclassical Hôtel

242
Hôtel Guimard, elevation and section

243
Hôtel Guimard, section

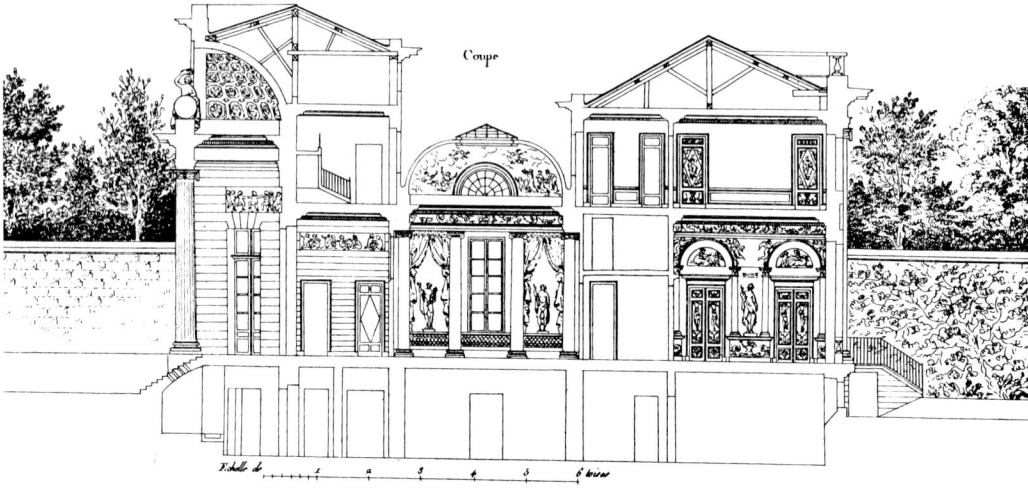

was formed a concave, semicircular niche. This giant niche was then screened by four columns and an entablature supporting a sculptural group, the Crowning of Terpsichore. The lack of correlation between facade and plan is especially striking in the Hôtel Guimard, where the powerful central form of the apse-like porch strongly suggests a centralized plan behind. Instead, the facade masks an asymmetrically organized interior. The opening on the central axis of the niche is not the entry door, but rather a window to the *cabinet des bains;* the real entry is off the axis to the right into an oval *antichambre,* which in turn leads to the *salle à manger* on the left and to the rectangular *salon de compagnie* in the rear. The barrel-vaulted dining room is screened from the second *antichambre* by a pair of columns forming an "interior facade," which recapitulates the exterior facade and thereby establishes a relationship between the interior public spaces that is analogous to the overall relationship of forecourt to house. The T-shaped figure formed by the public rooms thus disengages the bedroom area in the rear of the plan and the bathroom area in the front.

Ledoux is able to paradoxically invert the normal order of things and at the same time comment on the nature of his client. Normally, the private rooms are discreetly located and used to support and disengage public parts; but here it is the reverse—the public sequence is diverted in order to disengage the private elements, which are then given positions of prominence along the main axis of the house. Formally, the service areas are the habitable *poché* of the house; symbolically, they are figural. Unfortunately, the bankruptcy of one of her lovers forced Mlle Guimard to sell her house in 1786.[27] With poetic injustice, the house was destroyed in 1862 to accommodate the rearrangement of the streets around the site of Charles Garnier's new Paris Opera.

To the original model for the Neoclassical *hôtel,* the Petit Trianon, Ledoux added idiosyncratic plans, a freer interpretation of antiquity, and a personalization based on the client. This penetration of the abstract type by more fanciful interpretations of circumstance was not so much a collision between two opposing tendencies as a mingling in which empirical reality and the ideal became largely inseparable. If this system worked best when a unique client required a unique house, it also had more normative applications, because it became characteristic of late-eighteenth-century *hôtels.* On the whole, the clients of these *hôtels* were not as famous as Mlle Guimard, as important as the Montmorency, or as rich as Madame de Thélusson; but they did aspire to the same ideals, and they did desire approximately similar accommodations, if on a reduced scale. Thus, even by the early 1770s, Ledoux had provided models for the incredible number of *hôtels* that were to be constructed in the next thirty years.

In the last quarter of the eighteenth century, and especially during the 1770s and 1780s, the construction of domestic buildings in Paris reached a level so frenzied that Sebastian Mercier observed that a third of Paris had been rebuilt in thirty years.[28] This proliferation inevitably produced a wide variety of *hôtels,* but some general tendencies may be observed. Strongest is the preference for the block-like form of the Petit Trianon, a preference that asserts itself in suburban villas even when located on narrow or complicated sites. The plans of these buildings tend to be either two or three zones deep and three or five bays wide, with the two-by-three-bay plan apparently preferred. They are asymmetrically organized behind symmetrical and centralized facades, and the central bay of the plan is usually emphasized, implying a sequence from front to back. In most cases, the center bay is blocked, however, as in Ledoux's Hôtel Guimard and Boffrand's Hôtel d'Amelot, thus forcing a sequence—a *promenade*—around the center through a variety of rooms. Finally, the axis of symmetry is maintained from front to back even if the site is irregular, so that the recentering between forecourt and garden that was typical in the Baroque and Rococo *hôtel* is totally absent in the Neoclassical *hôtel.*[29]

But not all were the isolated block type; the more traditional courtyard types were also used, especially for large *hôtels.* Examples of these are the Hôtel de Salm (1782–85) by Pierre Rousseau, the Hôtel Soubise (1787–88) by Jacques Cellerier, and the Pavillon d'Orléans (1774),[30] Hôtel de Ste.-Foix (1775), and Hôtel Dervieux (1774)[31] by Alexandre-Théodore Brongniart. Two of Etienne-Louis Boullée's built works, the Hôtel Alexandre (1763–66) and the Hôtel de Brunoy (1775–79), also fall into this general category, as does François Franque's Maison Abbatiale of the Abbaye de Prémontrés at Villers-Cotterets.

The persistence of the courtyard type may be at least partially attributable to the conservative tradition of Blondel. From his *Architecture françoise* on, Blondel always relied on the traditional courtyard *hôtel* for his increasingly detailed descriptions of *la distribution.* For example, he used the abbot's house at Villers-Cotterets to illustrate the principles of *hôtel* design in his *Cours* (1771–77); and in his description of a private *apparte-*

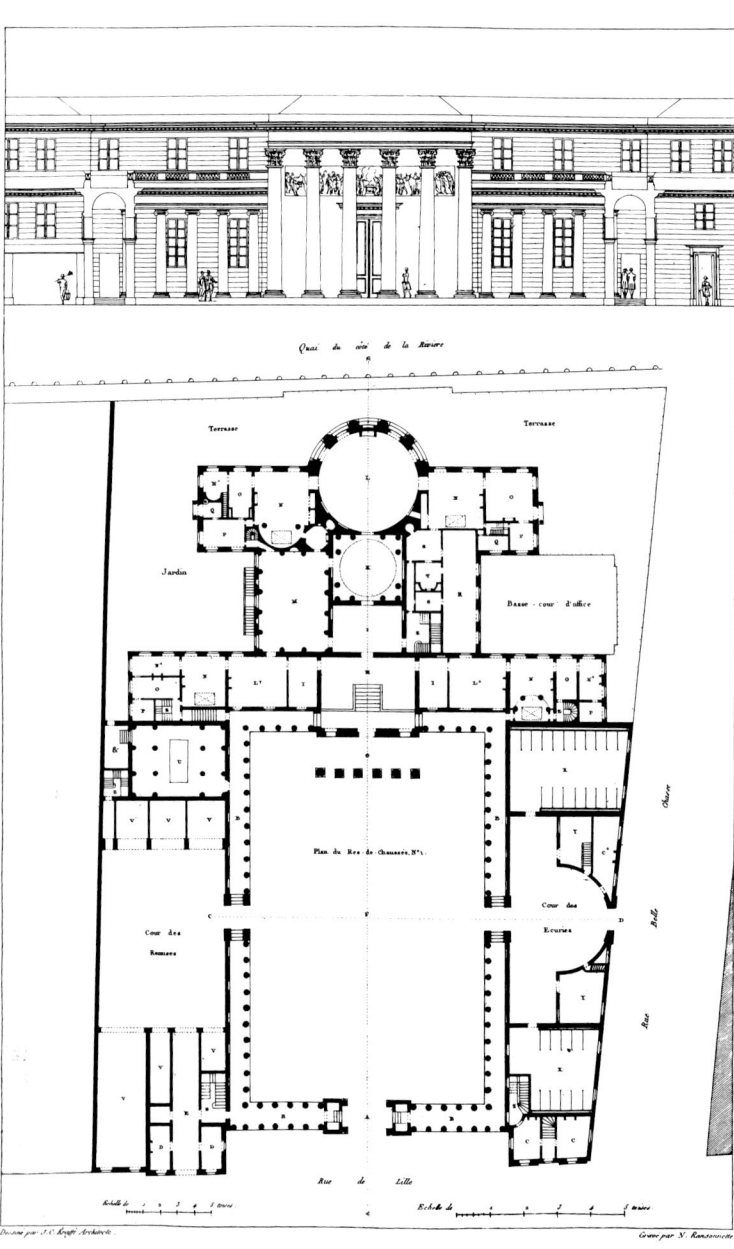

244
Hôtel de Salm, plan and section, Pierre Rousseau, 1782–85.
A. entry
B. circular gallery
C. Swiss guard
D. concierge
E. vehicular passage
F. court
G. peristyle
H. *vestibule*
I. *antichambre*
K. music room
L. small *salon*
M. dining room
N. *chambre à coucher*
O. *cabinet*
P. dressing room
Q. English wardrobe
R. *grande galerie*
S. *cabinet*
T. small study
U. billiards
V. carriages
X. stables
Y. harness room
Z. stair
&. small court

245
Pavillon d'Orléans, plan and garden elevation, Alexandre-Théodore Brongniart, 1774.

A. entry
AB. court defined by trellis
B. porch
C. gallery
D. first *antichambre*
E. second *antichambre*
F. *salon de compagnie*
G. dining
H. buffet
I. *cabinet*
K. *chambre à coucher*
L. stair
M. dressing
N. *boudoir*
O. *cabinet* and toilet
P. water basins
Q. greenhouse
R. small *salon*
S. water basin
T. lawn
T*. flower bed
U. garden music room
V. outdoor theater
X. arbor
Y. English garden
Z. pleasure garden

Theater:
A. vestibule
B. entry to boxes
C. stair
D. toilet
F. corridor
G. boxes
H. pit
I. orchestra
L. boxes
L. *dégagements*
M. proscenium
N. foyer
O. service stair
P. actors' boxes

tion announces his aim: "No one has yet written of the analogy of proportions with our senses,"[34] and he acknowledges that the more he examined nature, the more he recognized that "every object possesses its own special character, and that often a single line, a simple contour suffices to express it."[35] He argues that the outside and the inside of a building have "the most intimate relationship" and that the exterior "prepares the spirit" by indicating both the use of the building and what is to follow on the interior.[36] Thus, for Le Camus, the houses for a noble gentleman, a military man, a magistrate, or a rich private citizen should all be treated differently, and each should have a distinct character. Although the courtyard *hôtel* may have been a practical form for confined sites and extensive services, the freestanding body—the Neoclassical *hôtel*—was the ideal form for *l'architecture parlante*.

The adaptation of the ideal pavilion to the reality of Parisian sites, and the increased particularization of the plan, can be seen in several *hôtels* of the 1770s and 1780s. In most, the services are separated from the main block and are located on the street side of the forecourt. The central axis of the house is usually blocked, and the plans are two zones deep and either three or five bays wide. Most have picturesque gardens rather than formal geometric ones, and frequently the elevations show the building to be freestanding even if it is a party-wall building.[37]

For example, Brongniart's Hôtel de Monaco (1774–77), built for the mistress of the Prince de Condé on a site near the Hôtel de Lassay, is a freestanding block two zones deep and five bays wide. The site is wide enough to enable the garden walls to bypass the house, and the definition of the forecourt is completed by rows of pleached trees between the service block and the *corps-de-logis*. The central axis is blocked, creating a counterclockwise public sequence through a variety of rooms.

A more common version of the Neoclassical type was one in which a modest, square *corps-de-logis* three bays wide spanned the entire width of the site and was contained by lower garden walls. In the Hôtel d'Orliane (1789) by Pierre d'Orliane, the Neoclassical serenity of the facade masks a highly agitated and idiosyncratic plan that is a response to the decreasing size and increasing specialization of functional rooms. The Hôtel d'Orliane is the reverse of a Palladian plan: impacted, particularized, and rationalized. It is not that the large, stable, multi-use rooms of earlier periods were discarded, but rather that they were augmented by more specialized rooms. The Hôtel d'Orliane, for example, resembles a smaller version of the Palais Bourbon of sixty years earlier: the public rooms circle clockwise from the entrance around two sides of the stair and contrast with the small service spaces that fill the third side. The asymmetrical plan is stabilized by the large square *salon* on the garden side, which, with the porch and oversized stair, begins to hint at a level of grandeur beyond the expected capacity of so small a building.

Similar qualities of grandeur disproportionate to size exist in the Hôtel Courmont (1789) by Jean-François Chevalier, where the central figure of the elegant plan is reinforced by the three-dimensional articulation of the block. The entrance portico corresponds to the oversized central *salon* projecting into the garden, but the narrower bay of the entry and stair permits a large room to the right of the entrance, and therefore greater modulation of the spatial sequence. A beautiful oval bedroom completes the public sequence. A very small-scale commentary on this *hôtel* can be seen in the Hôtel L'Auchère (1801) by Charles Aubert, where each floor contains only one large room surrounded by support spaces.

The French Revolution temporarily disrupted architectural production, but for the construction of small houses, the interruption was brief. People were not about to sacrifice the pleasures of everyday life for long, and when production resumed, it resumed at more or less the same point at which it had ceased. One of the themes that continued after the Revolution was the interplay between classical and natural forms; and two small projects, one built during the Revolution, the other built after, illustrate to what degree the extravagances of the Hôtel de Thélusson were adaptable to more modest budgets. In the Hôtel Chenot (1790) by Brunau, the services and entry are located on street level around a courtyard that is articulated by rusticated pilasters of natural rock, while the public spaces are above the entrance on the next floor, facing a romantic garden. The garden is furnished with small temples, one of which acts as a transposed piece of the house by terminating the gallery and marking the center of the garden. In his own house (1799), the architect Ollivier inverted the normal order of the site, that is, the sequence of court–main block–garden; here, the single-zone main block sits at the very end of the site and faces the informal garden to the front. The entrance from the street is through a naturalistic arch of boulders into an oval space defined by small service buildings, and this space in turn leads to the garden and house beyond. The *hôtel* is conceived as a garden with a grotto-like gate and a thick,

164   Private Icons: The Neoclassical Hôtel

249
Hôtel de Monaco, plans, section, and elevation, Alexandre-Théodore Brongniart, 1774–77.

A. court
B. peristyle
C. *vestibule*
D. *antichambre*
E. dining
F. buffet
G. music room
H. *salon de compagnie*
I. *chambre à coucher*
K. boudoir
L. library
M. bath
N. dressing room
O. passage
P. toilet
Q. small stair
R. terrace
S. garden
T. flower garden
U. gazebo

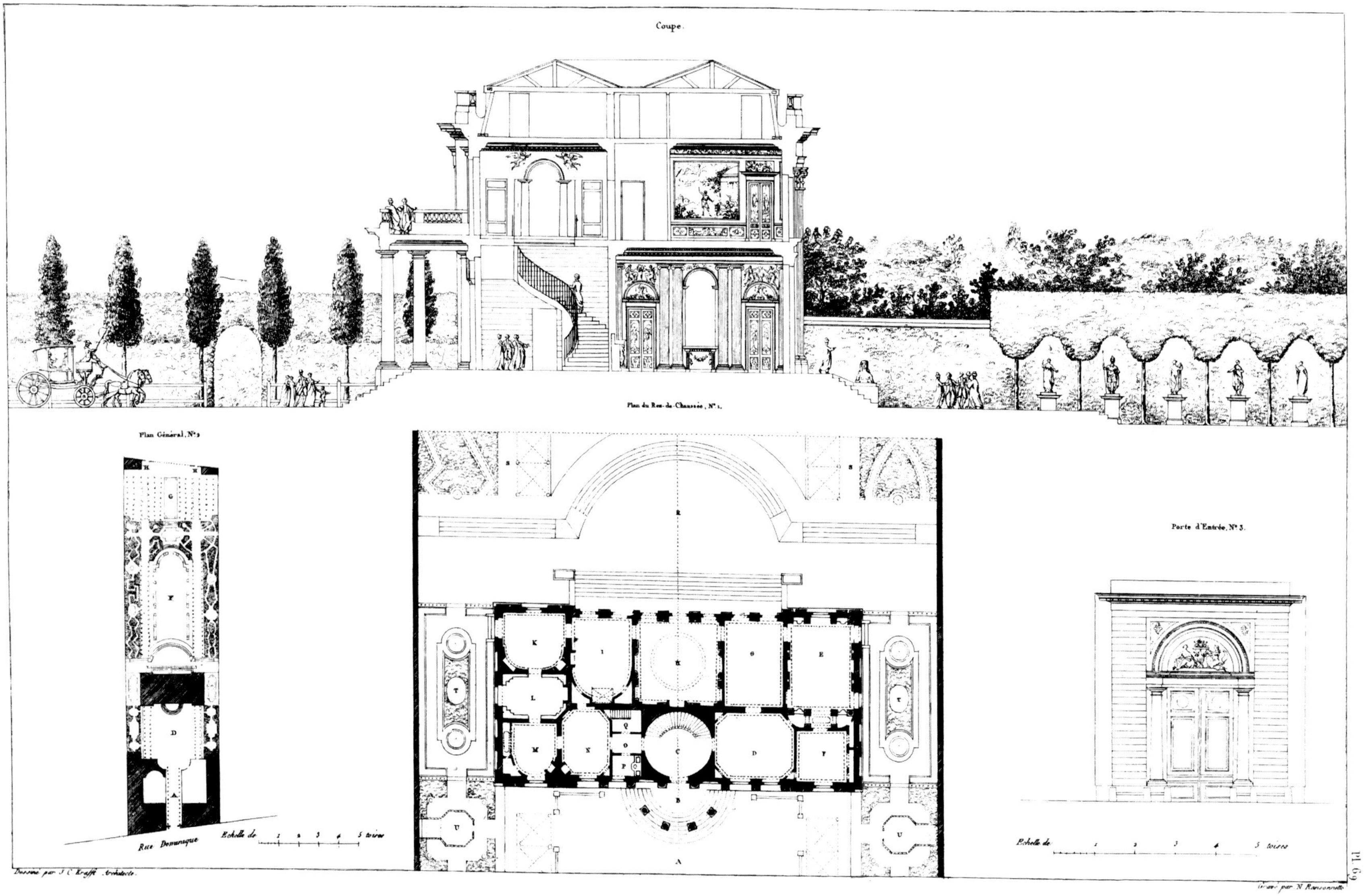

165 The Neoclassical Hôtel

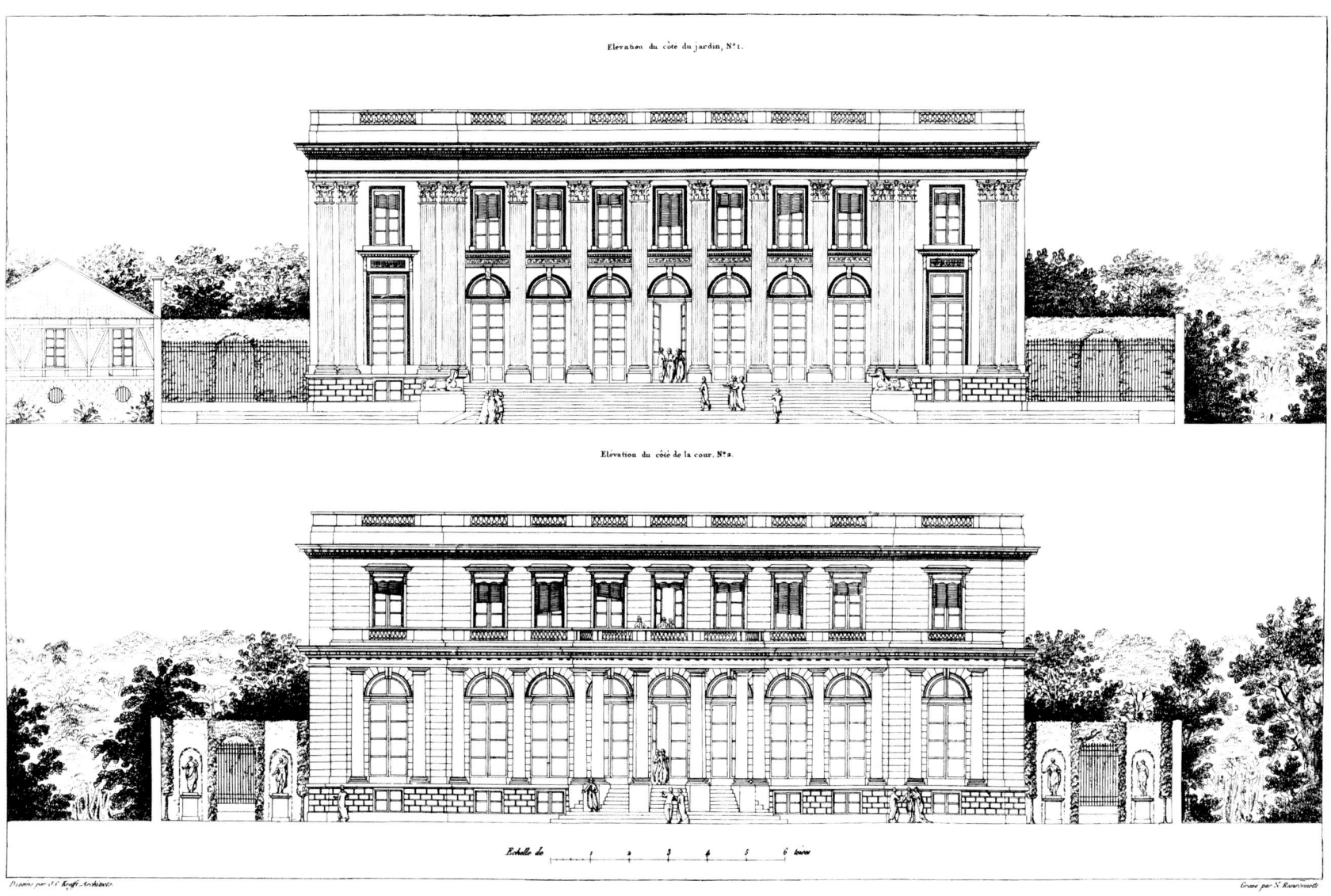

250
Hôtel de Monaco,
elevations

166 Private Icons: The Neoclassical Hôtel

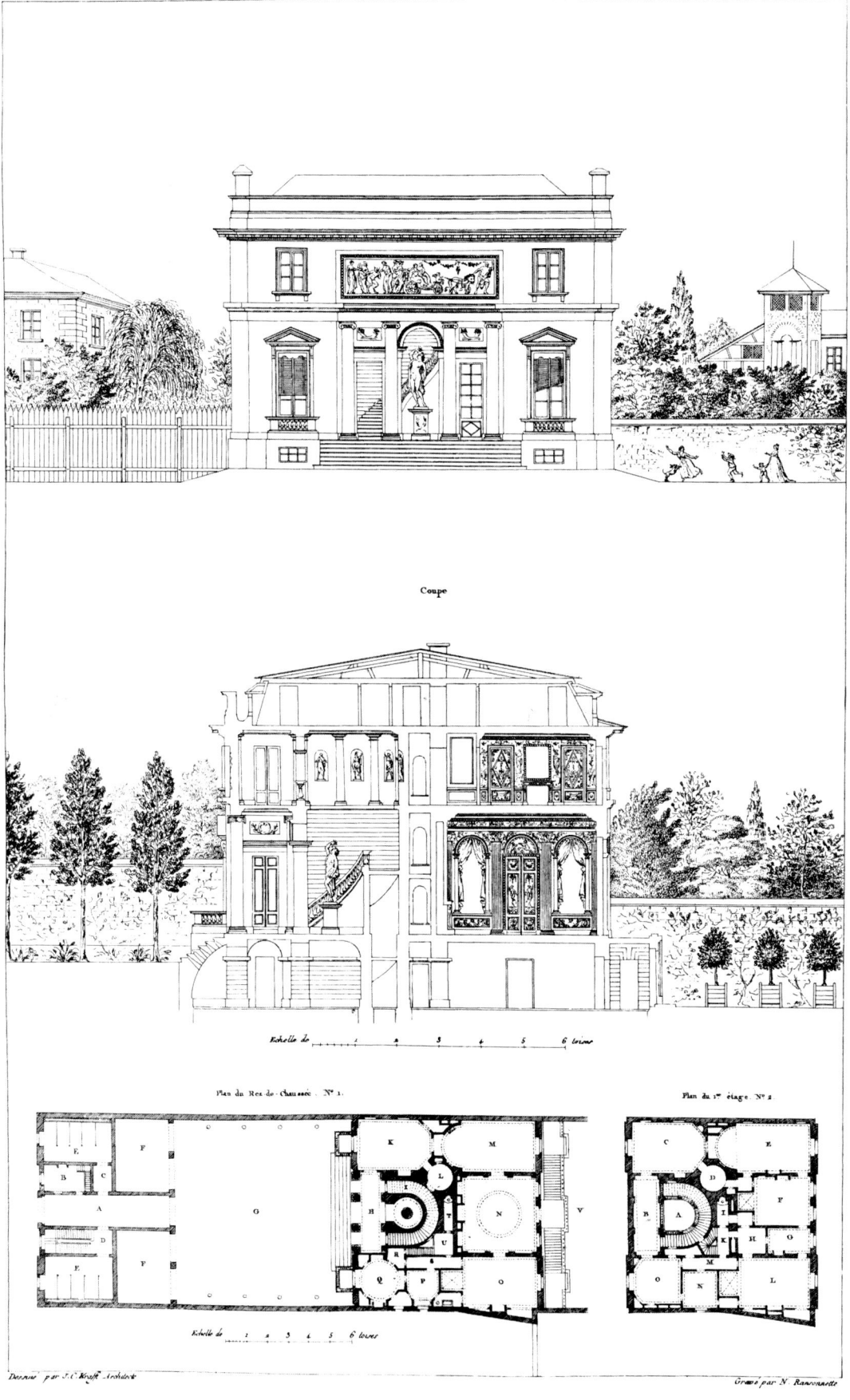

251
Hôtel d'Orliane, plans, section, and elevation, Pierre d'Orliane, 1789.

Ground floor:
A. entry
B. porter
C. *dégagement*
D. stair
E. stable
F. carriages
G. court
H. peristyle
I. stair
K. *antichambre*
L. office
M. dining
N. *salon de compagnie*
O. *chambre à coucher*
P. bath and dressing room
Q. *boudoir*
R. private stair
S. *dégagement*
T. toilet
U. wardrobe
V. garden

Upper floor:
A. stair
B. vestibule
C. *antichambre*
D. *dégagement*
E. salon
F. *chambre à coucher*
G. cabinet
H. wardrobe
I. toilet
K. private stair
L. *chambre à coucher*
M. *dégagement*
N. dressing room
O. *boudoir* and library

252
Hôtel Courmont, plans, section, and elevation, Jean-François Chevalier de Beauregard, 1789.

A. entry
B. porter
C. court
D. peristyle
E. *antichambre*
F. stair
G. dining
H. office
I. *salon de compagnie*
K. *chambre à coucher*
L. *cabinet*
M. *boudoir*
N. dressing room
O. toilet
P. *dégagement*
Q. garden
R. linen room
S. harness room
T. stable
U. latrines
V. carriages
X. well

253
Hôtel L'Auchère, plans, section, and elevation, Charles Aubert, 1801.

Ground floor:
A. *vestibule*
B. stair
C. dining
D. *salon de compagnie*
E. wardrobe
F. small *cabinet.*

Upper floor:
A. stair
B. *antichambre*
C. *salon* serving as *chambre à coucher*
D. dressing room
E. wardrobe
F. small *chambre à coucher*

Second floor:
A. stair
B. *antichambre*
C. billiard room
D. *cabinet*
E. toilet

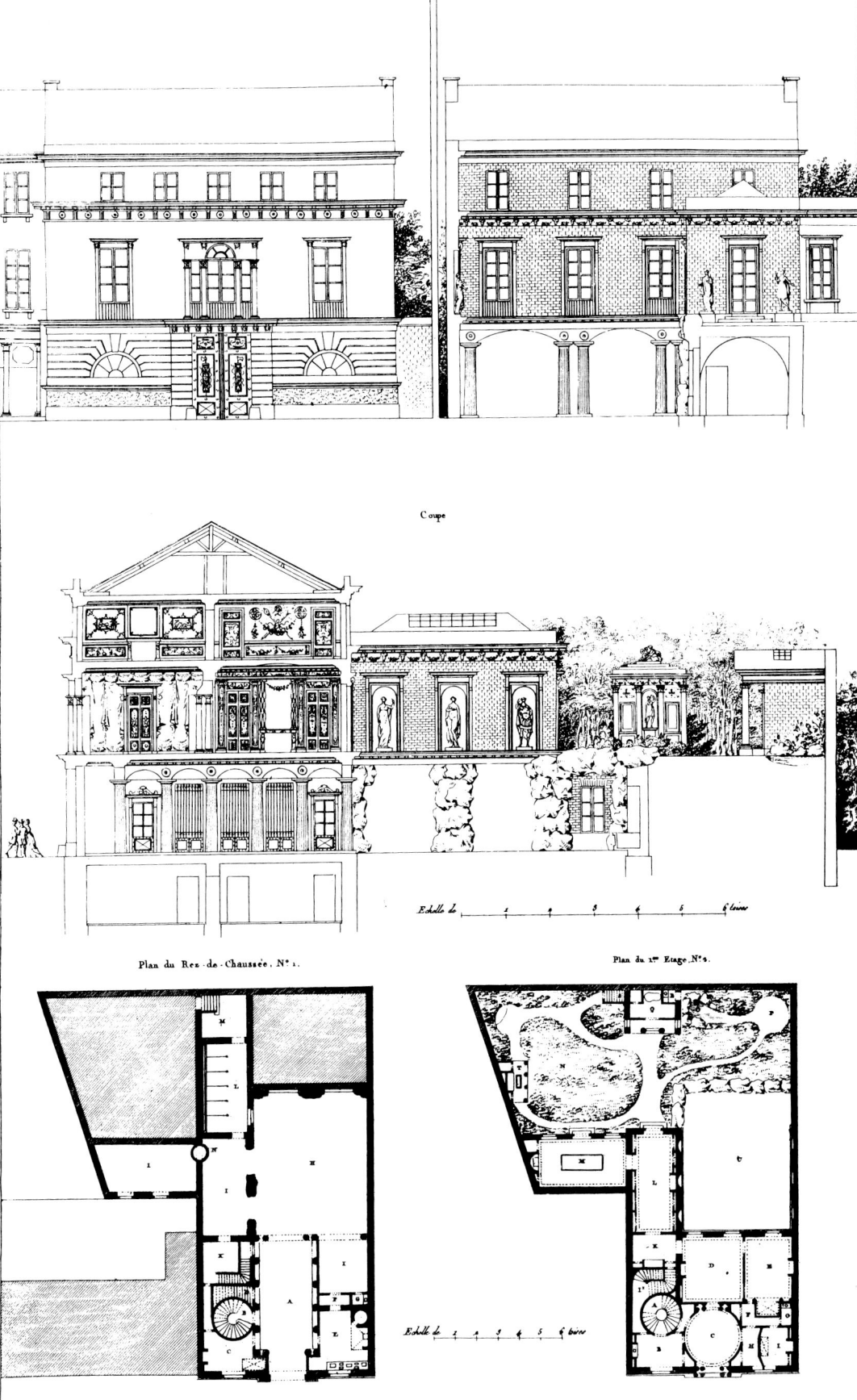

254
Hôtel Chenot, plans, sections, and elevation, Brunau, 1790.

Ground floor:
A. entry
B. stair
C. porter
E. kitchen
F. storage
G. toilet
H. court
I. carriages
K. harness room
L. stables
M. stair
N. well

Upper floor:
A. stair
B. *antichambre*
C. dining
D. *salon de compagnie*
E. *chambre à coucher*
F. *dégagement*
G. toilet
H. dressing room
I. *boudoir*
I*. stair to mezzanine
K. reading room
L. library
M. billiard room
N. English garden
O. water piece
P. *bosquet*
Q. bath
R. toilet
S. private stair
T. small temple

170 Private Icons: The Neoclassical Hôtel

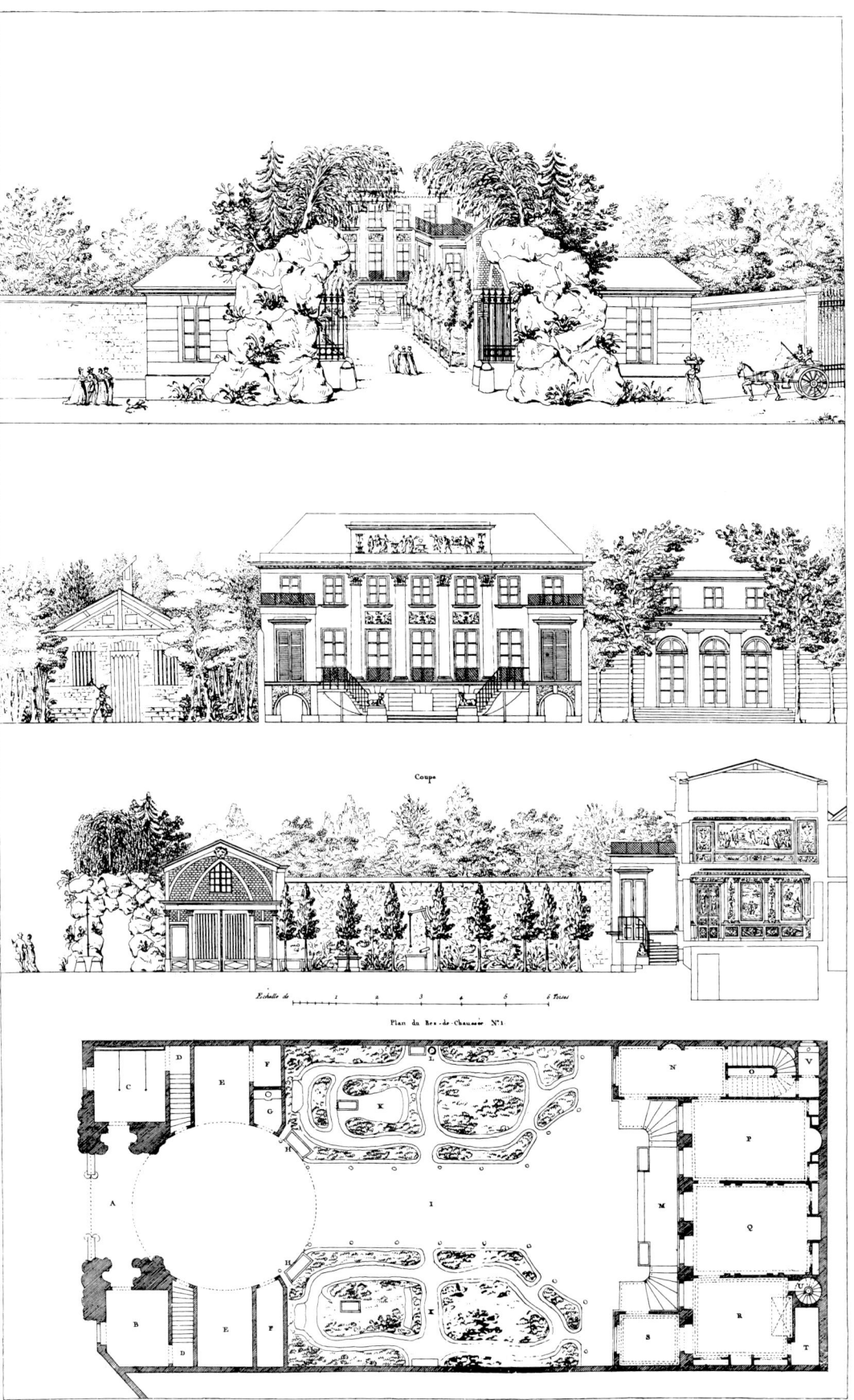

255
Hôtel Ollivier, plan, section, and elevations, Ollivier, 1799.
N. *antichambre*
O. stair
P. dining
Q. *salon de compagnie*
R. *chambre à coucher*
S. *boudoir*
T. wardrobe
U. private stair
V. toilet

habitable facade at the other end—a grand concept in spite of its simplicity and sentimentality.

In another variation of the Neoclassical *hôtel*, the main block sits free as a pavilion on a wide site and joins the service buildings to define a small forecourt. The Hôtel Lakanal (1795) by Henry is typical, as is the Hôtel Callet (1777) by Bernard Poyet. The basic plan of the Hôtel Callet is in itself uninspired, but the method of creating rooms is especially intriguing: through a series of "inserts" or "liners," the otherwise neutral rectangles of the plan are qualified and made specific. In the Hôtel Callet, the "liner" is sometimes transparent, as in the oval dining room; sometimes it is usable, as in the library; and sometimes it simultaneously defines the shape of the room and the *dégagement*, or private passage, behind and around the room. The development of these multifunctional areas of *poché* allowed endless variety, and in a sense they did for the private realm of the eighteenth century what the habitable *poché*, the Baroque *hôtel*, did for the public realm of the seventeenth century: they allowed discontinuity, disengagement, and mediation. Normally, they were the residue, but in the Hôtel Callet they were the active ingredient.

The art of residue was a special skill of eighteenth-century architects, and there was no greater test of this skill than the planning of round buildings. The circular *hôtel* was the ultimate pavilion, the ultimate object, the purest of the ideal forms; as such, it offered the most extreme contrast to the impure reality of daily life. Resistant to subdivision, the round building is, in terms of planning and geometry, essentially a problem of residue.

In 1788 the architect Henry built a round *hôtel* in the rue Pigalle for a M. Vassale. The service buildings in front defined a small forecourt, and to the rear was a simulated romantic garden typical of the time. Then in 1790, for unknown reasons, M. Vassale built a rectangular house on the adjacent site and had the two houses connected by a small bridge. The rectangular house is predictably less interesting, but the round one, for all its problems, is a virtuoso performance that offers a revealing connection and contrast to the late theoretical work of Ledoux—one which illuminates the two opposing tendencies manifested in the Petit Trianon.

The Hôtel Vassale was obviously inspired by Ledoux's Barrière de la Villette, but its plan might best be compared to Ledoux's project for a round country house. Both plans are generated by a nine-square grid superimposed over a circle, both maintain and articulate two central axes, and both have the stair in the same location. In Ledoux's plan as well as in Henry's, the main rooms occupy the central cruciform of the nine-square grid, and the secondary spaces are relegated to the remaining quadrants. But Ledoux's plan is bilaterally symmetrical about both of its axes so that there is an equality among rooms and an equality of the residual quadrants as well, whereas Henry's plan is asymmetrical about both axes, has rooms of varying size and shape—even in the residual quadrants—and has a formal progression of public spaces culminating in the oval *salon* that overlooks the garden. In Henry's plan there are elaborate adjustments to accommodate the extravagant array of rooms within the circle. In Ledoux's plan, no such adjustment takes place; the rectangular system and the circle simply coexist. Indeed, it is as if the one is the diagram of the type, the other its application, deformed by fashion and circumstance. If the upper floor of Henry's building suffers too much at the hands of circumstance, then perhaps the lower plan of Ledoux's suffers too little. As with the sixteenth-century examples of Du Cerceau and Lescot, the question might again be asked: is one an idealized improvement on the excesses of the other, or, conversely, has it been rendered dry and diagrammatic by its removal from circumstance?

The traditional view of these two buildings, and the most fashionable current one as well, would describe the project by Henry as representing the end of one architectural and social system, the Baroque, while the Ledoux project would be regarded as the beginning of another—more modern, more egalitarian, and thus implicitly better. However, as we have seen, the French *hôtel* was not a pure representation of the Baroque system; on the contrary, it represented a resistance to it. It was not the planning system of the French *hôtel* that died near the end of the eighteenth century, but rather the symbolic sovereignty of the classical vocabulary. Thus the projects by Henry and Ledoux update a long-standing French debate between idea and reality, between two states of mind, between two variations of the same type. If this debate had already been raging for at least 250 years, then, fortunately, it was to continue.

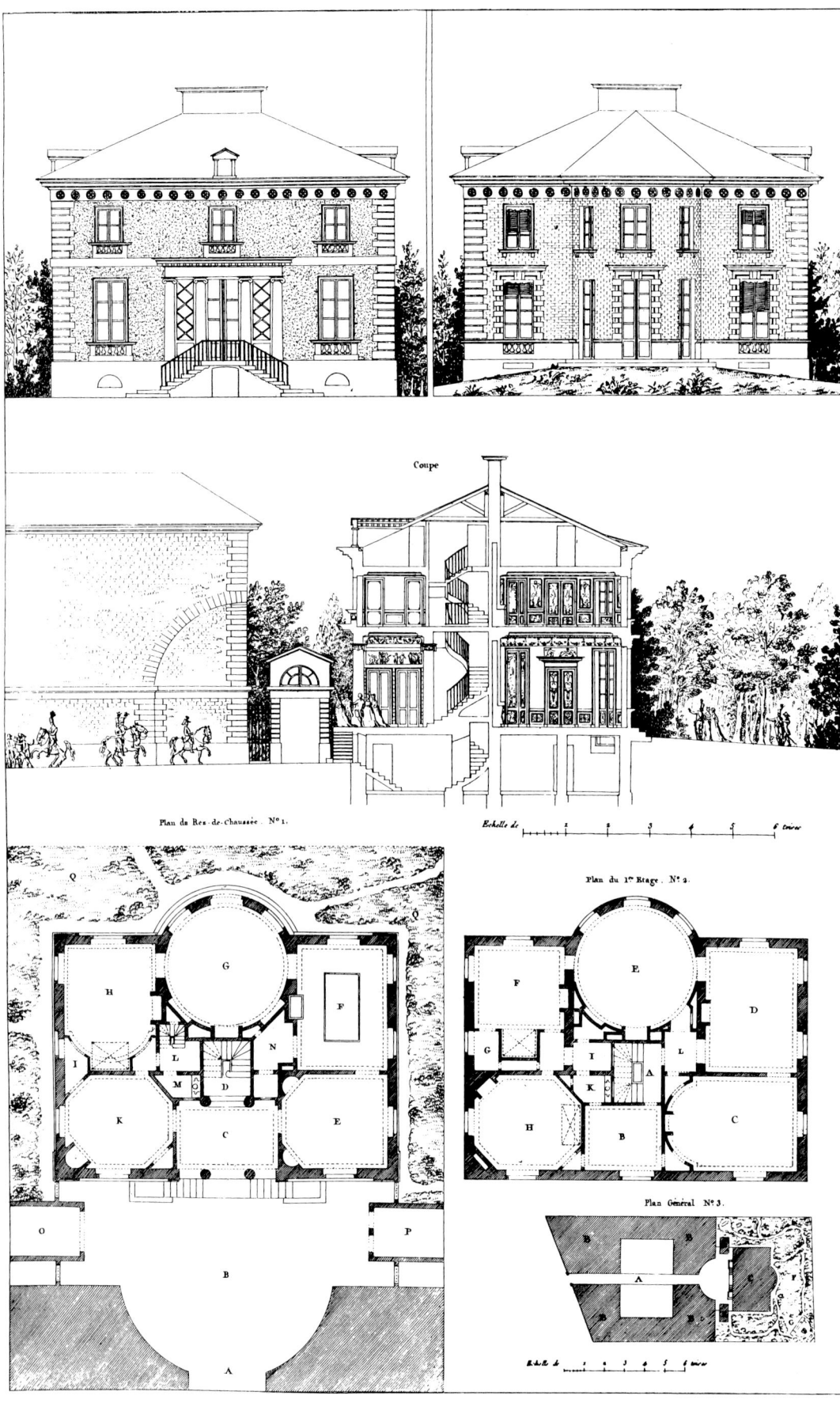

256
Hôtel Lakanal, plans, section, and elevations, Henry, 1795.

Ground floor:
A. entry
B. court
C. *vestibule*
D. stair
E. dining
F. billiards
G. *salon de compagnie*
H. *chambre à coucher*
I. dressing room
K. study
L. private stair
M. toilet
N. *dégagement*
O. carriages
P. stables
Q. English garden

First floor:
A. stair
B. *antichambre*
C. dining
D. library
E. *salon de compagnie*
F. *chambre à coucher*
G. dressing room
H. *cabinet*
I. wardrobe
K. toilet
L. *dégagement*

Site plan:
A. entry
B. private houses

257
Hôtel Callet, plans, section, and elevation, Bernard Poyet, 1777.

Ground floor:
A. court
B. stair
C. *antichambre*
D. *salon de compagnie*
E. dining
F. office
G. buffet
H. *chambre à coucher*
I. library
K. boudoir
L. dressing room
M. toilet
N. wardrobe
O. *dégagement*
P. chambermaid's room

Upper floor:
A. stair
B. *antichambre*
C. billiards
D. *chambre à coucher*
E. private stair
F. *dégagements*
G. toilet
H. *cabinet*

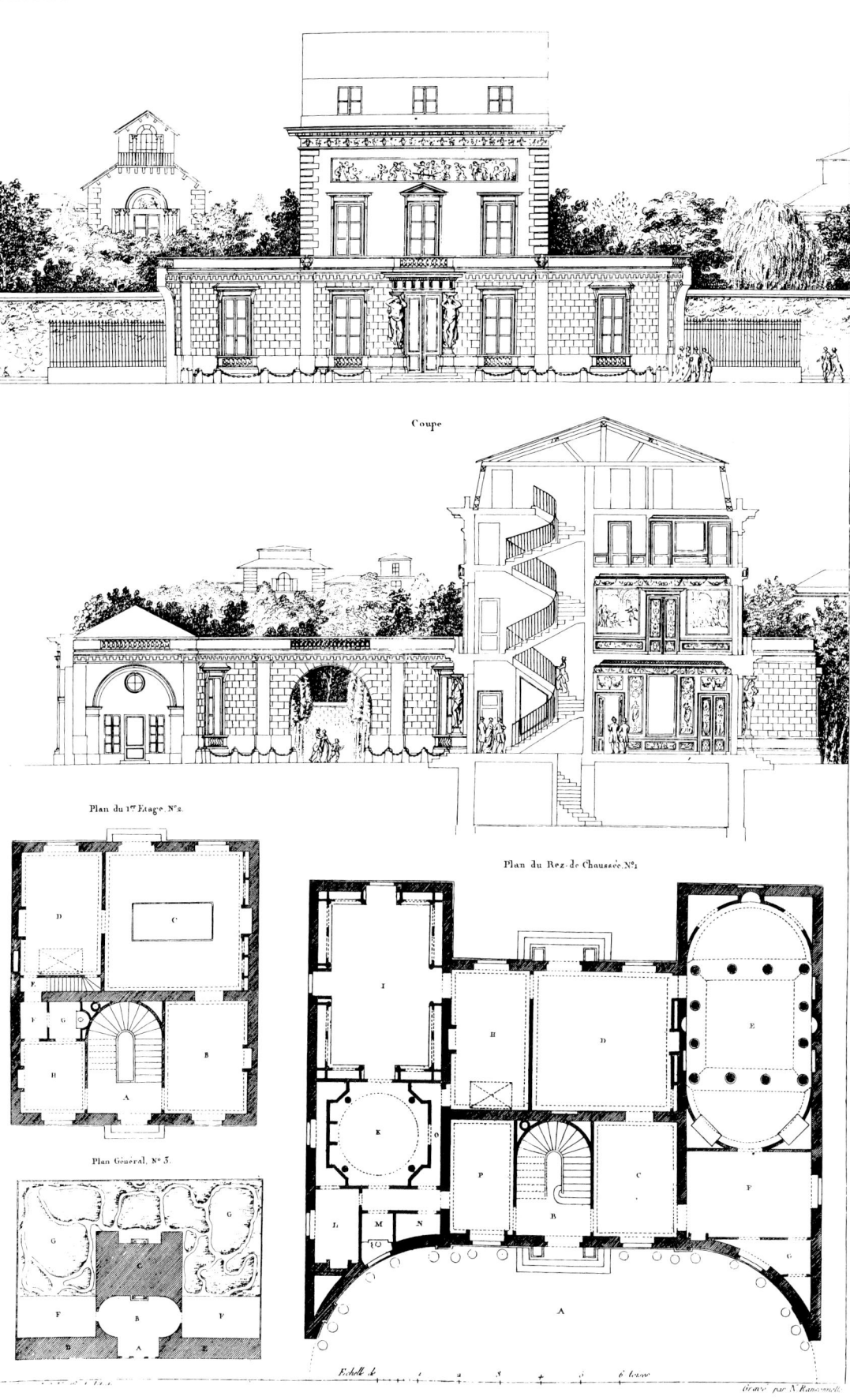

174 *Private Icons: The Neoclassical Hôtel*

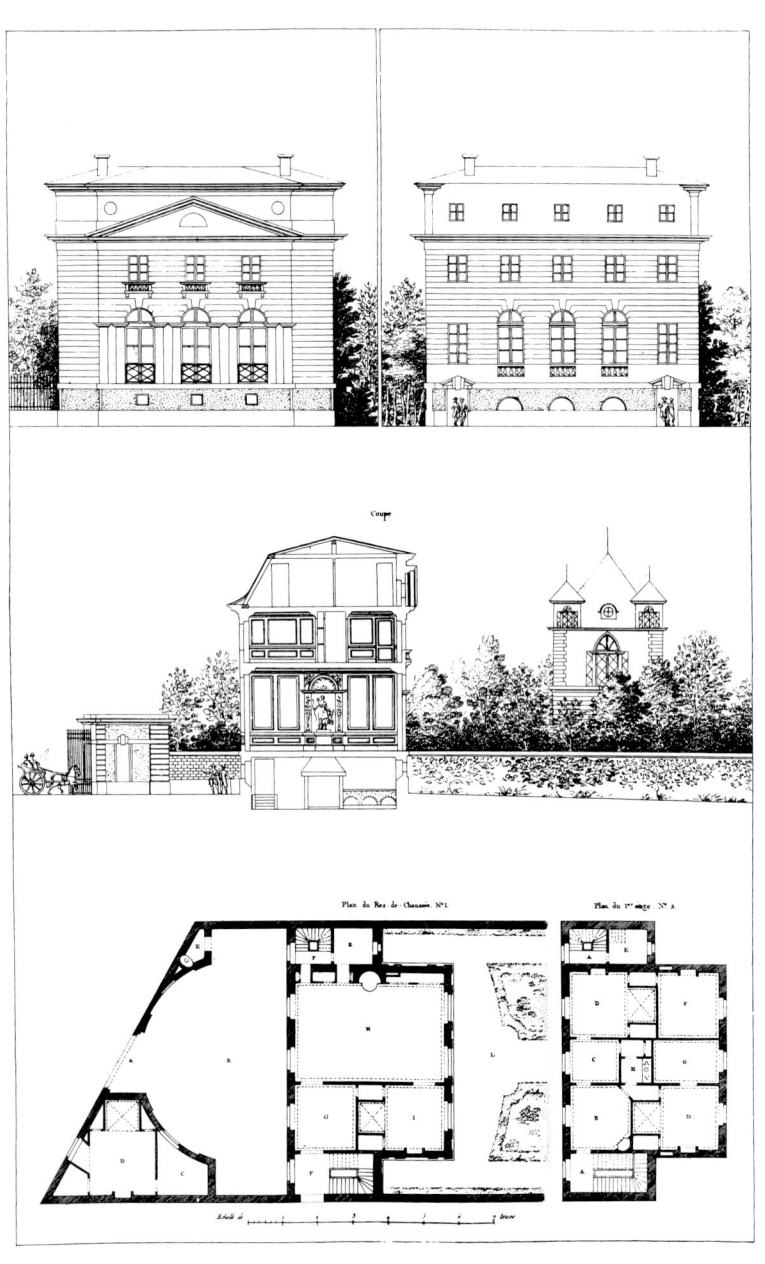
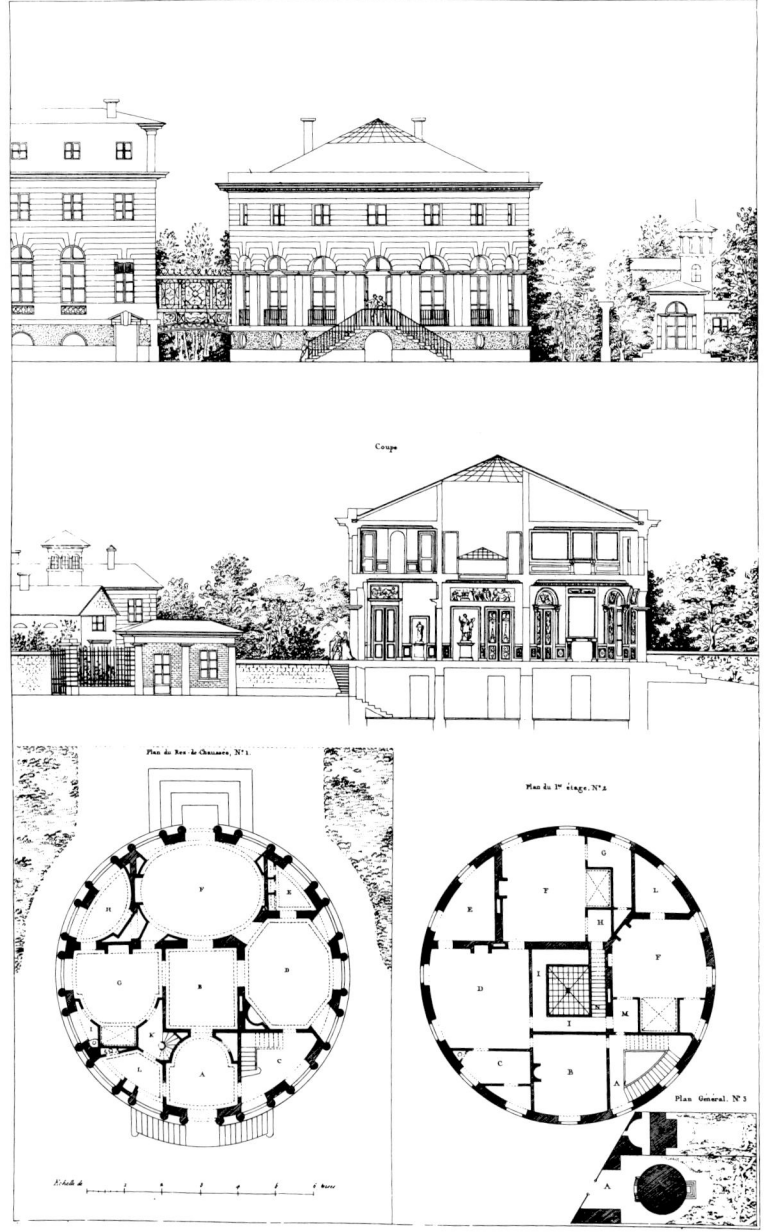

258
Hôtel Vassale, plans, section, and elevations, Henry, 1790.
Ground floor:
A. entry
B. court
C. porter
D. chambre à coucher
E. toilet
F. stairs
G. antichambre—dining
H. grand salon de compagnie and de jeu
I. boudoir
K. cabinet
L. garden

Upper floor:
A. stair
B. dining
C. cabinet
D. chambre à coucher
E. morning cabinet
F. study
G. cabinet
H. toilet

259
Hôtel Vassale, plans, section, and elevations, Henry, 1788.
Ground floor:
A. vestibule
B. antichambre
C. stair
D. dining
E. buffet
F. salon de compagnie
G. chambre à coucher
H. boudoir
I. toilet
K. private stair
L. dressing room

Upper floor:
A. stair
B. antichambre
C. cabinet
D. salon de compagnie
E. cabinet
F. chambre à coucher
G. dressing room
H. wardrobe
I. circulation
K. toilet
L. cabinet
M. dégagement
N. stair

260
The Barrière de la Villette, Claude-Nicolas Ledoux, 1785–87

261
Project for a country house, first and second floor plans, Claude-Nicolas Ledoux

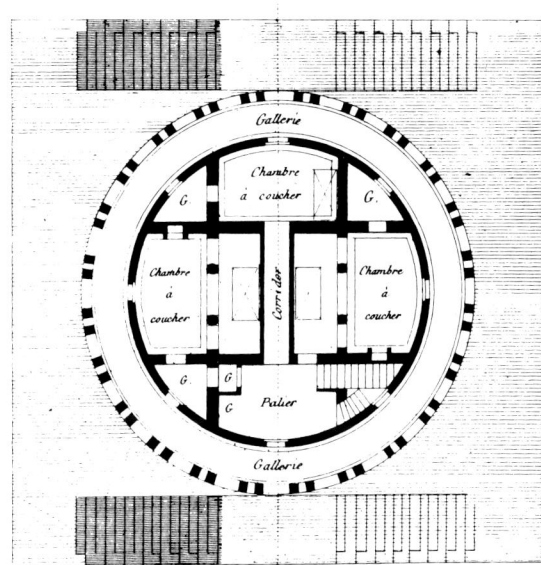

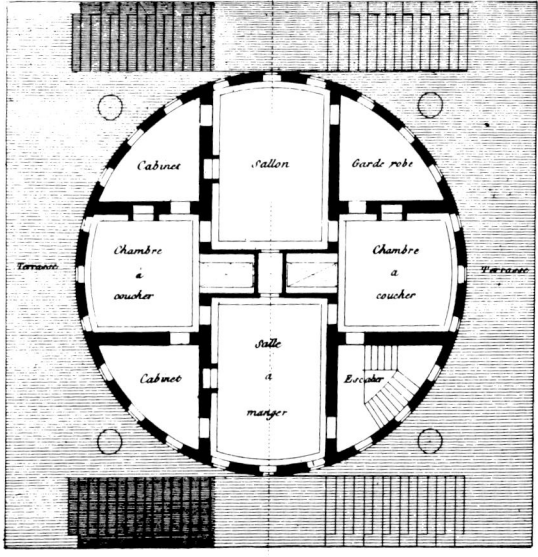

Krafft and Ransonnette

Although *hôtels* were still built after the French Revolution, even well into the nineteenth century, the form of the *hôtel* was essentially complete by 1800.[38] The Maire plan of 1808 therefore shows Paris at a complete stage of development, with all Neoclassical *hôtels* of the last quarter of the century indicated. These *hôtels* were published by Krafft and Ransonnette in *Plans, coupes, élévations des plus belles . . . hôtels . . . à Paris . . .* just after 1800 (1802?).[39] Unlike earlier eighteenth-century writers, Krafft and Ransonnette provide no theoretical text to accompany the plates. Their introduction and conclusion, however, published in French, German, and English, reveal their awareness of their historical context and serve as a summary of the three *hôtel* types. The passages quoted here are from their English text, but because both the English and French texts are somewhat garbled, small omissions and corrections (in brackets) are made for clarification. Simply stated, they argue that the *hôtels* of Louis XIV are highly developed on the exterior, but not the interior; that the *hôtels* of Louis XV are highly developed on the interior, but not the exterior; and that the *hôtels* of Louis XVI, which they are publishing, are highly developed on the exterior *and* the interior. They summarize the three periods, as follows:

In the century forever memorable of [Louis] XIV, wherein [the] sciences and polite arts made the most amazing progress, the art of Architecture was brought to a high degree of perfection, and France [was] embellished by a great number of monuments capable of immortalizing the nation. . . . But . . . architects thought themselves obliged to sacrifice everything to . . . external magnificence and [to the] embellishment of the cities. Especially the internal disposition of houses . . . was extremely neglected. The riches of architecture were spent on large vestibules, [great] staircases . . . long galleries and salons of state. It appeared that . . . architects [tried to arouse] the admiration of foreigners, rather than to provide for the private convenience of the inhabitants. . . . The architects of that time did [not] know the modern and proper distribution and disposition of . . . rooms, nor the various conveniences [provided in] edifices erected [since that time].

It was [only] during the reign of [Louis] XV that . . . architects began to unite the useful with the pleasing, and to furnish the internal parts of buildings with those conveniences of which they had been deprived hitherto. [Things were] even strained to such a pitch as to create . . . a new art . . . in building (*la distribution*). There were seen at once a great many palaces, country and pleasure houses, which, by the charms of their internal disposition, deserved the approbation and applause of . . . learned men, and threw . . . the French architecture such a lustre, as to engage most of the European princes to take . . . our architects into their service, or to draw them into their dominions.

Nevertheless, we must freely confess that . . . the internal disposition of buildings had . . . improved at the expense of . . . external beauty. . . . The architects . . . judged it proper to increase the number of windows in the rooms, to straighten their walls, and to diminish the extent and the height of the ceilings, in order to procure *galleries, entresols*, private staircases, dressing rooms, English privies and small bathing rooms; it was generally thought that for the proper distribution of all these [rooms] it would be necessary to have recourse to certain licenses often entirely contrary to the rules of real architecture. According to these principles . . . architects [frequently] mutilated some [rooms]; in the disposition of others [they followed] captious but false forms; and [they] sacrificed everything, even the external beauty itself, to the internal conveniences. . . .

It [is only] 25 or 30 years since the architects [tried] to unite the [principles] of ancient Architecture with what the conveniences seem to require. The progress . . . made has been such as to furnish us . . . with edifices which we . . . look upon as masterpieces.[40]

Finally, they acknowledge "the revolution, which has taken place in the arts," and explain their role in it:

Knowledge, which has spread itself throughout every class of society, a passion for travelling, and [education] have brought about [remarkable changes] in the art of building. . . . [A] great number of private houses [have been] erected in the new parts of town for opulent proprietors, who [have] brought back with them from their travels in Italy and other countries the taste for novelty, and a certain propensity for deviating from the old, servile method of building, [thus] freeing themselves from many received prejudices. This has totally changed the physiognomy of our architecture; and those foreigners, who fancy they acquire a perfect idea of this art [by] consulting old collections of our buildings (Marot, Blondel, etc.), or in deriving their principles from those treatises which have formerly dealt with this subject, are vastly mistaken.

We look upon it as an important service rendered to society to publish what may well be called the monuments of architecture regenerated in the nineteenth century, and those, which towards the end of the eighteenth [century], have prepared this regeneration.[41]

If Krafft and Ransonnette's summary of the three periods of *hôtel* building is clear from the traditional French point of view of *distribution* and *décor*, they totally avoid the relationship of those elements to a space/form transformation. The reference to the regeneration of architecture at the end of the eighteenth century is somewhat vague, but presumably refers to new freedom in

style and comfort, not to type; that is, the destruction of the classical system of absolute standards allowed for relativity, for choice, in matters of style and internal convenience. Ironically, it was the form—the preference for freestanding buildings—that facilitated this choice of style or character but that also facilitated the uncoupling of style and type: free buildings, like free bodies, could more easily be dressed in different suits of clothes, so the type emerges as merely a diagrammatic abstraction on which to hang the clothes. This can be seen clearly in L. A. Dubut's *Architecture civile* (1803), in which the same plan is illustrated with stylistically different elevations.[42] For the architect-*antiquaire* this was convenient; however, for the architect-*philosophe*, type was of fundamental importance and so intrinsically related to style and character that they were inseparable. Thus, the theoretical projects published by Ledoux in 1804 in his *L'Architecture* allow for neither stylistic eclecticism nor for internal deformation as a response to circumstantial reality. He applied the ideal rigors previously reserved for public buildings to private ones. This was not true, however, of his own built work, unpublished until much later,[43] nor of the real buildings published by Krafft and Ransonnette.

For J.-N.-L. Durand also, the regeneration of architecture was predicated on type rather than style and practical planning. His *Recueil* (1800) and *Précis* (1802–5) both propose type as the basis for architectural production, and his plans are as impervious to empirical nuance as are the theoretical ones of Ledoux and, later, of the Beaux-Arts. Common to these otherwise disparate points of view, however, is the overwhelming preference for freestanding iconic objects. Not

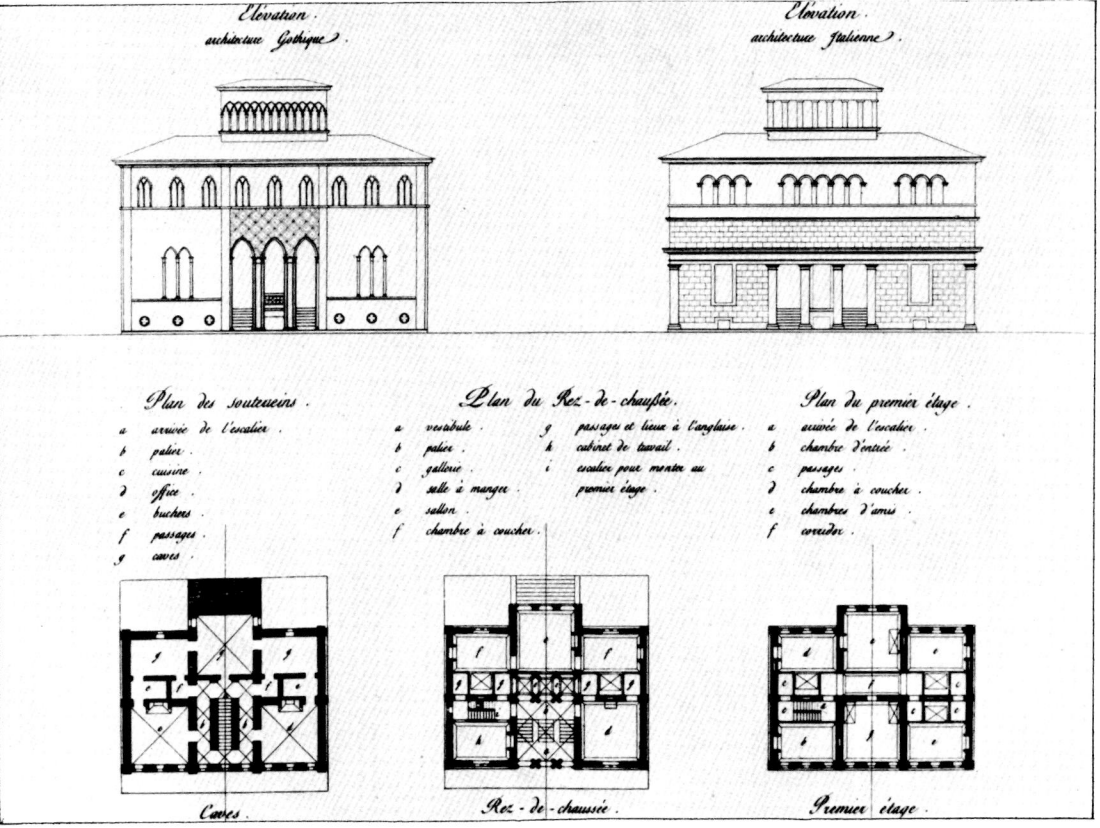

262
Execution of Louis XVI in the Place de la Concorde, January 21, 1793. Engraving by Berthault.

263
Designs for a house, L. A. Dubut, 1803

only were objects more ideal vehicles for conveying "the message" than spaces, but they were also easier to rationalize and categorize. This was of course a paradoxical condition, poised as it was on the edge of a period of unprecedented urban expansion, in which the management of urban space would be crucial; and it was to remain an underlying problem throughout the nineteenth century.

The Nineteenth Century

The great architectural preoccupation of nineteenth-century Paris was the development of the street and the apartment house, instead of the square and the *hôtel*. But the *hôtel* was not without influence. In a sense, the focus of domestic architecture simply shifted from housing for the aristocracy to housing for the bourgeoisie; the French *hôtel* planning system was applied to a new problem. The *hôtel* also provided two distinct models for the apartment building: one based on the principles of the Baroque *hôtel* type, the other based on the Neoclassical *hôtel* type. This may be seen in two late-eighteenth-century buildings: the Hôtel Beaumarchais and a building by François-Joseph Bélanger.

As an example of the Baroque *hôtel* type, the Hôtel Beaumarchais is a *pièce de résistance*. In 1790, on a long, narrow site in eastern Paris directly across from the Bastille, the playwright Caron Beaumarchais built an elaborate *hôtel* that surpassed in grandeur most of those of the aristocracy he had so relentlessly mocked in his plays. Properly speaking, however, Beaumarchais's estate was not a *hôtel* at all, but an apartment house, with a screen of shops and rental apartments on the street side facing the Bastille. This arrangement spared an artistic temperament daily exposure to the remainders of the Bastille and provided continual financial support for the poet's own quarters. The architect, Paul-Guillaume Lemoine, "le Romain," arranged Beaumarchais's apartment in a semicircle facing a long romantic garden designed by Bélanger, which bore the inscription: "This little garden was planted in the first year of liberty."[44] A circular colonnade completed the figure of the building on the lower level and thereby formed a continuous terrace off the main rooms of the *bel étage*. From the oval *porte-cochère* on the lower level, a circular stair led to a rectangular *antichambre* above, and through this to the domed *salon* on the central axis of the garden. This *salon* was the center of Beaumarchais's little world, analogous to the king's bedroom at Versailles, and was the setting for Beaumarchais's famous receptions and readings.[45] Its dominant position also enabled him to contemplate the garden—and man, nature, and revolution.

An example of the Neoclassical apartment type, and one response to the problem of housing for people of modest means, was a building Bélanger created in 1788. Here three small houses were designed to appear as one large one. The regular platonic volumes of the later *hôtels* were more readily combinable than the early irregular ones, and they lent themselves to endless possibilities of replication. In this building the three houses are joined by party walls. The two end ones are the three-bay type, similar to the Pavillon de Bagatelle, but the round *salon* of the Bagatelle becomes a court in the apartment building. The center house is a five-bay type similar to Brongniart's Hôtel de Monaco. The center house contains two apartments, each connected by narrow walkways to small, separate terraces and stepped gardens over the stables.

That the Neoclassical *hôtels* and the *folies*—the country pleasure pavilions of the very rich—should lend themselves so readily to the cause of mass housing is ironic. Bélanger's apartment building also suggests another prototype for housing, one that, unlike the Hôtel Beaumarchais, is fundamentally additive rather than reductive.

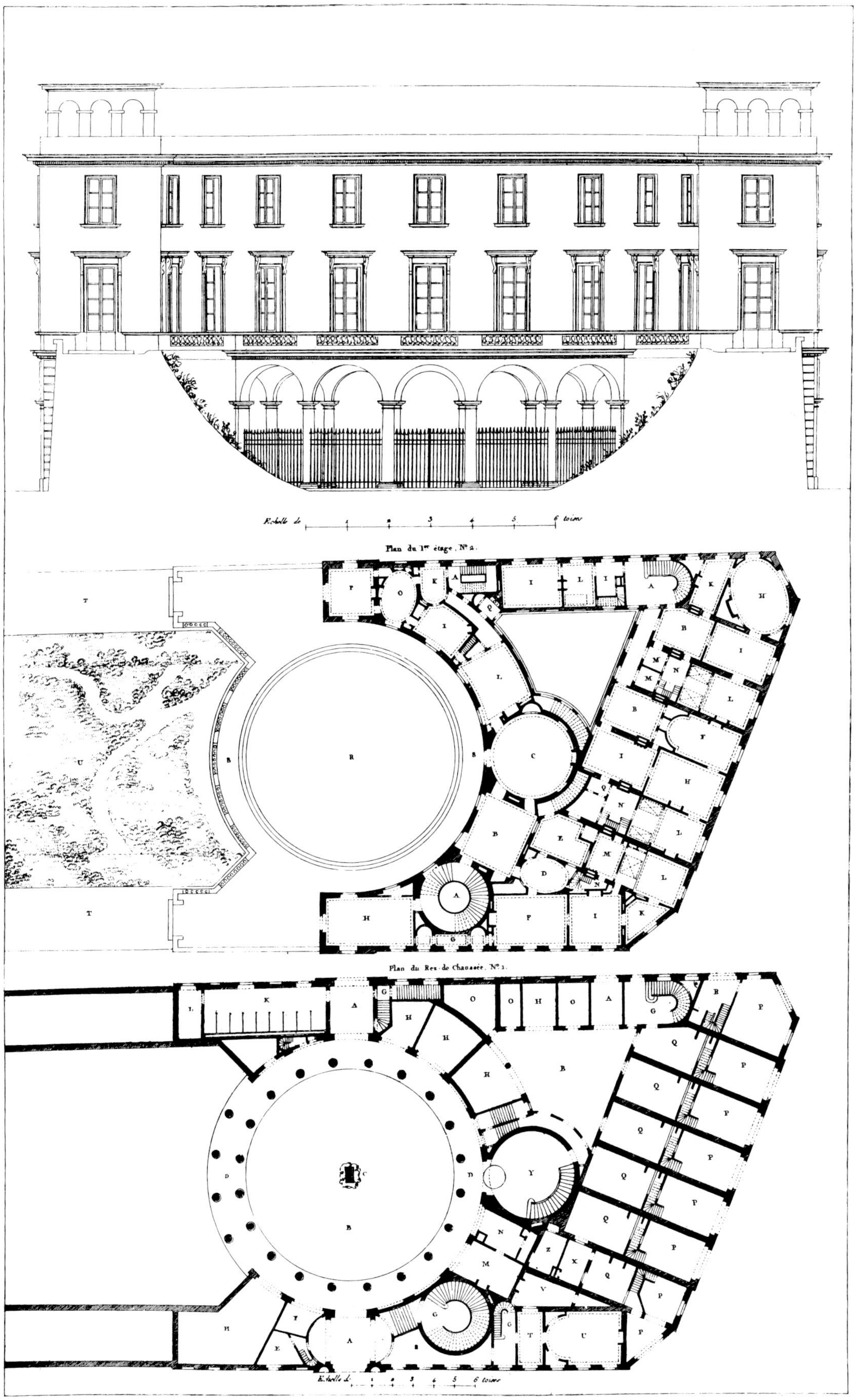

264
Hôtel Beaumarchais, plans and section, Paul-Guillaume Lemoine, 1790.

Ground floor:
A. entry
B. court
C. statue of gladiator
D. gallery
E. porter
F. storage
G. stair
H. carriages
I. garden
K. stables
L. harness room
M. work room
N. *dépendance*
O. storage
P. shop
Q. back room of shop
R. entry to shop
S. *dégagement*
T. *antichambre*
U. salon
V. kitchen
X. small court
Y. dining (stair to mezzanine)
Z. storage

Upper floor:
A. stair
B. *antichambre*
C. *salon de compagnie*
D. second *antichambre*
E. office
F. dining
G. *dégagement*
H. salon
I. cabinet
K. dressing
L. *chambre à coucher*
M. *arrière cabinet*
N. private stair
O. library
P. reading room
Q. toilet
R. court
S. terrace
T. pergola terrace
U. English garden

180 Private Icons: The Neoclassical Hôtel

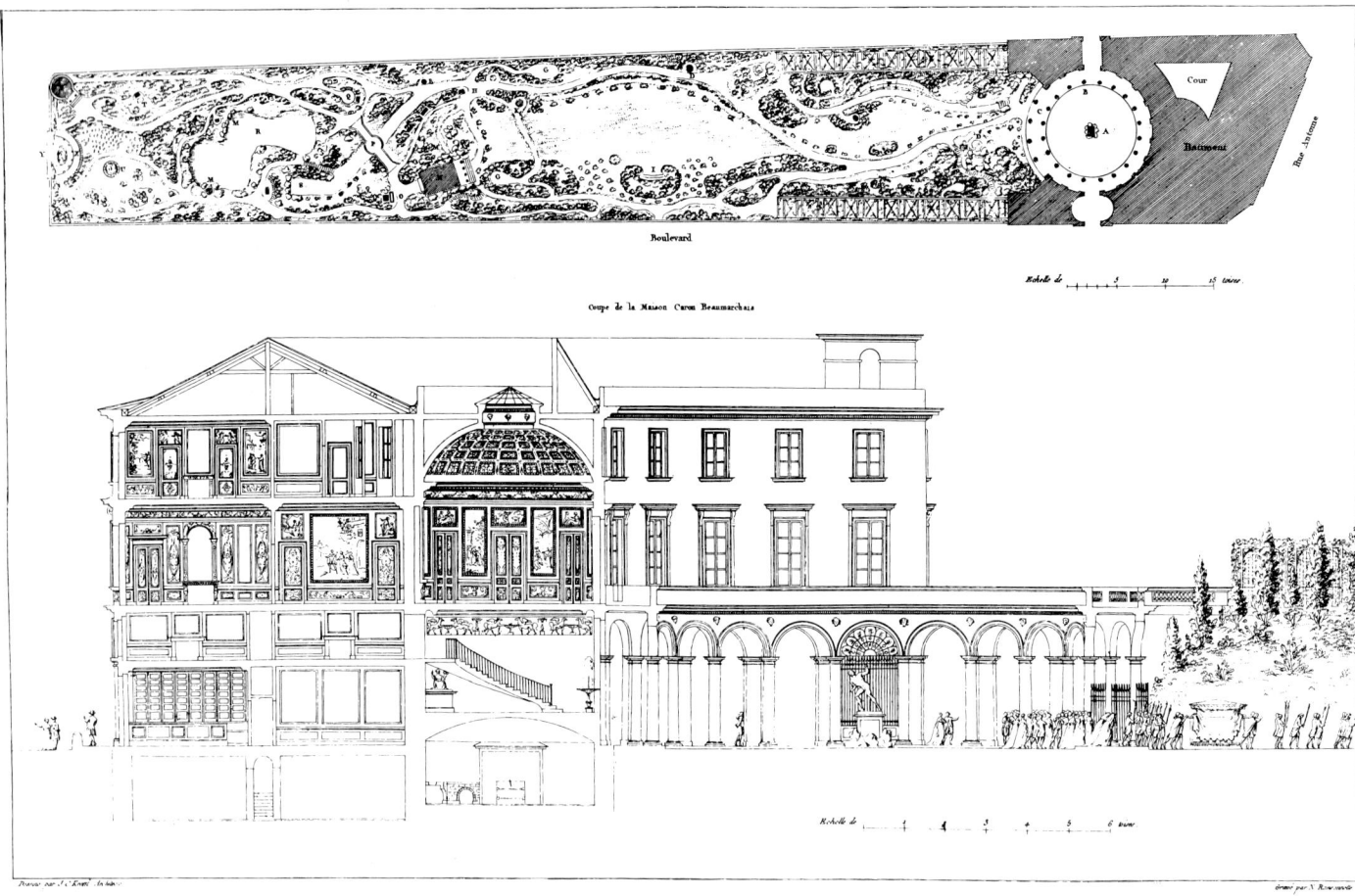

265
Hôtel Beaumarchais, section and site plan

266
Hôtel Beaumarchais, garden, François-Joseph Bélanger, 1790

181   The Nineteenth Century

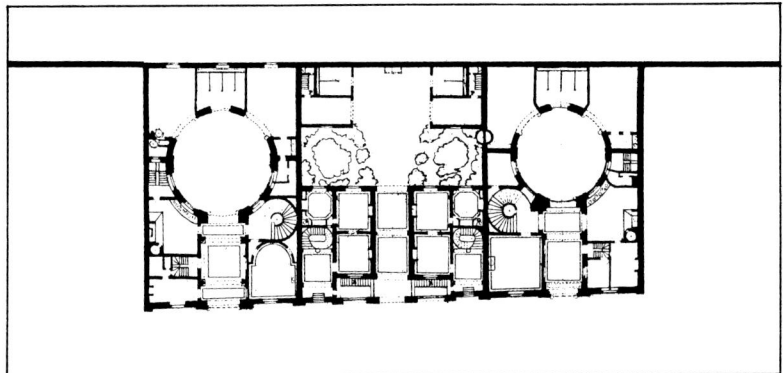

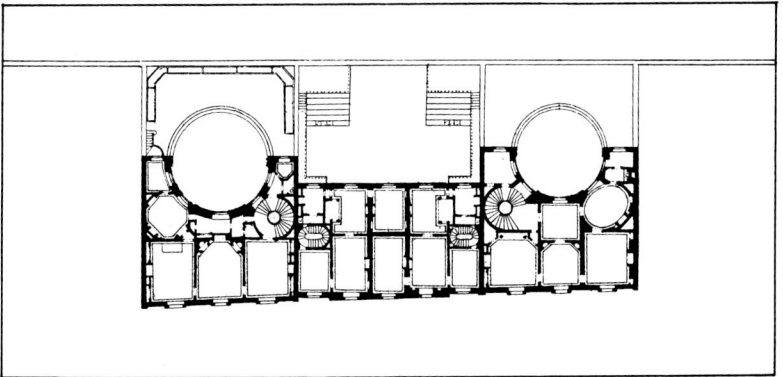

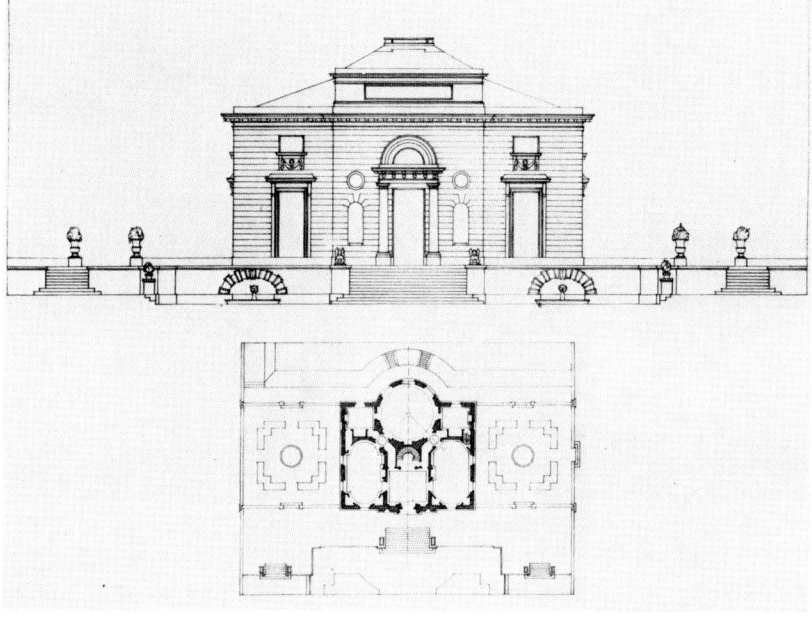

268
Pavillon de Bagatelle
(original state), plan and
elevation, François-
Joseph Bélanger, 1777

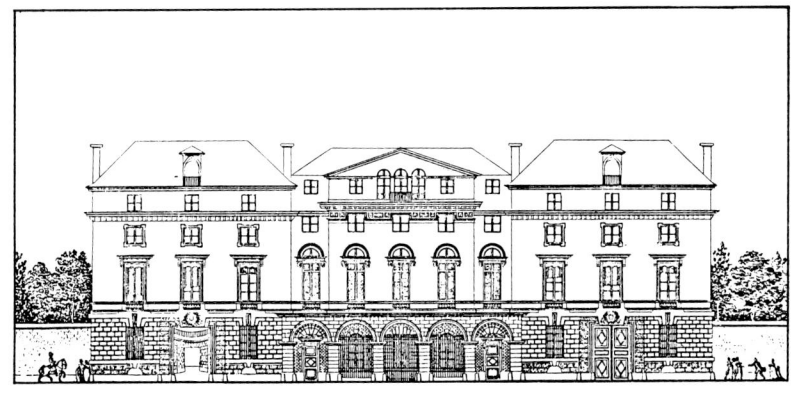

267
Three houses, plans and
elevation, François-
Joseph Bélanger, 1788

During the early decades of the nineteenth century, the Neoclassical *hôtel* type formed the basis for the development of several new districts in Paris. Hélène Lipstadt, in as yet unpublished research, calls attention to this aspect of Parisian urbanism, which for too long has been obscured by fascination with the development of the *galeries*. The formation of these small *quartiers*—usually organized around the idea of private streets[46]—in fact parallels the development of the *galerie* and the unified street. By 1840, however, the pressures of urban growth and the prominence of the bourgeoisie forced the apartment house, the *maison à loyer*, to the foreground. As an instrument of the urbanism of Haussmann and Napoléon III, the apartment house was better served by the principles of the urban, Baroque *hôtel* than by the suburban characteristics of the Neoclassical type.

The most important source for the principles of this building type at mid-century was César Daly's architectural journal the *Revue générale de l'architecture et des travaux publics* (1839–88). For over twenty years, Daly's journal supported Haussmannian urbanism by publishing articles on apartment house design, although among theorists—including Daly himself—the apartment house was not considered an ideal form of housing.[47] Theorists from Blondel to Durand and Viollet-le-Duc shared a disdain for the *maison à loyer*; it was regarded as at best an economic necessity and at worst, uncivilized.[48]

By 1864 Daly's earlier enthusiasm for the *maison à loyer*—the "result of a complete revolution" in domestic architecture—had changed to great reservation. His objections were primarily stylistic and social and centered on the repetitious and "banal" anonymity of the building type rather than the internal planning system. His reservations about the inhabitants and the appearance of the bourgeois apartment house are at the core of his *Architecture privée sous Napoléon III*, in which he illustrates not only the *maison à loyer*, but also the *hôtel moderne* and the detached *villa*.

For Daly, the *hôtel*, unlike the *maison à loyer*, was all physiognomy. Moreover, it had a sophisticated plan. As a home for an extended family, it could not only override the social association with the *hôtel* of the *ancien régime*, but also provide an ideal model for an intermediate housing type in the Fourierist system, halfway between the private house and the *phalanstère*. It should be emphasized that the *hôtel* referred to by Daly was the freestanding Neoclassical *hôtel*, not the urban party-wall type. Thus the extended family *hôtel* had a capacity for "expression" and carried the social implications of progressive "community," even if limited to branches of the same family.

Of the three dwelling types, Daly considered only the *villa* an ideal residence for the *bourgeoisie*. Inspired by the English, this picturesque descendant of the Roman country house was the perfect expression of a new suburban society. Free from the constraints of symmetry and anonymity, the *villa*—such as that by J. M. Duc at Croissy—was, as Lipstadt points out, "the very antithesis of the primitive hut: 'the House of the savage is the shadow; the House of Croissy, the light.'"[49] This single-family house in the suburbs was as anti-urban as it was anticlassical, for in addition to the differences in social connotations, there are crucial formal differences between the Neoclassical *hôtel* and the picturesque *villa*. Although both types were detached blocks, the Neoclassical *hôtel* still acknowledged the classical conventions of frontality, hierarchical sequence of space, and external symmetry—all of which made it a compatible urban form despite its suburban tendencies. Also, like the Bagatelle, the regular perimeter of the Neoclassic *hôtel* allowed for replication and recombination into larger organizations, whereas the external idiosyncracies of the picturesque *villa*, however expressive, prevented any such reinterpretation, thereby staunchly preserving its unitary status.

The point is that nineteenth-century architects and urbanists made great attempts to rationalize the traditional elements of street and square[50] and to extend the benefits of the city to a new class of society via the urban apartment house. But this renewed spatial city never completely obscured the dichotomy between it and the Enlightenment garden city—the city of private icons—spawned in the eighteenth century. Nor did it obscure the visions of social utopia of Fourier and others. Public space was implicitly traded for the private object somewhere near the middle of the eighteenth century, and if this was the beginning of the end of the *res publica*, then it was also surely the beginning of the long but steady rise to power of the *res privata*. All that was necessary to make one unified architectural and urban form system was to effect an inversion of interior space analogous to the eighteenth-century inversion of urban space. This would have to wait for Le Corbusier and the first decades of the twentieth century.

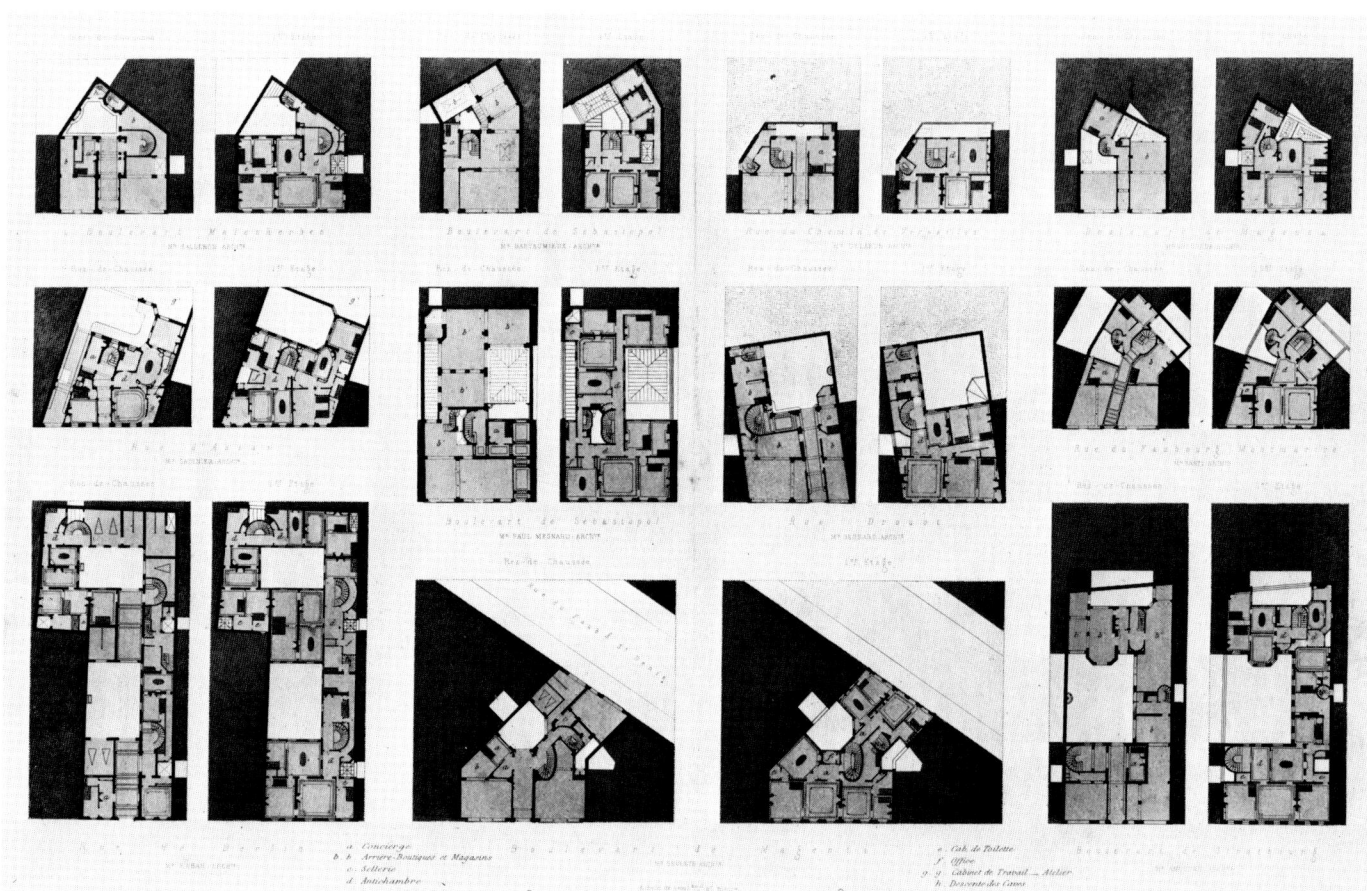

269
Apartment house plans, César Daly's second *parallèle* of the Second Order

270
Apartment house of the Second Order, elevation, Amoudru

271
Hôtel de Mr L. Fould, site plan, Henri Labrouste, 1850

272
Hôtel de Mr L. Fould

273
Croissy, The Villa of Light, perspective, J. M. Duc

274
Hôtel for a painter, plans, A. Jal (architect) and Jollivet (painter), 1858

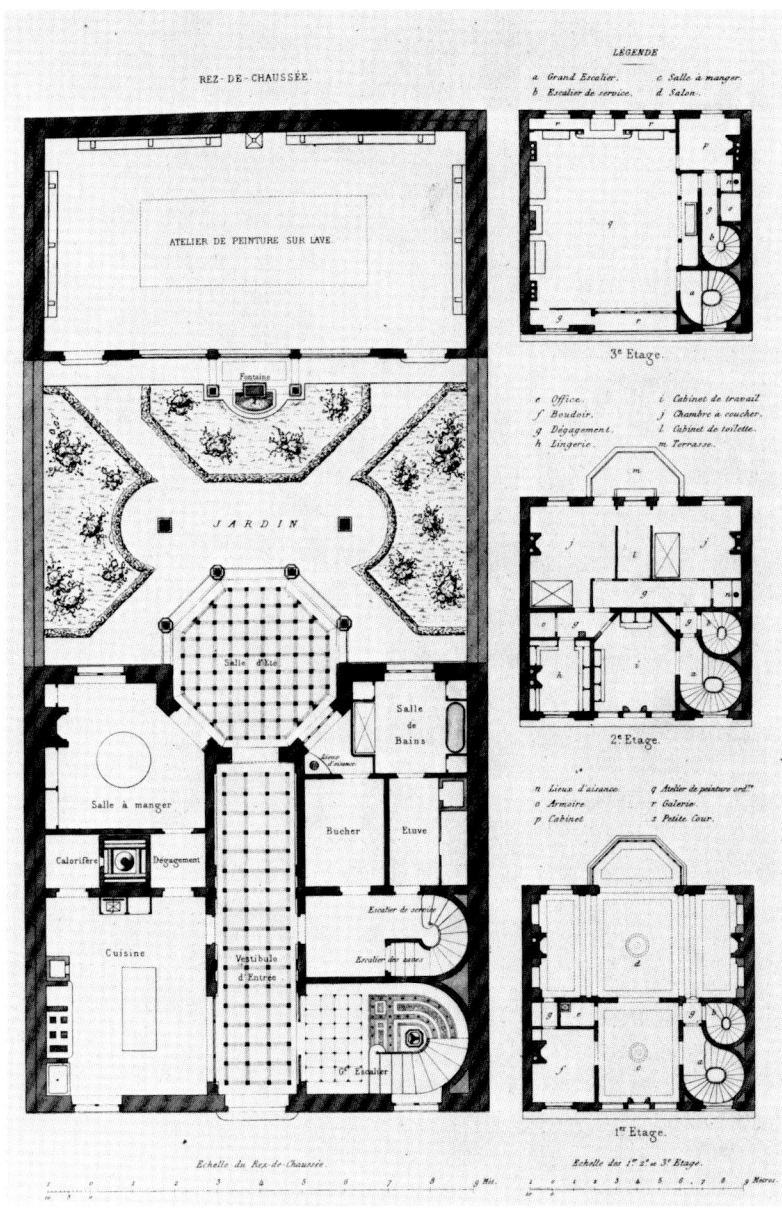

275
Hôtel for a painter, section

276
Hôtel for a painter, elevation

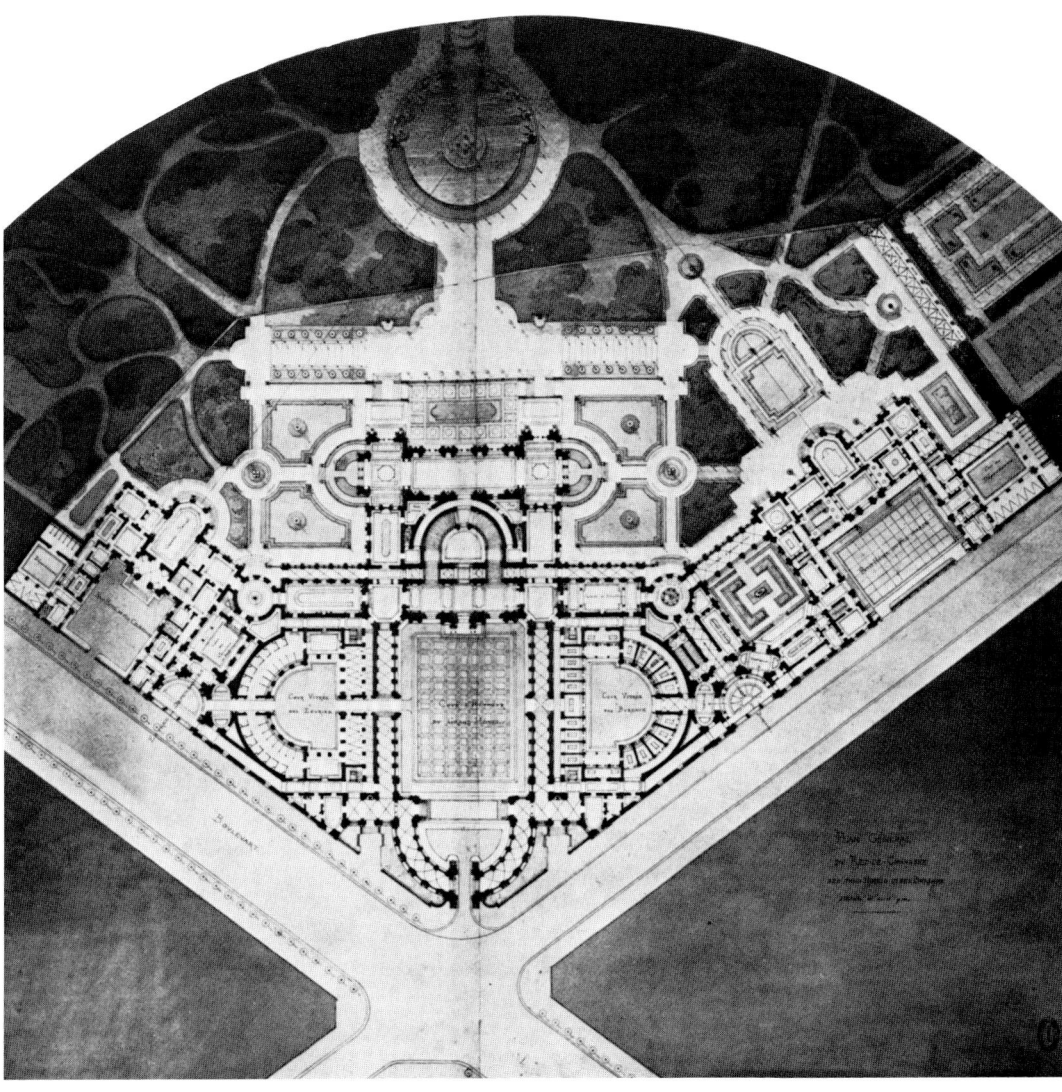

277
Hôtel for a rich banker, 1er Grand Prix, plan, Jean-Louis Pascal, 1866. A *hôtel* on an irregular urban site was a unique combination for nineteenth-century Beaux-Arts competitions.

278
Hôtel for a rich banker, 1er Grand Prix, elevation and section

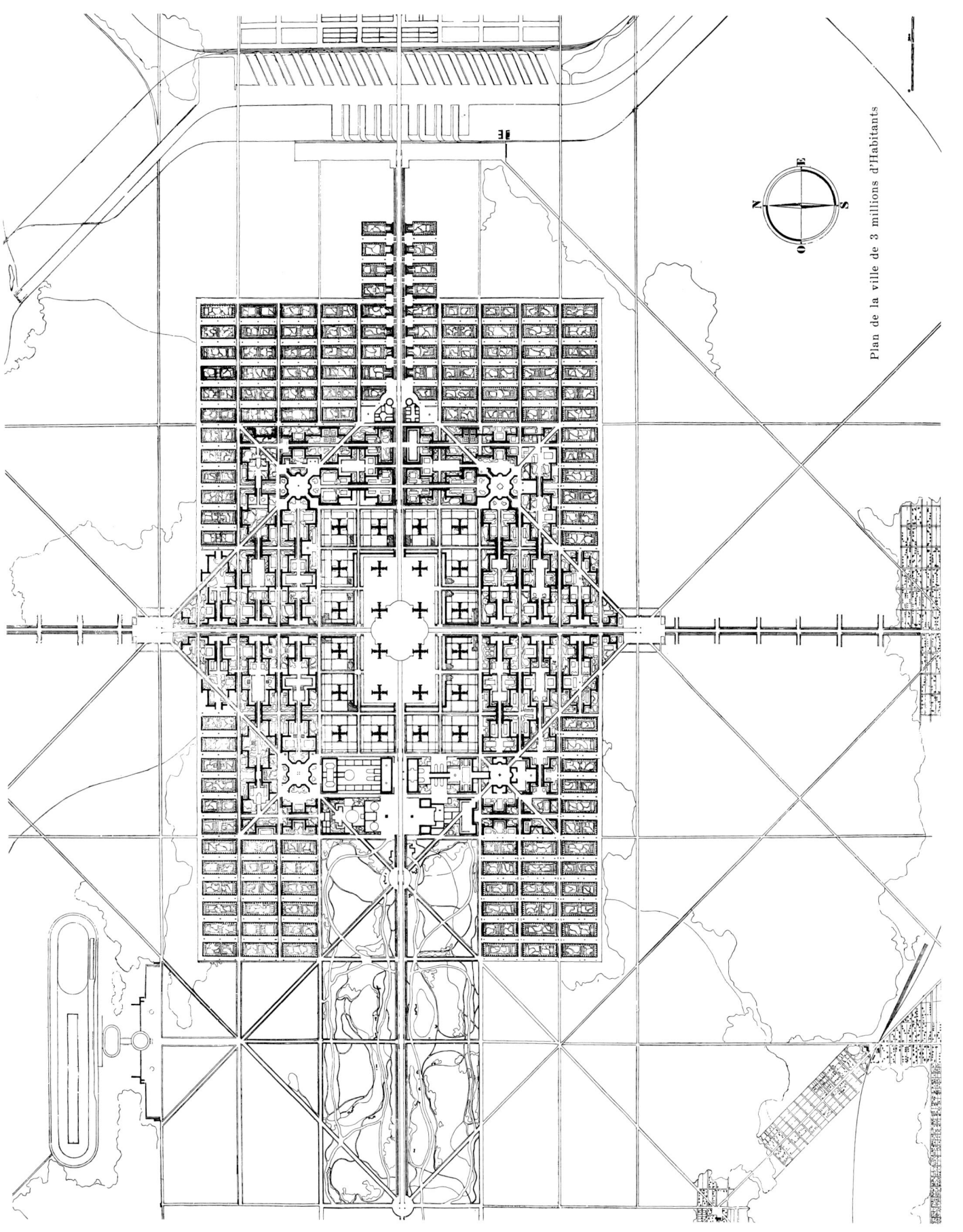

279
Ville contemporaine, plan, Le Corbusier, 1922

280
Dom-ino frame, Le Corbusier, 1914

6 Le Corbusier and the City of Modern Architecture

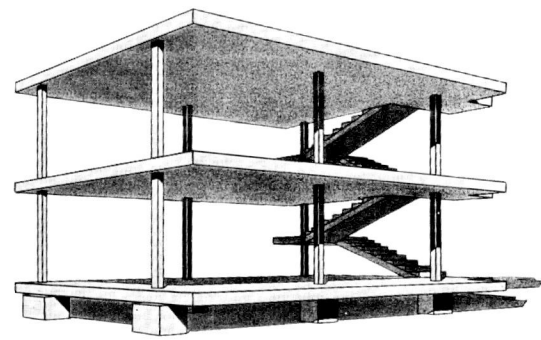

For years the shock of abstraction, assisted by carefully orchestrated polemics, obscured the conventional underpinnings of modernism and accentuated its invention. Now, however, it is evident that although modernism as a style was revolutionary, as a set of principles it was evolutionary. In architecture, for example, we can see that the utilitarian tradition represented by Hannes Meyer and the humanist tradition represented by Le Corbusier[1] share a common ancestry deeply rooted in the eighteenth century. In addition, Le Corbusier was also the eager beneficiary of an obvious formal legacy, despite his efforts to conceal it. This classical legacy, quite clearly French, included the typical French schism between theory and practice, between public architecture and domestic architecture. Le Corbusier thus appears as a sort of caricature of the eighteenth-century French tradition—a latter-day Ledoux, but with global impact.

Like his eighteenth-century counterparts, Le Corbusier was involved with ideal or utopian urbanism, with domestic architecture, and with illustrated architectural books, both treatises and handbooks. An important difference between him and his French predecessors, however, was sequence or timing. Ledoux outlined his agenda for the future near the end of his life and published it just before his death; Le Corbusier established his agenda rather early and then spent the rest of his life trying to explore and implement it. The earlier French sequence of urban intervention–a series of *hôtels*–publication was reversed: for Le Corbusier it was publication–series of houses–urban intervention. For him, theory preceded practice.

Shortly after the end of World War I, most of Le Corbusier's architectural and urban theories were in place. His *dom-ino* (1914) and *citrohan* (1920) prototypes for housing had been developed, and the first issue of the journal *L'Esprit nouveau*[2] appeared (October 1920). In 1922 his project for a *ville contemporaine de 3 millions d'habitants* was exhibited at the Salon d'Automne; in 1923 the first edition of *Vers une architecture* was published; and in 1925 the *Plan voisin*, an application of the principles of the *ville contemporaine* to the city of Paris, and the project for the *ville contemporaine* itself were both exhibited in the rotunda attached to the *Pavillon de l'Esprit Nouveau* (the *immeubles-villas* version of the *dom-ino* frame) at the Paris *Exposition des arts décoratifs*. Thus within five years, Le Corbusier outlined his architectural and urban theories, illustrated their application, and began to publicize them.

The first volume of his *Oeuvre complète*, covering the period 1910–29, illustrates a series of houses—some built, some projects—in which he explored the principles of the "New Architecture." In addition, there were several large projects, including the Palace of the League of Nations (1927–28), the Mundaneum (1929), and the project for the Centrosoyuz in Moscow (1929). By the early 1930s, Le Corbusier's war against the traditional street and everything that went with it was clear in both theory and practice. His project for the Palace of the Soviets in Moscow (1931) and the Salvation Army building in Paris (1932) both exhibit an anticonventional attitude toward the street; and the principles of modern town planning that were adopted at the fourth CIAM conference in Athens (1933) on the "rational city" were embedded in Le Corbusier's update of the *ville contemporaine*, *La Ville radieuse*, published in 1935.[3] A continuous series of town-planning interventions were proposed during the 1930s and after World War II, but none were built. In fact, it was not until after the war that even a fragment of the *ville radieuse* was constructed—as the *Unité d'habitation*. Finally, the only built example of Le Corbusier's town-planning theories—at least of any appreciable size—is the new capital city of the Punjab, Chandigarh, begun in 1950 and continued until his death in 1965. But it was not this new town, built near the twilight of his career, which revised urbanism; it was his theories and his projects. By the 1960s, the principles and models proposed by Le Corbusier had been accepted around the world, permeating the zoning codes and building practices of cities as diverse as Bogotá and New York. It was also during the 1960s that both the eighteenth-century roots and the anti-urban implications of the modern city began to be apparent.

The single most cogent and compelling image of the new utopia—the city of modern architecture—was, and still is, Le Corbusier's *ville radieuse*, which reconfirmed the formal and social tendencies that had been so revolutionary in the eighteenth century. The decadent, outmoded system of the traditional city was to be replaced by a "new" architecture and urbanism that promised freedom, honesty, and openly articulated elements. The ground plane and all space would belong to society and would serve the common good rather than the privileged few. In the new social state, rationalism would prevail, and everyone would have a salubrious and economical dwelling in a public garden, the street having been banished to the history books.[4] The city of platonic voids was to be replaced by the city of platonic solids; the city which contained parks was to become the city in the park;[5] the elements of the new city—the buildings, circulation systems, recreational system—were separated, articulated, and categorized into a rational and hierarchical system of types which would have made Diderot and d'Alembert smugly content; and the new city promised to be more healthy, socially as well as physically.[6]

The building blocks of the new city and the basis for the new architecture were, for Le Corbusier, the *citrohan* and *dom-ino* prototypes. Like Neoclassical pavilions, both could be used as isolated blocks or replicated vertically and horizontally. In both, the structural system facilitated a new freedom of planning and thus promoted a new vision of space. The *citrohan* prototype employed a directional plan and structural system, in which, ideally, the space formed by two parallel bearing walls could be spanned by simple framing members. Double-height spaces could be easily formed by omitting portions of the floor system, and since the "ends" were not load bearing, they could be walls of glass. Here the emphasis was on the vertical plane, and there were obvious references to primitive or vernacular architecture. This prototype, similar to the narrow frontage units of Du Cerceau and Le Muet, led directly to the units of the Marseille block and to the Jaoul and Sarabhai houses.

The *dom-ino* prototype emphasized the horizontal planes rather than the verticals, and its references were technological rather than vernacular. The columnar frame allowed a nondirectional plan in which the "sides" as well as the "front" and "back" could be open. The space formed by the horizontal planes of floor and ceiling could then be arranged at will. This prototype, like a small Neoclassical *hôtel particulier*, produced the Villa Savoye, the villa at Garches, and the Assembly Building at Chandigarh.

The *dom-ino* frame was crucial to the new architecture and urbanism. As the twentieth-century version of the primitive hut and the principal instrument of the *ville radieuse*, it was intended to liberate society as well as architects from the constraints, deceit, and closure of a centuries-old system by allowing the continuity of space not only around, but also through and under the building. In short, it was to be the new architecture of the free plan as the *ville radieuse* was to be the new urbanism of the free society. An ideal model to be adapted to circumstances, it answered an insistent social call: "Modern life demands, and is waiting for, a new kind of plan, both for the house and for the city."[7]

Le Corbusier proposed and used the theory of the *dom-ino* frame quite early (1914), but its architectural implications are best illustrated by the diagrams of the villa at Carthage II (1929). Here all the characteristics may be seen in their pure state: the regular grid of exposed columns that contains and orders the idiosyncratic elements of the free plan, the dominance of the horizontal layers of space, and the virtual elimination of the facade. The villa demonstrates what Le Corbusier called "the five points of a new architecture": the *pilotis*, the roof garden, the free plan, the horizontal window, and the free facade.[8]

Carthage II, however, is unique among the early works for its visible grid of round columns. In all the other small projects between 1910 and 1929, the small number of freestanding columns is remarkable. The sense of the frame seems to come primarily from the solid and void of the fenestration and from the layering and gridding of

191 Le Corbusier and the City of Modern Architecture

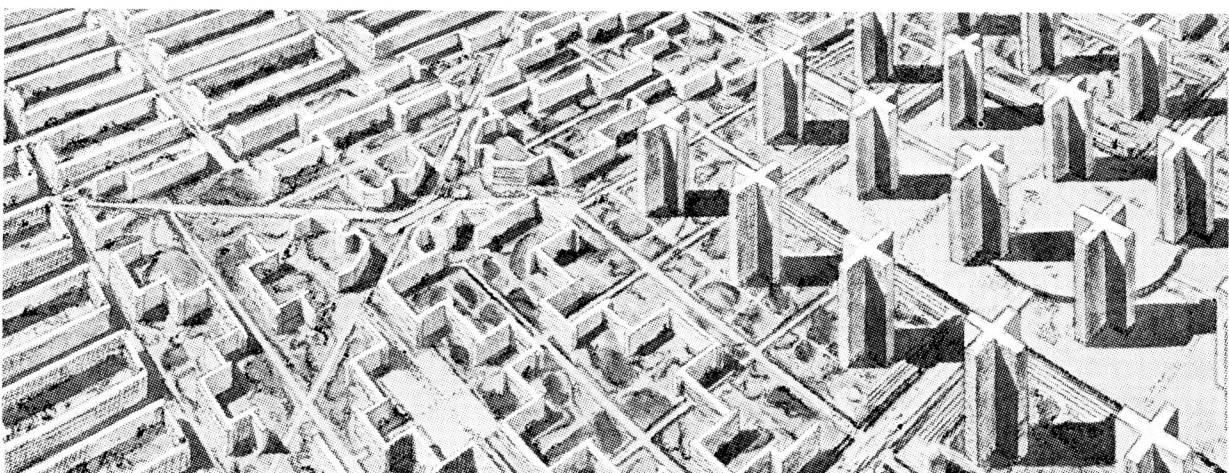

 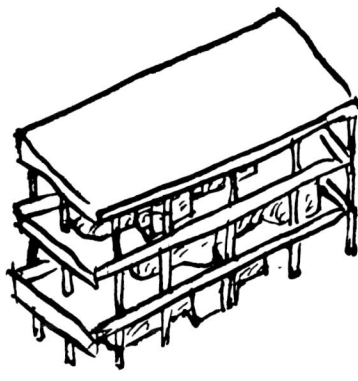

281
Manhattan and the *ville contemporaine*, Le Corbusier, 1922

282
Villa at Carthage II, diagrams, Le Corbusier, 1929

192 Le Corbusier and the City of Modern
Architecture

the space. Although the few freestanding round columns may play a role in the gridding, there is at least an equally strong tendency to read them, devoid of structural characteristics, as cylinders or sculptural objects inserted in a prism of space. Occasionally, they may also be used in pairs as a frame or portal or in groups of four to define a space within a space, but during this period only the large public buildings exploit the continuous grids of exposed columns that became the rule rather than the exception in Le Corbusier's later work. During the 1920s, his commissions were used as opportunities to develop the *dom-ino* and *citrohan* prototypes and to demonstrate a new vision of space. In these, Le Corbusier clearly demonstrated an uncanny knack for maintaining principles while reversing values.

The projects for the Maison de M. X. in Brussels (1929) and the Villa Meyer (1925), as examples of *citrohan* and *dom-ino*, respectively, show succinctly how Le Corbusier literally inverted interior space and gave new imagery and meaning to old principles. If the traditional plan can be seen as concave voids carved out of a solid, the new plans may be seen as convex solids inserted into a space. In the old plan, the spaces were figural and the solids served as ground. Both plans utilize the concept of *poché*, but in the traditional plan the *poché* is that which is left over after the spaces are particularized; in Le Corbusier's plans it is the *poché* itself that is particularized—the space is only defined, not enclosed. The rooms of the Hôtel d'Orliane have identity and closure, and it is easy to imagine them existing out of context, independent and free of the *poché* that shapes them. Conversely, it is impossible to imagine the space of Le Corbusier's plans without the solids that pressure and shape it; rather, it

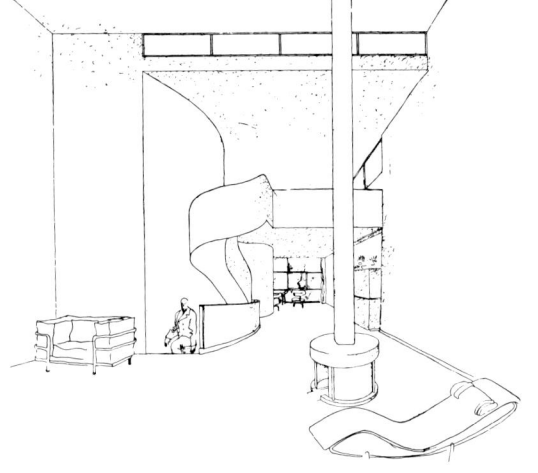

283
Brussels, Maison de M. X., perspective, Le Corbusier, 1929

284
Brussels, Maison de M. X., interior perspective

285
Brussels, Maison de M. X., plans

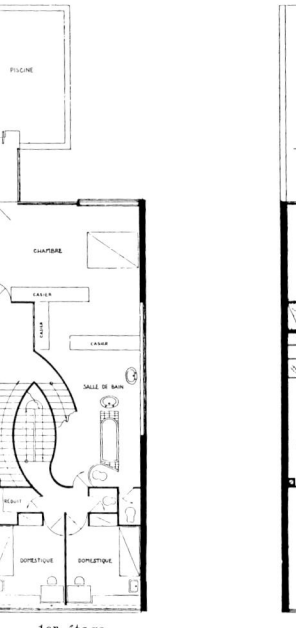 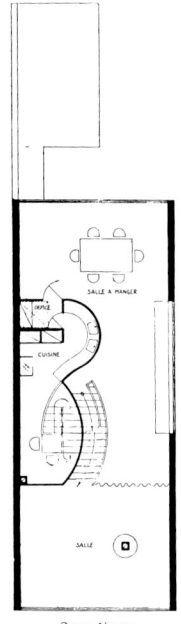 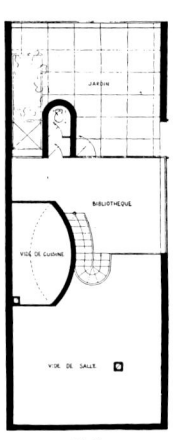

1er étage   2me étage   Toit

193 Le Corbusier and the City of Modern Architecture

286
Hôtel Dervieux, dining room, François-Joseph Bélanger, 1788

287
Villa Meyer, interior perspective, Le Corbusier, 1925

194 Le Corbusier and the City of Modern Architecture

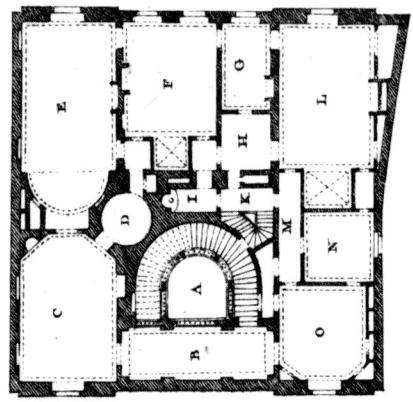
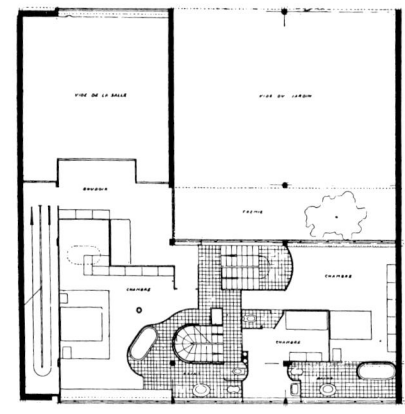
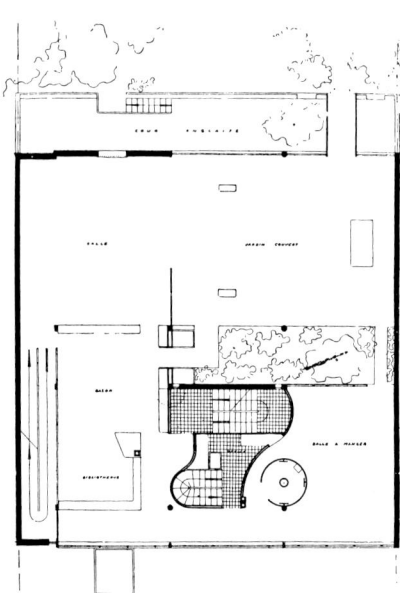
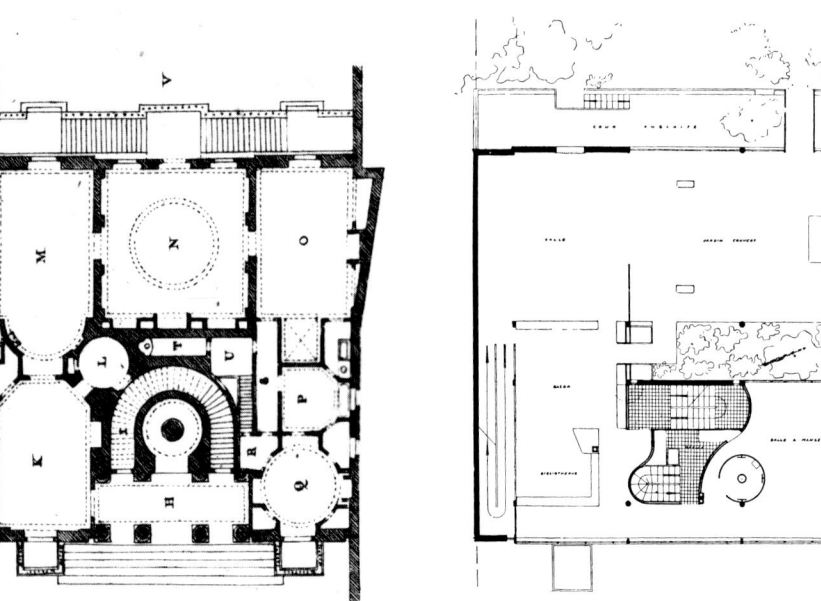

288
Hôtel d'Orliane, plans,
Pierre d'Orliane, 1789

289
Villa Meyer, plans

290
Villa Meyer, perspective
of terrace

is the solids that lend themselves to extraction and examination.

This preoccupation with freely articulated solids is first stated in Le Corbusier's project for the Villa Meyer. "The house," he says, "could be like an automobile: a simple envelope containing the organs of the plan in a free state." That "simple envelope" calls for different materials, for while "reinforced concrete would be too rough (*onéreux*) if one conserved the plan of the 'Louis' or of the Renaissance . . . in the small house it permits *the free plan:* the floors are not supported by the enclosing walls. They are free."[9] That critique becomes a curious jab at the French classical tradition when Le Corbusier notes: "A sharp observation: The [free] plan gets rid of the compromises of Classicism (the 'Louis' and the High Renaissance) to find again the spirited health of the gothic, gothic rationalism. But in new forms."[10] Pierre Patte would no doubt have approved of the *dom-ino* frame, because by eliminating the structural problems he associated with the superimposition of diverse floors, it freed the architect to "put the plan into turmoil" by using "a great number of forms, under the pretext of making the *appartement* more convenient."[11]

The inversion of the traditional interior spatial system can now be seen as the counterpart to the mid-eighteenth-century inversion of urban space; and if the *ville radieuse* represented the ultimate development of the new urban system, then the free plan was the analogous architectural condition. The free facade made it possible to directly relate and unify the inside and the outside; space could extend around, under, and through the building from horizon to horizon, providing a continuity, a unity, and a degree of total control that was unattainable by Baroque architects. In

291
Poissy, Villa Savoye, Le Corbusier, 1928–31

292
Versailles, Petit Trianon, Ange-Jacques Gabriel, begun 1762

196 Le Corbusier and the City of Modern Architecture

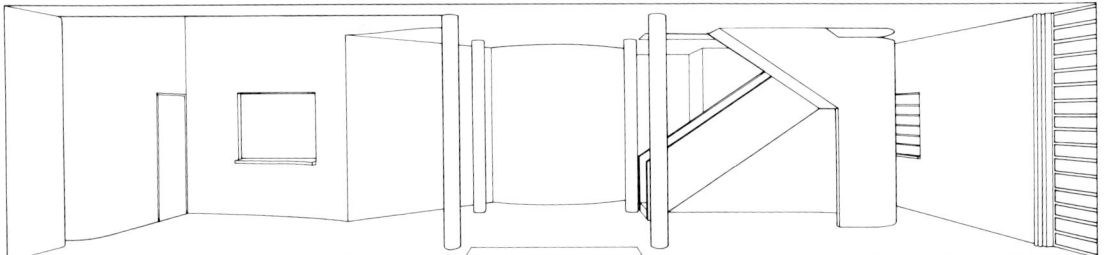

293
Ideal city square, Francesco di Giorgio (?), c. 1470

294
Ville contemporaine, perspective of the city center, Le Corbusier, 1922

295
Villa at Garches, perspective of entry hall, Le Corbusier, 1927

theory, the new system of architectural and urban space was complete.

There remains, however, the perplexing paradox of Le Corbusier the architect versus Le Corbusier the city planner, or, perhaps, the practitioner versus the theoretician. For example, the "architect–practitioner" never applied the *domino* frame literally, but always as idea.[12] The ideal building types were always deformed and qualified and never took form as freestanding buildings devoid of context. Since the domestic buildings were usually experimental prototypes that could be replicated, they tended to have perimeters that contained the interior agitation and that allowed the buildings to be modified and inserted into a variety of traditional party-wall urban conditions. The public buildings are another matter, for here the agitation is peripheral rather than central, and contextual adaptation is secondary to the building's role as a component of the *ville radieuse* and of a polemic against the street and the traditional city. Nevertheless, even buildings such as the Salvation Army, the Centrosoyuz, and the Palace of the League of Nations are, like their smaller contemporaries, intricately tuned responses to their contexts. The Salvation Army building may reject the street, but it acknowledges it. The "city planner–theoretician," however, was less accommodating: application of the forms and principles of the *ville radieuse* was literal and total, as in the *plan voisin* for Paris and the many urban proposals of the 1930s. The new city was to replace the old.

The calculated power of Le Corbusier's polemic has long obscured the allegiance of his practice to convention and tradition. Only recently have time and dissatisfaction with his urban theories allowed us to see his practice in new (old) ways. One of these is the connection between his domestic work and the French tradition. In spite of his stated aversion to the architecture of the "Louis," Le Corbusier's own work owes as much, in principle, to the French *hôtel* as to any other source. That the French *hôtel* is a precursor of his work can be seen by examining several of his domestic projects in terms of *parti, poché*, local symmetry, recentering, and hierarchical sequence.

In 1923, the same year in which the first edition of *Vers une architecture* was published, Le Corbusier built *deux hôtels particuliers à Auteuil:* the Maisons La Roche–Albert Jeanneret. This was the largest of Le Corbusier's built compositions to date, and its pedigree becomes clear when the plan of the first scheme is compared with the plan of the Hôtel de Biron illustrated by Le Corbusier in *La Ville radieuse*.[13] The *parti* of the building is clearly derived from the early *hôtel*, with the exception that the forecourt terminates in a convex curve rather than in a concave curve on the street side. The first scheme was more literal than the final version in that it was U-shaped rather than L-shaped and had both entrances in the far corners of the court. The curious corner entry remains in the final scheme, but at least there are not two of them, which might have been as confusing as the dual entrances in some of the early *hôtels*.

Here, despite the relatively modest size in comparison to a grand Rococo *hôtel* and despite a radically different social context from that of the *ancien régime*, Le Corbusier has continued the idea of a hierarchical sequence of public spaces—now called a *promenade architecturale*. The pretext was that the owner of the La Roche half of the house was a bachelor art collector and that his house would function as a kind of art gallery. Indeed, the name of the main room changed between the first and second schemes from *salon* to *galerie de tableaux*. Le Corbusier describes the house as an "architectural spectacle with a sequence or itinerary of perspectives of the exterior where one rediscovers the architectural unity of the composition."[14] We can only assume that after an initial shock caused by the building's abstraction, Le Camus de Mézières would be extraordinarily pleased by the building's harmonious proportions, its well-modulated sequence, the manner in which the exterior "prepares the spirit" for the interior, and finally the "intimate" relationship between the two.

If the Maisons La Roche–Jeanneret were inspired by the Rococo *hôtel*, the Maison Cook *(petit hôtel particulier à Boulogne-sur-Seine*, 1926) and the Maison Plainex (1927) are like modern updates of the Neoclassical *hôtel*. The Maison Plainex, for example, might be compared to Ledoux's Hôtel Guimard in that the strongly centralized street facade belies the asymmetrical main floor behind. The central projected bay that defines the overlap of the two adjacent buildings is reflected in the main floor plan only by two freestanding columns in the living room. The rest of the plan is asymmetrically organized, and, as in the Hôtel Guimard, the main space runs parallel to the facade rather than perpendicular, as implied by the centralized street facade. The services are articulated as convex solids, which, with the stair, can be read as an asymmetrical figure that intrudes upon the plan without heeding the suggestions of the facade. Likewise, the rear facade operates independently of the plan and resolves the slight splay of the site by recentering; that is, like many French *hôtels*, it is cen-

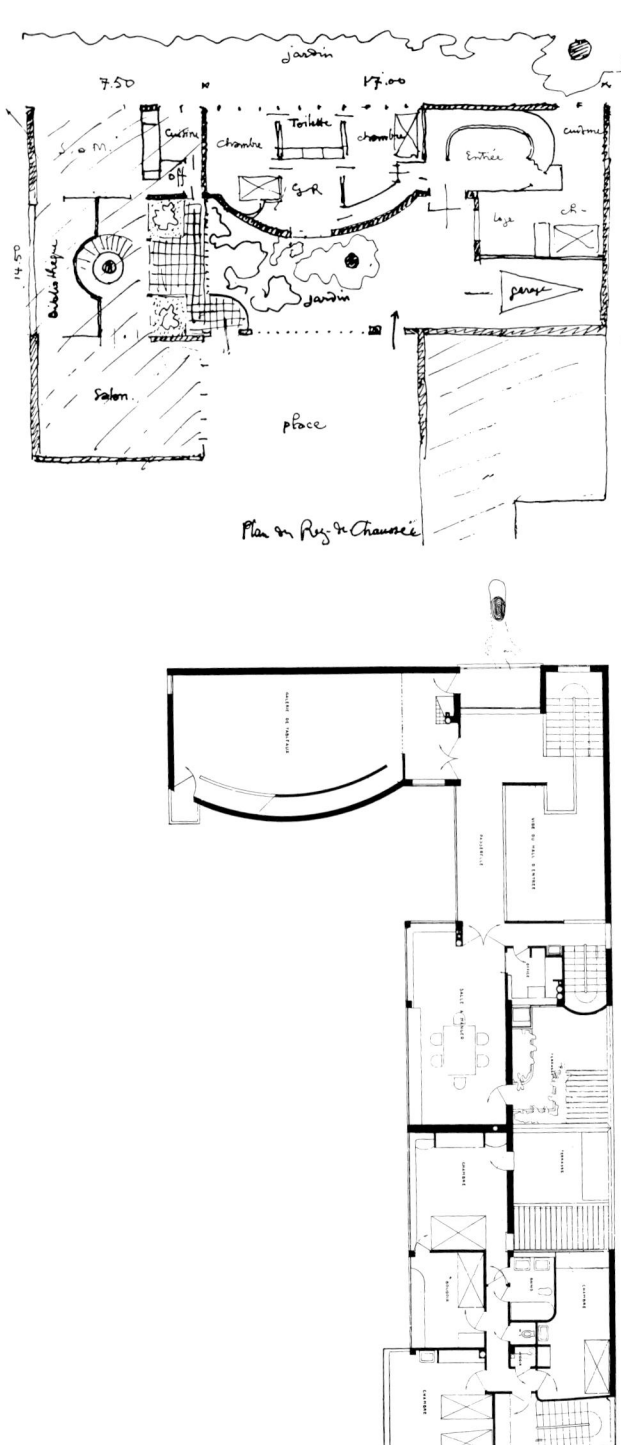
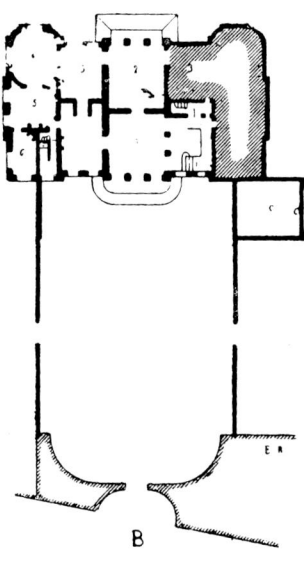

296
Maisons La Roche-Jeanneret, ground floor plan of first scheme, Le Corbusier, 1923

297
Maisons La Roche-Jeanneret, second floor plan of final scheme

298
Hôtel de Biron, plan. From *La Ville radieuse*. Le Corbusier's caption reads: "Faced with contemporary problems, traditional methods are insufficient."

199 Le Corbusier and the City of Modern Architecture

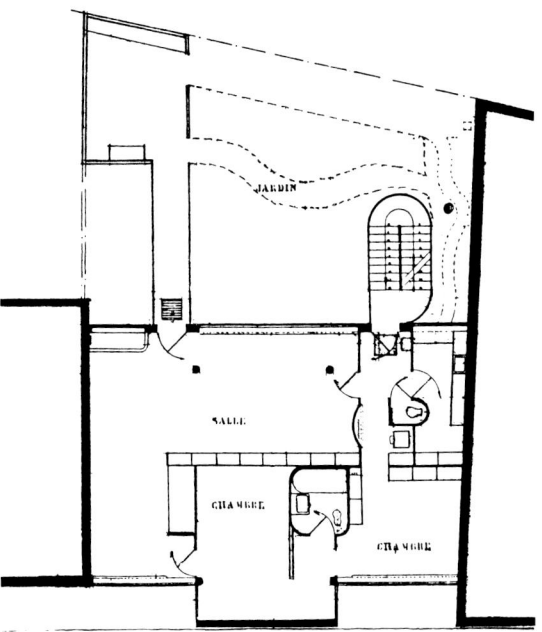

299
Maison Plainex, first floor plan, Le Corbusier, 1927

300
Maison Plainex, facade

301
Villa at Garches, view from entry gate, Le Corbusier, 1927

tered on the garden rather than the major divisions of the plan or the front facade. Admittedly, not much claim can be made for an elegant sequence of space, or *promenade architecturale*, when one is obliged to enter the building through the garage and then go outside again in order to ascend to the main floor, but the facade does provide a memorable urban image.

Le Corbusier's majestic villa at Garches, constructed for M. de Monzie in 1927 and then sold to Gertrude Stein, is not only his masterpiece of the 1920s, but it is also one of a few great houses of the twentieth century. This now familiar icon was elegantly related to Palladio, and therefore, implicitly, to the Venetian plan type, by Colin Rowe in "Mathematics of the Ideal Villa" (1947); but Rowe also suggests a connection to the French *hôtel*:

> For his plans he seems to find at least one source in those ideals of *convenance* and *commodité* displayed in the ingenious planning of the Rococo *hôtel*, the background of a social life at once more amplified and intimate. The French, until recently, possessed an unbroken tradition of this sort of planning; and, therefore, one may often discover in a Beaux-Arts utilization of an irregular site, elements which if they had not preceded Le Corbusier might seem to be curiously reminiscent of his own highly suave vestibules and boudoirs.[15]

Nowhere are these ideas more elaborately developed than in the villa at Garches. Although the building owes a great debt to Venice, particularly in its facades (see, for example, the Ca Farsetti and Ca Loredan on the Grand Canal), it is typical of the suburban Neoclassical French *hôtels*, such as Brongniart's Hôtel de Monaco, in which a detached rectangular block sits well back on a narrow site and has a semipublic forecourt in

200   Le Corbusier and the City of Modern
      Architecture

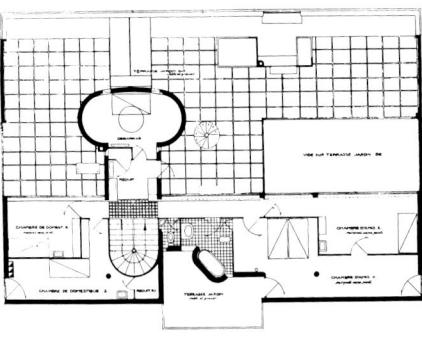

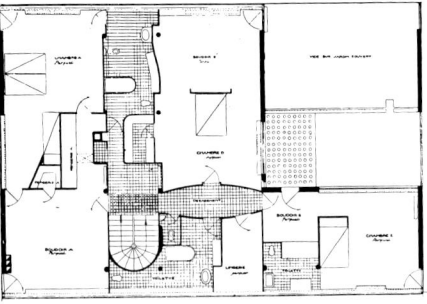

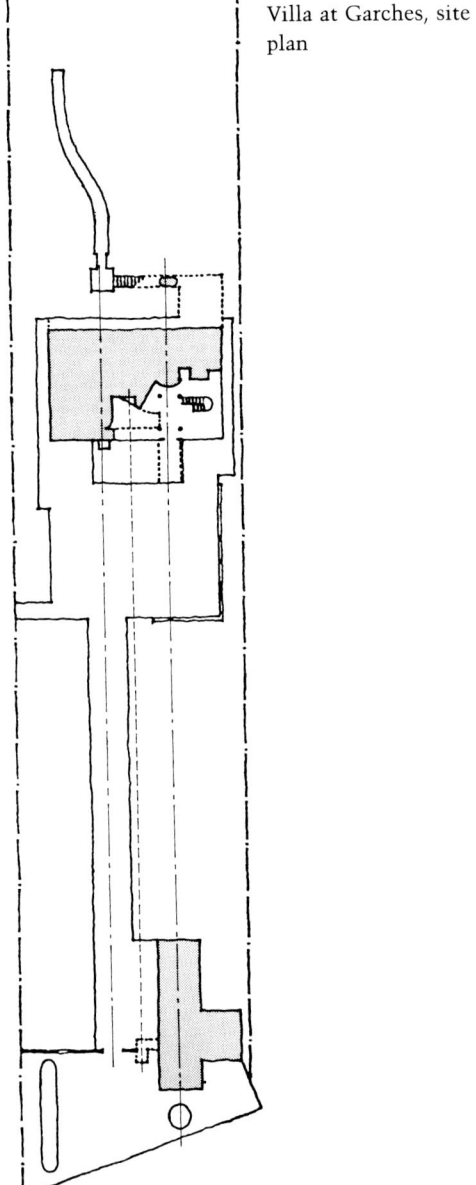

302
Villa at Garches, site plan

303
Villa at Garches, plans

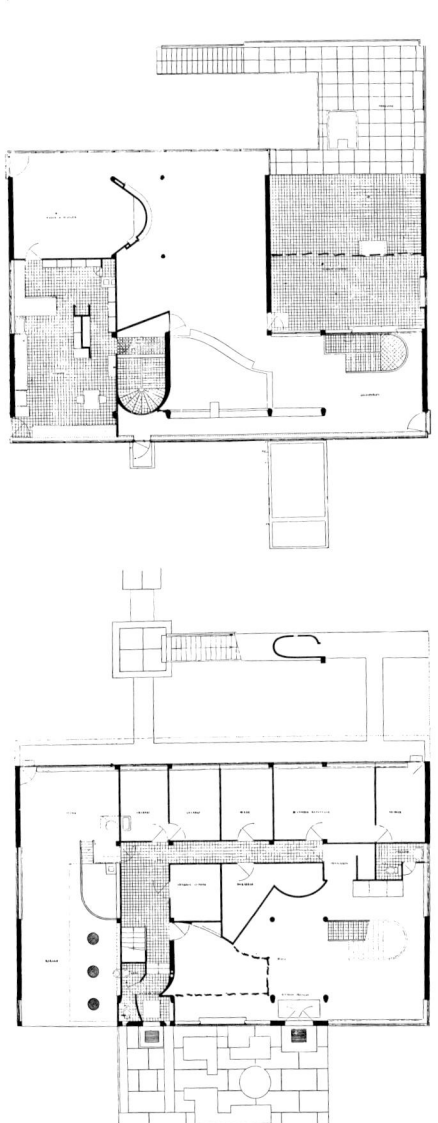

street to street through the site, and the unique elements are articulated as figural solids displayed against the slab. Free space replaces the *poché* of Perronne's plan. Perronne's plan seems generated primarily from the outside, with adjustments made to the inside, whereas Le Corbusier's plan appears to be generated from the inside, and adjustments are made to the exterior. Perronne's building responds to the convention of enclosing the space of the street; Le Corbusier's resists the convention of the street and is a fragment of an ideal building imposed on the site.

Similar comparisons could also be made between Perronne's traditional plan and other large projects of Le Corbusier, such as the Swiss Pavilion or the Centrosoyuz. For example, if one imagines the Perronne plan to be cracked open, the back zone of rooms rotated ninety degrees, and the services rationalized, then the inverse relation to Centrosoyuz is readily apparent. There are of course other differences between the traditional plan of Perronne and those of Le Corbusier—the most obvious being the frame and its exploitation—but the profile of the new urban system is the critical issue delineated by these projects. The exposure of the rationalized and articulated components of Centrosoyuz is surely intended to produce an urban landscape that is analogous to the interior landscapes of the domestic buildings like Villa Meyer; and if these early built projects were all contextually responsive, they were also, conceptually, the enemy of the traditional city.

In proposal after proposal, from the *plan voisin* for Paris to St. Dié and Berlin, Le Corbusier the "city planner" demonstrated the application of the *ville radieuse*. In each case, the application was more or less pure with minimal adjustment

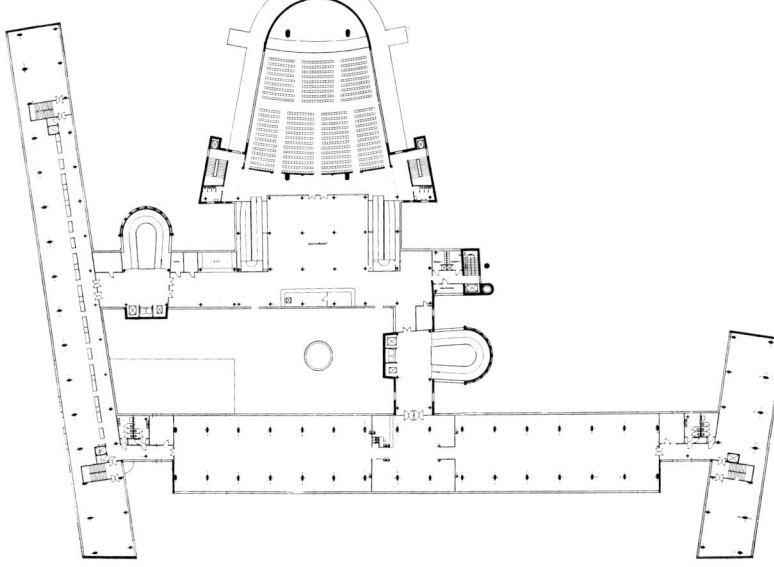

308
Moscow, Centrosoyuz, third floor plan, Le Corbusier, 1929

309
Chandigarh, assembly building, plan, Le Corbusier, begun 1953

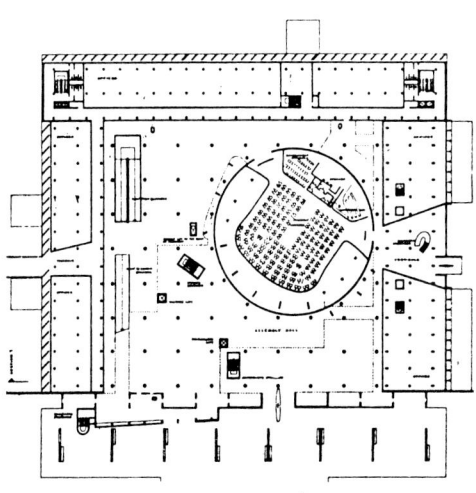

conditions. The Ozenfant studio cannot be understood without knowledge of its site, and the villa at Garches becomes much easier to understand when its site plan is reconstructed.

Le Corbusier could espouse the open plan with its emphasis on articulate solids, but the essence of his buildings is space; he could talk about buildings growing from within and design them in the reverse; and he could virtually eliminate the facade in theory and then insistently refashion it, relying on little more than pure principle. Most importantly, he could talk about total solutions, but produce individual works of architecture which were, above all, orchestrations of contradictions.

It is Le Corbusier's larger projects of the late twenties and early thirties, however, that, despite their contextual adjustments, begin to demonstrate the anti-urban implications of the new system. A comparison of the late-nineteenth-century Parisian apartment building by the architect Perronne and Le Corbusier's Salvation Army building illustrates this quite well. Both have irregular sites bounded by two streets, but the solutions are the inverse of each other. Perronne aligns the primary rooms of the apartments in vertical zones along the streets; the center part of the plan is occupied by an enclosed court or figural void; and the interstitial areas of the plan are fitted with service areas, secondary rooms, and stairs. The relationship to the Baroque *hôtel* is obvious; the difference is that there are now four separate apartments per floor and the floors repeat four or five times vertically, thus the outside zone of rooms is a kind of single-loaded slab facing the street. In the Salvation Army project, the living accommodations are organized in a freestanding, single-loaded slab that spans from

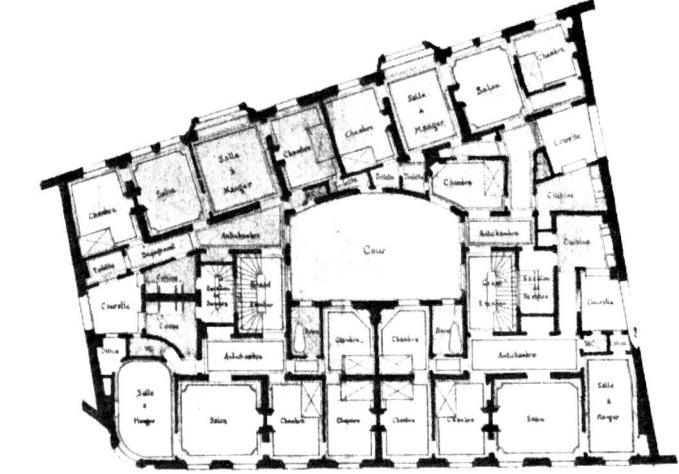

306
Paris, apartment building, Perronne, 1890s

307
Salvation Army, ground floor plan, Le Corbusier, 1930

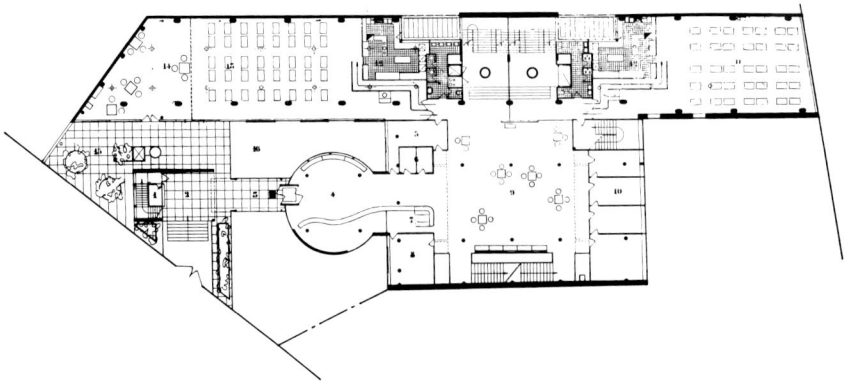

dining room behind the paired columns and convex curve. The private stair skewers the whole house and is the only connection to the bedroom floor with its "highly suave vestibules and boudoirs." The stair is contained within the *poché* of the ground floor, is expressed on the main floor, and culminates on the top floor, where the terrace overlooks the garden.

Le Corbusier's work is saturated with principles derived from traditional French architecture, but a complete analysis of the parallels is beyond the intent and scope of this work. That the French *hôtel* may be seen as both a precursor to and a critique of the free plan, however, deserves comment.

The free plan produced great spaces, but by definition it could not easily produce great rooms. Rooms need adequate closure, particularly of shape, and reasonably continuous wall surface; in the free plan, only the service spaces have these characteristics, as the public areas are residual. The traditional plan articulates the difference between spaces, while the free plan articulates the difference between objects. The consequent emphasis on spatial continuity and unity of the whole is bound to be at the expense of the identity of the part. Rooms therefore become "areas," and continually shifting relationships make a sense of place difficult to achieve. In the living room of the villa at Garches, for example, there can be no real sense of arrival but only an outward thrust toward the garden. Only the dining room and the porch have sufficient closure to establish stasis. The space of the living room is all for circulation, and even the "correct" furniture might be an intrusion.

The introduction of any incorrect image into such a space is in fact likely to be disruptive; for in spite of the supposedly conciliatory potential of the free plan, it tends to demand unrelenting consistency of image—specifically, abstract images thought to represent the future. Cubism and purism fractured familiar images into fragments that were reassembled into new and ambivalent relationships, but Le Corbusier and other architects eliminated traditional images entirely in favor of a more obtuse set of icons assembled in the new plan. Cubism offered a new vision of traditional images while the free plan offered a new vision of new images. The free plan did not just fracture and reassemble the old plan, it completely reversed it; and remnants of the old had no place in the new. More than anything else it was this reversal of images—the abstraction of the "message"—that obscured the relation to convention and made the *architecture parlante* of the twentieth century a misunderstood language.

The most elusive problem with the theoretical assumptions of the free plan, however, may very well be that of the facade. Implicitly, the free plan and the *dom-ino* frame eliminated the need for a continuous facade. But Le Corbusier himself, having eliminated its necessity, always insisted upon it; and usually he was able to charge both its opacity and its transparency with energy, prophecy, depth, and tension to a degree unattainable by or undesirable to his colleagues. For Mies, the problem of the facade was almost nonexistent. For Gropius, the facade was at best a nuisance. For Terragni, it may have been more important than the plan. But the facade as a mask, or mediator, between the public and private realms was without a doubt latently contradictory to the idea of the free plan, and consequently the demise of the vertical surface as an architectural and urbanistic concern was ultimately inevitable. Only Le Corbusier, and to a certain extent Terragni, realized the importance of this contradiction and continued to explore the art of the wall. Quite simply, the facade was not an issue for most modern architects. A list of great modern facades is a short list indeed, and this now seems all the more unfortunate given the exposure that the format of modern freestanding buildings provided. The modern descendants of *l'architecture parlante* lost their tongues.

This contradiction points out another problem: the difference between the accessibility of Le Corbusier's polemic and the cerebral but difficult genius of his practice. Unlike Phidias and Michaelangelo (his examples of genius), who transcended the ongoing matrix of orthodoxy to achieve great works, Le Corbusier literally inverted an orthodoxy, clothed it in an abstract new style, and propagated it around the world—expounding the polemic while obscuring the practice. Unfortunately, abstraction was unlike past styles in that it could exist without any architectural principles behind it, thus making bad buildings easy and good buildings difficult. Perfectly able practitioners, but lesser lights than Le Corbusier, were all too quick to pick up the style without its conventions and the theory rather than the practice.

While promoting the new city of freestanding buildings, Le Corbusier built contextually related buildings. Indeed, he was one of the great contextualists of the twentieth century. This is obscured in his publications of his own work, however. Rarely are site plans shown (Ozenfant, Garches, Museum of Contemporary Art Project in Paris, for example) so that only reconstruction or first-hand examination reveals the degree to which his projects are formulated relative to site

201 Le Corbusier and the City of Modern Architecture

304
Villa at Garches, garden facade

305
Villa at Garches, entry facade

front and a private garden behind. At Garches, the site is regular so there is no contextual reason for recentering, but the principle is elaborately exploited nonetheless: the front emphasizes the central bay and thus the center of the site, while the enclosed portion of the rear facade is symmetrical about the second bay and thus asymmetrical to the garden. The public and private entrances create local symmetries about the narrow bays, and then, together with the balcony on the top floor, they emphasize the center again. This system of overlapping and alternative readings is more than just facade manipulation, however; by subtly relating the exterior and the interior and by "preparing the spirit," the facades and the spatial development articulate a sequence through the entire site. By creating movement back and forth across the central axis via the smaller bays of the building, Le Corbusier is able to engage the spatial volumes in front and back in the processional sequence, and thereby subtly relates the exterior and the interior.

Within the villa, public and private circulation are completely segregated. Approximately three-quarters of the ground floor is service space, treated as *poché* in support of the public entry hall, whose agitated perimeter is stabilized by a central space formed by the four freestanding columns. The entry hall in the villa at Garches, as well as the similar one in the Villa Savoye, is like a small, localized analogue to the Hôtel de Beauvais, where the regular center formed by the four columns controls an idiosyncratic perimeter. The relative stability of this "space within a space" marks one's arrival within the building and initiates the interior public sequence, or *promenade architecturale*, that culminates in either the living area on the next floor or in the

205   Le Corbusier and the City of Modern Architecture

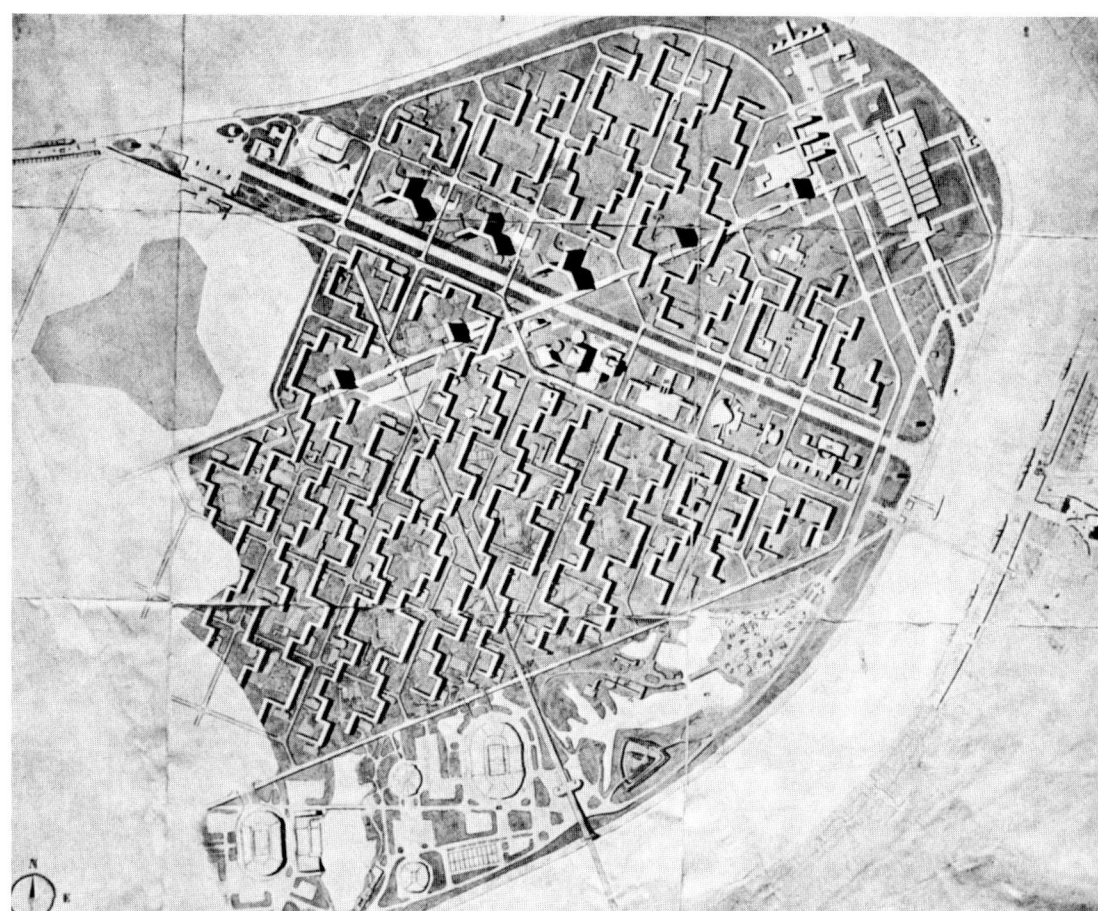

310
Anvers, urban plan, Le Corbusier, 1933

311
"Le Plan de Paris 37," *Ilot N. 6*, Le Corbusier, 1936

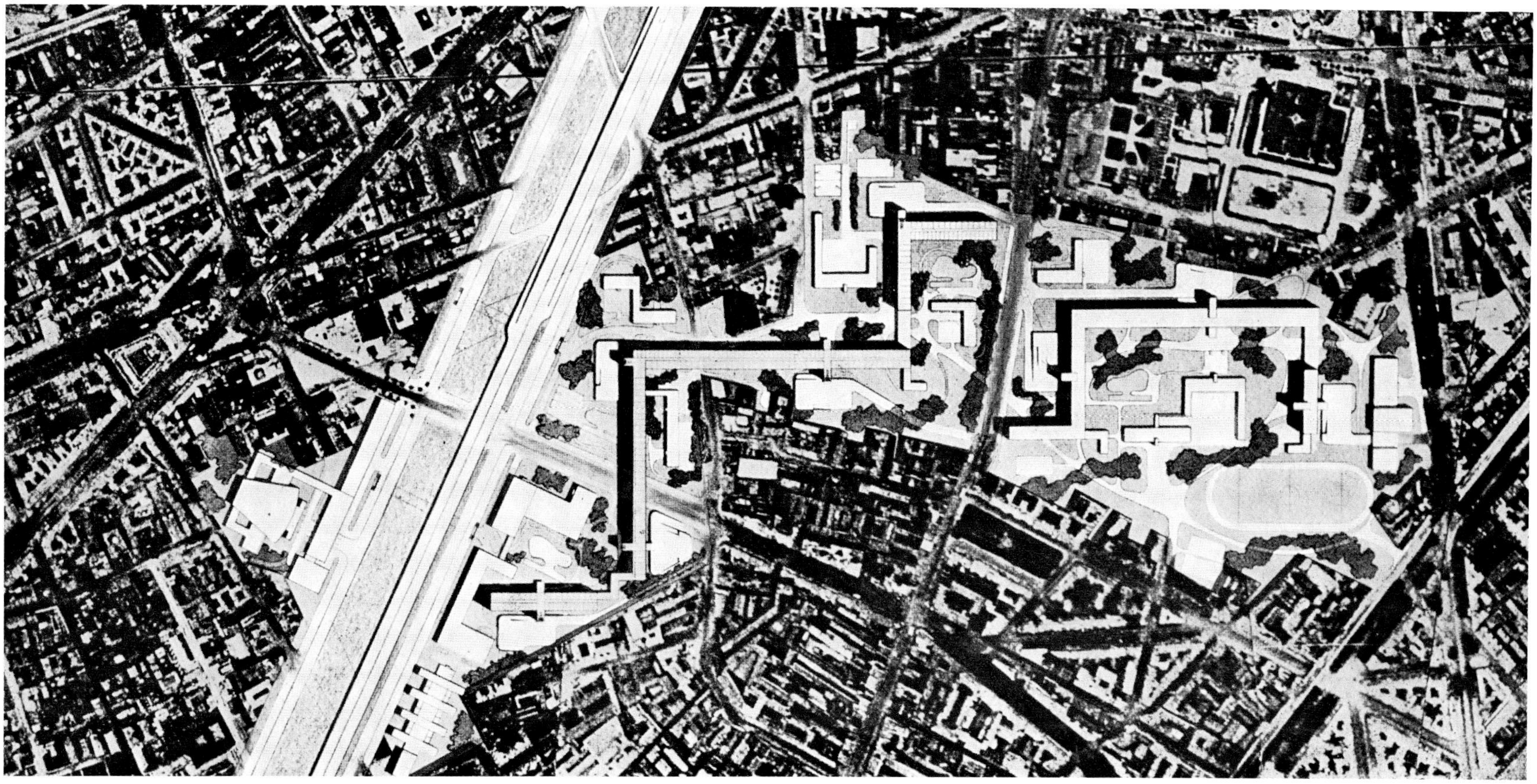

for local circumstance, and in each case the message was clear: the new system would have to totally replace the old; there was little or no place for the old in the new, for this was the city of the future—new, pure, and untainted. The relentless rationalism of his new town proposal for Anvers in 1933 only exaggerates the violence of his plan for Ilot no. 6 in Paris in 1937.

That Le Corbusier was aware of the historical system he was proposing to destroy, as well as of the source of the destruction, is confirmed in *Concerning Town Planning* (1946):

> The Palais de l'Institut in Paris (formerly Collège Mazarin). This act of will in the heart of the tangle of streets and contorted areas of Paris created a special mode of architectural treatment. Many masterpieces of invention have been provoked by the restraints of the site.
>
> This is to become the special whim of the Parisian school: the practice (perhaps, the love) of sterile problems.
>
> Against all sense, the habit of aligning buildings on the streets is to persist, creating the present practices: *alignment on the streets* and *enclosed courts and light wells*, two forms entirely contrary to human well-being, and to which the "Athens Charter" has opposed the principle of architectural development from within to without.
>
> Place Vendôme, Paris (previously [Place] Louis-le-Grand). Here the streams of architecture and town-planning have joined to form a lake of repose in the bristling town compressed within its military walls; an architectural fashion owing much to the interior decorator and the scenic designer flowered in the salons and anterooms. Salons to the glory of kings and princes. A fashion that soon flourished in the provinces, abroad, wherever courts were held and courtiers dwelt.
>
> Paris, Invalides and Ecole Militaire. Buildings on unrestricted sites developed on other lines. The spirit of order and commandment is the

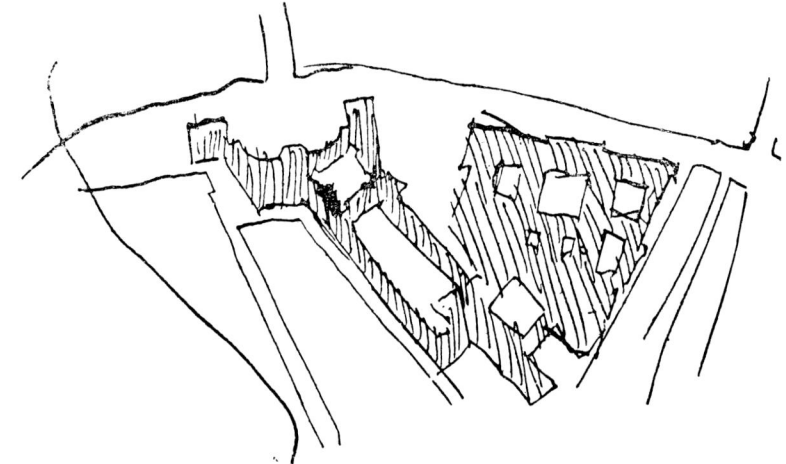

312
Paris, Palais de l'Institut, sketch by Le Corbusier

313
Paris, Place Vendôme, sketch by Le Corbusier

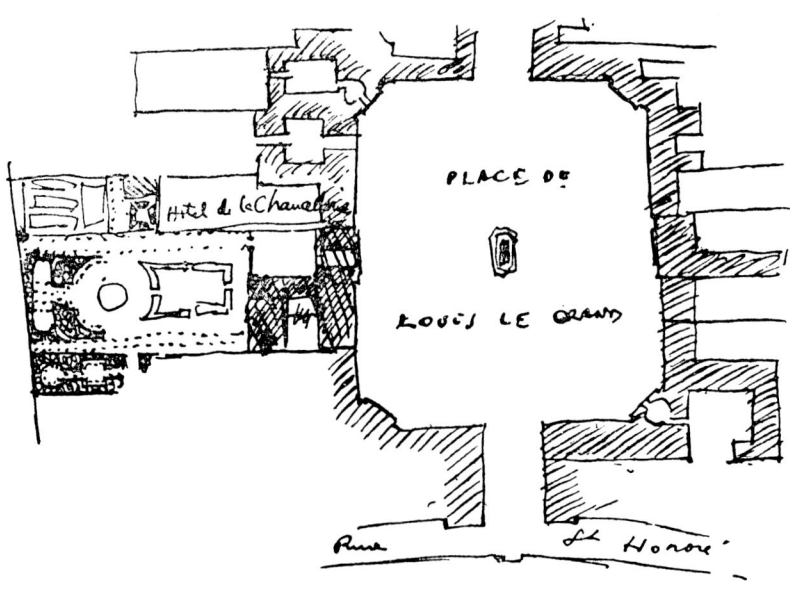

207   Le Corbusier and the City of Modern Architecture

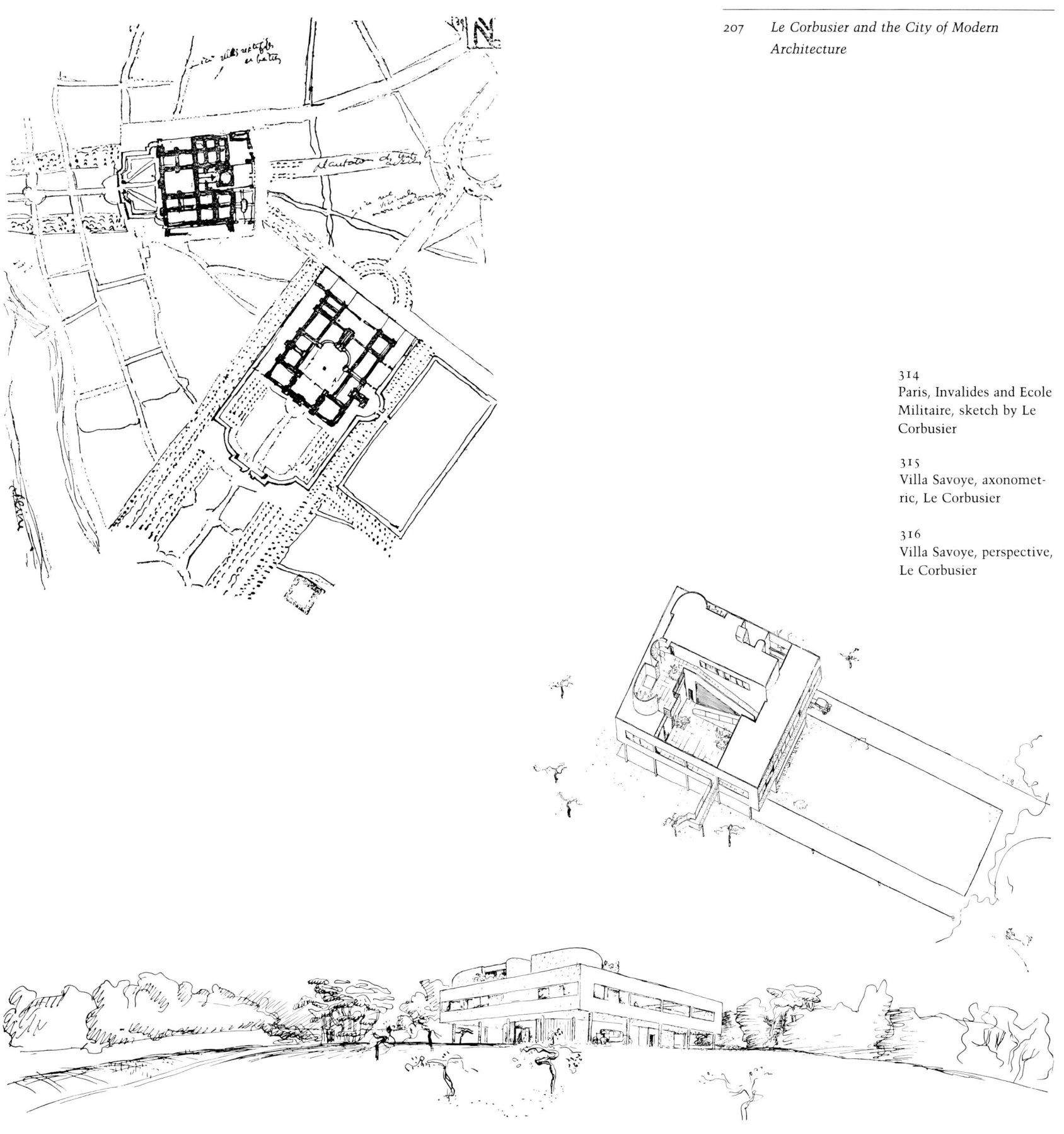

314
Paris, Invalides and Ecole Militaire, sketch by Le Corbusier

315
Villa Savoye, axonometric, Le Corbusier

316
Villa Savoye, perspective, Le Corbusier

same, the same verve and grandeur, but in place of successive ante-chambers walling out the slums (hollows), palaces rise, growing from within to without, composing blocks of dwellings, naves and domes, surrounded by space, and now offering to the eye volumes under the sun (solids).

Hollows or solids are both lawful forms when they occur as expressions of a way of life.[16]

That "alignment on the streets" and "enclosed courts" are "contrary to human well-being" appears, for better or for worse, to have eluded architects and laymen alike for thousands of years. And that this is in opposition to the principle of "architectural development from within to without" also apparently escaped a great many traditional architects. By now the temptation is to regard all of this as a bad joke played on his colleagues of CIAM, but the net legacy of Le Corbusier's urban theory remains. The belief in, and search for, total solutions still predominates. Space is still that which is left over after the solids are rationalized and designed. Buildings are still primarily generated by the "program," and the words *street* and *facade* are barely intelligible professional terms to most architects. What has clearly changed, however, is the idea of the city. We no longer want a totally new replacement for the old; we want a city to be what it has always been, a combination of new and old, an accumulation. The architectural parallel to this is, of course, that the imagery of buildings is not limited to the future alone, but, like the city, can reflect the past as well. Thus we can believe that the free plan was, and may still be, a marvelously useful invention, but must acknowledge that the *ville radieuse* was one of the most disastrous events in the history of urbanism.

317
Plan voisin, model, Le Corbusier, 1925

318
Versailles and *ville contemporaine*, montage

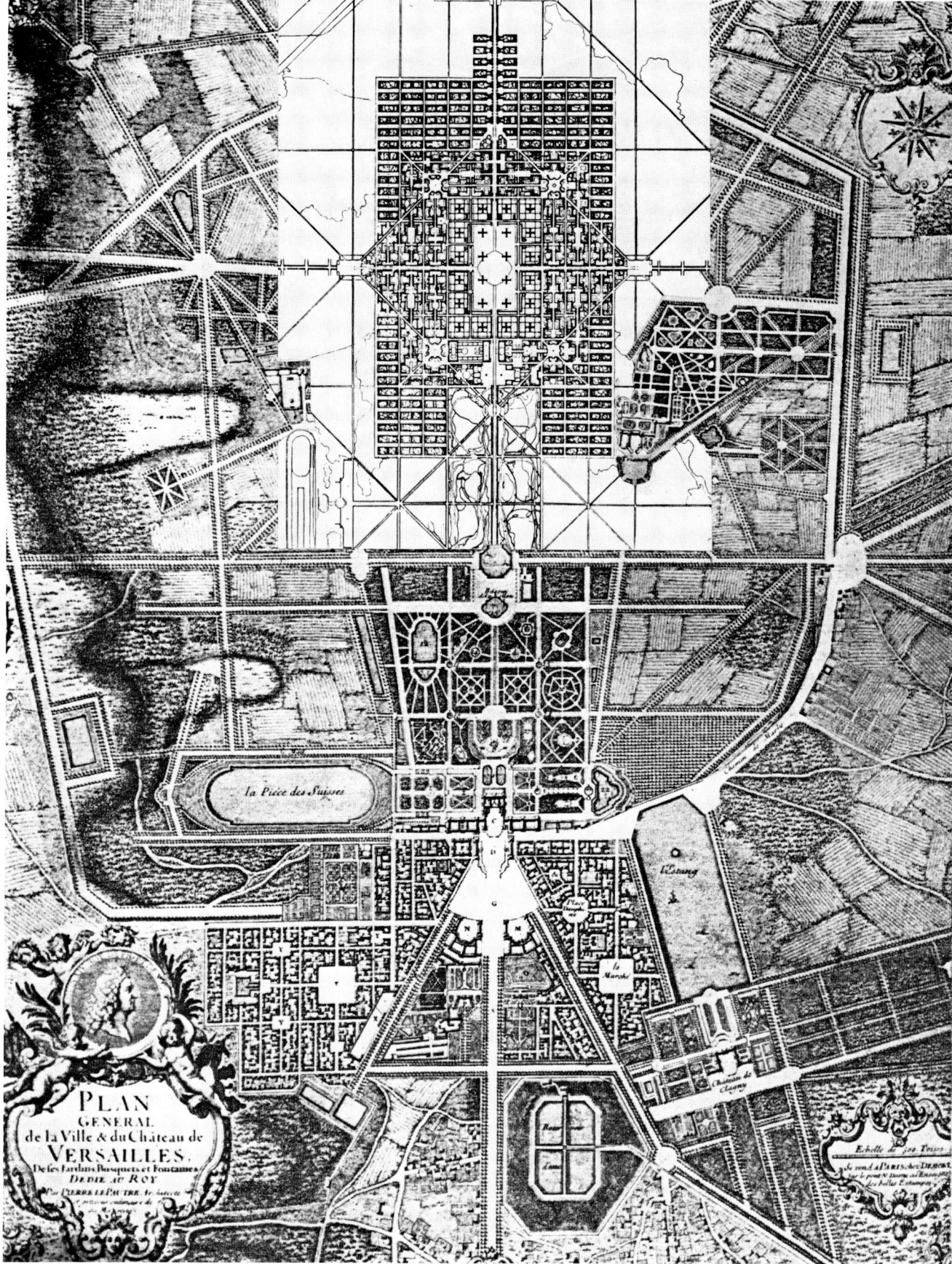

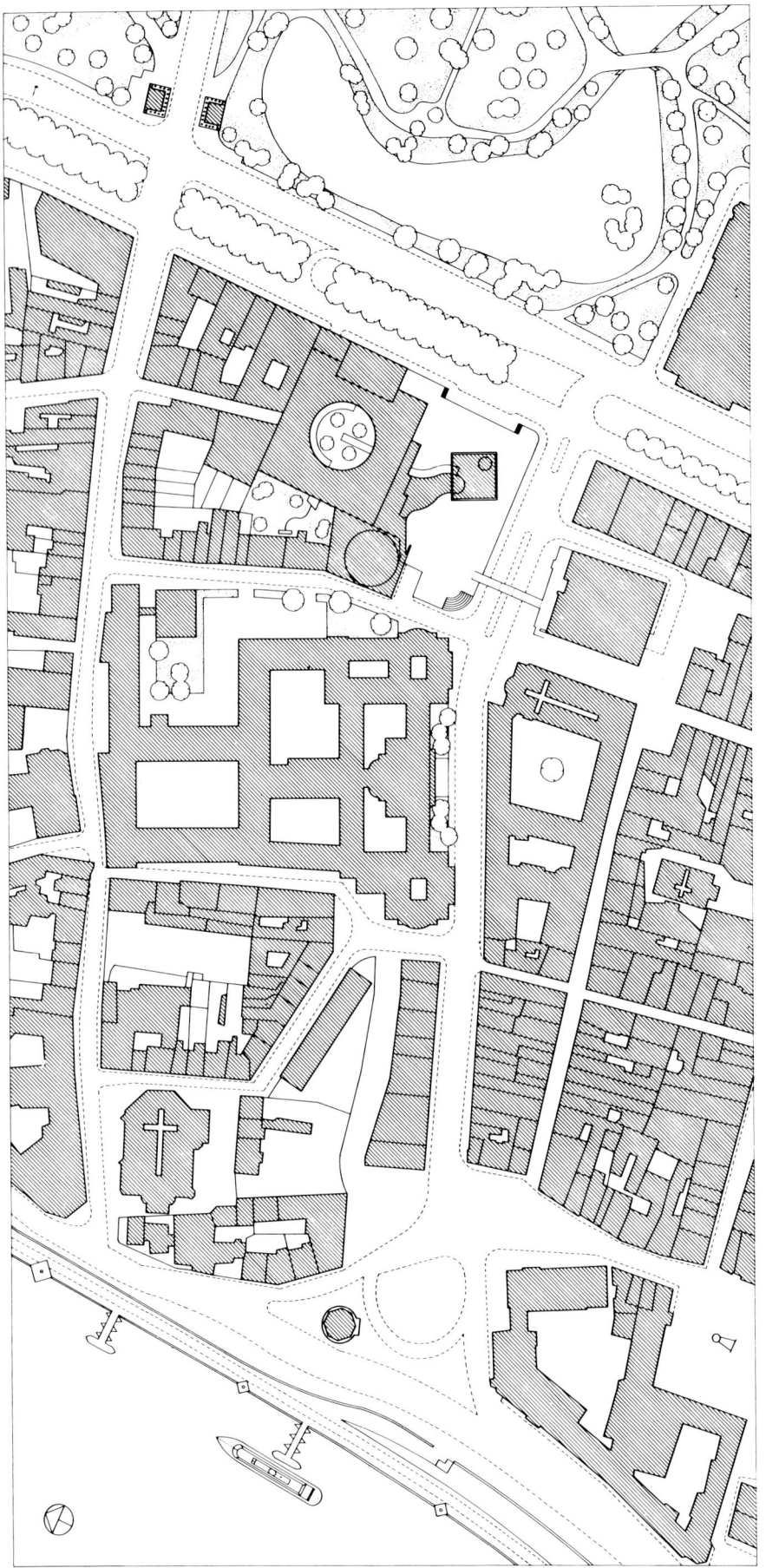

319
Competition for the Northrhine-Westphalia Art Museum, Düsseldorf, site plan, James Stirling, 1975

320
Competition for the Northrhine-Westphalia Art Museum, Düsseldorf, main floor plan, James Stirling, 1975

7 Architecture and the Cumulative City

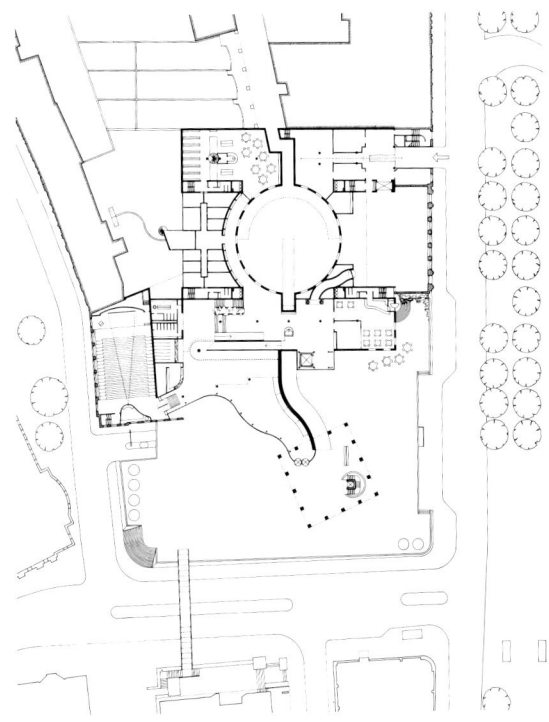

Yet another significant change in art and culture is taking place. Indeed, there is widespread consensus, admittedly without consistent enthusiasm, that the values of the final quarter of the twentieth century are as distinct from those of the previous half century of modernism as the values of modernism were presumed to be from the periods that preceded it. Clearly modernism has been absorbed by history; it is no longer revolutionary, but has become an established tradition—identifiable, orthodox, real, and, to a certain extent, measurable in its successes and failures. That it has come under fashionable attack is to be expected, but recent reactions to modern architecture may be of greater historical and cultural significance than a mere change of architectural clothes—from cardboard Corbusier to cardboard Classicism. The change that is now taking place in our ideas may ultimately prove to be as profound as that which took place during the first quarter of the twentieth century, and, possibly, as that which began to take place during the 1750s. Interpretations of this change vary, however; and whether it is viewed with suspicion or enthusiasm depends to a large extent on how history and modernism are viewed.

It is undeniably useful to see Western history as a succession of unitary or monolithic world views, each a quest for unity and continuity and each more or less absolute in its own orthodoxy. Obviously, no single period is totally consistent, but there are predominant tendencies, such as the Medieval, Renaissance, and Enlightenment cosmologies summarized earlier. Even the apparent pluralism of the nineteenth century may be seen as a series of separate and mutually incompatible monolithic world views, each with its own closure and internal consistency. The dominant characteristics of modern architecture are probably consistent with this predilection for total unitary order.

The change that occurred in the arts, and particularly in architecture, during the first quarter of the twentieth century is admittedly difficult to overstate. But if modern architecture presented itself as the inversion of all that went before, it now seems not the revolutionary beginning of a totally new world at all, but rather the ultimate expression of Enlightenment principle. Ideas of progress, utility, mechanism, and total order—characteristics of mainstream modernism—are all deeply embedded in the rationalist construct of the eighteenth century. Both the modern form system and the modern method of thought have their roots there.

Near the middle of the eighteenth century, public space was implicitly traded for the private object, a deal that, formally, represented the beginning of the end of the *res publica.* Parallel to this formal exchange was an integrally related intellectual exchange that became no less tyrannical. Despite the demolition of the absolute canons of the classical aesthetic system and the substitution of the relativity of taste, rational description of the natural world became the dominant method of thought and eventually something of an absolute in itself—the absolute of science. Objects are more easily quantifiable than spaces or people, so it is not surprising to find that architecture lent itself as easily to rational determinism as it had to classical canon. It might now be said that the art of science was traded for the science of art near the middle of the eighteenth century and that modern architecture can be seen, fundamentally, as the product of that exchange.

Modern architecture was evolutionary rather than revolutionary in its principles, and in this sense continuity was as important as discontinuity. On the other hand, by the early years of the twentieth century, the abstract masses and surfaces of architects like Ledoux and Boullée had long been obscured by an endless succession of "styles," so that the shock of abstraction—be it the abstraction of Picasso, Stravinsky, Wright, or Le Corbusier—was indeed discontinuous and revolutionary. Surely it was abstraction that drove the strongest wedge between modernism and the past and between the *avant-garde* and the bourgeoisie, even though it may have been the logical remains after the stylistic trappings of the old order (principally the classicism of the *ancien régime*) were shed. In any case, mechanism and abstraction, though not inseparable, formed the dominant tradition of modern architecture. When this simple tradition is deprived of its historical roots—when it is perceived as even more simplistic than it was—dissatisfaction and prescription become especially problematic.

Revolutions depend on continuity; it is the very fabric which gives them meaning and allows change. If modernism is seen only in terms of its mechanistic and abstract characteristics, and if it is seen only as an historical aberration, then reaction is likely to be once again total, the prescriptive choices limited, and history doomed to be reenacted, but with less-than-resonant voices. As a reaction to the mechanism of modern architecture, we should not be surprised to find a kind of mindless, stripped-down Neoclassicism, nostalgic for the life and forms of pre-industrial cities. Reactions to the abstraction of modern architecture, however, are likely to inspire a kind of mindless eclecticism, rootless and sugarcoated for easy consumption. In the Neoclassical mode, tragedy is in abundance; in eclecticism, comedy prevails. With the one, abstraction renders a muted ideal with diagrammatic but total clarity, whereas the other succumbs with equal thoroughness to a vigorous frenzy of picturesque and circumstantial reality. That this argument is a caricature of the late eighteenth century is no accident, but simply to reenact the play with latter-day "antiquaires" and "philosophes" would seem to severely misread history in general and modernism in particular. Moreover, either of these attitudes unnecessarily divorces production from the continuity needed for significant change.

Fortunately, other aspects of history and a more complex tradition of modernism exist that are less clear and less obvious, but potentially far more interesting, than those described above. Specifically, we can find evidence of another attitude, another state of mind, perhaps even another tradition—fragmentary but identifiable—parallel to, and critical of, mainstream ideas. This attitude may be found in individuals such as Ledoux (the "practitioner") or Le Corbusier (the "architect"), in subthemes of history such as the French *hôtel* tradition, and occasionally in whole periods of production such as Italian Mannerism. It is an attitude almost always marked by simultaneous acknowledgment and distrust of absolute canon; it usually chooses to represent multiple and discontinuous aspects of reality; it may place a special premium on virtuosity, cleverness, and invention, but—despite the relativity of its argument (or because of it)—it is never independent of the notion of rational or "ideal" order. This alternative state of mind simply does not require the total and exclusive presence of a single ideal. On the contrary, the possible interpretations of order increase geometrically as clarity and ambiguity converge.

In the twentieth century, this multi-ordinal and uncertain interpretation of reality may be the only truly revolutionary aspect of modernism. The embracing of relativity as well as rationalism in this century removed the burden of an absolute value system from the Enlightenment construct and thereby transformed irreconcilable and destructive inner conflict into a whole new set of possibilities. Conflict still existed, but it could be positively exploited. Multiple orders were attainable. This, more than any other aspect of modernism, seems especially fresh and compelling today. At the very least it offers an alternative tradition of modern architecture—more complex, more contradictory, more useful.

The alternative stream is most notably represented by Alvar Aalto and Le Corbusier and is in sharp contrast to the tradition of Walter Gropius, Hannes Meyer, and Frank Lloyd Wright. For Aalto and Le Corbusier, physical form expressed not total unity and a consistent, integrated world, but the simultaneous presence of more than one reality. Aalto and Le Corbusier both elaborated rational and relative themes, they invited, even demanded, a dialogue between abstraction and empathy, between man and nature. Both exhibited a state of mind which, despite Le Corbusier's prescriptive polemic to the contrary, could accept discontinuity as well as continuity. Thus after at least five hundred years of preemptive questing for total solutions, modernism—or one stream of it—proposed an alternative to one unitary view of the cosmos. This was revolutionary.

The principle of discontinuity was inevitably as important to this new order as the principle of continuity had been to the old. Before 1917, T. E. Hulme wrote in *Speculations*:

> One of the main achievements of the nineteenth century was the elaboration and universal application of the principle of *continuity*. The destruction of this conception is, on the contrary, an urgent necessity of the present.
>
> Originally urged only by the few, it has spread—implicit in the popular conception of evolution—till it has attained the status of a category....
>
> When any fact seems to contradict this principle, we are inclined to deny that the fact really exists. We constantly tend to think that the discontinuities in nature are only *apparent*, and that a fuller investigation would reveal the underlying continuity. This shrinking from a *gap* or jump in nature has developed to a degree which paralyzes any objective perception and prejudices our seeing things as they really are. For an objective view of reality we must make use both of the categories of continuity and discontinuity. Our principal concern then at the present moment should be the re-establishment of the temper or disposition of mind which can look at a *gap* or chasm without shuddering.[1]

If Le Corbusier and Aalto did possess the temper or disposition to "look at a *gap* or chasm without shuddering," then Hannes Meyer, Frank Lloyd Wright, and Walter Gropius evidently did not. These two groups identify, more or less precisely, the two different traditions of modernism. And while one of these traditions may now seem less than totally plausible, the other may offer renewed promise for a convincing mode of operation in the present day. Indeed, it may be argued that the absolute value system of the Enlightenment was *not* explicitly destroyed in the early years of the twentieth century; that both the form system and the intellectual system of the eighteenth century remained the dominant operational mode until recently; and that consequently the current state of confusion and change may represent a kind of delayed reaction, a kind of playing out of the tyranny of the Enlightenment. This suggests that we are indeed at such a historic watershed as the one that occurred some two hundred years ago.

But if we perceive a renewed philosophical connection with the early twentieth century, its unique promise must find new formal manifestations. For Le Corbusier's inversion of formal and spatial values produced a system that was opposite, but not equal, to its classical predecessor: the absolute exchange of positive void for positive solid was in the end one of considerable social and artistic limitation, not liberation. The free plan alone was hardly a useful vehicle for the modern program; and the columnar frame, even as used by Le Corbusier, could never provide the reassuring stability of platonic space, although it could on occasion quietly delineate the perspective structure of it. More importantly, however, modern high-tech versions of the Petit Trianon can hardly be expected to constitute an appropriate urban fabric for an elaborate society. Le Corbusier may not have been the philosophical prisoner of the Enlightenment, but he was, probably, the formal prisoner of a Neoclassical legacy. For all his pursuit of the collective ideal, his methods—his form system—did help to promote one of the great tragedies of the twentieth century: the collapse of the public realm.

The language of modern architecture was alien to the traditional city by design as well as by default. If one of the results of this language was the destruction of the city, then surely one of our principal tasks is the development of a language capable of its reconstruction. In fact, the current revival of interest in traditional cities and the search for an expanded architectural and urban vocabulary seem to represent a new sensibility common to several otherwise diverse groups of architects and urbanists. One obvious litmus test of this changing sensibility is a renewed interest in the street. Rationalized in the nineteenth century and banished by Le Corbusier and most of CIAM in the twentieth, the street is undergoing a revival that would have been unthinkable twenty years ago. The following remarks should be sufficiently illustrative:

"The street wears us out. And when all is said and done we have to admit it disgusts us."
LE CORBUSIER, 1929[2]

"The first thing to do is abolish the *rue corridor* with its rigid lines of buildings and its intermingling of traffic, pedestrians, and houses."
SIGFRIED GIDEON, 1941[3]

"Against all sense, the habit of aligning buildings on the streets is to persist, creating the present practices: *alignment on the streets* and *enclosed courts and light wells*, two forms entirely contrary to human well-being."
LE CORBUSIER, 1946[4]

"The problem of re-identifying man with his environment... cannot be achieved by using historical forms of house-groupings, streets, squares, greens, etc., as the social reality they presented no longer exists."
ALISON SMITHSON AND PETER SMITHSON, 1953[5]

"The street and the square represent the only necessary model for the reconstruction of a PUBLIC REALM."
LEON KRIER, 1978[6]

In other terms as well, traditional urban values are being rediscovered and examined. Indeed, it is the attitude toward the city that most clearly distinguishes the last quarter of the twentieth cen-

214   Architecture and the Cumulative City

321
Venice, Tablino della
Caritá, Andrea Palladio

322
Poissy, Villa Savoye, entry hall, Le Corbusier, 1928–31

tury from the preceding half of modernism. If anything is in a positive sense "postmodern," it might be the city rather than architecture.

But architecture can never be separated from urbanism, and it is not surprising that the object building, the *dom-ino* frame, and the free plan should be inadequate as sole instruments in the formation of the city. However, a return to purely traditional techniques ("Neo-Trad" or "B.C. Beaux-Arts") is equally untenable. What might be proposed instead is a hybrid architecture for a hybrid city, an architecture of traditional rooms as well as "modern" space, of facades as well as frames—an architecture that *makes* urban space as well as consumes it. If the reintroduction of enclosed urban space is the essence of the post-modern city, and if inclusion of both the present and the past is a desirable urban condition, then something similar should define the architecture that is to form this city.

Fortunately, we are now in possession of not one but two architectural and urban traditions—premodern and modern—and although they may conflict, they are not necessarily mutually exclusive. Both traditions may on occasion be useful; they might be made to complement each other; and neither need necessarily be disposed of as obsolete cultural debris, nor nostalgically preserved as solution-by-default. Rather, they might be realigned and reexamined as mutually beneficial adjacencies.

In the premodern (would pre-Enlightenment be more accurate?) tradition, the city is generally composed of a hierarchy of articulated spaces supported by a more or less continuous urban fabric or texture. Except for a very few important public buildings, space takes precedence over object. Streets and squares are sacrosanct; and it is

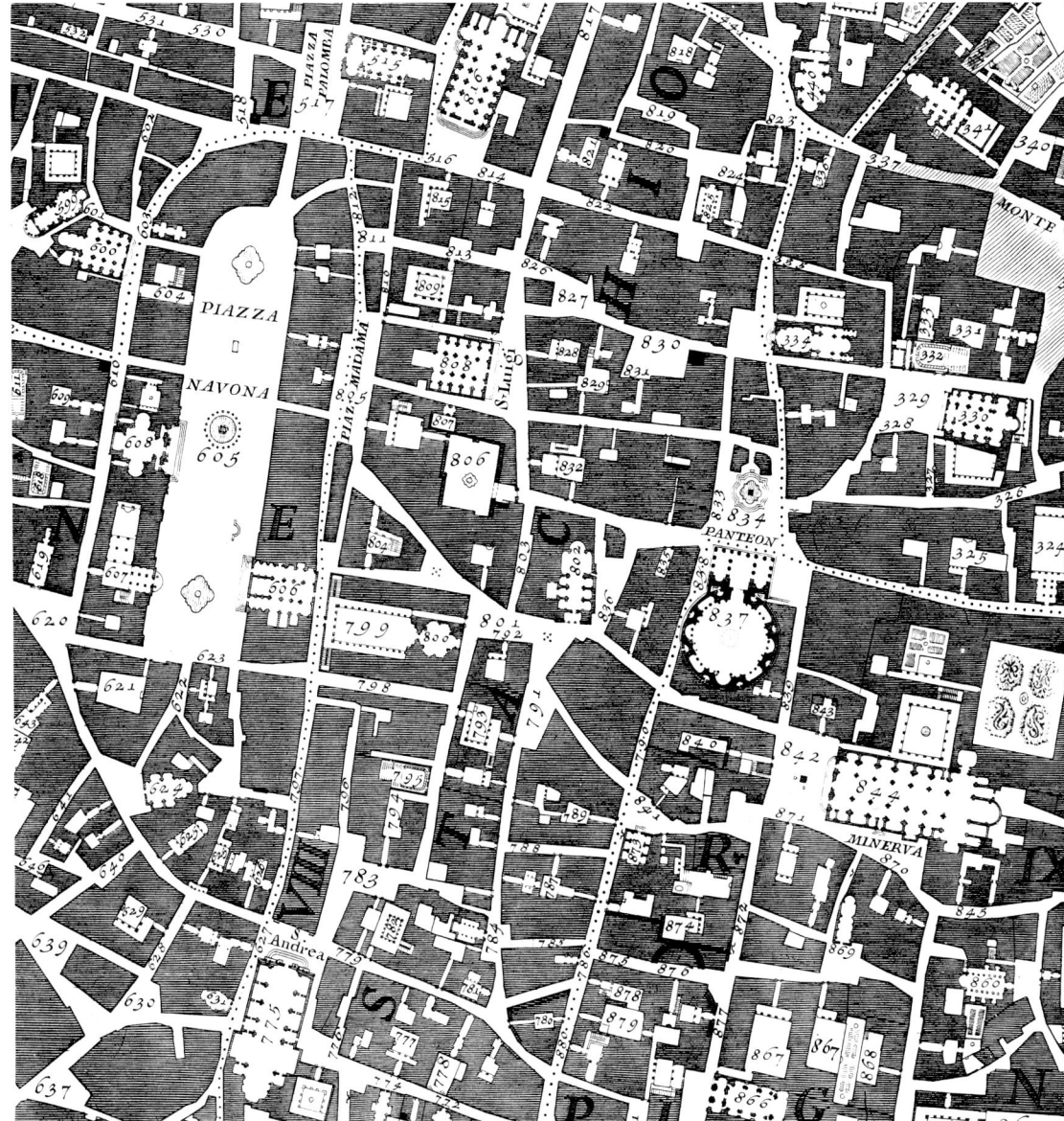

323
Rome, detail of the Nolli plan, 1748

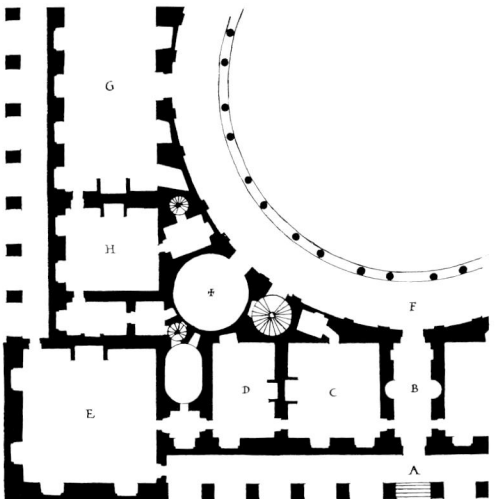

324
Detail of a plan for a country house, Sebastiano Serlio, 16th c.

usually the solids, or buildings, that must absorb and accommodate any urban idiosyncracies. The architectural analogy to this city is a series of discrete rooms articulated by thick, load-bearing walls. Primary spaces are rationalized, and if anything is left over or subordinate, it is absorbed by solid material or service elements. In the premodern city, the facade mediates between the public and private realms, providing both public closure and private symbol.

The modern city is the opposite of its ancestor in almost every respect. If the "solid city" of the past and its architecture embody a value system that requires determination from the outside in, then the "tower city" of modern architecture reveals a value system that specifies development from the inside out. This system favors rationalized and articulate solids instead of defined spaces and freestanding buildings instead of contiguous ones. As a result, the quantifiable aspects of buildings, such as the structure and service elements, are rationalized and expressed, while the habitable spaces are left over. This same condition is generally true on an urban level, where buildings are articulated as free objects in continuous and largely undifferentiated space. In the modern city, open space absorbs any urban idiosyncrasy; and, because the street has disappeared as an enclosed space, the facade functions only as private symbol.

Together these two traditions constitute a rich legacy, not a confusing obstacle. They are the conventions that allow invention, and need only will and the recognition of necessity to be activated. Here temper or disposition of mind is critical, for neither system is wholly acceptable. The city requires both public and private accommodation, and it is architecture that must

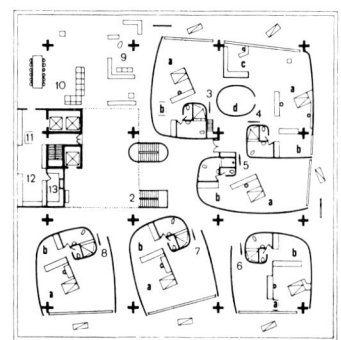

326
Chandigarh, early plan for the governor's house, Le Corbusier, 1952

325
Plan voisin for Paris, Le Corbusier, 1925

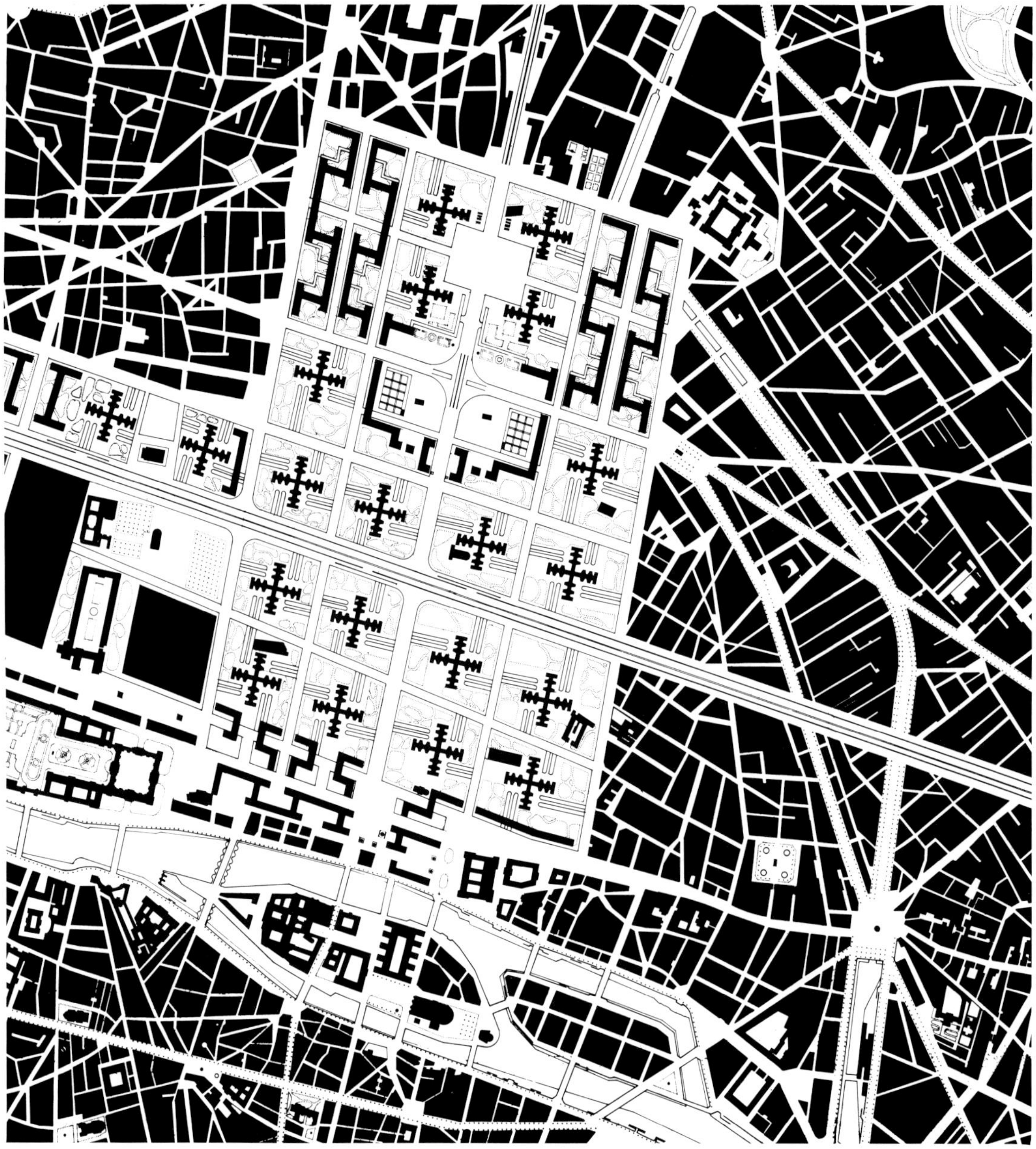

mediate between the two related but not integrated realms. If the two realms are at odds with each other, so much the better; for necessity may then encourage will; and thus a particular state of mind—one which has the capacity to function without the assist of necessity or program—may escape the guilt of capriciousness and be reassured by having acted with social and civic responsibility.

Both the ideal and the circumstantial require acknowledgment, and if there is a gap or chasm between them, we need only remember that much of the most interesting seventeenth- and eighteenth-century French architecture was generated from just such a schism (aided of course by the occasional odd site). Le Corbusier may have been correct when he said that "many masterpieces of invention have been provoked by the restraints of the site,"[7] but it is difficult to believe that the Hôtel de Beauvais is solely a product of the collision of Louis XIV with medieval Paris. Rather, it can be imagined that if such collisions did not occur, it might occasionally be useful to invent them. Certainly the last word has not yet been written about the relationship between form and function.

Le Corbusier understood when he defined "the special whim of the Parisian school" as "the practice (perhaps the love) of . . . problems."[8] That the built work of Ledoux is fundamentally more interesting than his theoretical work may be debated, but the built Ledoux *is* symptomatic of the peculiarly French predilection for dialectic—that is, for finding or posing a problem, often where none exists, in order to solve it with demonstrable virtuosity. In French plans one is somehow always aware of the existence of the problem, whereas in those of Palladio, one scarcely imag-

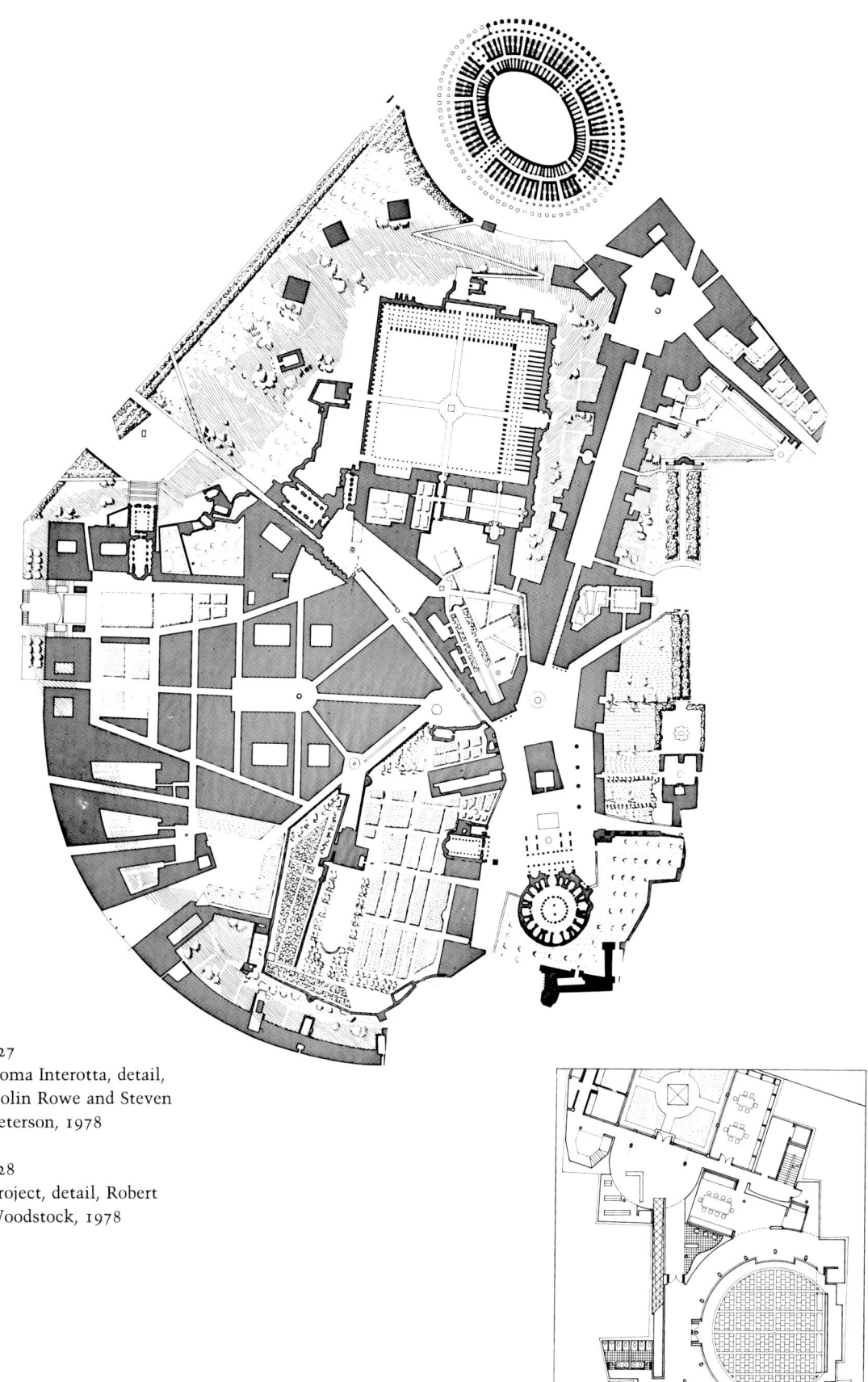

327
Roma Interotta, detail, Colin Rowe and Steven Peterson, 1978

328
Project, detail, Robert Woodstock, 1978

ines a problem existed at all. Whatever the reason, French plans are unique, and changing urban sensibilities offer a convenient excuse (should one be needed) to look at them anew.

It might be useful to rearrange history a bit and shake out revised definitions of "old" and "new." Comparing the projects of Le Corbusier and August Perret for the Palace of the Soviets competition offers reversed definitions. That Le Corbusier may be artistically better only heightens the architectural challenge in the search for the architecture of the cumulative city. James Stirling's project for the Northrhine–Westphalia Art Museum competition in Düsseldorf (1975) provides an equally important pivot in the late twentieth century. Through its collage of ideas and its acknowledgment of the traditional urban elements of street and square, Stirling's project confirms a revised agenda for architecture and the city.

In the search for the obliging solid and the assertive void, traditional plans of the nineteenth century take on renewed significance; and the extremely beautiful modern ones of Michel Roux-Spitz are tantalizingly stimulating to contemplate once free of the absolute dogma of modern architecture. One might, for example, look at the Garot plan and imagine it gently provoking an open site; one might look at a Roux-Spitz plan and fantasize about its analogous city; and as an example of a plan with allegiance to multiple masters, the Caffé Pedrocchi is more than a little suggestive of postmodern possibilities.[9] It is almost the plan of both free and figural space—or is sufficiently close at least to allow us to imagine that a new space might just be possible.

Individual response to principles and precedents varies considerably, of course, but in addition to modernism, we have found the tradition

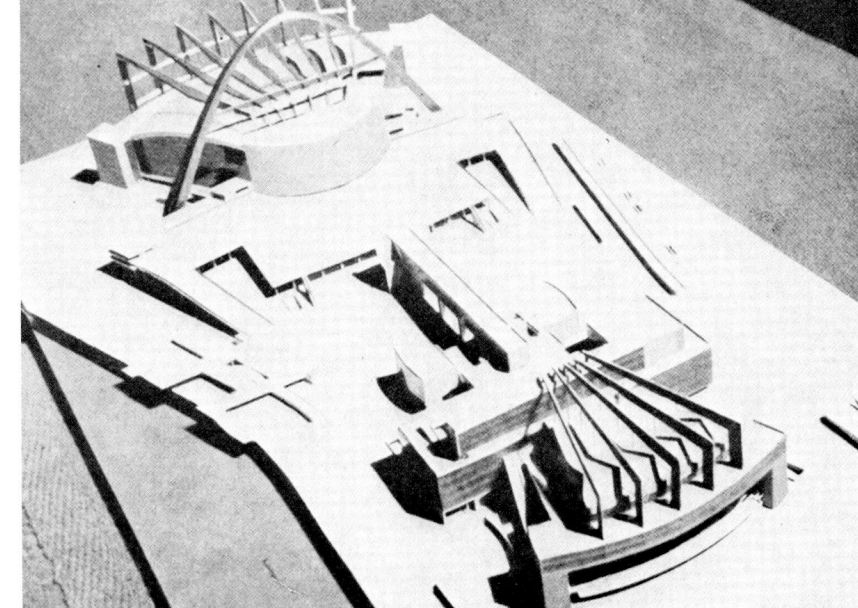

329
Palace of the Soviets competition, model, Le Corbusier, 1931

330
Palace of the Soviets competition, August Perret, 1931

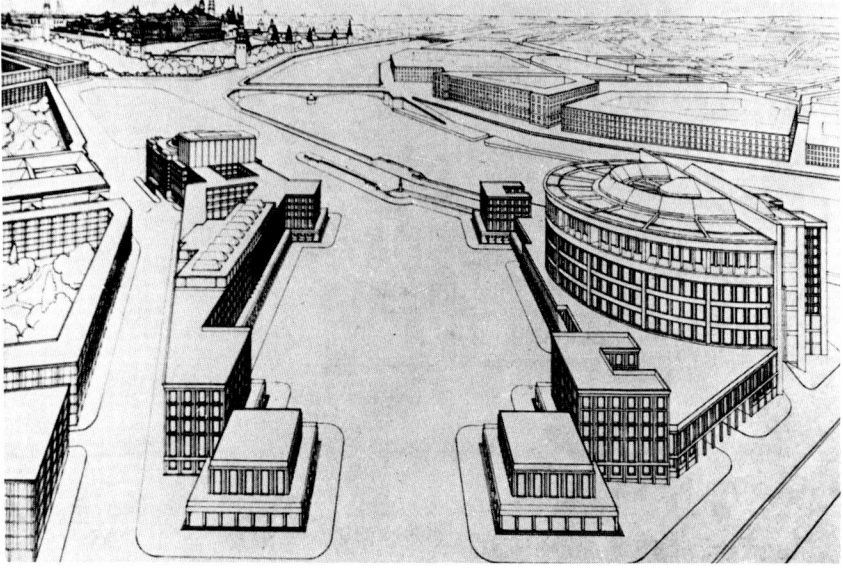

of the *hôtel* a particularly expansive source of ideas for our own work. Ironically perhaps, it was the urban *hôtel* type that informed the project for the new University Art Museum on the lush suburban campus of the University of California at Santa Barbara, while the competition for the new Paris Opera at the Place de la Bastille—an urban problem par excellence—provided a poignant opportunity for the exploration of recurrent French themes of architectural urbanism.[10] But if the city of contiguous solids appears to be served best by the principles of the Baroque *hôtel* type, then surely the Rococo and Neoclassical types may still offer informative lessons in the simultaneous provision for *convenance* and *commodité*, for display and retreat. And if greater awareness of the public realm were again to prevail, the Neoclassical *hôtel*, as an urban villa, might find renewed life as a fertile source for urban form[11]—especially in America.

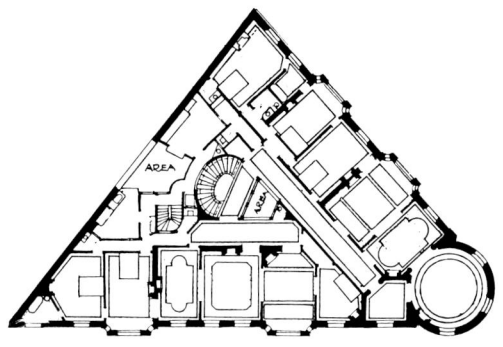

331
Paris, apartment house, plan, Thion

332
Paris, apartment house, plan, Perronne, 1890s

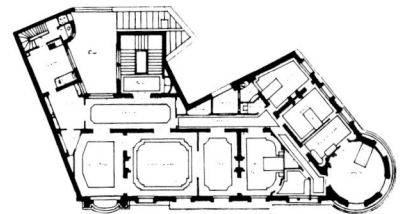

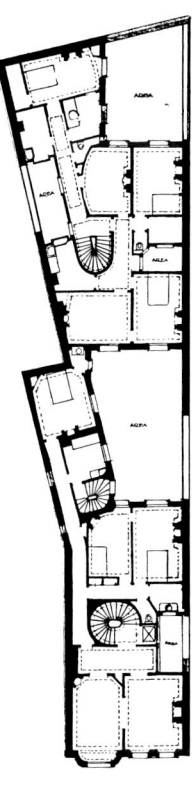

333
Paris, apartment house, plan, Blavette

334
Paris, apartment house, plan

335
Paris, apartment house, plan, Emile Garot

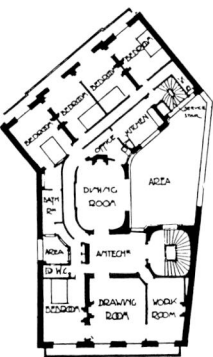 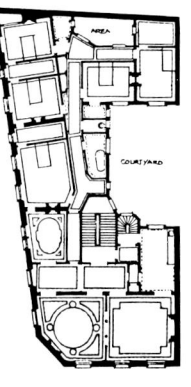

336
Paris, apartment house, plan, Henri Sauvage, 1928

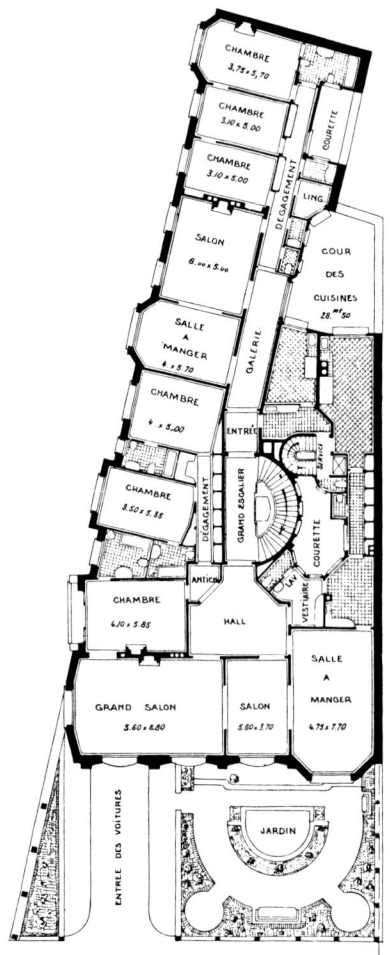

337
Newport, Rhode Island, E. D. Morgan house "Beacon Rock," 1889–91

338
Paris, apartment house in rue Guynemer, ground and typical floor plans, Michel Roux-Spitz, 1925

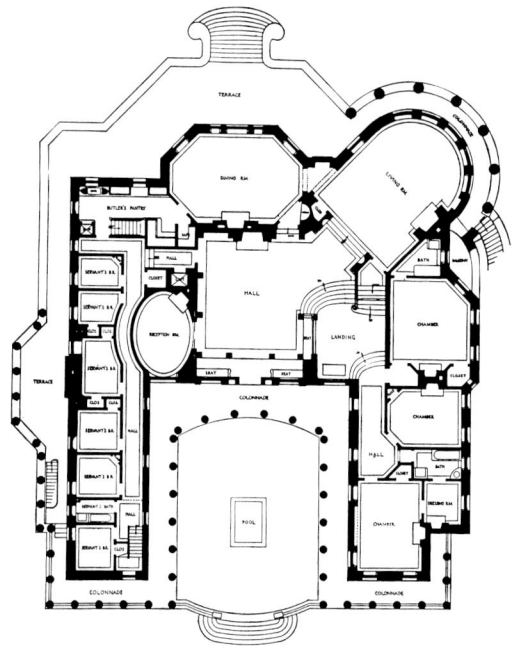

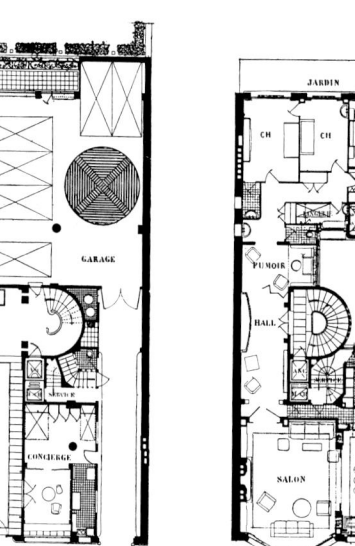

221 Architecture and the Cumulative City

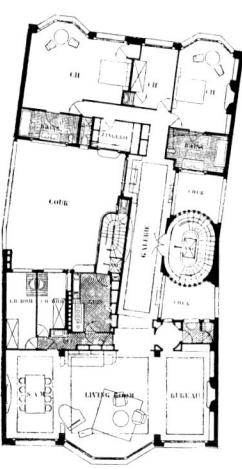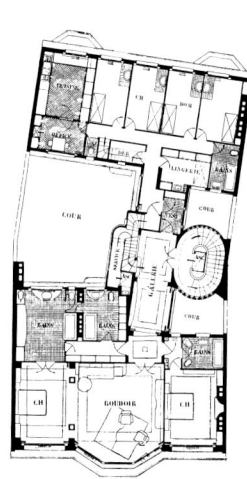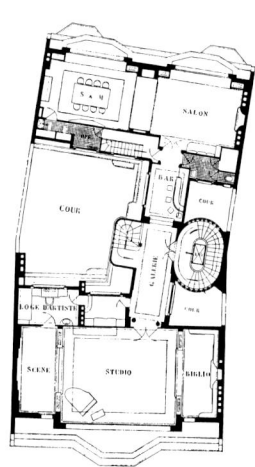

340
Paris (Neuilly), apartment house in boulevard d'Inkermann, ground and typical floor plans, Michel Roux-Spitz, 1929–31

341
Paris, apartment house in boulevard du Montparnasse, typical floor plan and plan of seventh-floor studio, Michel Roux-Spitz, 1930–31

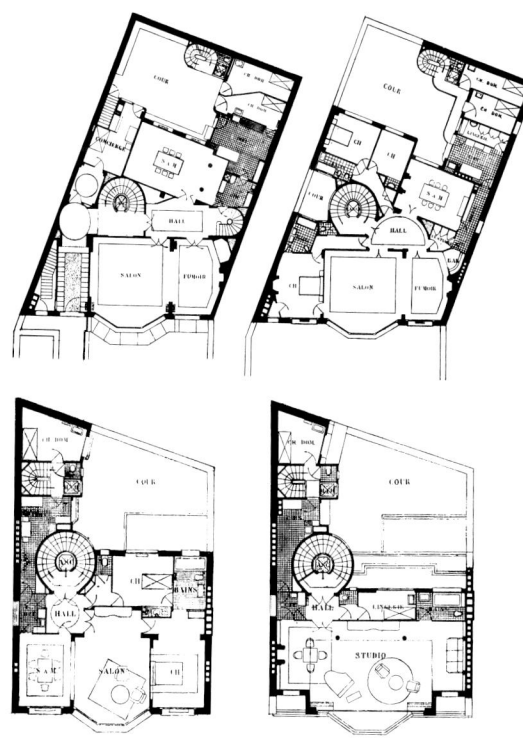

342
Padova, Caffé Pedrocchi, ground floor plan, Giuseppe Jappelli, 1831.
1. central red room
2. green room and white room
3. stock exchange room
4. gallery
5. and 6. north loggias
7. south loggia
8. toilet
9. serving area
10. storage
11. grand stair to the casino
12. stair to the casino
13. stairs to basement
14. stairs to basement
15. circulation

343
Padova, Caffé Pedrocchi, upper floor plan (casino d'nobili), Giuseppe Jappelli.
17. grand stair
18. Etruscan room
19. Greek room by de Min
20. room by Caffi
21. Renaissance room by Gazzotto
22. Herculaneum room by Paoletti
23. Egyptian room
24. secondary entrance from the round stair
26. Rossini ballroom
27. orchestra
28. service
29. Moorish sitting room
30. Corinthian gallery
31. attic stair
32. terraces above the Doric loggias

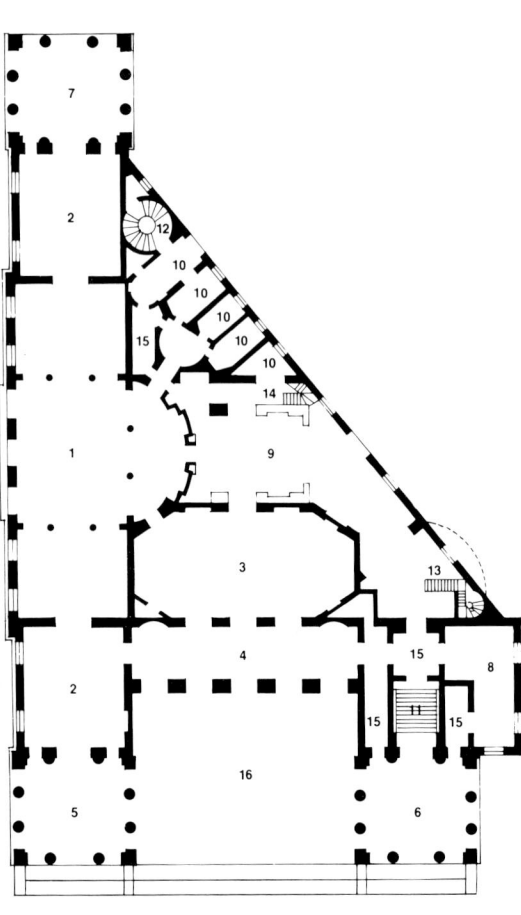

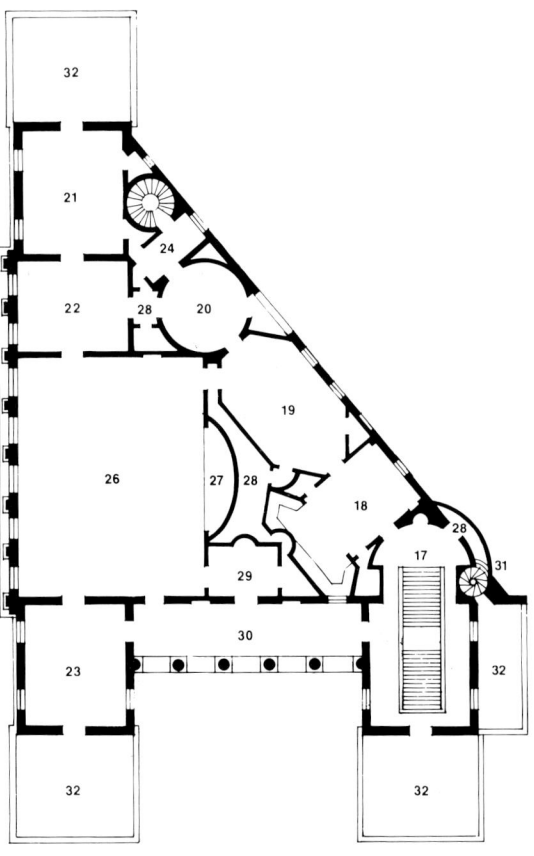

344
University of California at Santa Barbara, Art Museum, site plan, Michael Dennis and Jeffrey Clark, 1983

223 *Architecture and the Cumulative City*

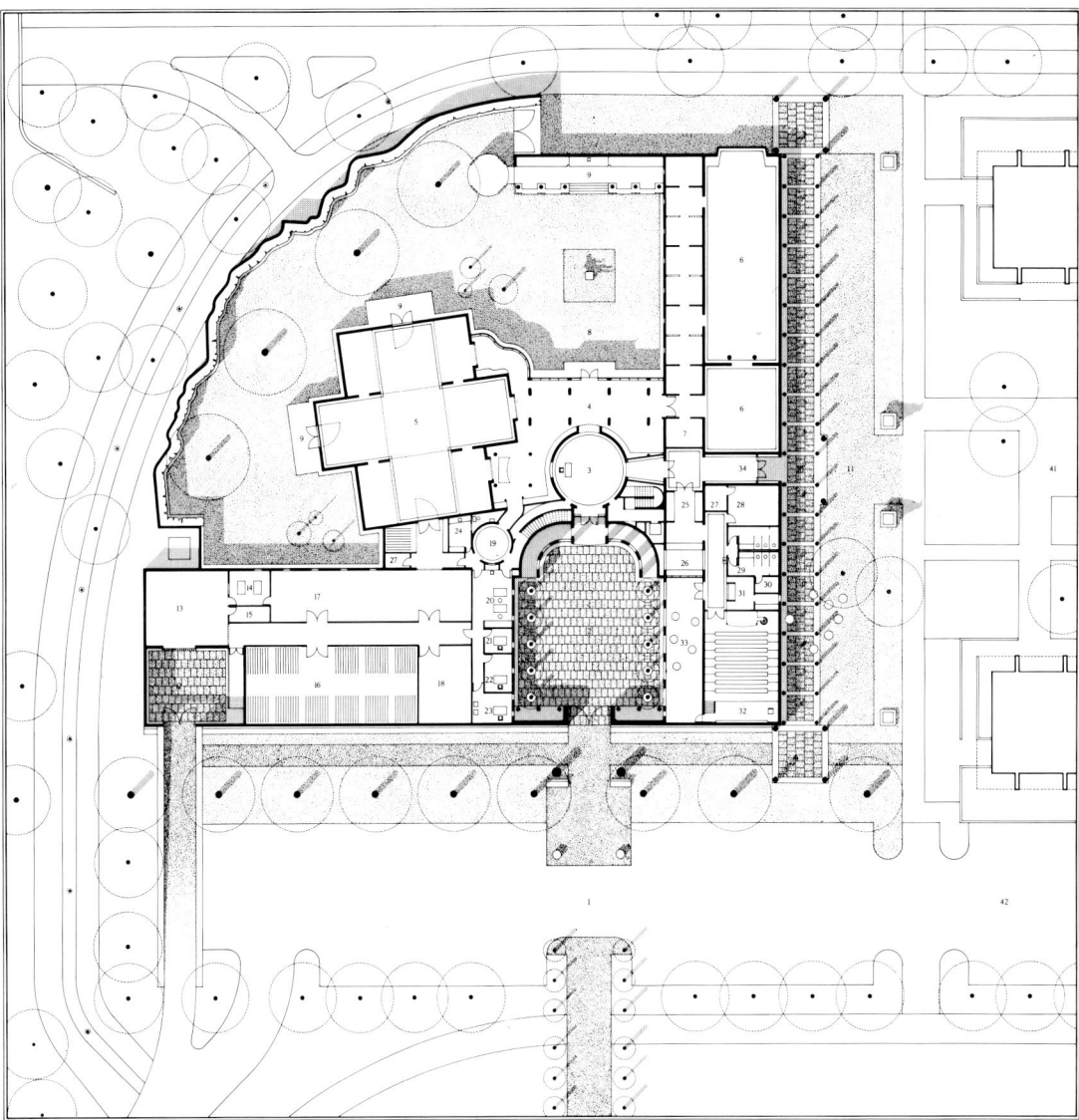

345
University of California at Santa Barbara, Art Museum, ground floor plan.

1. parking
2. entry court
3. rotunda
4. hall
5. changing exhibits
6. permanent collections
7. study collection
8. garden
9. green room
10. pergola
11. sculpture terrace
12. service court
13. receiving
14. registrar
15. storage
16. vault
17. preparation
18. conservation
19. reception
20. clerical
21. administrator
22. curator
23. director
24. office machines
25. coats
26. bookstore
27. electrical
28. boiler
29. toilets
30. custodian
31. café
32. lecture room
33. loggia
34. east entrance

Prints, architectural drawings, and a conference room are above spaces 25–31.

224 Architecture and the Cumulative City

346
University of California
at Santa Barbara, Art
Museum, axonometric

347
University of California
at Santa Barbara, Art
Museum, perspectives

348
University of California
at Santa Barbara, Art
Museum, axonometric

349
University of California
at Santa Barbara, Art
Museum, perspectives

225 Architecture and the Cumulative City

350
University of California at Santa Barbara, Art Museum, model

351
University of California at Santa Barbara, Art Museum, perspective of rotunda

352
University of California at Santa Barbara, Art Museum, perspective of hall

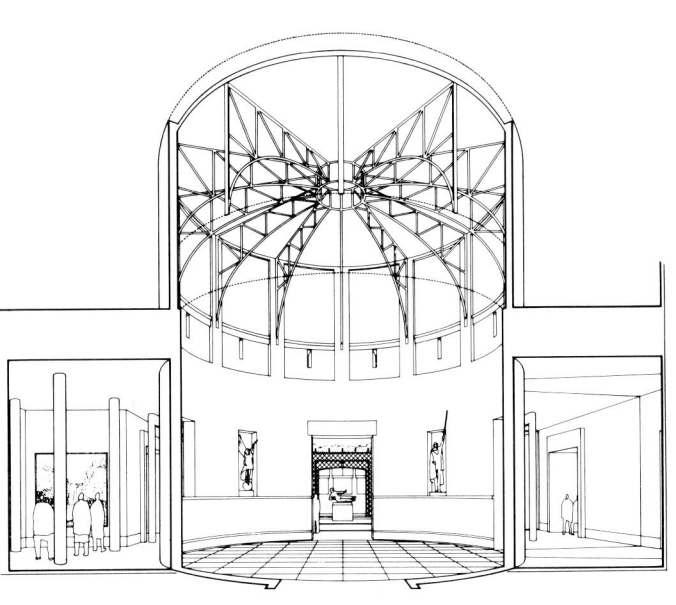

226 Architecture and the Cumulative City

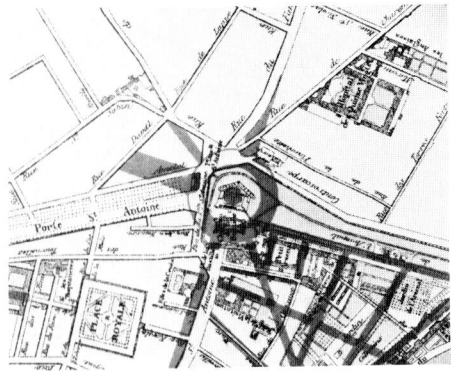

353
Place de la Bastille. Detail from the Artists' plan, 1793.

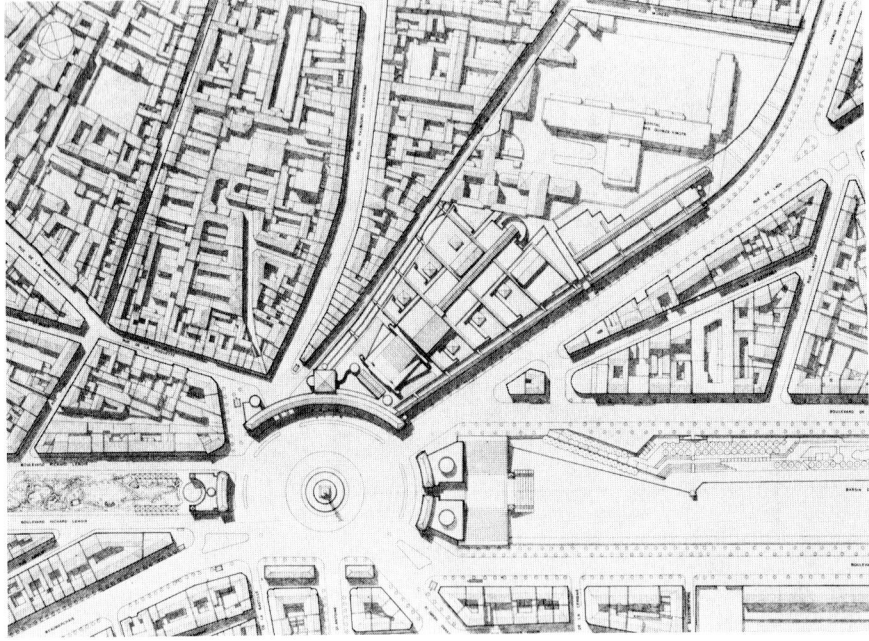

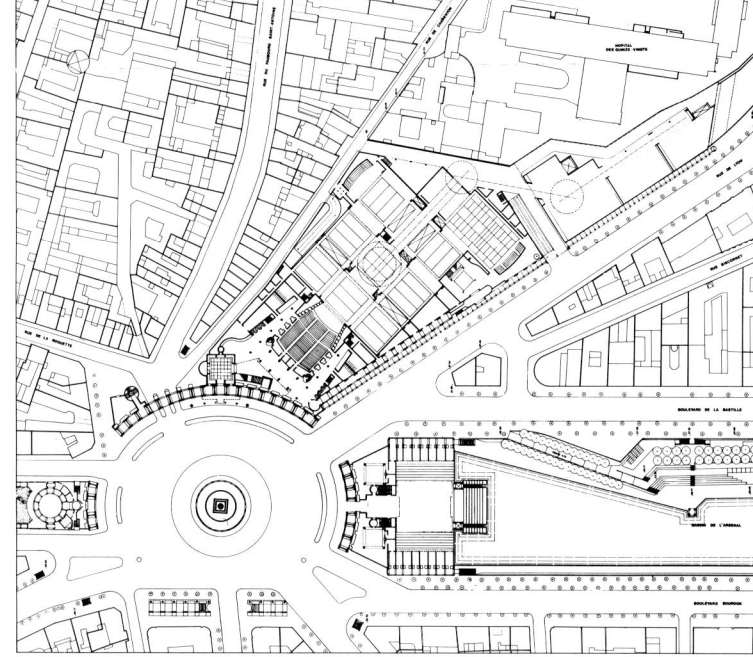

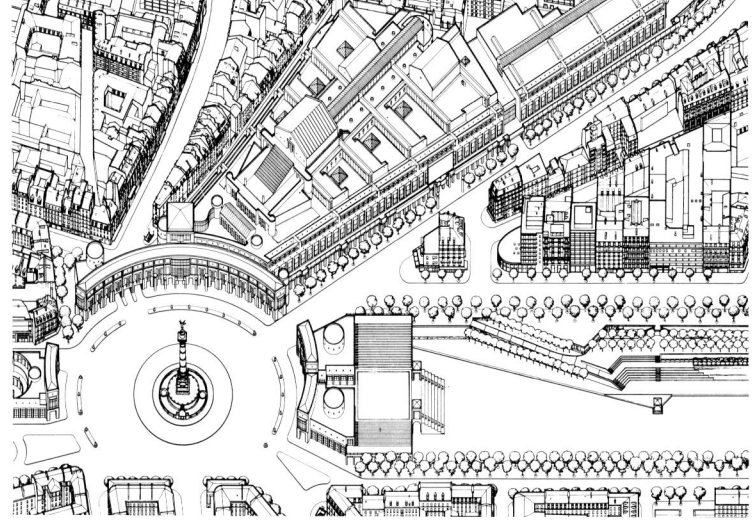

354
Opera de la Bastille competition, site plan, Michael Dennis and Jeffrey Clark, 1983

355
Opera de la Bastille competition, ground floor plan

356
Opera de la Bastille competition, axonometric

Architecture and the Cumulative City

357
Opera de la Bastille competition, plan of Paris

358
Opera de la Bastille competition, aerial view

359
Opera de la Bastille competition, entry facade

360
New Haven, Connecticut, plan in 1824

361
The White House, as pictured on a twenty-dollar bill

362
Versailles, Petit Trianon, view of the south facade, Ange-Jacques Gabriel, begun 1762

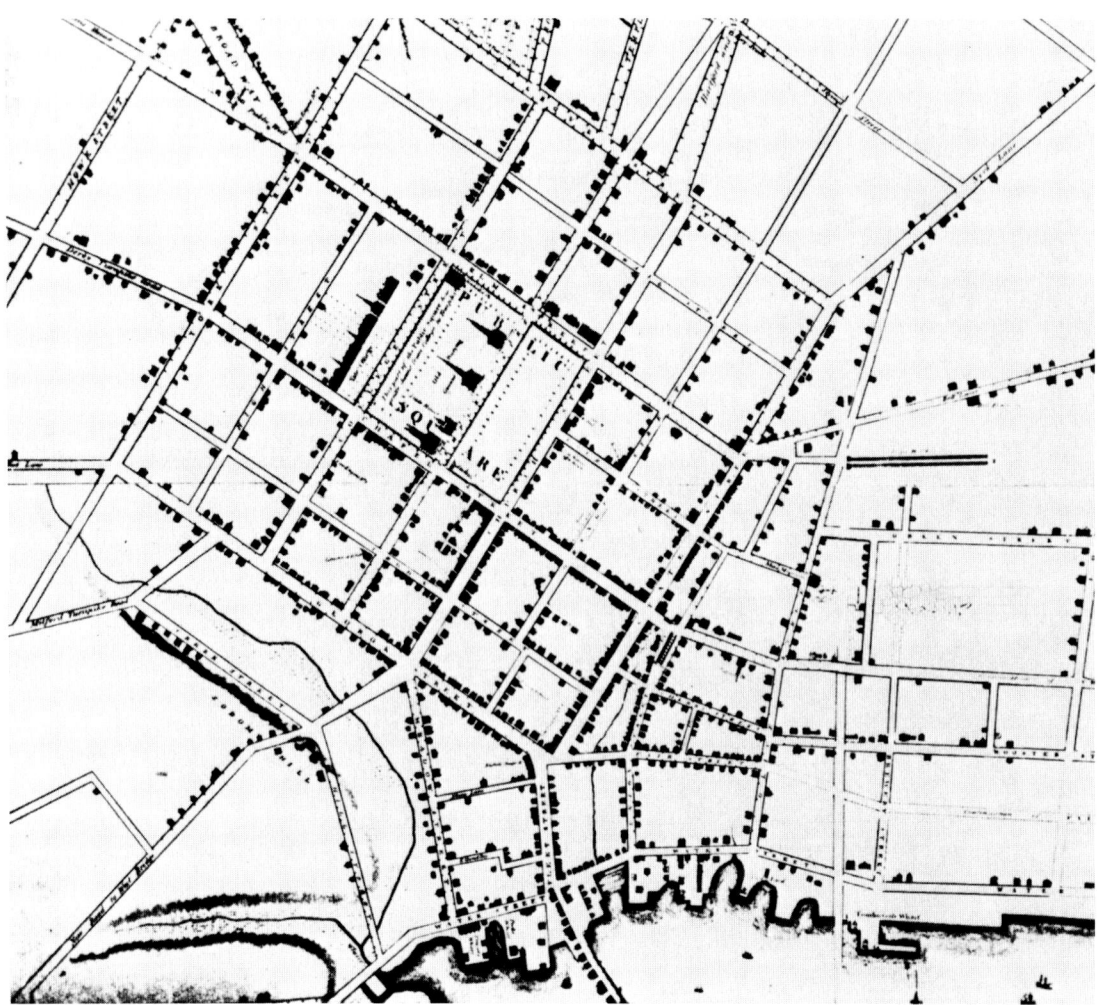

8 Excursus Americanus

The United States of America was not among the last Roman colonies, but then the idea that it was could appear equally plausible. Across the entire country there is evidence of a rational and powerful society, the background of which could have been Greco-Roman. If the town grids exhibit a lack of closure and an occasional confusion about cardo and decumanus, and if temples to unknown deities are rivaled in their freedom of distortion only by the greatness of their numbers, then all of this might only too easily be explained by remoteness of original models and the relative lateness of colonization. But in spite of insistent visible evidence of grid towns and temples—and even an occasional pantheon—there is no trace, crucially, of forum or agora, thus assuring that the United States is a product of another time and another culture, that its Roman ties are indirect, assumed, or both.

From the absence of a strong tradition of enclosed urban space (that is, of forum or agora), we can conclude that America was principally the product of Neoclassicism, not of Classicism, and that the profile of urban America, with its notably fragile tradition of urban space, is therefore more a result of chronology than of geography or genetics. Both the landscape and its distance from the centers of Western civilization contributed to the basic psychology of the place—to what Vincent Scully describes as "a feeling at once of liberation and of loss"[1]—but it was Neoclassicism that provided the urban system for the emerging nation. It was precisely that urban system, applied in the special geographic and psychological context, that turned the ideal of the Enlightenment garden city into reality in the New World.

At the time of its birth in 1776, the United States of America had a total population of approximately 2.25 million. By 1790 this had increased to almost 4 million, but the total urban population was only slightly more than 200,000 people and only two cities were larger than 25,000.[2] The whole country was regarded as something of a wilderness by foreign visitors, and there were no professionally trained American architects. (Benjamin Latrobe, arriving in 1796, was the first.) Urbanism was barely an ideal, much less a developed tradition or even a necessity. The principal architectural element in the colonies had been the detached house; and even by the time of the Revolution, only the northern cities evinced some pattern of town houses with potentially common walls. The character of the towns was still distinctly medieval. Between this innocent time and the era of aspiring to an expansive future, a second wave of European influence appeared—one that would be of incalculable importance to the urbanization, and subsequent deurbanization, of America. By 1900 this relatively primitive arcadia would be transformed: almost half of the total population of 87,832,000 would be urban, and three cities would be larger than one million.[3]

This second wave of European influence, which swept America during the 1790s, is analogous to the second wave of Italian influence introduced to medieval France in the 1540s. The principal difference is that this time the imported taste and culture were not Italian but English and French; the imported spatial sensibilities were not those of the Renaissance but of the Enlightenment; and two of the three principal couriers were not foreign, as were Vignola and Serlio, but native Americans: Charles Bulfinch and Thomas Jefferson. Both men were gentlemen-amateur architects, each returned from an extended stay in

Europe in the late 1780s, and each tried to introduce an appropriate architecture and urban culture to the developing United States of America. The architectural language of both men was Neoclassicism, but for Bulfinch the tradition was English, whereas for Jefferson it was French—and Roman.[4]

After returning in 1787 from almost two years in Europe, Charles Bulfinch devoted himself for some thirty years to providing his provincial hometown of Boston with an urban architecture. His sources, like his background, were English, primarily Robert Adam and William Chambers. Although his projects for Park Street, Colonnade Row, and the Tontine Crescent no longer exist, they provided the inspiration for many surviving projects that still place Boston closer than most American cities to the European urban tradition. The partially realized Tontine Crescent was especially significant. Planned around 1793, it was the first (and almost the only) American example of a unified enclosed urban space. Although there were earlier squares and greens, such as those of Savannah, Philadelphia, and New Haven, they were neither enclosed nor unified; and although there were subsequent examples of unified enclosed squares, there were very few, and fewer still outside of Boston.

The Tontine Crescent was originally designed as two opposing crescents of regular houses with an oval park in the middle and the Franklin Theater at one end. As finally realized, the northern crescent was replaced by a straight row of houses, but the integrity of the composition was maintained. The Tontine Crescent could have been the prototype for an American tradition of enclosed urban spaces; that this was ultimately not the case may be due as much to the project's En-

363
Boston, Tontine Crescent, Charles Bulfinch, c. 1793

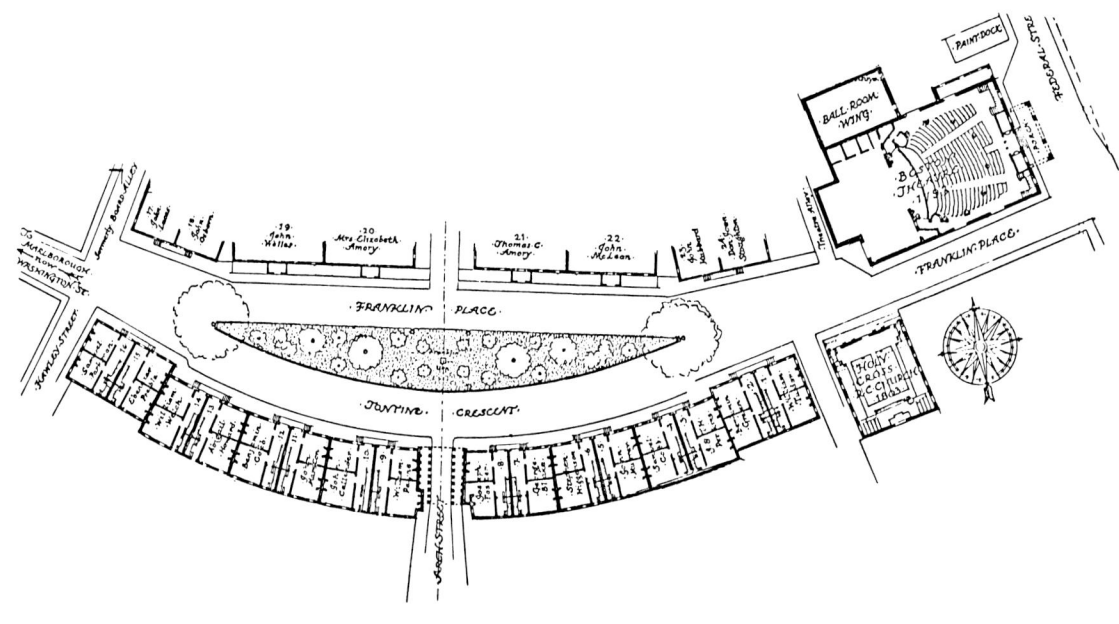

364
Boston, Tontine Crescent, plan

glish derivation as anything else. Bulfinch's Crescent, along with his other projects, renewed the connection to English architecture and culture that had been broken for thirty years. But while the English tradition may have been highly coveted in Boston, it was predictably less so in the rest of the country. Having just broken away from England through revolution, the rest of America certainly did not want an English architecture as a symbol of their new nation. It may have been more than the Britishness of Bulfinch's Boston, however, that made its acceptance difficult.

America was born on a cusp of history, a philosophical and architectural turning point between the spatial tradition of the Renaissance and the iconic stirrings of the Enlightenment; and although it would be disingenuous to suggest that the country as a whole was consciously aware of it, there was a general longing for expression. Architects were seeking an American architecture, one that was both an instrument of and an appropriate symbol for a country that was a product of the Enlightenment, not the Renaissance. Of course, the ironies of the gardens of Versailles serving as the model for the capital city of a new democracy have often been noted, but even this ultimate symbol of the *ancien régime* took on a different meaning when it was reinterpreted by New World Neoclassicism. Washington, D.C. established the importance to America of the French tradition, which, embodied in the French Enlightenment, had its greatest impact on American architecture and urbanism. In this respect, it was Jefferson, and not Bulfinch or Latrobe, who played the role of Serlio to the New World.

Jefferson was an idealist as well as a practical man, and he provided the most poignant architectural and "urban" expression for the new democracy. The expression was so compelling that it still permeates the American psyche and therefore remains problematic to this day, perhaps as much for its symbolic implications as for its anti-urban ones. Early in his career, Jefferson consciously rejected the English architectural tradition for its political associations, and, with the exception of the English landscape garden which he guardedly admired, turned instead to Roman architecture as understood through books, especially those on Palladio. After his stay in Paris, his style became a kind of Franco-Romanism that he considered an appropriate cultural expression.

Jefferson's well-known rejection of the city appeared quite early and was modified only when, late in his life, he grudgingly accepted its necessity. Even as late as 1800, after five years in Paris, he viewed "great cities as pestilential to the morals, the health and the liberties of man."[5] Indeed, Paris not only failed to change Jefferson's anti-urban convictions, it reinforced them. Paris demonstrated to him that the Neoclassical pavilion in a romantic landscape had the potential to serve as the ideal fabric of a civilized agrarian democracy.

Jefferson replaced Benjamin Franklin as Minister to the Court of France and lived in Paris from August 1784 to September 1789. The experience had a profound effect not only on him, but also on America through the ideas he imported. The influence was almost immediate: after seeing his first and only important Roman temple, the Maison Carrée in Nîmes, Jefferson reinterpreted it, with the help of the French architect Clérisseau, as America's first Roman temple, the Virginia State Capitol (1785–89). To point out that Jefferson mistook the Maison Carrée for a repub-

365
Nîmes, France, Maison Carrée, 16 B.C.

366
Richmond, Virginia, the State Capitol, Thomas Jefferson, 1785–89

lican monument would verge on pettiness about symbolism; what caught Jefferson's eye was the monument's beauty and perfection. In any case, its symbolism is probably close enough.

But "Jefferson's Paris" was not really Roman Paris or even seventeenth-century Paris; rather, it was Paris of the 1780s—frenzied, elegant, avant-garde, Neoclassical Paris—the Paris of Ledoux, of the Palais Royal, and of the pavilions in the new quarters beyond the *boulevards*.[6] Paris was a vital, active place during Jefferson's five years there, and thanks to his fanatical record keeping, we are aware of his visits and his interests. Two of the most influential were the newly completed Palais Royal and the new domestic architecture. Both had an enormous impact on Jefferson. As models, they represented extreme opposites: one, the ultimate public gesture, an elaborate urban organism providing both textural continuity and conspicuous spatial focus; the other, the ultimate private icon, prelude to the *machine à habiter*, the internally responsive, externally expressive solid.

Naturally, it was the latter that had the most pervasive influence on Jefferson's work. During his first year in Paris, he lived in the new Chaussée d'Antin section beyond the *boulevards*, and since Ledoux's Hôtel de Montmorency and Hôtel Guimard were just around the corner, Jefferson must have known them. He appreciated the sophistication of French planning, and nowhere is this more apparent than in the development of his own house at Monticello. Before Paris, Monticello was an incomplete and slightly awkward combination of a symmetrical English plan with simple rooms and a modified Palladian facade. Afterward, it was not just completed but transformed into an elaborate Franco-Roman villa in-

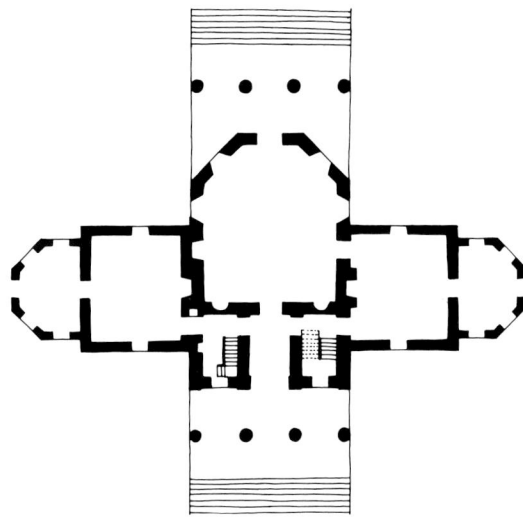

367
Monticello, view from the garden, Thomas Jefferson, 1770–1808

368
Monticello, ground floor plan, before 1772

369
Monticello, final first floor plan, 1809

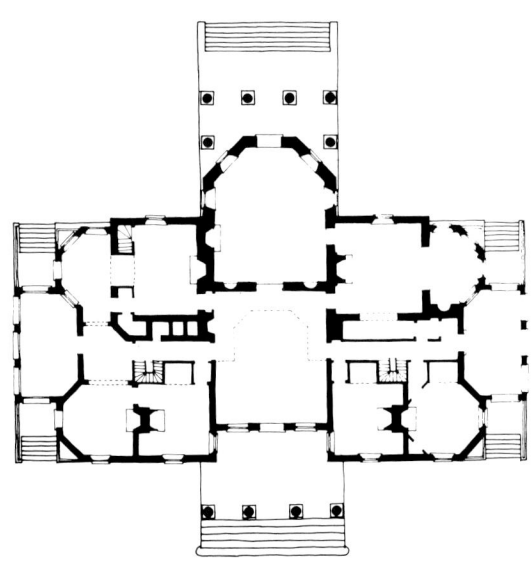

corporating all the latest developments from Neoclassical Paris. The outside was modified to read as a one-story pavilion like the Hôtel de Salm, which he had much admired; and the inside was extended and particularized to a degree achieved only in the best French plans. The house has a great variety of rooms, highly developed service areas, and a separation and contrast between the public and private sequences resulting from the ingenious arrangement of the private rooms in two tiers around the double-height public rooms.

All of these are distinctly French traits, yet one glance reveals that the plan is not French, but something quite different. In the typical Neoclassical French plan, the idiosyncrasies and irregularities are always contained within a rectangular configuration—simple on the outside, complex on the inside—and the central axis of the building is almost always blocked. Jefferson's final plan for Monticello is the opposite. The central Palladian axis is maintained through the sequence of regular public rooms, and the smaller, more specific private rooms are thrown to the outside of the plan. In addition, the perimeter of the plan is loose, articulate, particular; here the center is simple, the perimeter complex. It is as if a French plan had been modified by English influence, rather than the reverse. Later, this kind of modification actually happened when the influence of the English *cottage ornée* loosened the French perimeter and made the axes of the plan even more casual. Then, in the late nineteenth and early twentieth centuries, the Americans reestablished the axes again while maintaining the English preference for the picturesque perimeter. Thus Jefferson's little house may be seen as a historical shortcut and a magnifi-

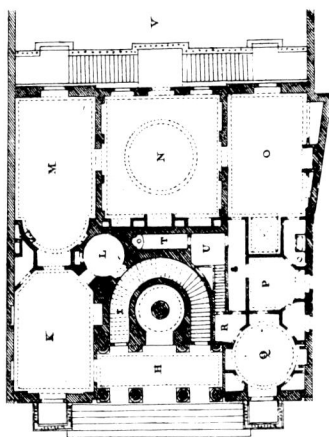

370
Paris, Hôtel d'Orliane, first floor plan, Pierre d'Orliane, 1789

371
Paris, Hôtel de Salm, river facade, Pierre Rousseau, 1782–85

cent preview of what would be one of America's most poetic urban inventions—the one-family house on Elm Street.

The Palais Royal, Jefferson's other Parisian fascination, had become what Mercier called "the capital of Paris" by the time Jefferson arrived in 1784. Indeed, it was at that time a complex, multifunctional public building, although this had not always been the case. Until 1780, the building proper had been a royal palace facing gardens that were always accessible to the public. The new owner, later to become the Duc d'Orléans, decided to capitalize on the potential of the property and hired Victor Louis to transform the palace complex into a vast multi-use commercial center. The gardens were surrounded and enclosed with arcaded galleries, to the understandable outrage of the public, especially the surrounding property owners. When the building was opened in 1784, however, it was an instant success. Full of shops, restaurants, theaters, and apartments, it became the social center of Paris. The public garden remained, and was even equipped with a subterranean circus. Jefferson visited the Palais Royal frequently and was sufficiently moved to propose a similar complex for Richmond, Virginia, which would be "a whole square in Richmond improved on some such plan, but accommodated to the circumstances of the place."[7]

It is tragic that this idea came to naught, however casual its suggestion may have been, for it would have joined the Tontine Crescent in introducing conspicuous urban space to America. The Palais Royal is an invaluable resource both as a fragment and microcosm of the city, and had it been realized, its American counterpart might have been an equally suggestive model for the rapidly growing country. Fortunately, however, this persuasive image informs Jefferson's most important work, the University of Virginia, in a subtle yet profound way.

The University of Virginia sometimes evokes references to Roman fora; it almost always invites comparisons with the original plan (1812) for Union College in Schenectady, New York, by the French émigré architect Jean-Jacques Ramée; and its similarity to the Château de Marly (begun 1679) by J. H. Mansart has occasionally been noted. Yet Jefferson's project is unlike any of these. It is less enclosed and less unified than a Roman forum or Union College; and although it bears a striking resemblance to the arrangement at Marly, its form and its meaning are completely different. The Château de Marly, intended as an escape from the totalitarian rigors of Versailles, is formed of separate but equal pavilions axially related to a similar but larger one for the king, all of which are set in a terraced, formal French garden. At Marly the order is singular and unified, and the part, although expressed, is still controlled by the whole. The University of Virginia, on the other hand, exhibits a more complex order in which the part and the whole exist in a suggestive balance, with many intermediate shades of interpretation. Both the immutability of public truth and the transcendental license of private adjustment are debated at all levels of the organization. It is as if the best qualities of the French Enlightenment and the French Renaissance—of the Neoclassical pavilions and the Palais Royal—had been fused by Jefferson into one spectacular and distinctly American expression.

For political and religious reasons, Jefferson studiously avoided the English university models, and he also avoided the early American

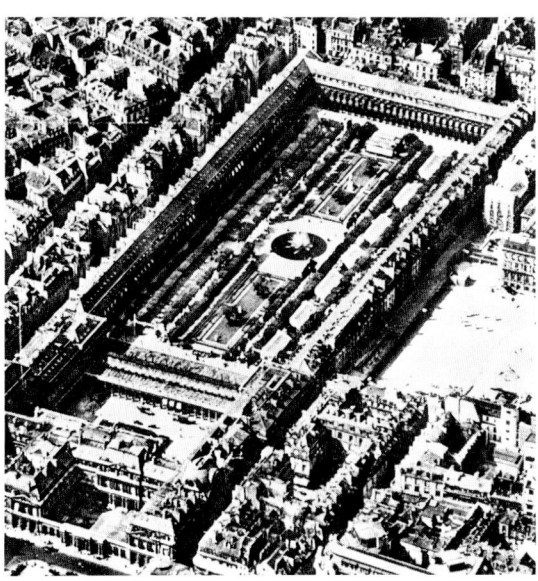

372
Paris, Palais Royal, aerial view

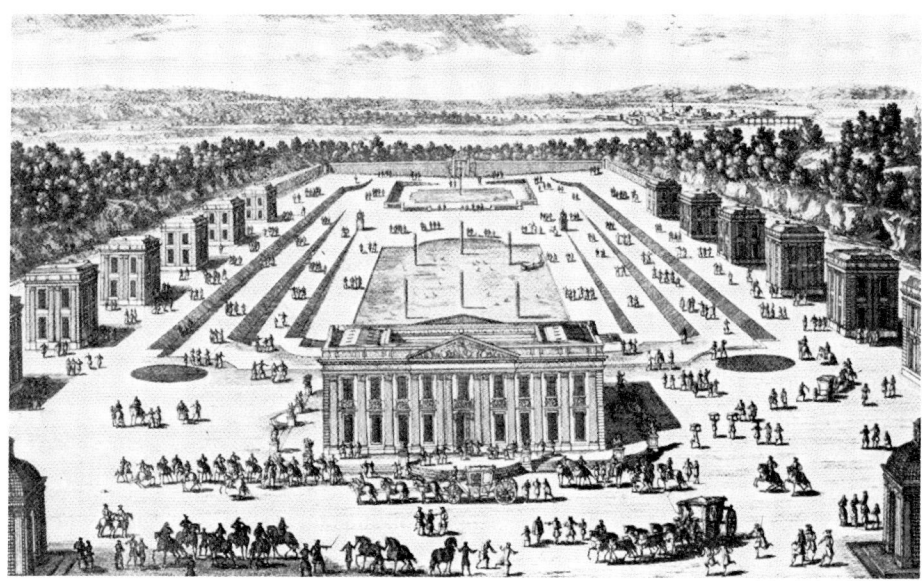

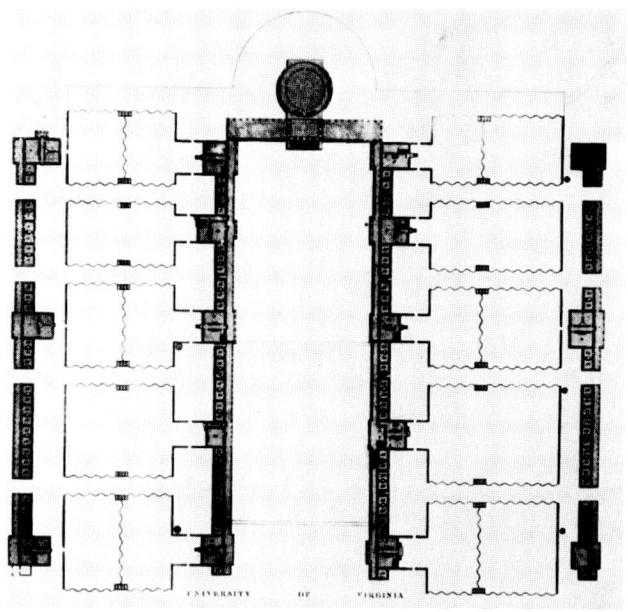

373
Château de Marly, Jules Hardouin Mansart, begun 1679. Engraving by Perelle.

374
Charlottesville, Virginia, The University of Virginia, aerial view, Thomas Jefferson, 1817–26

375
Charlottesville, Virginia, The University of Virginia, plan. Engraving by Peter Maverick, 1825.

campus models because of their ad hoc, inconsequential freedom. Instead, he provided for Virginia a great central space defined by colonnades and individual pavilions. Planted with grass and lined with trees, this space was open on the lower end, and, at Latrobe's suggestion, focused on the library at the upper end. Supporting the space on either side was a rich system of gardens, paths, and an outer range of service buildings. Like a democratic version of the Château de Marly, the University of Virginia was at once more subtle and more suggestive. It is no accident that Jefferson referred to his plan as an "academical village," for it is, if anything, a metaphor of society and the city—a Neoclassical ideal "adapted to the circumstances of the place." It certainly is as close as Jefferson came to a coherent idea about the city, and it did provide the United States with a sublime spatial model of the city.

I do not mean to portray Thomas Jefferson as the sole source of American architecture and urbanism, nor to slight Benjamin Latrobe. Rather, I would simply argue that at a critical time in its history—at its birth as a nation—the United States inherited an architectural language that was fundamentally not urban, but suburban; that the principal source was not English, Spanish, or American Indian, but French; and that the most persuasive purveyor of that language was Thomas Jefferson.

Fortunately, this inherited language was not absolutely pure; like most products of revolution, it contained traces of the previous system. Thus, although Jefferson's work and French Neoclassicism demonstrated Enlightenment preference for the evocative solid, there was still a trace of the Renaissance in the faint structure of urban space.

For example, in late-eighteenth-century French engravings, such as those by Krafft and Ransonnette,[8] or Ledoux,[9] domestic pavilions were rendered in an apparently continuous romantic landscape, whereas the real buildings that they depict—the pavilions of suburban Paris—were always contained by walls and the streets were defined by gates and service buildings. It can be argued that in France it was necessity that compromised the new ideal—necessities of space, economics, and tradition—and to a certain extent this may be true. The United States, however, was hardly encumbered by these circumstances, which makes it all the more remarkable that Jefferson considered both the symbolic power of the buildings and the sublime presence of space to be, to some degree, necessary to the formulation of the public realm. This may in fact be Jefferson's most important legacy: the continued insistence on both the ideal and the circumstantial, even in the absence of obvious necessity. For Jefferson, circumstance seems to validate the ideal and, furthermore, the ideal only seems to achieve meaning within that union. From the Neoclassical propensities of the American constitution to the anatomy of the small American town, this debate is inextricably present as principle and as fact. Though in the United States the balance may be tipped in favor of the private and the circumstantial over the public and the ideal, there was, for at least a century and a half, a dialogue.

Jefferson's interpretation of the French tradition in his two principal works, the University of Virginia and Monticello, relates directly to what can only be described as two uniquely American contributions to urbanism: the American college campus and the essence of the small American town, Elm Street.

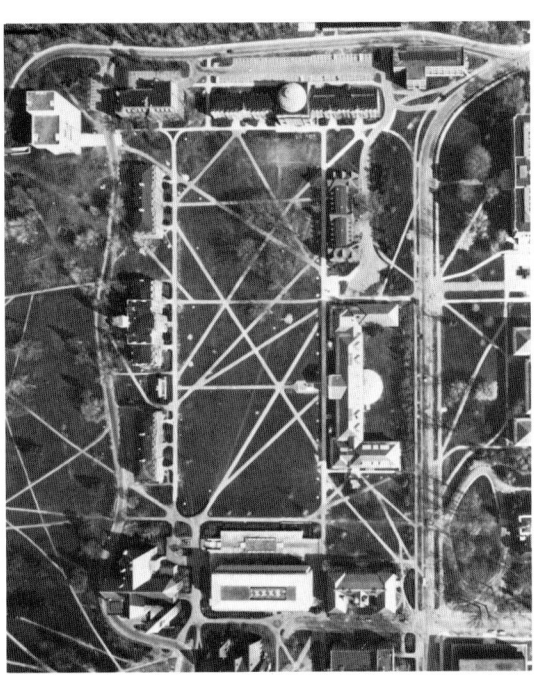

376
Ithaca, New York, Cornell University, Arts Quadrangle, aerial plan

377
Ithaca, New York, Cornell University, Arts Quadrangle, aerial view

378
Satyric street scene, Sebastiano Serlio

379
"Elm Street" (New Haven, Connecticut, Temple Street), c. 1863

From the earliest colleges of the colonial era to the land-grant universities of the frontier, the American campus has been a simulated city that, with few exceptions, is distinctly unlike European models. Loose arrangements of freestanding buildings meld with the landscape to suggest an almost urban space. Not all campuses possess clearly defined quadrangles, but the ones that do seem to be more focused and provocative. They also represent the most tangible tradition of enclosed urban space in the United States, and that is directly attributable to Thomas Jefferson. The image of Jefferson's Virginia lawn is imprinted on countless campuses in America, from Bowdoin to Cornell to Columbia to Minnesota. The order is usually less rigorous than the original, but the stable presence of public space remains, enriched and tirelessly supportive of peripheral freedoms. On campus one has a veiled sense of being in some kind of primitive urban laboratory, where urbanism is being dissolved into landscape or perhaps reconstituted in spite of it. And is not the campus almost always more substantial, more urban than its host body, and a continual commentary upon it? As a model of the city, the American campus may well be more suggestive than the real thing; certainly it is one of America's truly original contributions to urbanism.

For all their vitality, American cities are still derivative of the European urban tradition and invite frequently unfavorable comparison. But the American small town is dream town, not to be found in Europe and therefore not comparable. It is the Enlightenment garden city rendered in infinite variations. If the Town Green is not always sublime, Church Street is usually redeeming, though Main Street may in desperation steer very close to toy town. But Elm Street—Elm Street elevates it all, occasionally to the level of poetry. With Elm Street, European hegemony in the development of urban streets is challenged, and in the process Serlio's "Satyric Scene," long ignored by Europe, is resurrected, civilized, and brought center stage. Elm Street is the quintessential tree-lined residential street. It is the Neoclassical street that the French could never or would never build, the penultimate stage in a long process of formal and social inversion. That process of inversion may be traced by examining a series of street types.[10]

In a typical street in the Marais section of Paris, one such as the rue des Francs-Bourgeois, the space of the street is emphatically defined by a continuous mass of urban *hôtels*. Even when the forecourt of the *hôtel* is screened from the street by only a wall and a gate, the ends of the service wings are of sufficient mass to positively define the street. The private world is completely screened from the public world, and clearly defined forecourts serve as transitional spaces.

A distinct difference may be noted in a typical Rococo street, such as the rue de Grenelle in the Faubourg St.-Germain. Although the plans of the *hôtels* appear similar to those of the Marais, the forecourts are defined by low service wings, and the main living blocks tend to assert themselves as pavilions between the forecourt and the garden. As a result, the street is defined primarily by gates and screen walls. Here the private realm has become more emphatic, the public realm has become less so. From the Rococo street to the American suburb is a surprisingly short jump, but there is one important intermediate step.

In the Neoclassical streets north of the *boulevards*, such as the rue Poissonnière, a condi-

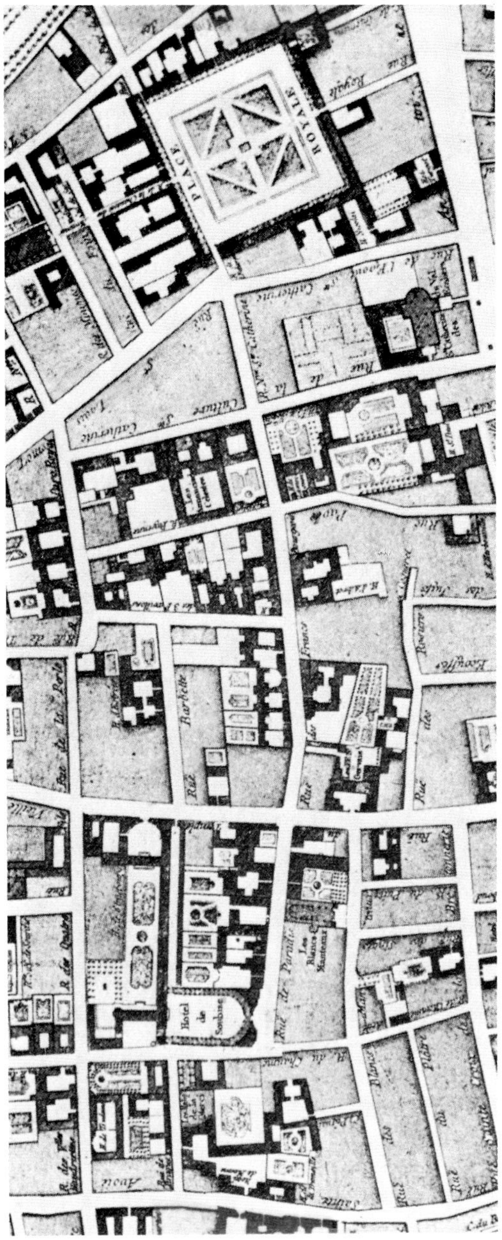

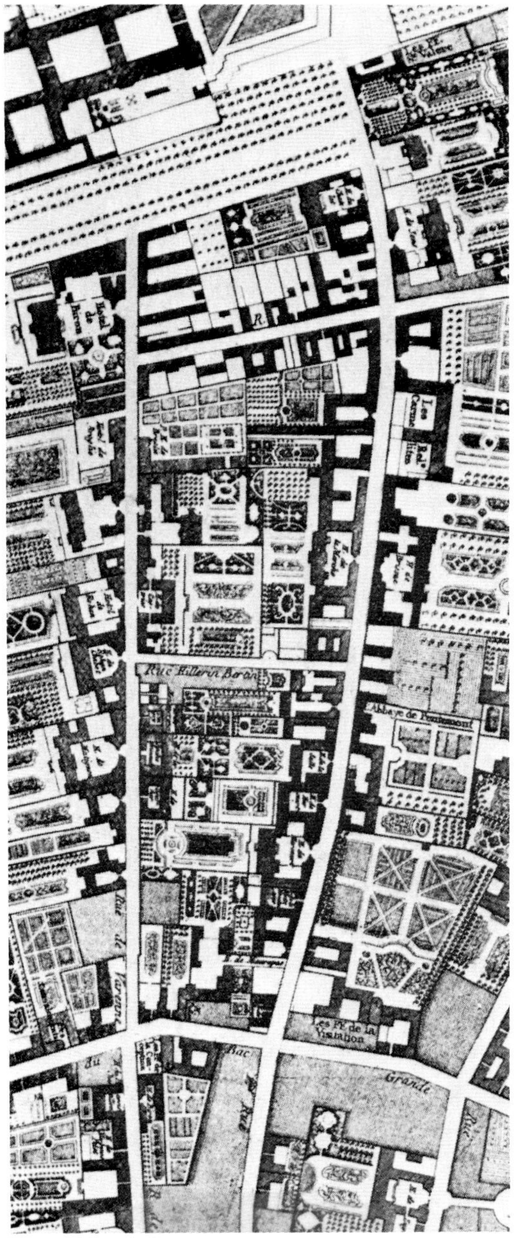

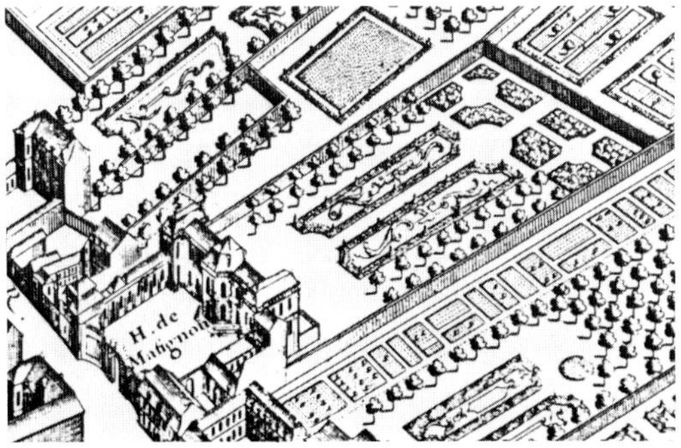

380
Paris, rue des Francs-Bourgeois. From the Jaillot plan.

381
Paris, Hôtel de la Vrillière, François Mansart, begun 1635. Engraving by Marot.

382
Paris, rue de Grenelle. From the Jaillot plan.

383
Hôtel de Matignon, Jean Courtonne, 1722–24. From the Turgot plan.

384
Paris, rue Poissonnière. From the Jaillot plan.

385
Hôtel Guimard, facade, Claude-Nicolas Ledoux, 1770

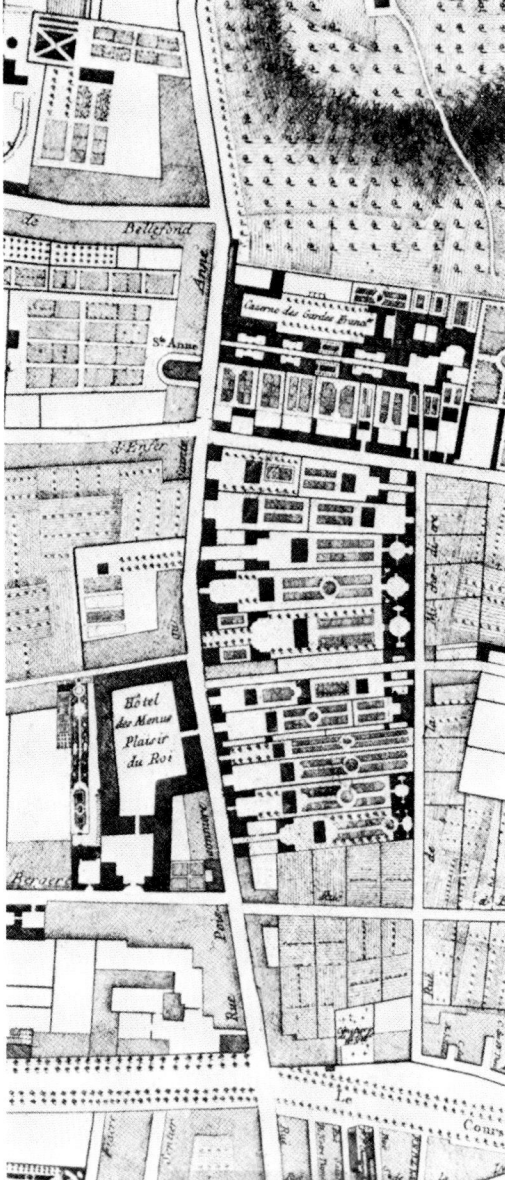

386
New Haven, Connecticut, Hillhouse Avenue, plan, 1879

387
New Haven, Connecticut, Hillhouse Avenue, The Skinner House, Town and Davis, 1830. Engraving.

tion of detached, independent houses is finally achieved. The service wings have disappeared, and the houses generally sit free. They are still separated by garden walls, however, and the street is still defined by rather substantial service buildings and gates. Formally and socially, these Neoclassical *hôtels* are the inverse of those of the Marais: void has become solid, yet the positive armature of the public realm is insistently maintained.

On Elm Street, however, there is no need for even the gates and party walls of the rue Poissonnière: the forecourt has become the front yard, the garden the backyard. As in idealized French Neoclassical renderings, the house sits free in continuous Arcadia, discreetly varying but always addressing the great colonnade of trees that structure the public realm. Here public and private are both accommodated in a respectful dialogue; and adherence to the conventions of street, sidewalk, front yard, porch, and public rooms is precisely what allows invention and private variation.

Unfortunately, the very characteristics that give the small American town its positive qualities are also those that make it extremely vulnerable. Endless nuance and interpretation are possible as long as the delicate balance of solids and voids is maintained. But the Neoclassical system is inherently biased in favor of the private icon, so balance is doubly dependent on maintenance of the public realm, the underpinnings of which are still, however faint, those of the classical structure of space—of street and square. What is not defined by the buildings must be completed by the trees, and slight weakening of either element can result in serious erosion of the system. The devastation caused by Dutch Elm disease

388
Ithaca, New York, Aurora Street

389
Ithaca, New York, Dewitt Park

and its professional equivalent, urban renewal, just after mid-century was rivaled in the extent of damage only by modern architecture.

Growing slowly, quietly maturing, modern architecture in America was like a time bomb planted during the Enlightenment, armed during the 1920s, and set to explode after World War II. And explode it did. Indeed, in some ways it is difficult to believe that America was not the theater of World War II. Even the damage caused by Dutch Elm disease seems minor when compared to that caused by architects and city planners who, in a spirit of postwar optimism, began to dismantle American towns and cities with reckless abandon. Urban renewal prepared the way by removing significant portions of existing urban fabric, but modern architecture delivered the *coup de grâce* with its insistence on the mute object and its rejection of the convention of street and square. Neoclassicism may have carried with it traces of the Renaissance in the faint structure of its urban space, but with modern architecture those traces—the public component of urbanism—disappeared as both idea and fact.[11]

The triumph of modern architecture in postwar America thus marks the last stage of a long transformation from a kind of tyranny of the public realm in the heyday of Louis XIV at Versailles to an equally demanding tyranny of the private realm in postwar Houston, or Los Angeles, or St. Louis. And if one cherishes the advance of individual liberty after the *ancien régime*, then, equally, one just as readily laments the passage of civic responsibility and the urban forms that express and promote it. Ideally (as in the *ville radieuse*), the city of modern architecture was to be totally public. As commandeered by the Americans, however, it became totally private.

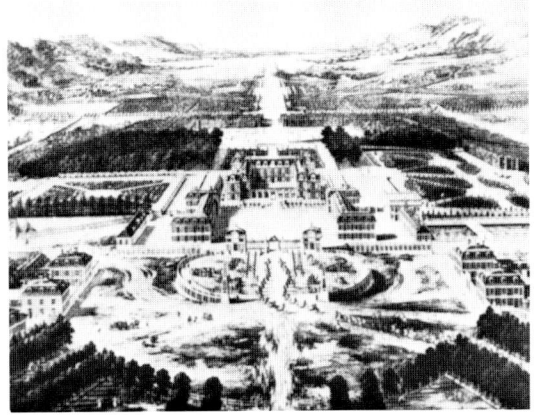

390
Versailles in 1666. Painting by Patel.

391
New Haven, Connecticut, Oak Street Connector, aerial view

392
Subdivision near Oakland, California, aerial view

Even wealth, which before had carried civic responsibility, became private indulgence at all levels of society. Everything now appears to have been cheapened and made more superficial in the heady optimism following World War II: the *plan voisin* before the war begat Boston's Prudential Center after the war; Radburn before the war became Levittown after the war. And to compare the serpentine streets and ranch houses of postwar suburbia to the eloquence of Elm Street would be unbearable if it did not again illustrate that it was in America in the third quarter of the twentieth century that the public realm finally collapsed—formally, socially, psychologically. From Versailles to Berkeley took approximately three hundred years; small wonder there is confusion in the ranks of the architectural profession.

At this point, it is easy to say that the reconstruction of the city—or the reurbanization of American cities—is our principal task in the last quarter of the twentieth century. But the nagging question remains: Is there again a growing desire for public expression, which merely lacks the appropriate means, or is there simply no desire and therefore no possibility of retrieval? Faced with this choice—paradise or apocalypse—one cannot be other than optimistic. As an architect and as a citizen, one can only choose paradise and believe that America does once again anticipate an urban architecture.

Creating a new architecture will be neither quick nor easy. Nor will it be the same as that required in Europe, for our towns and cities *are* different. On the other hand, we can no longer feign youth and naiveté as an excuse, nor should we. If the circumstances of our birth gave us an insufficient urban language, then we have the power and the knowledge to expand it. Indeed, we have the responsibility to do so. The pre-Enlightenment tradition in Western Europe is also our own inheritance; America need not have been born two hundred years earlier or been legitimately a late Roman colony to claim that legacy.

America did make some surprising urban contributions in a little over a hundred years,[12] despite any limitations of language and a fundamental antipathy toward the city. In fact, until well into the twentieth century, there was a nascent urbanism, a public sensibility desperately trying to come to terms with itself and the landscape. After all, Boston's Commonwealth Avenue and Union Park (Square) need no apologies; they are world class by anyone's standards. And in another of the world's many ironies, it was the United States that produced Rockefeller Center, perhaps the twentieth century's most significant urban space. But these and other examples were far from the norm; this nascent but distinct American urbanism was little more than a promise when it was snuffed out. If it is to be nurtured again, we can only hope that it will be informed by the brilliant Neoclassical balance of the American Constitution, by a dialogue between the public and private realms, and by Jefferson's insistence on the inextricable relationship between idea and circumstance.

393
Paris, Palais Royal, garden, view

394
Charlottesville, Virginia, The University of Virginia, Thomas Jefferson, 1817–26

243   *Excursus Americanus*

1
The Legrand plan, Paris in 1380 (nineteenth-century plan)

Plans of Paris

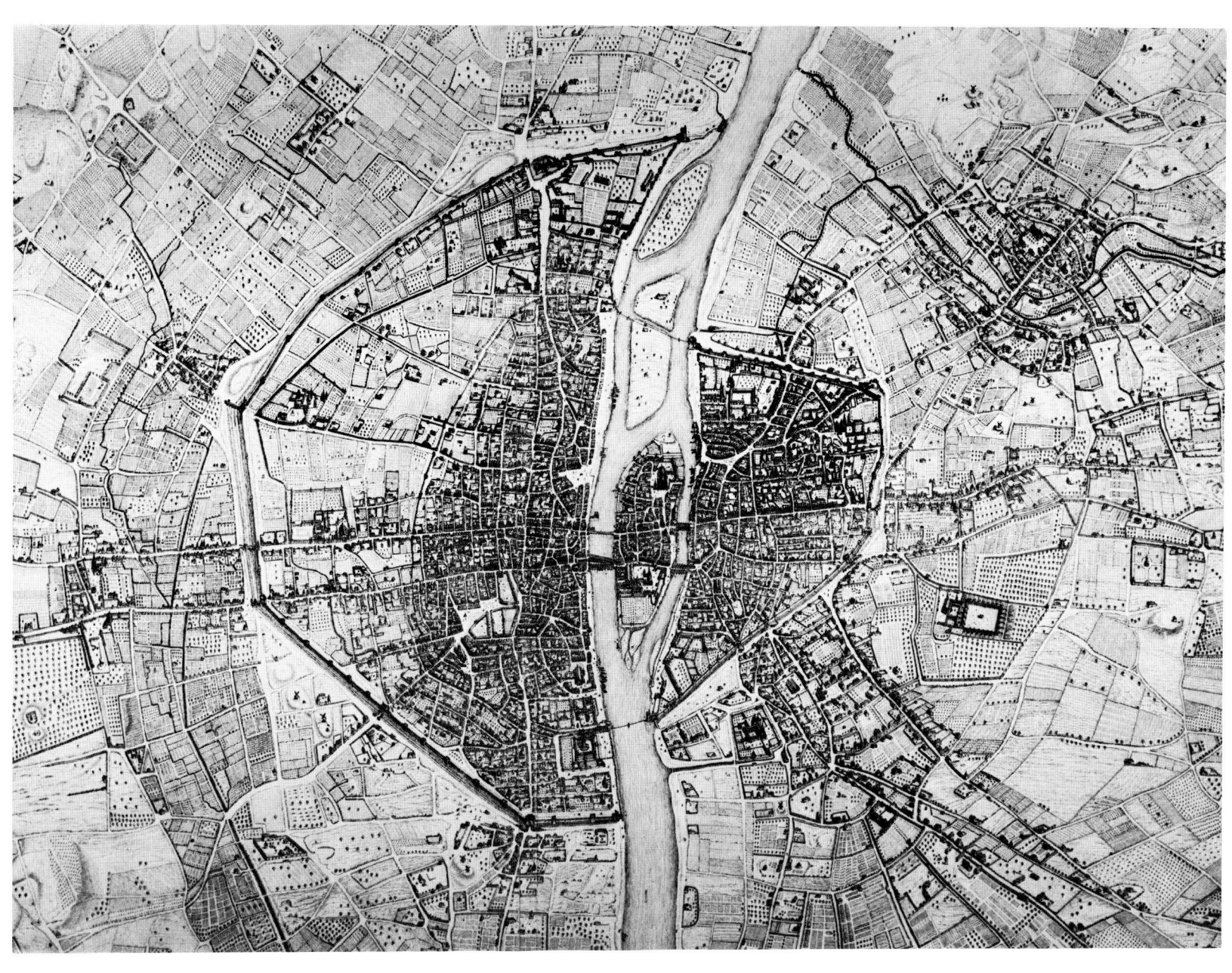

246 Plans of Paris

2
The Braun plan, called
"Aux Trois Person-
nages," Paris c. 1540

3
The Merian plan, 1614

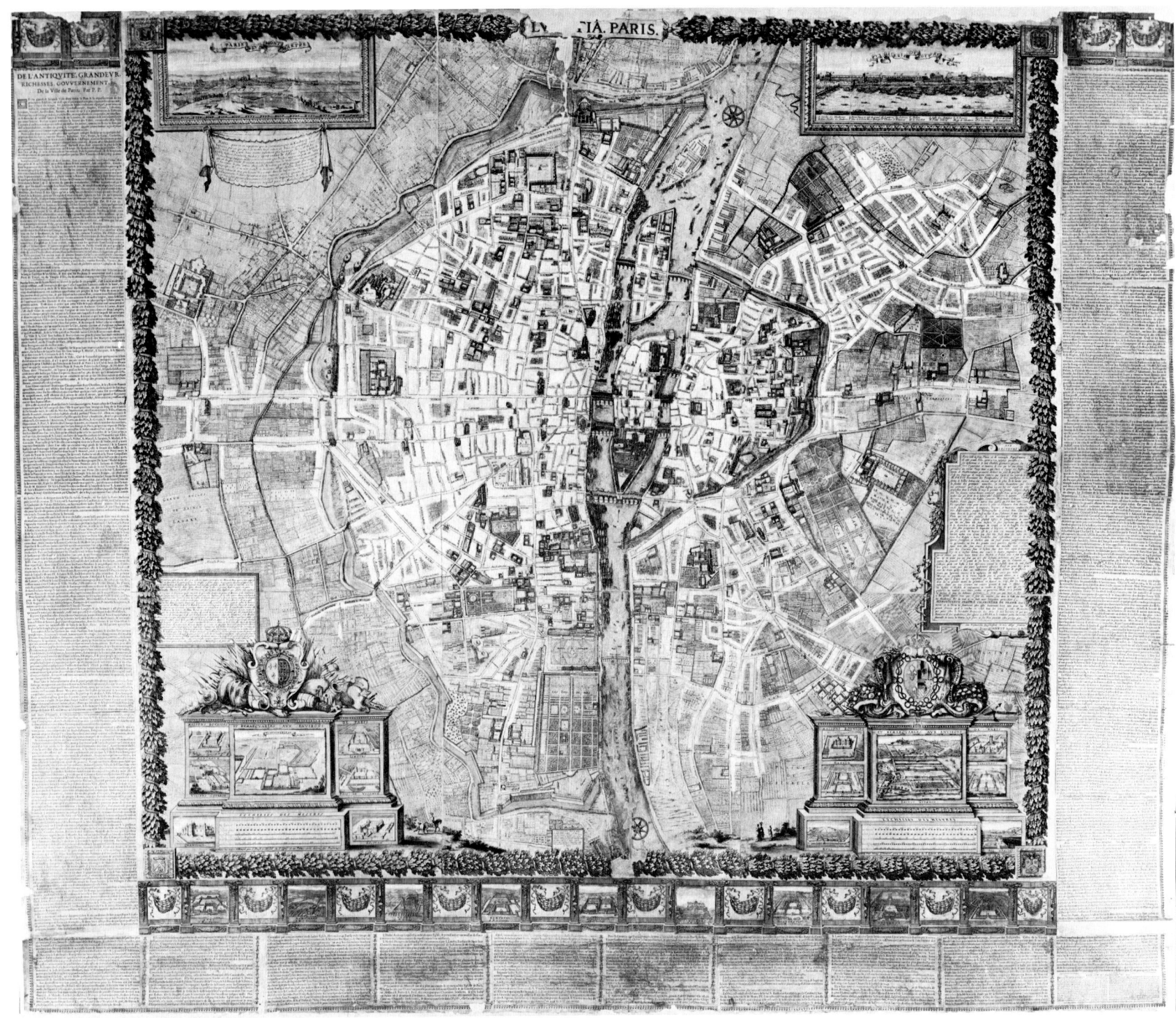

4
The Gombust plan, 1652

5
The Jouvin de Rochefort
plan, 1676

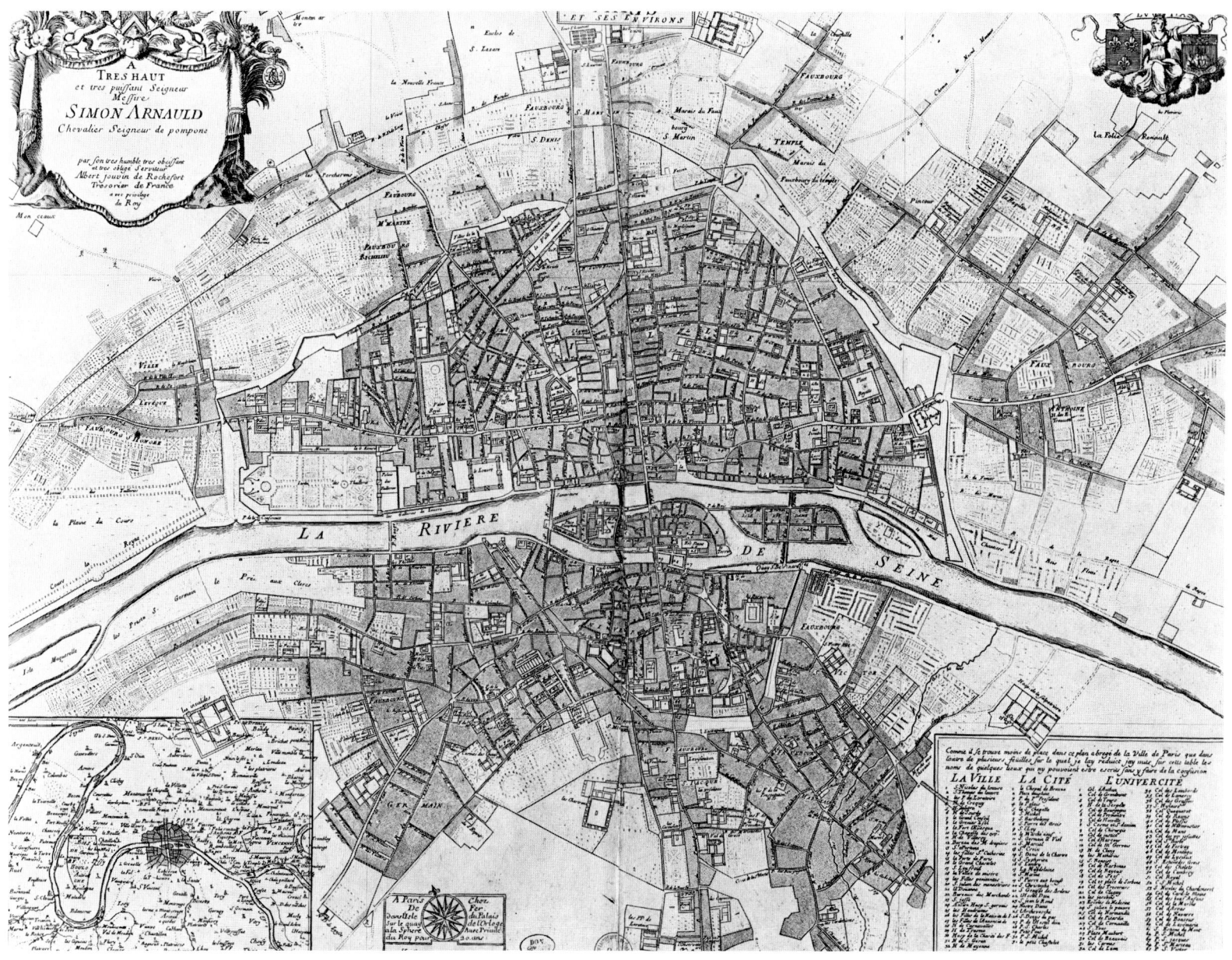

6

The Nicolas de Fer plan, 1697

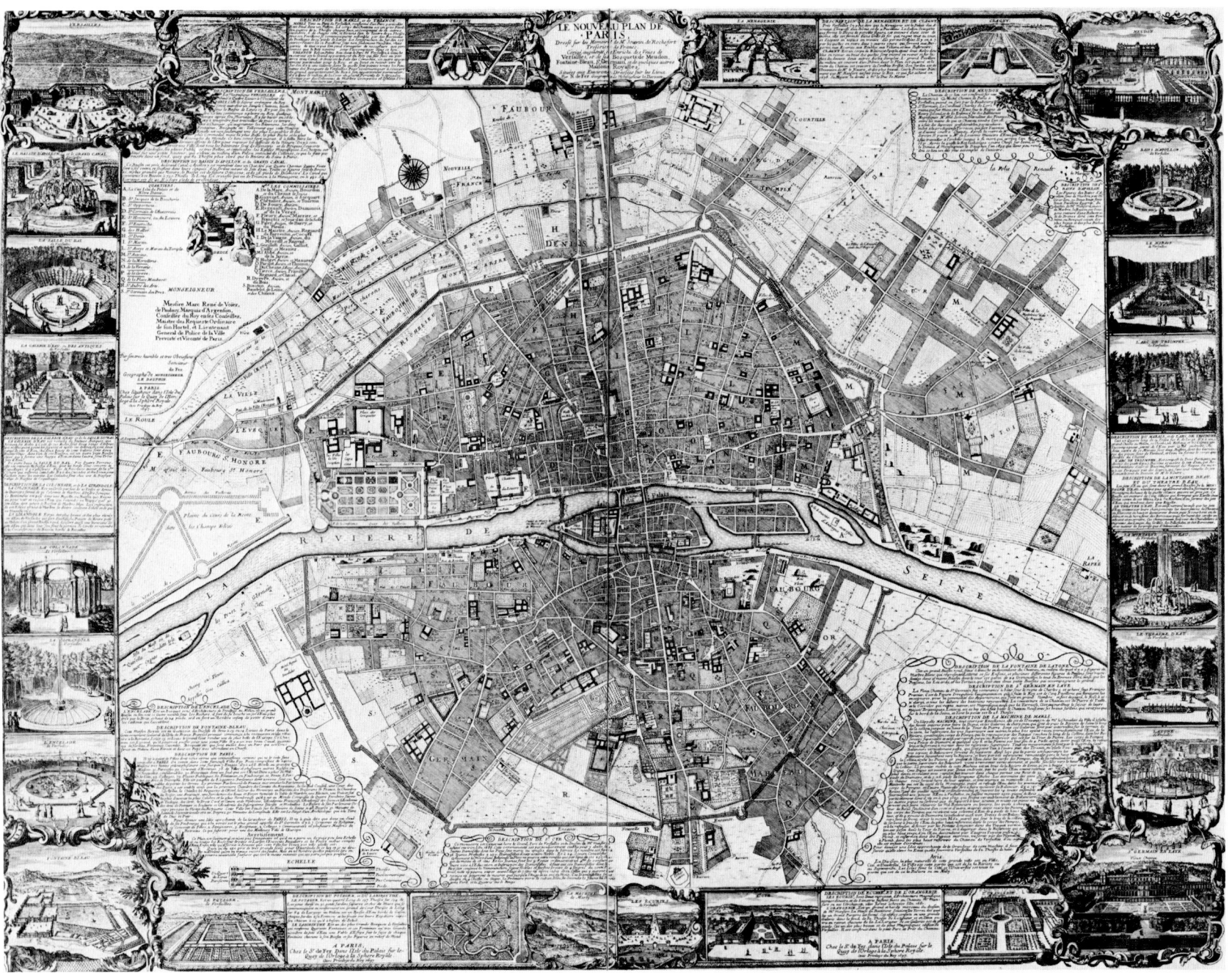

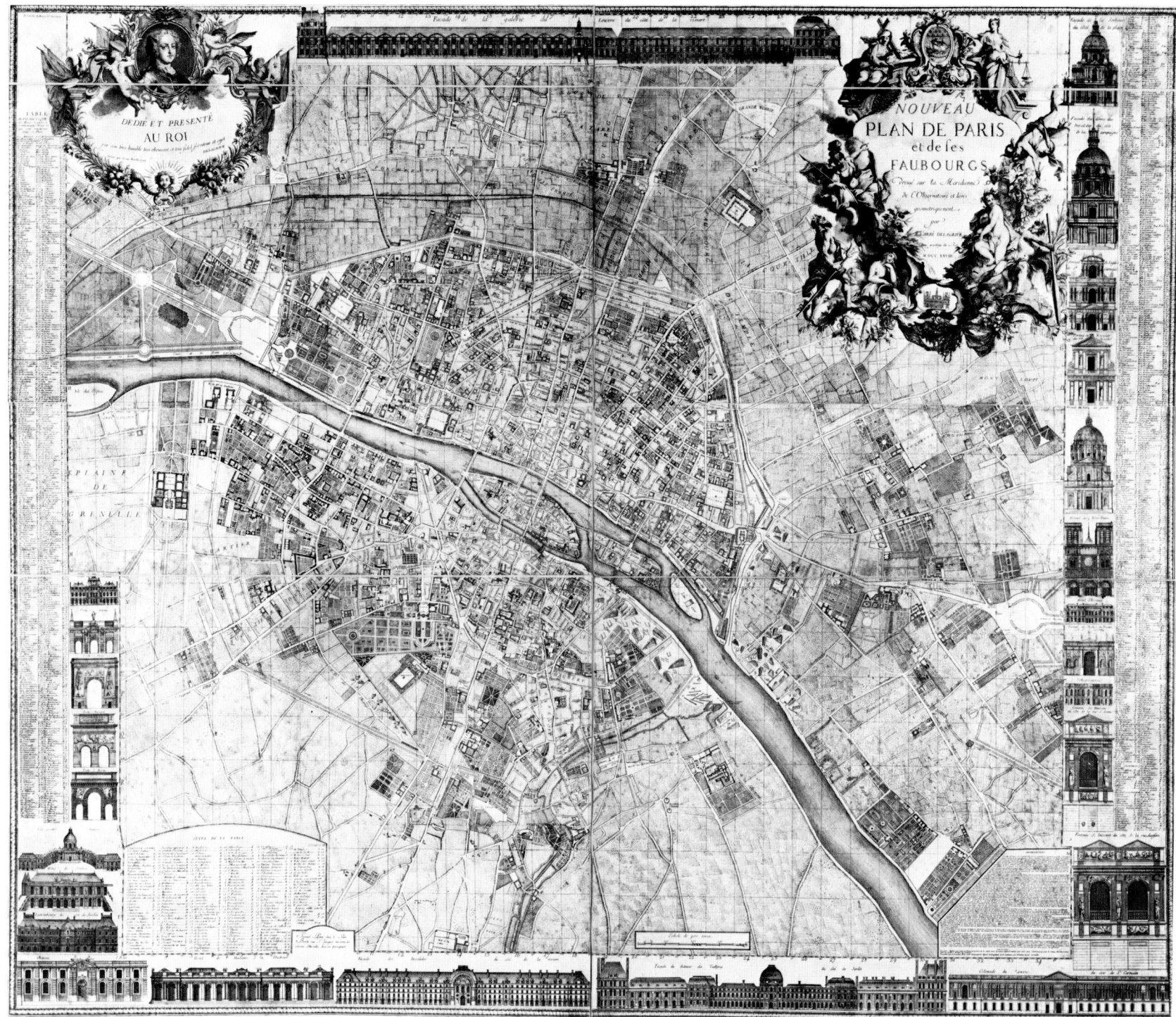

7
The Delagrive plan, 1728

8
The Bretez plan, called
"Turgot," 1734–39

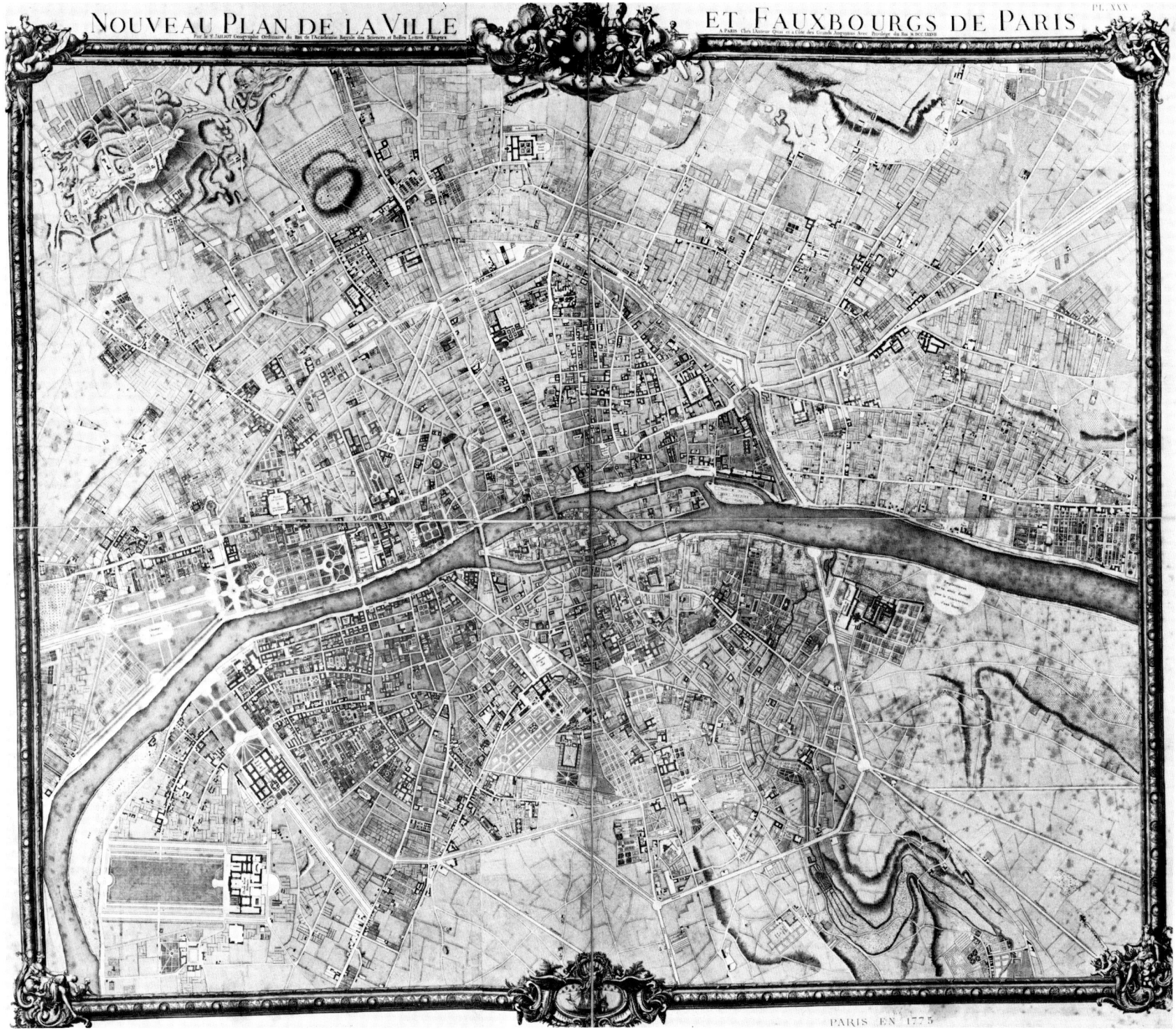

9
Jaillot plan, 1778

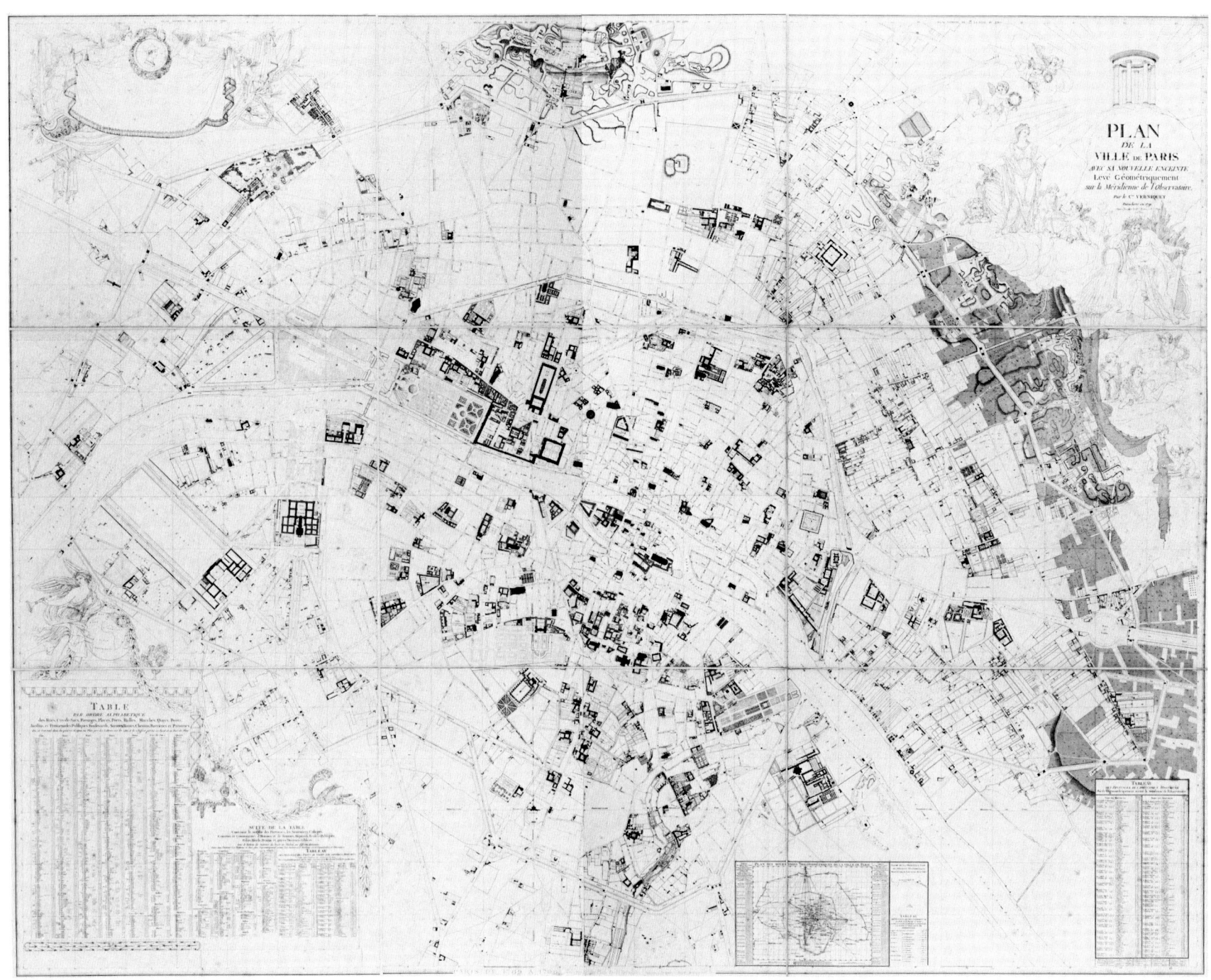

10
The Verniquet plan,
1791–99

11
The Artists' plan, 1793
(nineteenth-century plan)

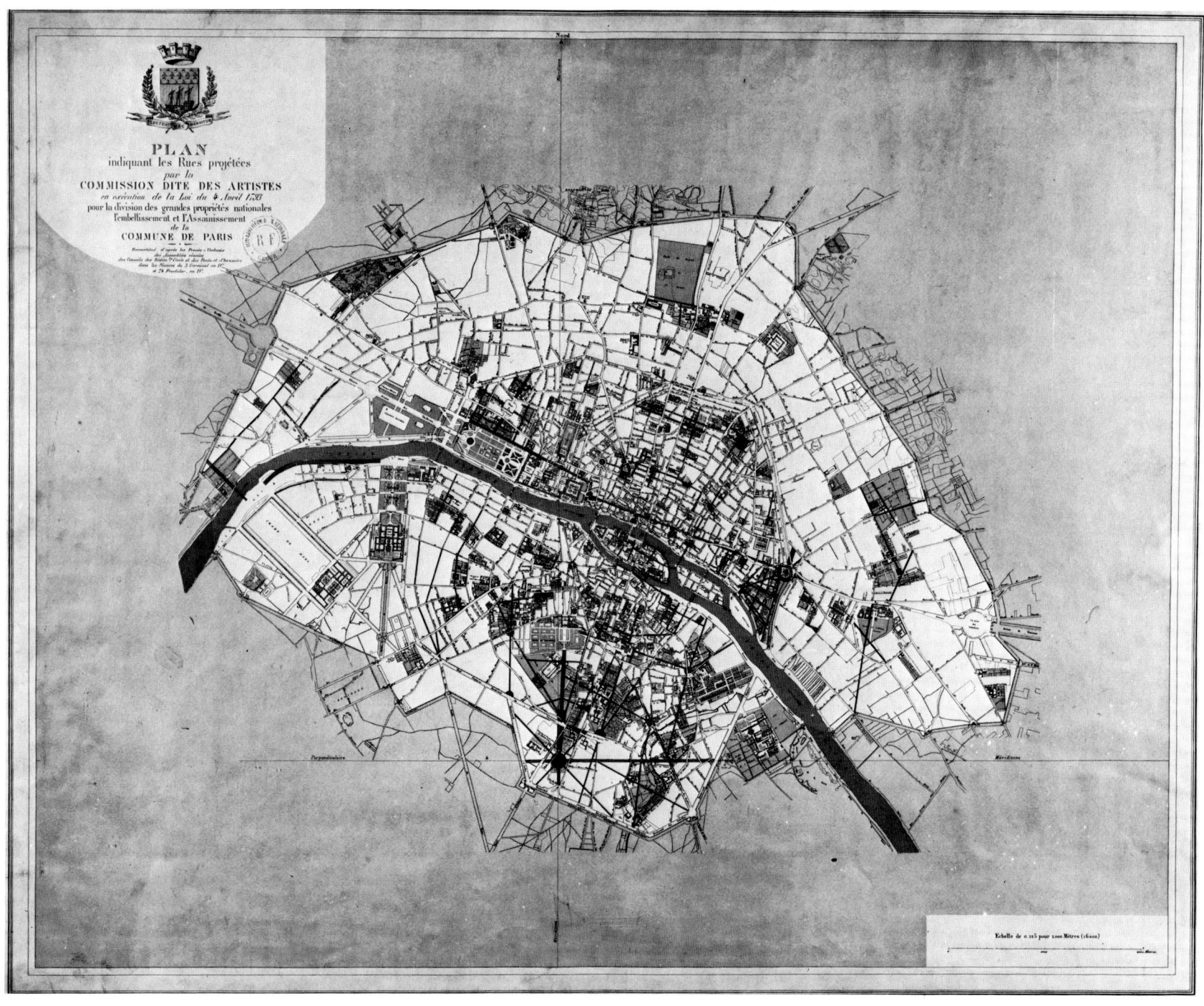

12
Plan showing successive
enclosing walls of Paris,
1787

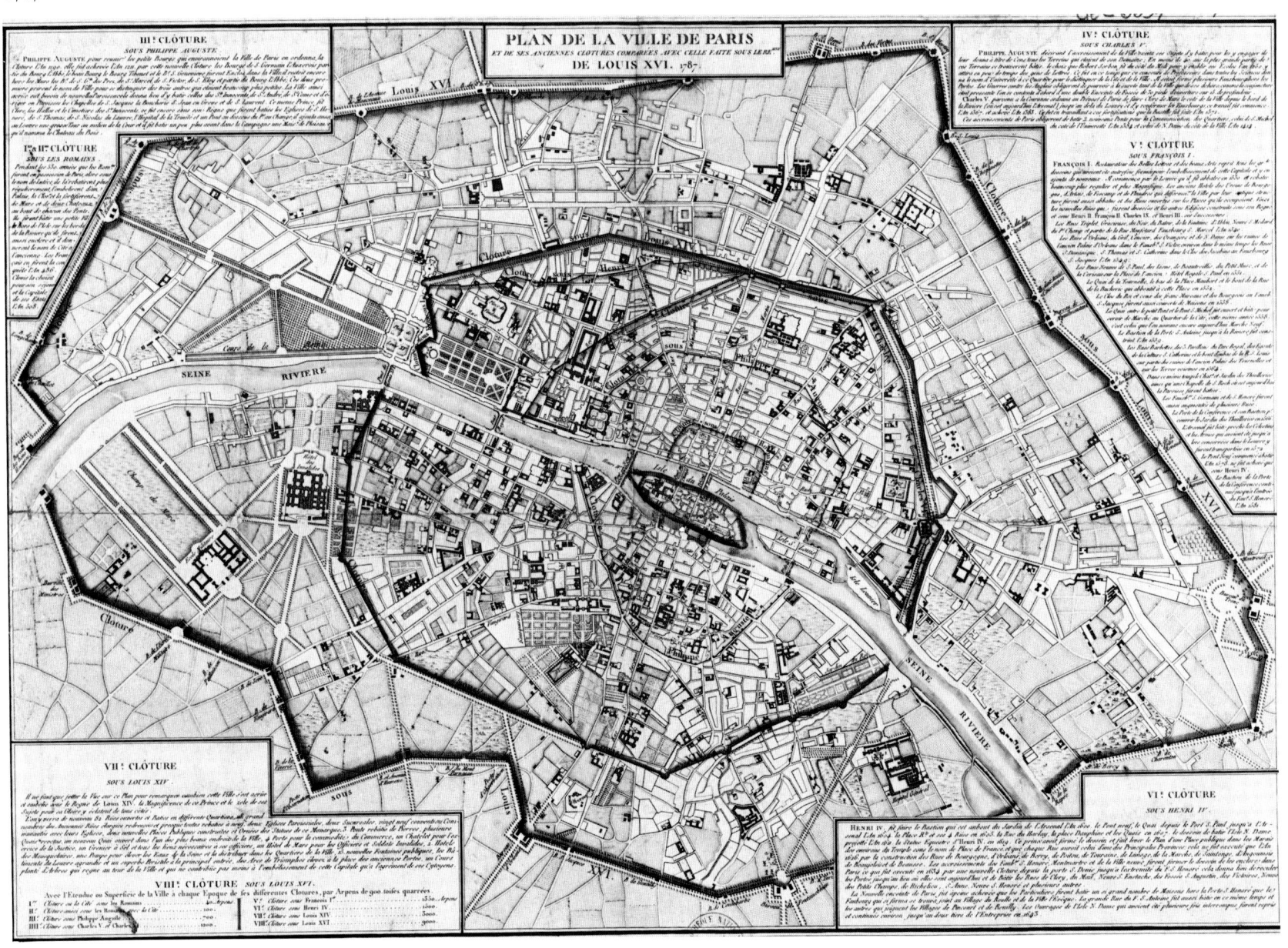

13
The Maire plan, 1808,
key plan showing the
assembly of the twenty
detail sections

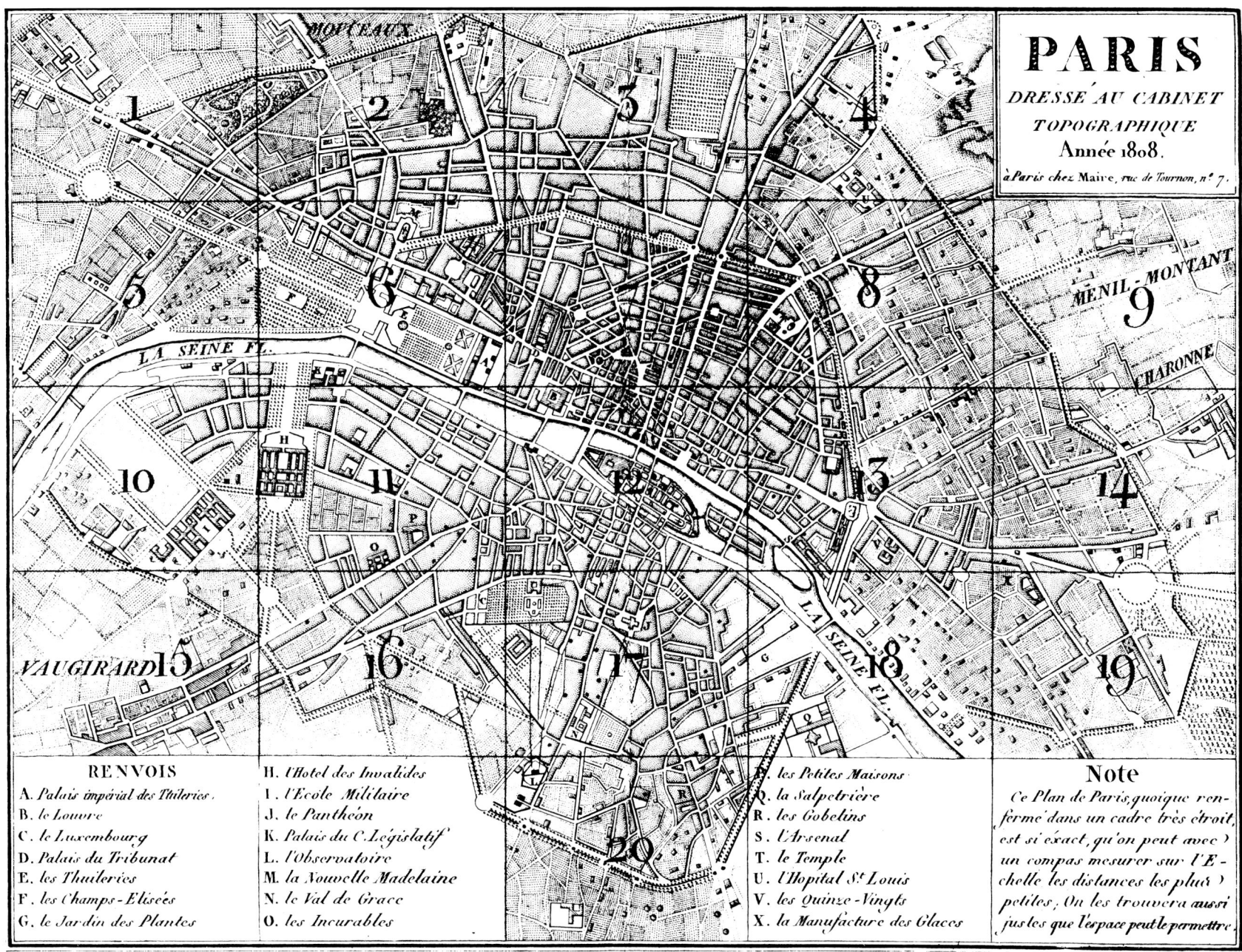

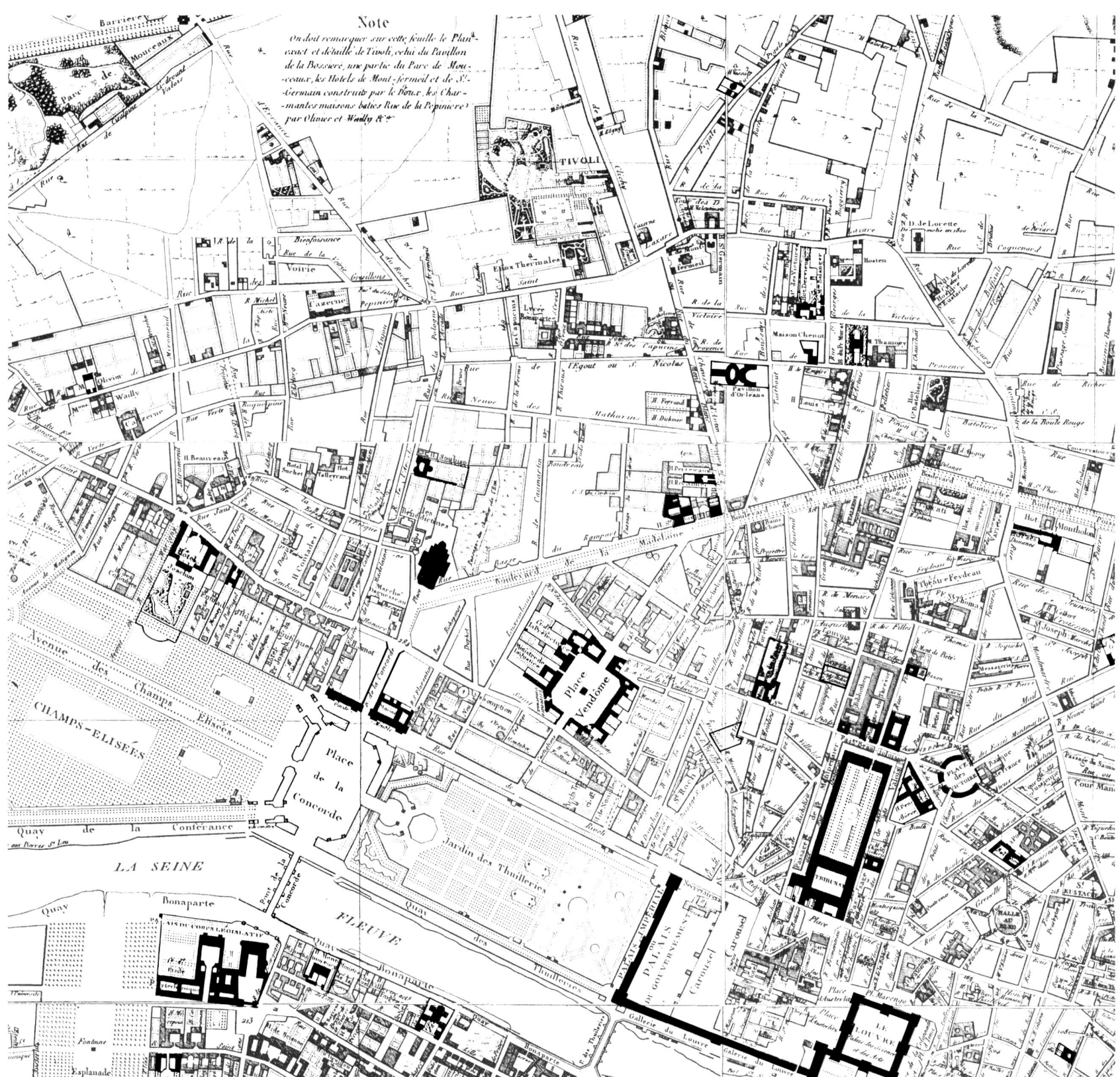

14
The Maire plan, detail sections showing the northwestern area of Paris

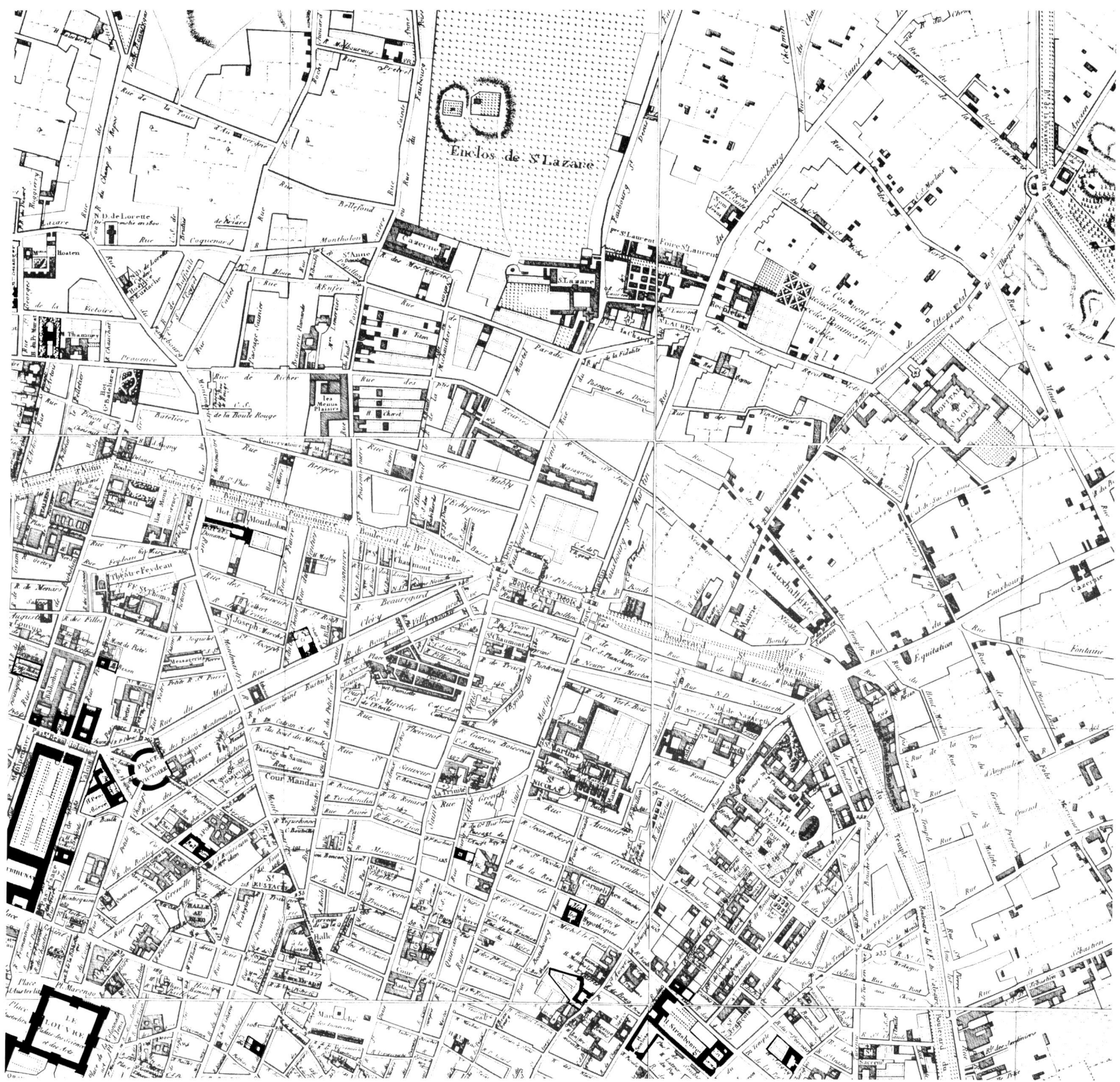

15
The Maire plan, detail sections showing the northeastern area of Paris

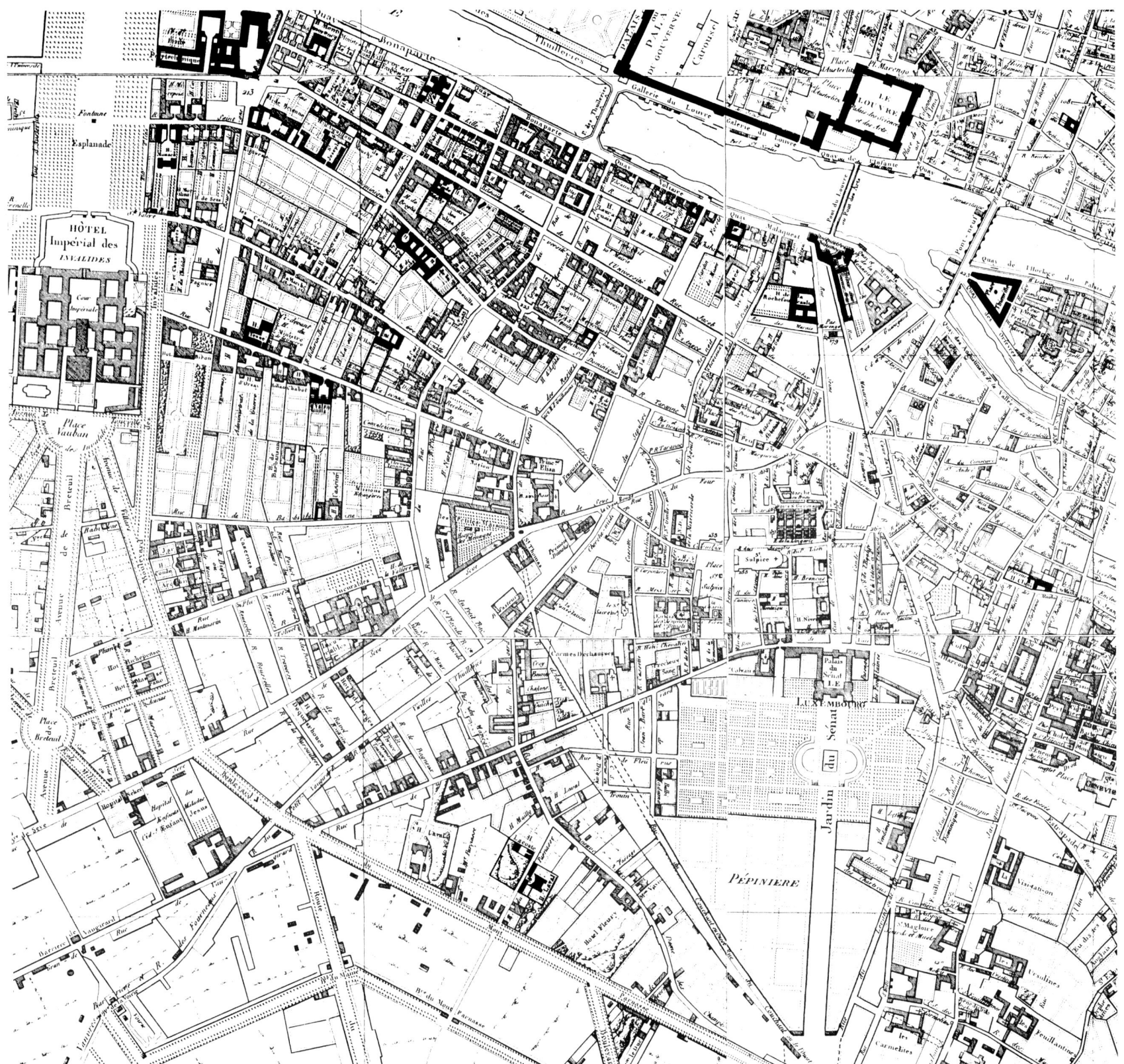

16
The Maire plan, detail
sections showing the
southwestern area of
Paris

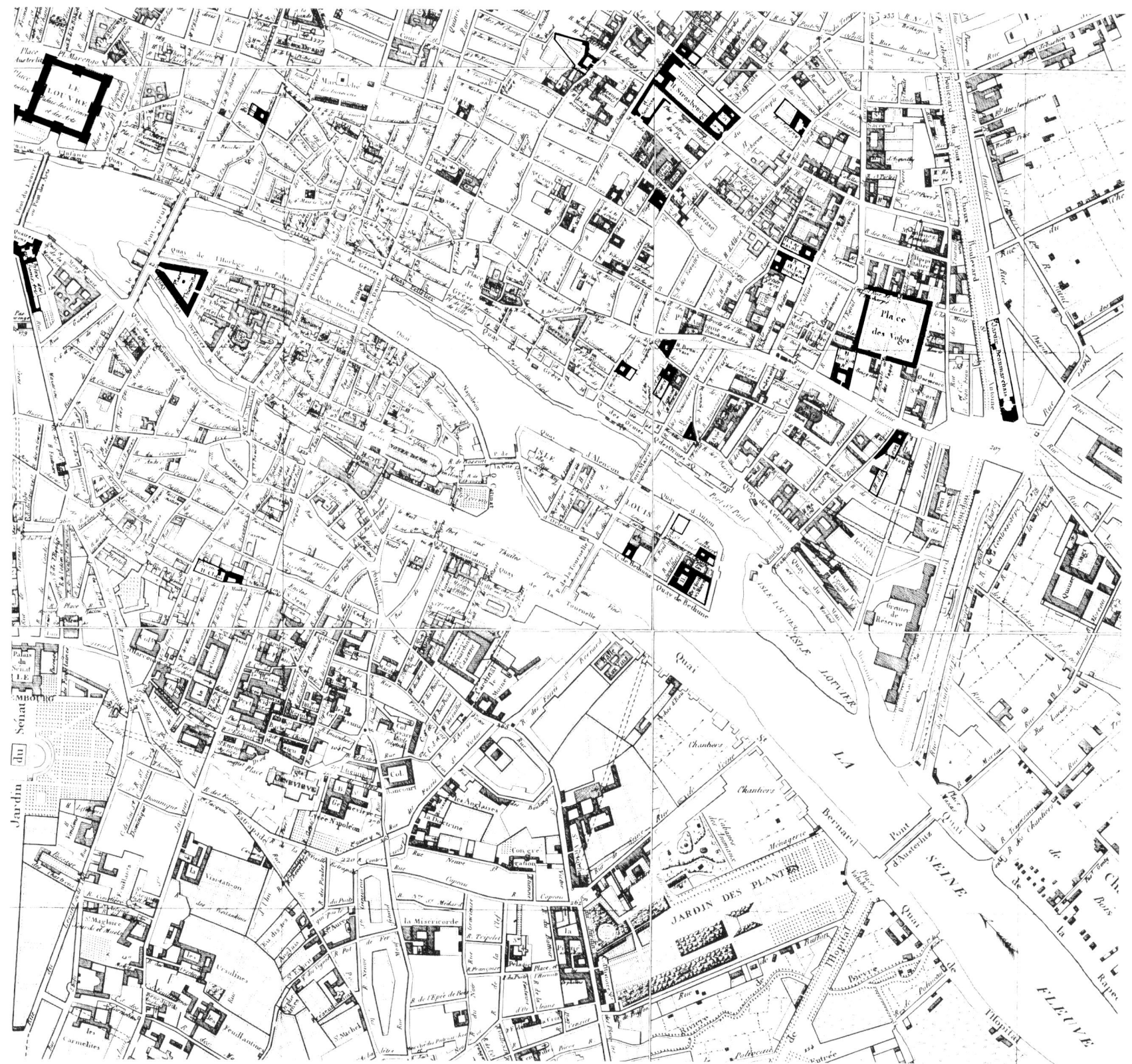

17
The Maire plan, detail
sections showing the
southeastern area of Paris

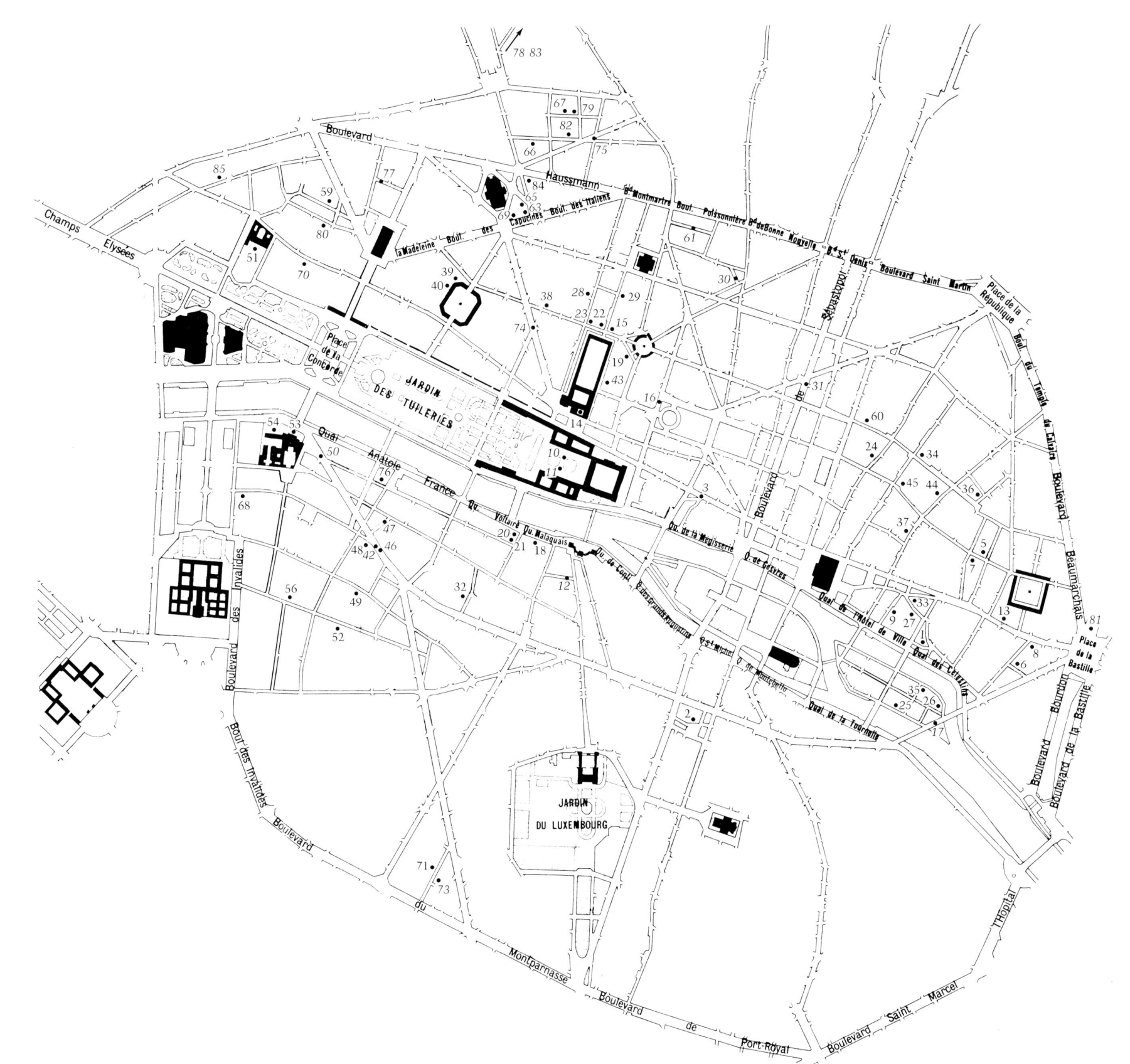

Chronology of Hôtels Discussed and/or Illustrated

Numbers at left refer to maps; hôtels in italics no longer exist. Alternate names for the hôtels are given in parentheses.

1. Sens (de), 1 rue du Figuier, 1475–1507
2. Cluny (de), rue des Mathurins, 1485–1510
3. *Le Gendre, rue des Bourdonnais, c. 1506*
4. *Ferrare (de), Fontainebleau, Serlio, 1542–46*
5. Carnavalet, 23 rue de Sévigné, begun 1540s
6. *L'Orme (de), rue de la Cerisaie, de L'Orme, c. 1557*
7. Angoulême (d') (Lamoignon), 24 rue Pavée, B. Du Cerceau, 1584
8. Mayenne (de), 21 rue St.-Antoine, Du Cerceau, 1613
9. Chalons-Luxembourg, 26 rue Geoffroy-l'Asnier, 1608–15
10. *Rambouillet (de), rue St.-Thomas-du-Louvre, Rambouillet*
11. *Chevreuse (de), rue St.-Thomas-du-Louvre, Métezeau, after 1622+*
12. *Liancourt (de), 14–18 rue de Seine, de Brosse and Lemercier, 1610–23+*
13. Sully (de), 62 rue St.-Antoine, Du Cerceau, 1624–29
14. *Cardinal (Palais de), rue St.-Honoré, begun 1632*
15. *Bautru de Serrant, 6 rue des Petits-Champs, Le Vau, 1634–37*
16. *Séguier (Bellegarde), 45–51 rue Jean-Jacques Rousseau, Du Cerceau, 1612–34+*
17. Bretonvilliers (de), 4 rue de Bretonvilliers, Du Cerceau, 1635–40
18. La Bazinière (de), 17 quai Malaquais, F. Mansart, 1635
19. *Vrillière (de la) (Toulouse), 1–3 rue de la Vrillière, Mansart, begun 1635*
20. *Falcony (Vartenaër), 21–23 quai Malaquais, Du Cerceau, 1640*
21. *Falcony (Montmorency), 7–7 1/2 rue des SS.-Pères, Jean Du Cerceau, 1640*
22. Duret de Chevry (Mazarin), 8 rue des Petits-Champs, Jean Thiriot, 1635–41
23. *Tubeuf, rue des Petits-Champs, Le Muet, before 1643*
24. Avaux (d'), 71–73 rue du Temple, Le Muet, 1640
25. Hesselin, 24 quai de Béthune, Le Vau, 1641–42
26. Lambert, 2 rue St.-Louis-en l'Ile, Le Vau, 1642–44
27. Aumont (d') (Scarron), 7 rue de Jour, Le Vau, 1648–49
28. *Jars (du), rue de Richelieu, F. Mansart, 1648*
29. Tubeuf, 12–16 rue Vivienne, Le Muet, 1649
30. *Roland, rue Cléry, Desargues*
31. *Pasquier, rue Bourg-l'Abbé, Richer*
32. L'Aigle (de) (Laigue), 16 rue St.-Guillaume, Le Muet
33. Beauvais (de), 68 rue François Miron, Le Pautre, 1652–55
34. Guénégaud (de), 60 rue des Archives, F. Mansart, 1653
35. Lauzun (de), 17 quai d'Anjou, Le Vau, 1656–57
36. Salé, 5 rue de Thorigny, Builler, 1656
37. Amelot de Bisseuil (d'), 47 rue Vieille du Temple, Cottard, 1657–60
38. *Lionne (de), rue des Petits-Champs, Le Vau, 1662+*
39. Evreux (d'), 19 Place Vendôme, Bullet, begun 1700
40. Crozat, 17 Place Vendôme, Bullet, begun 1702
41. *Maison (à bâtir), address unknown, Mansart, before 1708*
42. *Varanjeville (de), rue St.-Dominique, Gabriel, 1704*
43. *Argenson (d'), rue des Bons Enfants, Boffrand, 1704–5*
44. Rohan (de), 87 rue Vieille-du-Temple, Delamair, 1705–8
45. Soubise, 60 rue des Francs-Bourgeois, Delamair, 1705–9
46. *Béthune (de), rue St.-Dominique, Lassurance, 1708*
47. *Auvergne (d'), 53 rue de l'Université, Lassurance, 1708*
48. Amelot (d'), 1 rue St.-Dominique, Boffrand, 1712
49. Estrées (d'), 79 rue de Grenelle, de Cotte, 1713
50. *Humières (d'), rue de Bourbon, Mollet, 1715*
51. Evreux (d'), rue St.-Honoré, Mollet, 1718
52. Matignon (de), 57 rue de Varenne, Courtonne, 1722–24
53. Bourbon (Palais), 126 rue de l'Université, 1722+
54. Lassay (de), 128 rue de l'Université, 1724
55. Villefranche (de), Avignon, Franque, c. 1740(?)
56. Villeroy (de) (Desmares), 78 rue de Varenne, Leroux, 1746
57. Brethaus (de), Bayonne, Meissonier, ?
58. Petit Trianon, Versailles, Gabriel, begun 1762
59. Alexandre, 16 rue de la Ville-l'Evêque, Boullée, 1763–66
60. Hallwyl (d'), 28 rue Michel-Le Compte, Ledoux, c. 1764–66
61. *Uzès (d'), rue Montmartre, Ledoux, 1764–67*
62. Abbatiale (Maison), Villers-Cotterets, Franque, 1765(?)
63. *Montmorency (de), rue du Mont-Blanc, Ledoux, 1769–70*
64. Louveciennes (de), Louveciennes, Ledoux, 1770–71
65. *Guimard, rue de la Chaussée d'Antin, Ledoux, 1770–72*
66. Orléans (d'), 17 rue de Provence, Brongniart, 1774
67. Dervieux, rue Chantereine (44 rue Victoire) Bélanger and Brongniart, 1774–89
68. Monaco (de), 59 rue St.-Dominique, Brongniart, 1774–77
69. St.-Foix (de), rue Basse-du-Rempart, Brongniart, 1775
70. Brunoy (de), rue St.-Honoré, Boullée, 1775–79
71. *Orliane (d'), 28 rue du Montparnasse, d'Orliane, 1777*
72. Bagatelle (Pavillon de), Bois de Boulogne, Bélanger, 1777
73. *Callet, rue Montparnasse, Poyet, 1777*
74. *Evry (d'), rue Ventador, Ledoux, 1772–80 (?)*
75. *Théluson (de), rue de Provence, Ledoux, 1778–81*
76. Salm (de), 64 rue de Lille, Rousseau, 1782–85
77. *Soubise, 22 rue de l'Arcade, Cellerier, 1788*
78. *Vassale, rue Pigalle, Henry, 1788*
79. *Trois Maisons, rue St.-George, Bélanger, 1788*
80. *Courmont, rue de Surène, Chevalier, 1789*
81. *Beaumarchais, Porte St.-Antoine, Lemoine, 1790*
82. *Chenot, 50 rue de Provence, Brunau, 1790*
83. *Vassale, rue Pigalle, Henry, 1790*
84. *Lakanal, rue du Mont-Blanc (20 rue de la Chausée d'Antin), Henry, 1795*
85. *Ollivier, rue de la Pépinière, Ollivier, 1799*
86. *Auchère (l'), Chaillot, Aubert, 1801*

Notes

Introduction

1. W. Goehner, "Architecture as an Integral Part of the City," *The Cornell Journal of Architecture* 1 (1981), 69.
2. E. Kaufmann, *Architecture in the Age of Reason: Baroque and Postbaroque in England, Italy and France* (Cambridge, Mass., 1955), 128.
3. For a remarkable study of the centralization of power under Louis XIV—the "closure" that made the system function and also caused its demise—see N. Elias, *The Court Society* (New York, 1983); first published as *Die höfisch Gesellschaft* (Darmstadt and Neuwied, 1969).
4. C.-A. d'Aviler, *Cours d'architecture* (Paris, 1691), II, 355.
5. Robert Venturi was one of the first to resurrect the term *poché* in his *Complexity and Contradiction in Architecture* (New York, 1966), 78–82. See also C. Rowe and F. Koetter, *Collage City* (Cambridge, Mass., 1978), 78–79; and S. Peterson, "Space and Anti-Space," *The Harvard Architecture Review* (1980), 89–199.
6. D'Aviler, *Cours*, I, 180.
7. I am well aware of the problems and pitfalls of nomenclature: if the system is too coarse, it is not an accurate reflection of the material; if it is too fine, it becomes unhierarchical, bland, and useless. And historians have long known that the styles called Louis XIV, Louis XV, and Louis XVI do not match the reigns of their namesake monarchs; for example, the style commonly called Louis XVI was fully mature before Louis XVI took the throne. The same is true of the French *hôtel*; most of those called "the Baroque type" were completed before Louis XIV took the throne in 1661. Indeed, if the *hôtels* are categorized by style, there might have to be four or five varieties in order to acknowledge distinct shifts around 1630 and 1723. But in the interests of simplicity and clarity I have chosen to categorize them by form type and to name these types according to the general period in which they were developed. Thus the term "Baroque type" is extended backward in time to cover the late-sixteenth-century *hôtels*, which might otherwise be referred to as Classical, or Renaissance.
8. See R. Etlin, "*Les dedans* Jacques-François Blondel and the System of the Home, c. 1740," *Gazette des Beaux-Arts* (April 1978), 137–47.

1 Public versus Private

1. R. Wittkower, "Classical Theory and Eighteenth-Century Sensibility," in *Palladio and English Palladianism* (New York, 1983), 193–204; first published 1974.
2. R. Wittkower, *Architectural Principles in the Age of Humanism* (London, 1949), 73.
3. Wittkower, "Classical Theory," 196.
4. T. Hamlin, *Architecture Through the Ages* (New York, 1940), 464.
5. Letter to the Duke of Noailles, September 18, 1713; L. Benevolo, *The Architecture of the Renaissance* (Boulder, 1978), II, 388.
6. Kaufmann, *Architecture in the Age of Reason* (Cambridge, Mass., 1955), 127.
7. Ibid., 125–26.

2 The Prototypes

1. For a discussion of the architecture of this difficult period, see D. Thomson, *Renaissance Paris* (Berkeley, 1984).
2. See W. Lotz, *Studies in Italian Renaissance Architecture* (Cambridge, Mass., 1977), 74–139.
3. L. Benevolo, *The Architecture of the Renaissance* (Boulder, 1978), I, 543.
4. Thomson, *Renaissance Paris*, 35.
5. A. Blunt, *Art and Architecture in France 1500–1700* (London, 1953), 42.
6. Ibid. See also J.-P. Babelon, "Du 'Grand Ferrare' à Carnavalet, Naissance de l'Hôtel classique," *Revue de l'art* 40–41 (1978), 83–108.
7. Two manuscripts exist for Serlio's unpublished *Sesto libro de architettura*: the Munich manuscript has been published in facsimile with an introduction and notes by M. Rosci as *Il Trattato di architettura di Sebastiano Serlio* (Milan, 1967); the Columbia University manuscript has been published in facsimile with a foreword by A. K. Pla-

czek, an introduction by J. S. Ackerman, and a text by M. N. Rosenfeld as *Sebastiano Serlio on domestic architecture* (New York, c. 1978).
8. W. B. Dinsmoor, "The literary remains of Sebastiano Serlio," *The Art Bulletin* 24 (1942), 55ff.
9. J.-A. Du Cerceau, *Livre d'architecture* (Paris, 1559), I.
10. See Blunt, *Art and Architecture*, p. 82 and p. 259, note 25 for Hôtel de Soissons, 1572; Hôtel de Sandréville; Hôtel de Condé, 1584; Hôtel de Nevers, after 1572; Hôtel d'Angoulême, later Hôtel de Lamoignon, 1584. See P. Couperie, *Paris through the Ages* (New York, 1968) for Hôtel Scipion Sardini, 1565. For other *hôtels* of the period and an extensive bibliography, see Babelon, "Grand Ferrare," 83–108.

3 *Public Spaces: The Baroque Hôtel*

1. Although Louis XIV did not immediately take the court to Versailles upon taking the throne, he did begin to go there for picnics and parties. He gradually began to move the court there during the 1670s and made it the official seat of the court in 1682.
2. Sir R. Blomfield, *History of French Architecture 1661–1774* (London, 1911), II, 141.
3. Regarding the Place des Vosges, see the following: L. Arretche, M. Marot, and B. Vitry, "Renovation urbaine Le Marais," *Architecture aujourd'hui* 138 (June/July 1968), 86–87; J.-P. Babelon, "L'Urbanisme d'Henri IV et de Sully à Paris," *L'Urbanisme de Paris et de l'Europe 1600–1680* (Paris, 1969); E. Baudson, "La Place Royale de Paris et la Place Ducale de Charleville," *Bulletin de la société de l'histoire de l'art français* (1935), 204–16; A. Blunt, *Art and Architecture in France* (London, 1953), 97; L. Hautecoeur, *Histoire de l'architecture classique en France* (Paris, 1966), I, 3.1, 297–300; K. Joffet, "Paysages de la Place des Vosges," *La Vie urbaine* (1957), 1–16; P. Lavedan, *Nouvelle histoire de Paris* (Paris, 1975), 231–35; and A. E. J. Morris, *History of Urban Form* (London, 1972), 140.
4. Babelon, *L'Urbanisme*, 59.
5. Lavedan, *Nouvelle histoire*, 231–40.
6. This corner was opened in the nineteenth century.
7. Blunt, *Art and Architecture*, 98.
8. Ibid. Also, according to Baudson ("La Place Royale," 204–16), the architect of the Place Ducale at Charleville, Clément Métezeau, was the brother of Louis Métezeau, whose name appears in relation to the Place Royale in Paris.
9. Regarding the Place Dauphine, see Blunt, *Art and Architecture*, 160; and Lavedan, *Nouvelle histoire*, 202–11.
10. Regarding the Place de France, see Blomfield, *French Architecture*, II, 44–46.
11. Hautecoeur, *Architecture classique* (1967), I, 3.2, 693.
12. J.-P. Babelon, *Demeures parisiennes sous Henri IV et Louis XIII* (Paris, 1965), 185.
13. Blomfield, *French Architecture*, II, 141–44.
14. Hautecoeur, *Architecture classique* (1943), I, 573.
15. Blunt, *Art and Architecture*, 119. The *hôtel* was destroyed in the nineteenth century.
16. Regarding the development of the Ile St.-Louis, see L. Benevolo, *The Architecture of the Renaissance* (Boulder, 1978), II, 704.
17. Blunt, *Art and Architecture*, 135. The *hôtel* was destroyed in the nineteenth century.
18. In 1643, upon the death of Louis XIII and a year after that of Richelieu, the young Louis XIV moved into the palace with his mother; the name was changed to Palais Royal. For a description of the development of the palace see Benevolo, *Architecture* II, 708; and H. Saalman, *Haussmann: Paris Transformed* (New York, 1971), 38.
19. For a similar, but symmetrical, *hôtel* from the same period, see the Hôtel de la Bazinière (1635) in the *Petit Marot*. This *hôtel* is now part of the Ecole des Beaux-Arts.
20. Cf. the Hôtel de l'Aigle, by Le Muet, illustrated in the *Grand Marot*; the Hôtel d'Avaux (before 1647) by Le Muet, illustrated in his *Manière*, pt. 2, pp. 2–5; Hôtel Pasguier, by Richer, *Grand Marot*; Hôtel Roland, by Gerard Desargues, *Petit Marot*; and the Hôtel Enselin (Hesselin), by Le Vau, *Grand Marot*.
21. Hautecoeur, *Architecture classique* (1967), I, 677.
22. For the planning system of the seventeenth-century *hôtel*, see Babelon, *Demeures*, 184–200; Hautecoeur, *Architecture classique* (1967), I, 693–714, and II, 197–204; also C.-A. d'Aviler, *Cours d'architecture* (Paris, 1691), I, 172–80, for a codification of the system of the *appartements* at the end of the century, and vol. II for a glossary of terms.
23. L. Savot, *Architecture françoise* (Paris, 1624), 46.
24. Hautecoeur, *Architecture classique*, II, 203.
25. N. Elias, in *The Court Society* (English translation, Oxford, 1983, 48, n. 15), refers to an incident described by Voltaire's secretary Longchamp, a former servant of his mistress, the Marquise de Châtelet: "The Marquise showed herself naked before him in her bathroom in a way that caused him the utmost embarrassment, while she scolded him with total unconcern for not pouring the hot water properly." The point of the incident is that privacy—and embarrassment—was relative to social class; the Marquise's servant was not of the *monde*, and his presence therefore did not disturb her privacy, nor embarrass her.
26. Babelon, *Demeures*, 196.
27. Ibid., 190.
28. Hautecoeur, *Architecture classique* (1967), I, 710.
29. Ibid., 711.
30. Ibid., II, 201.
31. Regarding Madame de Beauvais, R. W. Berger, in *Antoine Le Pautre* (New York, 1969), 37, states: "This ugly and lascivious woman bears the delicate distinction of having provided the young Louis XIV with his first heterosexual experience."
32. Ibid., 38.
33. For an eloquent description of this phenomenon, see C. Rowe and F. Koetter, *Collage City* (Cambridge, Mass., 1978), 79.

4 *Display and Retreat: The Rococo Hôtel*

1. For a brilliant analysis of court society, etiquette, and ceremony and their relation to the architecture of the *hôtel*, see N. Elias, *The Court Society* (English translation, Oxford, 1983), particularly the chapters "Structure of Dwellings and Social Structure," "The Court-Aristocratic Figuration," and "Etiquette and Ceremony." It should be pointed out, however, that the *hôtel* Elias uses in his superb analysis is a very large hypothetical one by J.-F. Blondel that was illustrated in Diderot's *Encyclopédie* ("Recueil de Planches," II, "Architecture,"

plate 23) and therefore does not reflect the realities and diversities of the *hôtel* during the *ancien régime*. That is, if taken too literally, it leads to excessively mechanistic assumptions about the relationship between form and ritual.
2. Regarding the development of the Place des Victoires, see A. Blunt, *Art and Architecture in France* (London, 1953), 224; A. Boislisle, "Notices historiques sur la place des Victoires et sur la place Vendôme," *Memoires de la société de l'histoire de Paris et de l'Ile-de-France* 15 (1888), 1–272; P. Lavedan, *Nouvelle histoire de Paris* (Paris, 1975), 215–19; and A. E. J. Morris, *History of Urban Form* (London, 1972), 142.
3. Morris, *History*, 142.
4. Regarding the development of the Place Vendôme, see Blunt, *Art and Architecture*, 124–25; Boislisle, "Notices," 1–272; R. Josephson, "Les Projets pour la place Vendôme," *L'Architecture* (1928), 83–91; Lavedan, *Nouvelle histoire*, 219–27; M. Le Moel, "Archives Architecturales Parisiennes en Suede," in *L'Urbanisme de Paris et de l'Europe 1600–1680* (Paris, 1969), 105–92; and Morris, *History*, 142–43.
5. Lavedan, *Nouvelle histoire*, 221–23.
6. Ibid., 222.
7. Ibid., 222–26.
8. E. Langenskiold, *Pierre Bullet the Royal Architect* (Stockholm, 1959).
9. H. Saalman, *Haussmann: Paris Transformed* (New York, 1971), 42–43.
10. T. Hamlin, *Architecture Through the Ages* (New York, 1940), 464–65.
11. Ibid., 469.
12. J.-F. Blondel, *L'Architecture françoise* (Paris, 1752), V.
13. Blunt, *Art and Architecture*, 282, n. 22.
14. W. G. Kalnein and M. Levey, *Art and Architecture of the Eighteenth Century in France* (Harmondsworth, 1972), 203 and fig. 1.
15. See R. Evan's excellent study of circulation relative to social habits, "Figures, Doors, and Passages," *Architectural Design* 4 (1978), 267–78.
16. Kalnein and Levey, *Art and Architecture*, 224.
17. Regarding the domestic work of Robert de Cotte, see R. Neuman, "French Domestic Architecture in the Early 18th Century: The Town Houses of Robert de Cotte," *Journal of the Society of Architectural Historians* 39, 2 (May 1980), 128–44.
18. As Kalnein points out (*Art and Architecture*, 380, n. 33), Blondel considered the Palais Bourbon the beginning of "modern" French planning (J.-F. Blondel, *Architecture françoise* I, 267, and P. Patte, *Monuments érigés à la gloire de Louis XV* (Paris, 1765), 6).
19. François Blondel's *Cours d'architecture* (1675–98) dealt only with the intricacies of the orders, not with domestic architecture. For other treatises of this period, see Hautecoeur, *Architecture classique*, II, 467.
20. C.-A. d'Aviler, *Cours d'architecture* (Paris, 1691), II, 355.
21. Ibid., II, 375.
22. Ibid., I, 180.
23. Ibid. (1710 edition), I, 185 *1.
24. Le Blond's system of the *appartement* (*de parade*) is the traditional one, but expanded to the following sequence: *vestibule*—gives access to the grand stair and serves as a waiting room for the servants in the summer; *première antichambre*—the waiting room for servants in the winter, furnished with stoves to keep out the cold air from comings and goings; *seconde antichambre*—a waiting room for people of higher rank that may also serve as a dining room; *salon*—a grand room for receiving important visitors, for dining with distinction, or for concerts—the most distinguished place in the *appartement*; the *chambre à coucher*—for show (*parade*) rather than use, although in the summer it could be used for sleeping, though in the winter the smaller rooms were more comfortable; *grand cabinet*—the place where business was transacted; it should be arranged with a small *antichambre* so that it could be entered without passing through the *enfilade* of the other rooms; *second cabinet*—a study or workroom with a desk; if possible, a *galerie* should be attached so that one could get away from work; *galerie*—a long room for art and precious objects; *arrière cabinet* or *serre-papier*—placed beside the *second cabinet*, for papers, money, and other valuables and usually closed by a grill; they are arrived at only through the *grand cabinet* and did not require a *dégagement*; *garde-robes*—places of *commodité* near the bedrooms requiring their own *dégagements* and private entrances so that the servants could avoid passing through the private *appartement* of the master; they could be on the *entresol*; *grande garde-robe*—contained the *toillet*, the clothes, and the linens and was where the valet or chambermaid slept; *troisième garde-robe*—a place of convenience for the *chaise percée*, or better still, for the *siège d'aisance* or *soupape*, a flush toilet in which the trap was opened by raising the seat; it was then flushed by water; lowering the seat closed the trap again. Le Blond then states that the smaller *appartements* had fewer rooms and smaller dimensions, and goes on to outline in equal detail the practicalities of the rooms of the kitchen and stable areas (D'Aviler, *Cours* (1710 edition), I, 185 *7–10).
25. The most important governmental activity during this period was the financial system of John Law. (See A. Cobban, *History of Modern France* (Harmondsworth, 1963), I, 23–26.) At this time the financial position of many of the nobility began to weaken significantly, and the display required by the social pressures of the court aristocracy was about to increase. As a result, it was a period of ever-increased blurring of the line between the rich bourgeoisie and the *noblesse de l'epée*.
26. See Kalnein and Levey, *Art and Architecture*, 242.
27. R. Etlin, "*Les dedans* Jacques-François Blondel and the System of the Home, c. 1740," *Gazette des Beaux-Arts* (April 1978), 137–47.
28. See note 17 above.
29. E. Kaufmann, *Architecture in the Age of Reason* (Cambridge, Mass., 1955), 160 and 206.
30. M. Gallet has called attention to this area of domestic architecture in *Stately Mansions* (New York, 1972), 63–68; and in "Quelques étapes du Rococo dans l'architecture parisienne," *Gazette des Beaux-Arts*, 6th pér., LXVII (1966), 145ff; see also Kalnein and Levey, *Art and Architecture*, 267–68.
31. The year 1730 is generally accepted as the end of the Regency style and the beginning of the Rococo proper. See Kalnein and Levey, *Art and Architecture*, 237.
32. A third treatise of the same period dealt with the middle-class house: A.-C. Tiercelet, *Architecture*

moderne ou l'art de bâtir pour toutes sortes de personnes ... (Paris, 1728).
33. J. Courtonne, *Traité de perspective pratique avec les remarques sur l'architecture* (Paris, 1725), 97.
34. Ibid., 94.
35. Ibid., 93.
36. Sir R. Blomfield, *History of French Architecture*, IV, 88–89.
37. W. H. Ward, *The Architecture of the Renaissance in France* (London, 1911), 381.
38. R. Etlin has called attention to a third source during this time: J.-F. Blondel, *Abrégé d'architecture concernant la distribution, la décoration, et la construction des batiments civils* (unpublished, c. 1740); see Etlin, "Les dedans," 137–47.
39. Hautecoeur, *Architecture classique*, III, 200.
40. Blomfield, *French Architecture*, IV, 88–89.
41. This was essentially a new edition of Mariette's *Architecture françoise* of 1727, with a full accompanying text. Blondel had collaborated on the original volumes as a young man.

---

5 Private Icons: The Neoclassical Hôtel

1. W. G. Kalnein and M. Levey, *Art and Architecture of the Eighteenth Century in France* (Harmondsworth, 1972), 238, and 378 n. 6, 7.
2. T. Hamlin, *Architecture Through the Ages* (New York, 1940), 474.
3. H. Honour, *Neo-classicism* (Harmondsworth, 1968), 18.
4. Ibid., 17.
5. For an extensive outline of French rationalism, see R. Middleton and D. Watkin, *Neoclassical and 19th Century Architecture* (New York, 1980), chapter 1.
6. J.-F. Blondel wrote the section on architecture. The first volume of plates, which included architecture, appeared in 1761.
7. J. Rykwert, *On Adam's House in Paradise* (New York, 1972), 49.
8. For an extensive discussion of space as a reflection of man's attitude toward the environment, see W. Worringer, *Abstraction and Empathy* (New York, 1953), first published in 1908.
9. For the *forum:acropolis* equation, I am indebted to C. Rowe and F. Koetter, *Collage City* (Cambridge, Mass., 1978), 83.
10. See P. Patte, *Monuments érigés à la gloire de Louis XV* (Paris, 1765). Patte illustrates the provincial royal squares as well as the Parisian one and some competition entries.
11. Ibid.
12. M.-A. Laugier, *An Essay on Architecture* (Los Angeles, 1977), 95.
13. Patte, *Monuments*. The designs not published by Patte are published in *La Vie urbaine*, 1962.
14. P. Lavedan, "Le IIe centenaire de la Place de la Concorde," *La Vie urbaine* (July-Sept. 1956), 161–76. See also S. Granet, "Le Livre de vérité de la Place Louis XV," *Bulletin de la société de l'histoire de l'art français* (1961); P. Lavedan, *Nouvelle histoire de Paris* (Paris, 1975), 243–51; and E. Lambert, "Un projet de Place Royale à Paris en honneur de Louis XV," *Bulletin de la société de l'histoire de l'art français* (1938), 85–97.
15. According to Lavedan ("Place de la Concorde"), the prince brought great pressure to bear on the king and the ministers to acquire his property. Lavedan speculates that the unknown author, Gabriel de l'Estrade, may even have been the pen name of the prince himself.
16. Laugier, *Essay*, 96–97.
17. W. H. Ward, *The Architecture of the Renaissance in France* (London, 1911), 425.
18. E. Kaufmann, *Architecture in the Age of Reason* (Cambridge, Mass., 1955); see also E. Kaufmann, "Three Revolutionary Architects, Boullée, Ledoux, and Lequeu," *Transactions of the American Philosophical Society* 42 (1952), part 3.
19. The first volume of Ledoux's *L'Architecture* appeared in 1804 and contained primarily his theoretical projects. The second volume appeared after his death and illustrated his actual commissions, although frequently much altered in accordance with his later taste.
20. For a more thorough description of Madame de Thélusson, see A. Braham, *The Architecture of the French Enlightenment* (London, 1980), 186–87.
21. Ibid., 189.
22. For a documentation of Ledoux's projects, see M. Gallet, *Claude-Nicolas Ledoux* (Paris, 1980).
23. For a rejected version of the courtyard, see M. Gallet, *Stately Mansions* (New York, 1972), 114.
24. The Hôtel d'Uzès was destroyed in the late nineteenth century, but some of the interior panels are in the Museum of Fine Arts, Boston.
25. For a description of Ledoux's clients, see Braham, *French Enlightenment*.
26. Ibid., 173.
27. Ibid.
28. Gallet, *Stately Mansions*, 4.
29. The principle source for the Neoclassical *hôtels* is J.-C. Krafft and N. Ransonnette, *Plans, coupes, élévations* ... (Paris, c. 1802?).
30. This flamboyant building was built for the Duc d'Orléans on a corner site in the northern part of Paris, adjacent to the house of his wife (also by Brongniart). Although the two houses had separate entrances, they were interconnected and shared the gardens (Braham, *French Enlightenment*, 211–13).
31. The Hôtel Dervieux was built for an actress who later became the wife of Bélanger. Bélanger made some additions to the house.
32. J.-F. Blondel, *Cours d'architecture* (Paris, 1771–77), IV, 367–82.
33. Laugier, *Essay*, 81–90.
34. Le Camus de Mézières, *Le Génie de l'architecture ou l'Analogie de cet art avec nos sensations* (Paris, 1780), 1.
35. Ibid., 3.
36. Ibid., 80.
37. The English influence on garden design and on the Neoclassical *hôtel* form has often been noted. See F. Kimball, *The Creation of the Rococo* (Philadelphia, 1943), 208–22.
38. For the later *hôtels*, see Hautecoeur, *Architecture classique*, V, 325–32; VI, 123–25; and VII, 228–55. An urban *hôtel* was even given as the subject of the competition for the Prix de Rome in 1866; it was one of the few urban contextual projects given at the Ecole des Beaux-Arts.
39. Krafft also published several subsequent books dealing with gardens, country houses, facades, etc.
40. Krafft and Ransonnette, *Plans* (English text), *Conclusion*.

41. Ibid., *Avertissement*.
42. For a lucid discussion of style, character, and type during this period, see D. Porphyrios, "The 'End' of Styles," with an introduction by A. Vidler, *Oppositions* 8 (Spring 1977), 118–33.
43. The plates of Ledoux's built work were completed before his death in 1806, but remained unpublished until 1847 when D. Ramée published both volumes as *L'Architecture de C.N. Ledoux*.
44. Gallet, *Stately Mansions*, 108.
45. Braham, *French Enlightenment*, 236.
46. One such quarter is illustrated in J.-C. Krafft, *Choix des plus jolies maisons de Paris et des environs...* (Paris, 1829; enlarged edition, 1849).
47. H. Lipstadt, "Housing the Bourgeoisie: César Daly and the Ideal Home," with an introduction by A. Vidler, *Oppositions* 8 (Spring 1977), 33–47.
48. Ibid., 35–36.
49. Ibid., 43. The ideas preceding this quotation rely heavily on Lipstadt's research.
50. See G. Shayne, "The revival of the street: Birth and decline from the Renaissance to today," *Lotus International* 24 (1979), 103–14.

6 Le Corbusier and the City of Modern Architecture

1. See K. Frampton, "The humanist versus the utilitarian ideal," *Architectural Design* 38 (March 1968), 134–36.
2. Edited by Dermée, Le Corbusier, and Ozenfant.
3. For an outline of the street in the twentieth century, see G. Shane, "The Street in the Twentieth Century; Three Conferences: London (1910), Athens (1933), Hoddesdon (1951)," *The Cornell Journal of Architecture* 2 (1982), 20–41.
4. See G. Shane, "The revival of the street; Birth and decline from the Renaissance to today," *Lotus International* 24 (1979), 103–14.
5. See T. Schumacher, "Contextualism: Urban Ideals and Deformations," *Casabella* 359/360 (1971), 79.
6. For a more complete description of the *ville contemporaine*, forerunner to the *ville radieuse*, see P. Blake, *Le Corbusier; Architecture and Form* (Harmondsworth, 1963), 37–42; originally published in *The Master Builders*, 1960.
7. Le Corbusier, *Towards a New Architecture* (London, 1946), 9.
8. Le Corbusier, *Oeuvre complète 1910–1929* (Zurich, 1960), 128.
9. Ibid., 91.
10. Ibid., 87.
11. See chapter 4, n. 39.
12. See C. Rowe, "The Chicago Frame," *The Mathematics of the Ideal Villa and Other Essays* (Cambridge, Mass., 1976), 89–117; first published in the *Architectural Review*, 1956.
13. Le Corbusier, *La Ville radieuse* (Paris, 1964), 30.
14. Le Corbusier, *Oeuvre complète 1910–1929*, 60.
15. Rowe, *Mathematics*, 14.
16. Le Corbusier, *Concerning Town Planning* (London, 1947), 22.

7 Architecture and the Cumulative City

1. T. E. Hulme, *Speculations* (New York, 1927), 3–4; first published in 1924.
2. Le Corbusier, *Oeuvre complète 1910–1929* (Zurich, 1960), 118. The quote is from "The Street," which originally appeared in *L'Intransigéant* in May 1929.
3. S. Gideon, *Space, Time and Architecture* (Cambridge, Mass., 1941), 548.
4. Le Corbusier, *Concerning Town Planning* (London, 1947), 22.
5. A. Smithson and P. Smithson, *Team 10 Primer* (Cambridge, Mass., 1974), 78.
6. L. Krier, *Rational Architecture* (Brussells, 1978), 58.
7. Le Corbusier, *Concerning Town Planning*, 22.
8. Ibid., 22.
9. The Caffé Pedrocchi is for Jorge Silvetti, who first put me on to it.
10. The basic equation of the competition for the new Paris Opera was not without contradiction and irony: a socialist government proposed to build a monumental opera house on a small, off-hand infill site adjacent to the irresolute but historically important Place de la Bastille at the opposite end of the main east-west route through Paris from the Place de l'Etoile. For political reasons construction was limited to the designated site boundaries, and unfortunately, this was a fatal flaw. The problem of an opera house at the Place de la Bastille is not so much an architectural problem as it is an urban problem in the most profound formal and cultural sense.
11. Regarding the detached building as an urban system, see "Paris discret ou l'autre systeme," *Les Cahiers de la recherche architecturale* 3 (Paris, 1979).

8 Excursus Americanus

1. Vincent Scully, *American Architecture and Urbanism* (New York, 1969), 12.
2. A. E. J. Morris, *History of Urban Form* (London, 1972), 219, 222.
3. Ibid., 222.
4. For the various phases of American Neoclassicism, see William H. Pierson, Jr., *American Buildings and Their Architects: The Colonial and Neoclassical Styles* (New York, 1970).
5. P. L. Ford, ed., *Works of Thomas Jefferson* (New York, 1904), 9:146–47.
6. For a complete description of "Jefferson's Paris," see Howard Rice, Jr., *Thomas Jefferson's Paris* (Princeton, 1976).
7. Ibid., 15. Letter to James Currie, February 5, 1785.
8. J.-C. Krafft and N. Ransonnette, *Plans, coupes, élévations...* (Paris, c. 1802?).
9. C.-N. Ledoux, *L'Architecture considérée sous le rapport de l'art, des moeurs et de la législation* (1804).
10. Each of the Parisian streets and their *hôtels* may be seen on the Maire plan of Paris, 1808.
11. Awareness of the problem is not recent; see V. Scully, *American Architecture and Urbanism* (New York, 1969), 245.
12. Regarding this antipathy toward the American city, see Morton White and Lucia White, *The Intellectual Versus the City: From Thomas Jefferson to Frank Lloyd Wright* (Cambridge, Mass., 1962).

Bibliography

The sources are listed by category and in chronological order of publication, rather than in alphabetical order by author. This is far from a definitive bibliography; only the most important sources are listed. Articles and books of special use—such as books on individual architects—are cited in the notes, and many of the sources listed below have extensive bibliographies themselves.

The Ancien Régime

1856
TOCQUEVILLE, A. DE. *L'Ancien Régime et la Révolution.* Paris, 1856. Several English translations.

1879–1928
BOISLISLE, A. *Mémoirs de Saint-Simon.* Paris, 1879–1928. Several English translations and abridgments.

1911
LAROUSSE (ed.). *Histoire de France . . .* II. Paris, 1911. See also 1954 edition by M. Reinhard.

1953
FORD, F. *Robe and Sword: The Regrouping of the French Aristocracy after Louis XIV.* Cambridge, 1953.

1953
LEWIS, W. H. *The Splendid Century: Some Aspects of French Life in the Reign of Louis XIV.* London, 1953.

1957
COBBAN, A. *A History of Modern France, 1715–1789.* Harmondsworth, 1957.

1969
ELIAS, N. *Die höfische Gesellschaft.* Darmstadt and Neuwied, 1969. English translation, *The Court Society,* Oxford, 1983.

1977
SENNETT, R. *The Fall of Public Man.* New York, 1977.

Selected Plans of Paris

Most of the plans listed here are contained as reduced facsimile engravings in the *Atlas des anciens plans de Paris* (Paris, 1880).

1380	Legrand Plan (nineteenth-century plan)
1540+	Braun Plan ("Aux Trois Personnages")
1614	Merian Plan
1652	Gombust Plan
1697	Nicolas de Fer Plan
1728	Delagrive Plan
1734–39	Bretez Plan ("Turgot")
1778	Jaillot Plan
1793	Artists' Plan
1799	Verniquet Plan
1808	Maire Plan

The Royal Squares

In addition to the general sources listed here, the notes refer to articles giving more detail on the royal squares.

1943+
HAUTCOEUR, L. *Histoire de l'architecture classique en France.* Five volumes. Paris, 1943–53. New edition of Volume I, Paris, 1963–67.

1948
AUZELLE, R. *Encyclopédie de l'urbanisme.* Paris (1948?)–1968.

1971
SAALMAN, H. *Haussmann: Paris Transformed.* New York, 1971.

1972
MORRIS, A. E. J. *History of Urban Form.* London, 1972.

1975
AYMONINO, C., G. FABBRI, and A. VILLA. *Le citta capitali del XIX secolo–Parigi e Vienna.* Rome, 1975.

1975
LAVEDAN, P. *Nouvelle histoire de Paris: Histoire de l'Urbanisme à Paris.* Paris, 1975.

Contemporary Treatises on the French Hôtel

Only treatises that deal in whole, or in substantive part, with domestic French Classical architecture—the *hôtel*—are listed. For example, F. Blondel's *Cours d'architecture* (Paris, 1675) deals only with the orders and consequently is not listed. Sources noted by an asterisk are the publications of the *hôtels* after each phase of development.

1550s
SERLIO, S. *Sesto libro de architettura.* (Unpublished, n.d.; before 1554). Two manuscripts exist for this book: the Munich manuscript has been published in facsimile with an introduction and notes by M. Rosci as *Il Trattato di architettura di Sebastiano Serlio* (Milan, 1967); the Columbia University manuscript has been published in facsimile with a foreword by A. K. Placzek, introduction by J. S. Ackerman, and a text by M. N. Rosenfeld as *Sebastiano Serlio on Domestic Architecture* (New York, c. 1978).

1559+
DU CERCEAU, J.-A. *Livre d'architecture.* Paris, 1559, 1561, 1582. Facsimile reprint, New Jersey, 1965.

1567
L'ORME, P. DE. *L'Architecture.* Paris, 1567. Facsimile edition, London, 1967.

1576+
DU CERCEAU, J.-A. *Les plus excellents bastiments de France....* Paris, 1576–79. Facsimile reprint, Paris, 1868.

1623+
LE MUET, P. *Manière de bastir pour toutes sortes de personnes.* First edition, Paris, 1623. Facsimile reprint, New Jersey, 1972.

1624+
SAVOT, L. *Architecture françoise....* First edition, Paris, 1624.

1647
LE MUET, P. *Manière de bien bastir pour toutes sortes de personnes.* Second enlarged edition, Paris, 1647.

c. 1660
*MAROT, J. *Recueil des plans, profiles et élévations de plusiers palais... bâtis dans Paris (Petit Marot).* Paris, c. 1660–70. Facsimile reprint with an introduction by A. Blunt, New Jersey, 1969, and Paris, 1970.

c. 1670
*MAROT, J. *L'Architecture françoise (Grand Marot).* Paris, c. 1670. Facsimile reprint, Paris, 1970. An invaluable related study is A. Mauban, *Jean Marot: Architecte et Graveur Parisien.* Paris, 1944.

1691
D'AVILER, C.-A. *Cours d'architecture.* First edition, Paris, 1691.

1710
D'AVILER, C.-A. *Cours d'architecture.* Second edition (enlarged edition by A. Le Blond), Paris, 1710.

1725
COURTONNE, J. *Traité de perspective pratique avec les remarques sur l'architecture.* Paris, 1725.

1727
*MARIETTE, J. *L'Architecture françoise.* Paris, 1727. Four volumes. Enlarged edition of the *Grand Marot* as volume 4. Fifth volume in larger format in 1738. Reprint of volumes 1–3, Paris and Brussels, 1927–29. See A. Mauban, *L'Architecture Française de Jean Mariette.* Paris, 1954.

1728
BRISEUX, C.-E. *Architecture moderne, ou l'art de bien bâtir pour toutes sortes de personnes.* Paris, 1728.

1737
BLONDEL, J.-F. *De la distribution des maisons de plaisance, et de la décoration des édifices en général.* Paris, 1737–38.

c. 1740
BLONDEL, J.-F. *Abrégé d'architecture concernant la distribution, la décoration, et la construction des batiments civils.* (Unpublished manuscript, Bibliothèque Mazarin, Paris, ms. 3691). Paris, c. 1740. See R. A. Etlin, "Les dedans Jacques-François Blondel and the System of the Home, c. 1740," *Gazette des Beaux-Arts*, April 1978, 137–47.

1743
BRISEUX, C.-E. *L'Art de bâtir des maisons de campagne, où l'on traite de leur distribution, de leur construction, et de leur décoration....* Paris, 1743. Facsimile reprint, Farnborough, 1966.

1751
DIDEROT, D., and J. D'ALEMBERT. *Encyclopédie, ou Dictionnaire raisonné des sciences des arts et des métiers.* Paris–Amsterdam, 1751–77.

1752
*BLONDEL, J.-F. *Architecture françoise.* Paris, 1752, 1754, 1756. Facsimile reprint, Paris, 1904.

1753
LAUGIER, M.-A. *Essai sur l'architecture.* Paris, 1753. English translation, *An Essay on Architecture*, Los Angeles, 1977.

1765
PATTE, P. *Monuments érigés à la gloire de Louis XV.* Paris, 1765.

1771
BLONDEL, J.-F. *Cours d'architecture* (continued by Patte). Paris, 1771–77.

1780
LE CAMUS DE MEZIERES, N. *Le Génie de l'architecture ou l'Analogie de cet art avec nos sensations.* Paris, 1780.

c. 1802
*KRAFFT, J.-C., and N. RANSONNETTE. *Plans, coupes, élévations des plus belles maisons et des hôtels construits à Paris et dans les environs.* Paris, n.d. (c. 1802?). Facsimile reprint, Paris, 1909.

1802
DURAND, J.-N.-L. *Précis des leçons d'architecture.* Paris, 1802–5.

1804
LEDOUX, C.-N. *L'Architecture considérée sous le rapport de l'art, des moeurs et de la législation.* Paris, 1804. Enlarged edition by D. Ramée, *L'Architecture de C.-N. Ledoux*, Paris, 1847. Facsimile reprint of the Ramée edition, *C.-N. Ledoux: L'Architecture,* with an English translation of Ledoux's *Prospectus* and an introduction by A. Vidler, Princeton, 1983.

1806
KRAFFT, J.-C. *Recueil d'architecture civile.* Paris, 1806–7.

1829
KRAFFT, J.-C. *Choix des plus jolies maisons de Paris et des environs . . . .* Paris, 1829. Enlarged edition, 1849.

1839
DALY, C. (ed.). *Revue générale de l'architecture et des travaux publics.* Paris, 1839–88.

1864
DALY, C. *Architecture privée au XIXième siècle sous Napoléon III; nouvelles maisons de Paris et des environs.* Paris, 1864.

Modern Works

1911
BLOMFIELD, SIR R. *History of French Architecture 1494–1661.* Two volumes. London, 1911.

1921
BLOMFIELD, SIR R. *History of French Architecture 1661–1774.* Two volumes. London, 1921.

1943
KIMBALL, F. *The Creation of the Rococo.* Philadelphia, 1943. French translation, *Le Style Louis XV*, Paris, 1949. Reprinted as *The Creation of the Rococo Decorative Style*, New York, 1980.

1943+
HAUTECOEUR, L. *Histoire de l'architecture classique en France.*
I. *La formation de l'idéal classique.* Paris, 1943.
II. *Le Règne de Louis XIV.* Paris, 1948.
III. *Première moitié du XVIIIe siècle—Le Style Louis XV.* Paris, 1950.
IV. *Seconde moitié du XVIIIe siècle—Le Style Louis XVI.* Paris, 1952.
V. *Révolution et Empire 1792–1815.* Paris, 1953.
VI. *La restauration et le gouvernement de juillet 1815–1848.* Paris, 1955.
VII. *La fin de l'architecture classique 1848–1900.* Paris, 1957.

1953
BLUNT, A. *Art and Architecture in France 1500–1700.* London, 1953.

1955
KAUFMANN, E. *Architecture in the Age of Reason: Baroque and Postbaroque in England, Italy and France.* Cambridge, 1955.

1963+
HAUTECOEUR, L. *Histoire de l'architecture classique en France.*
I.1. *La Première Renaissance 1495 à 1535–40.* Paris, 1963.
I.2. *La Renaissance des humanistes 1535–40 à 1589.* Paris, 1965.
I.3. *L'Architecture sous Henri IV et Louis XIII.* Part 1, Paris, 1966, part 2, 1967.

1964
GALLET, M. *Demeures parisiennes l'époque de Louis XVI.* Paris, 1964. English translation, *Stately Mansions*, New York, 1972.

1965
BABELON, J.-P. *Demeures parisiennes sous Henri IV et Louis XIII.* Paris, 1965.

1972
KALNEIN, W. G., and M. LEVEY. *Art and Architecture of the Eighteenth Century in France.* Harmondsworth, 1972.

1980
BRAHAM, A. *The Architecture of the French Enlightenment.* London, 1980.

1984
THOMSON, D. *Renaissance Paris: Architecture and Growth 1475–1600.* Berkeley, 1984.

Guides and Topographical Histories

1612
DU BREUL, J. *Le Théâtre des antiquités de Paris.* First edition, Paris, 1612. Enlarged edition, Paris, 1639.

1641
CHASTILLON, C. *Topographie françoise.* Paris, 1641.

1684
BRICE, G. *Description de la ville de Paris.* First edition, Paris, 1684. Ninth edition, Paris, 1752. Reproduction of ninth edition, Paris, 1971.

1685
LE MAIRE, C. *Paris ancien et nouveau.* Paris, 1685.

1724
SAUVAL, H. *Histoire et recherches des antiquités de la ville de Paris.* Paris, 1724. Reproduced in facsimile, London, 1969.

1725
FELIBIEN, M. *Histoire de la ville de Paris.* Paris, 1725.

1736
PIGANIOL DE LA FORCE, J. *Description de Paris.* First edition, Paris, 1736.

1749
DEZALLIER D'ARGENVILLE, A. N. *Voyage pittoresque de Paris.* First edition, Paris, 1749.

1781
LA BORDE, J.-B. DE. *Voyage pittoresque de la France.* Paris, 1781–84.
MERCIER, L.-S. *Tableaux de Paris.* Paris, 1781.

1787
THIERY, L.-V. *Guide des amateurs et des étrangers voyageurs à Paris.* Paris, 1787.

1806
LEGRANDE, J.-G., and C.-P. LANDON. *Description de Paris et de ses édifices.* Paris, 1806.

1866
BERTY, A., et al. *Topographic historique du vieux Paris.* Paris, 1866–68.

1875
HOFFBAUER, F. *Paris à travers les ages.* Paris, 1875–82.

1929
DUMOLIN, M. *Etudes de topographie parisienne.* Paris, 1929–31.

1963
HILLAIRET, J. *Dictionnaire historique des rues de Paris.* Paris, 1963.

1964
CHRIST, Y., J. S. DE SACY, and P. SIGURET. *Le Marais.* Paris, 1964.

1968
COUPERIE, P. *Paris au fil du temps.* Paris, 1968. English translation, *Paris through the Ages.* New York, 1968.

Picture Books

Engravings

1697
PERELLE, A. *Vues des belles maisons de France, fait par Perelle.* Paris, n.d. (1697?).
SILVESTRE, I. *Vues de Paris.* Paris. Reprint with an introduction by J.-P. Babelon, Paris, 1977.

1783
PERELLE, G. *Les Délices de Paris et de ses environs ou Recueil des vues perspectives des plus beaux monuments de Paris . . . .* Paris, 1783.

1867
SAUVAGEOT, C. *Palais, châteaux, hôtels et maisons de France du XVe au XVIIIe siècle.* Paris, 1867.

Photographs

1910
SELLIER, C. *Les anciens hôtels de Paris.* Paris, 1910.

1920
VACQUIER, J., et al. *Les vieux hôtels de Paris.* Paris, 1920–30.

1945
PILLEMENT, G. *Les Hôtels de Paris.* Paris, 1945.
PILLEMENT, G. *Les Hôtels du Marais.* Paris, 1945. Revised edition, Paris, 1948.

1948
LE FRANCOIS, P. *Paris à travers les siècles.* Paris, 1948–56.

1962
CONNOLLY, C., and J. ZERBE. *Les Pavillons. French Pavilions of the Eighteenth Century.* London, 1962.

c. 1974
SIGURET, P., et al. *Le Faubourg Saint-Germain.* Paris, c. 1974.
SIGURET, P., et al. *L'Ile de la cité . . . .* Paris, c. 1974.

The French Garden

Both of these sources have extensive bibliographies.

1978
WIEBENSON, D. *The Picturesque Garden in France.* Princeton, 1978.

1979
ADAMS, W. H. *The French Garden 1500–1800.* New York, 1979.

Illustration Sources and Credits

Illustrations by the author are not cited. Complete citations for published works appear in the bibliography.

Abbreviations:
B.N.–C.E.: Bibliothèque Nationale–Cabinet Estampes: call number (photo number)

B.N.–C.P.: Bibliothèque Nationale–Cartes et Plans: call number (photo number)

O.C. '10–29: Le Corbusier, Oeuvre Complète 1910–1929

2. Musée National du Château de Versailles.
3. Courtesy of Fred Koetter.
6. The Turgot plan.
8. Claude Perrault translation of Vitruvius, *Les dix livres d'architecture* (Paris, 1673).
9. Blondel, *Architecture*, II, 236. Photo by permission of the Houghton Library, Harvard University.
10. P. Portoghesi, *Rome of the Renaissance* (New York, 1972), 68.
11. F. Borsi, *Leon Battista Alberti* (New York, 1977), fig. 240. Photo courtesy of Electa Editrice, Milano.
13. A. Salvador, *101 Buildings to See in Venice* (Venice, 1969), 90.
14. G. Perocco and A. Salvadori, *Civiltà di Venezia* (Venezia, 1973), 360.
16. After a study by Palladio.
17. After Palladio.
18. After R. Wittkower.
19. J. Ackerman, *Palladio* (Harmondsworth, 1966), fig. 22. Photo by permission of James Ackerman.
21. Palladio, *Quattro Libri*.
23. Le Pautre.
24. Blondel, *Architecture*, IV, 481. Photo by permission of the Houghton Library, Harvard University.
25. Perelle, *Vues*, pl. 164. Photo by permission of the Francis Loeb Library, Harvard Graduate School of Design.
26. Simpson, *History*, III, fig. 260.
27. N. Pevsner, *Outline of European Architecture*, 6th edition (Harmondsworth, 1963), 353. Photo by permission of Aerofilms Ltd.
28. *Grand Marot*. B.N.–C.E.: Ha 7d (cl. 85.C.171324).
30. P. Lelievre, *L'Architecture française* (Paris, 1963), 98. (Cl. Henrard Air Photo).
31. B.N.–C.E.: Va 261a (cl. 69.B.48704).
32. Blondel, *Architecture*, II, 153. Photo by permission of the Houghton Library, Harvard University.
33. The Turgot plan.
34. *Atlas des anciens plans de Paris.*
35. W. Lotz, *Studies in Italian Renaissance Architecture* (Cambridge, MA, 1977), fig. 44. Photo by Vigevano, Verga, courtesy of Bibliotheca Herziana (Max-Planck-Institute).
36. L. Benevolo, *The Architecture of the Renaissance* (Boulder, 1978), 549.
37. L. Benevolo, *The Architecture of the Renaissance* (Boulder, 1978), 549.
38. A. Blunt, *Art and Architecture*, pl. 8(A). (British museum).
39. A. Blunt, *Art and Architecture*, pl. 19(A).
41. B.N.–C.E.: Va 248c (cl. 56.C.12139).
42. Viollet-Le-Duc, *Dictionnaire*, 6, 286.
43. Hautecoeur, *Architecture Classique*, I, 1, 265, fig. 185. Photo by permission of the Caisse Nationale des Monuments Historiques et des Sites.
44. Viollet-Le-Duc, *Dictionnaire*, 6, 283.
45. Viollet-Le-Duc, *Dictionnaire*, 6, 285.
46. Du Cerceau, *Bastiments*. Photo by permission of the Houghton Library, Harvard University.
47. A. Blunt, *Art and Architecture*, pl. 28(B).
49. Redrawn from Serlio's *On Domestic Architecture* (Avery ms. M^{O}XI).
51. *Petit Marot*, pl. 34. B.N.–C.E.: Ha 7b (cl. 85.C.171325).
52. Blondel, *Architecture*, II, 278. Photo by permission of the Houghton Library, Harvard University.
53. Blondel, *Architecture*, II, 280. Photo by permission of the Houghton Library, Harvard University.
54. A. Blunt, *Art and Architecture*, pl. 29(B).
55. Du Cerceau, *Livre*, XIIII.
56. A. Blunt, *Art and Architecture*, pl. 61(B).
57. Du Cerceau, *Livre*, XXXVIII.
58. The Turgot plan.
59. B.N.–C.E.: Ve 9 Rés. (cl. 73.B.62057).
60. *Atlas des anciens plans de Paris.*
61. *Atlas des anciens plans de Paris.*

62. B.N.–C.E.: (cl. C.59774).
63. B.N.–C.E.: Va 251b (cl. 61.B.27114).
64. A. Blunt, *Art and Architecture*, pl. 71(A).
65. *Architecture d'Aujourd'hui* 138 (June/July 1968), 87. (Alain Perceval).
66. *Atlas des anciens plans de Paris*.
67. The Turgot plan.
68. B.N.–C.E.: (cl. C.25958).
69. B.N.–C.E.: (cl. C.109883).
70. The Turgot plan.
71. B.N.–C.E.: Va 251b (cl. 66.A.14597).
72. J.-P. Babelon, *Demeures Parisiennes*, 185.
73. B.N.–C.E.: Ed 30 Rés. (cl. 65.B.37952).
74. B.N.–C.E.: Ed 30 Rés. (cl. 56.C.11524).
75. Le Muet, *Manière*, 41.
76. Le Muet, *Manière*, 43.
77. *Petit Marot*. Photo by permission of the Houghton Library, Harvard University.
78. *Petit Marot*. Photo by permission of the Houghton Library, Harvard University.
79. A. Blunt, *Art and Architecture*, fig. 129.
80. A. Blunt, *Art and Architecture*, fig. 129.
81. M. Fleury, and others, *Paris: de Lutece à Beaubourg* (Paris, 1979), fig. 55. (Photo by Max and Albert Hirmer).
82. B.N.–C.E.: Ha 7c (microf. p. 5813) (cl. 85.C.171330).
83. *Petit Marot*. Photo by permission of the Houghton Library, Harvard University.
84. B.N.–C.E.: Ha 7c (cl. 69.C.39161).
85. B.N.–C.E.: Ed 30 Rés. (cl. 63.C.20681).
86. *Petit Marot*. Photo by permission of the Houghton Library, Harvard University.
87. A. Blunt, *Art and Architecture*, fig. 168.
88. The Turgot plan.
89. B.N.–C.E.: Ha 7c (cl. 70.B.51665).
90. *Grand Marot*. B.N.–C.E.: Va 232e (cl. 71.C.50743).
91. *Grand Marot*. B.N.–C.E.: Ha 7c (cl. 77.C.84262).
92. B.N.–C.E.: Va 230a (cl. 78.B.81885).
93. *Grand Marot*. B.N.–C.E.: Ha 7d (f.70) (cl. 85.C.171331).
94. *Grand Marot*. B.N.–C.E.: Ha 7c (cl. 77.C.82877).
95. Le Muet, *Manière*, 2. B.N.–C.E.: Ha 5 (cl. 85.C.171334).
96. Le Muet, *Manière*, 3. B.N.–C.E.: Ha 5 (cl. 85.C.171335).
97. Le Muet, *Manière*, 5. B.N.–C.E.: Ha 5 (cl. 85.C.171336).
98. Le Muet, *Manière*, 26. B.N.–C.E.: Ha 5 (cl. 85.C.171327).
99. Le Muet, *Manière*, 27. B.N.–C.E.: Ha 5 (cl. 85.C.171328).
100. Le Muet, *Manière*, 29. B.N.–C.E.: Ha 5 (cl. 85.C.171326).
101. Le Muet, *Manière*, 73.
102. Blondel, *Architecture*, III, 358. Photo by permission of the Houghton Library, Harvard University.
103. P. Lavedan, *Nouvelle histoire*, fig. 59. By permission of the Bibliothèque d'Art et d'Archéologie (Fondation Jacques Doucet).
104. Blondel, *Architecture*, II, 241. Photo by permission of the Houghton Library, Harvard University.
105. Blondel, *Architecture*, II, 241. Photo by permission of the Houghton Library, Harvard University.
107. A. Blunt, *Art and Architecture*, pl. 102(A).
108. A. Blunt, *Art and Architecture*, pl. 105(A).
109. Blondel, *Architecture*, II, 235. Photo by permission of the Houghton Library, Harvard University.
110. Blondel, *Architecture*, II, 236. Photo by permission of the Houghton Library, Harvard University.
114. *O.C. '29–34*, 24. © S.P.A.D.E.M., Paris/V.A.G.A., New York, 1985.
115. *O.C. '29–34*, 25. © S.P.A.D.E.M., Paris/V.A.G.A., New York, 1985.
119. P. Kjellberg, *Le Guide du Marais* (Paris, 1967), 51. Photo: Connaissance des Arts, courtesy of La Bibliothèque des Arts.
120. R. W. Berger, *Antoine Le Pautre*, pl. 56. (J. C. Vaysse).
121. A. Blunt, *Art and Architecture*, 237.
122. B.N.–C.E.: Ha 7d (cl. 74.C.63775).
123. The Turgot plan.
124. The Turgot plan.
125. *Atlas des anciens plans de Paris*.
126. The Turgot plan.
127. P. Lavedan, *Nouvelle histoire*, fig. 96. Photo by permission of the Archives Nationales.
128. The Turgot plan.
129. B.N.–C.E.: Va 230e (cl. C.9038).
130. *Atlas des anciens plans de Paris*.
131. *Atlas des anciens plans de Paris*.
132. B.N.–C.E.: Va 234 (cl. 77.C.83723).
133. B.N.–C.E.: Va 234a (cl. 85.C.171019).
134. B.N.–C.E.: Va 234a (cl. 67.C.31200).
135. B.N.–C.E.: Va 234 (cl. 77.C.83724).
136. B.N.–C.E.: Va 234 (cl. 66.B.38985).
137. B.N.–C.E.: Va 234 (cl. 51.B.8704).
138. The Turgot plan.
139. *Atlas des anciens plans de Paris*.
141. Courtesy of Bruno Fortier.
142. After Blondel, *Architecture*, III, 388 and 393.
143. After Blondel, *Architecture*, III, 389 and 395.
148. A. Blunt, *Art and Architecture*, pl. 175(B).
149. Blondel, *Architecture*, II, 267. Photo by permission of the Houghton Library, Harvard University.
150. Blondel, *Architecture*, II, 269. Photo by permission of the Houghton Library, Harvard University.
151. Blondel, *Architecture*, I, 58. Photo by permission of the Houghton Library, Harvard University.
152. Blondel, *Architecture*, I, 59. Photo by permission of the Houghton Library, Harvard University.
153. Blondel, *Architecture*, I, 71. Photo by permission of the Houghton Library, Harvard University.
154. Blondel, *Architecture*, III, 341. Photo by permission of the Houghton Library, Harvard University.
155. Blondel, *Architecture*, III, 332. Photo by permission of the Houghton Library, Harvard University.
156. *Atlas des anciens plans de Paris*.
157. Blondel, *Architecture*, I, 61. Photo by permission of the Houghton Library, Harvard Library.
158. C. Norberg-Shulz, *Late Baroque and Rococo Architecture* (New York, 1985), fig. 76. Photo by Bruno Balestrini, courtesy of Electa Editrice, Milano.
159. Blondel, *Architecture*, I, 40. Photo by permission of the Houghton Library, Harvard University.
160. Blondel, *Architecture*, I, 109. Photo by permission of the Houghton Library, Harvard University.
161. Blondel, *Architecture*, I, 29. Photo by permission of the Houghton Library, Harvard University.
162. Kalnein, *Art and Architecture*, pl. 223.
163. The Turgot plan.
165. D'Aviler, *Cours*, pl. 62.
166. D'Aviler, *Cours*, pl. 62.
167. *Atlas des anciens plans de Paris*.
168. Blondel, *Architecture*, III, 439. Photo by permission of the Houghton Library, Harvard University.

277 Illustration Sources and Credits

169. Blondel, *Architecture*, I, 99. Photo by permission of the Houghton Library, Harvard University.
170. The Turgot plan.
171. Blondel, *Architecture*, I, 97. Photo by permission of the Houghton Library, Harvard University.
172. H. Coutant, *Le Palais Bourbon* (Paris, 1905), facing 128.
173. Marchand, *Le Palais Bourbon* (Paris, 1962), 106.
175. Marchand, *Le Palais Bourbon* (Paris, 1962), no. 28.
176. R. Cameron and P. Salinger, *Above Paris* (San Francisco, 1984), 73. Photo by permission of Cameron and Company.
177. J.-M. Pérouse de Montclos, *Les Prix de Rome* (Paris, 1984), 38.
178. Blondel, *Architecture*. Photo by permission of the Houghton Library, Harvard University.
179. Lavedan, *Pour connaître les monuments de France*, no. 843. © Photo Archives Editions Arthaud, Paris.
180. Blondel, *Architecture*. Photo by permission of the Houghton Library, Harvard University.
181. D. Diderot and J. D'Alembert, *Encyclopédie* (Paris–Amsterdam, 1751–77), I, XXV.
182. J.-F. Blondel, *Cours*, 4, pl. XLVI.
183. Meissonier, *L'Oeuvre*, pl. 25.
184. Meissonier, *L'Oeuvre*, pl. 28.
185. Meissonier, *L'Oeuvre*, pl. 28.
186. Briseux, *L'Art de bâtir*, I, pl. 3.
187. Briseux, *L'Art de bâtir*, II, pl. 142.
188. Briseux, *L'Art de bâtir*, II, pl. 143.
189. Blondel, *Distribution*, I, pl. 32. Photo by permission of the Houghton Library, Harvard University.
190. Blondel, *Distribution*, I, pl. 33. Photo by permission of the Houghton Library, Harvard University.
191. Blondel, *Distribution*, I, pl. 35. Photo by permission of the Houghton Library, Harvard University.
192. Blondel, *Distribution*, I, pl. 85. Photo by permission of the Houghton Library, Harvard University.
193. Blondel, *Distribution*, I, pl. 82. Photo by permission of the Houghton Library, Harvard University.
194. Blondel, *Distribution*, I, pl. 10. Photo by permission of the Houghton Library, Harvard University.
195. Blondel, *Distribution*, II, pl. 86. Photo by permission of the Houghton Library, Harvard University.
196. Blondel, *Distribution*, II, pl. 86. Photo by permission of the Houghton Library, Harvard University.
197. Blondel, *Distribution*, II, pl. 86. Photo by permission of the Houghton Library, Harvard University.
198. The Turgot plan.
199. Ledoux, *L'Architecture*.
200. M.-A. Laugier, *Essai* (Paris, 1755).
201. Patte, *Monuments*, pl. XXXIX. Photo by permission of the Houghton Library, Harvard University.
202. Patte, *Monuments*, pl. XXXIX. Photo by permission of the Houghton Library, Harvard University.
204. Patte, *Monuments*. Photo by permission of the Houghton Library, Harvard University.
205. Patte, *Monuments*, pl. II. Photo by permission of the Houghton Library, Harvard University.
206. B.N.–C.E.: Va 277 (cl. 70.C.43137).
207. B.N.–C.E.: Va 277 (cl. 75.C.73037).
208. B.N.–C.E.: Va 277 (cl. 64.C.23972).
209. *Atlas des anciens plans de Paris*.
210. G. Gromort, *L'Architecture de la Renaissance en France* (XVI, XVII, XVIII siècles) (Paris), 182.
211. N. Pevsner, *Outline of European Architecture*, pl. 247. By permission of Bildarchiv Foto Marburg.
212. Editions "Guy."
213. G. Gromort, *Choix des Plans*. Photo by permission of the Frances Loeb Library, Harvard Graduate School of Design.
214. B.N.–C.E.: Ha 57 (cl. 75.C.70636).
216. M. Gallet, *Ledoux*, 38. By permission of Archives de Seine-et-Marne, collection Estampes.
217. Ledoux, *L'Architecture*, pl. 254.
218. Ledoux, *L'Architecture*, pl. 287.
220. Ledoux, *L'Architecture*, pl. 165.
222. J.-C. Krafft, *Maisons de Campagne*.
223. Ledoux, *L'Architecture*, pl. 161.
224. Ledoux, *L'Architecture*, pl. 163.
225. Ledoux, *L'Architecture*, pl. 166.
226. Gallet, *Ledoux*, 198. (Commission du Vieux Paris [Clichés E. Michot]).
227. Ledoux, *L'Architecture*, pl. 158.
228. Ledoux, *L'Architecture*, pl. 156.
229. A. Braham, *Architecture*, 163.
230. Ledoux, *L'Architecture*.
231. Ledoux, *L'Architecture*, pl. 207.
232. Ledoux, *L'Architecture*, pl. 207.
233. Ledoux, *L'Architecture*, pl. 208.
234. Ledoux, *L'Architecture*, pl. 152.
235. Ledoux, *L'Architecture*, pl. 154.
236. Ledoux, *L'Architecture*, pl. 153.
237. Krafft, *Plans*, pl. 40. Photo by permission of the Frances Loeb Library, Harvard Graduate School of Design.
238. Ledoux, *L'Architecture*, pl. 159.
239. *Atlas des anciens plans de Paris*.
240. Ledoux, *L'Architecture*, pl. 175.
241. Ledoux, *L'Architecture*, pl. 177.
242. Krafft, *Plans*. Photo by permission of the Frances Loeb Library, Harvard Graduate School of Design.
243. Ledoux, *L'Architecture*, pl. 175.
244. Krafft, *Plans*, pl. 74. Photo by permission of the Frances Loeb Library, Harvard Graduate School of Design.
245. Krafft, *Plans*, pl. 29. Photo by permission of the Frances Loeb Library, Harvard Graduate School of Design.
246. Krafft, *Plans*, pl. 5. Photo by permission of the Frances Loeb Library, Harvard Graduate School of Design.
247. Krafft, *Plans*, pl. 7. Photo by permission of the Frances Loeb Library, Harvard Graduate School of Design.
248. B.N.–C.E.: Ha 58 (cl. 80.B.88939).
249. Krafft, *Plans*, pl. 69. Photo by permission of the Frances Loeb Library, Harvard Graduate School of Design.
250. Krafft, *Plans*, pl. 70. Photo by permission of the Frances Loeb Library, Harvard Graduate School of Design.
251. Krafft, *Plans*, pl. 19. Photo by permission of the Frances Loeb Library, Harvard Graduate School of Design.
252. Krafft, *Plans*, pl. 57. Photo by permission of the Frances Loeb Library, Harvard Graduate School of Design.
253. Krafft, *Plans*, pl. 58. Photo by permission of the Frances Loeb Library, Harvard Graduate School of Design.
254. Krafft, *Plans*, pl. 50. Photo by permission of the Frances Loeb Library, Harvard Graduate School of Design.
255. Krafft, *Plans*, pl. 3. Photo by permission of the Frances Loeb Library, Harvard Graduate School of Design.

278 Illustration Sources and Credits

256. Krafft, *Plans*, pl. 11. Photo by permission of the Frances Loeb Library, Harvard Graduate School of Design.
257. Krafft, *Plans*, pl. 37. Photo by permission of the Frances Loeb Library, Harvard Graduate School of Design.
258. Krafft, *Plans*, pl. 27. Photo by permission of the Frances Loeb Library, Harvard Graduate School of Design.
259. Krafft, *Plans*, pl. 16. Photo by permission of the Frances Loeb Library, Harvard Graduate School of Design.
260. A. Braham, *Architecture*, 195. Photo by permission of the Caisse Nationale des Monuments et des Sites.
261. Ledoux, *L'Architecture*.
262. M. Reinhard, *Nouvelle Histoire de Paris: La Révolution* (Paris, 1971), XIII^2 (cl. Hachette).
263. L. A. Dubut, *Architecture civile* (Paris, 1803).
264. Krafft, *Plans*, pl. 23. Photo by permission of the Frances Loeb Library, Harvard Graduate School of Design.
265. Krafft, *Plans*, pl. 24. Photo by permission of the Frances Loeb Library, Harvard Graduate School of Design.
267. Krafft, *Plans*, pl. 17. Photo by permission of the Frances Loeb Library, Harvard Graduate School of Design.
269. C. Daly, *Architecture Privée*.
270. C. Daly, *Architecture Privée*, I, ex. 2, pl. 1.
271. *Revue Générale*, 1858, XVI, pl. 5.
272. *Revue Générale*, 1858, XVI, pl. 6.
273. *Revue Générale*, 1876, XXXIIIv pl. 53.
274. *Revue Générale*, 1858, XVI, pl. 15.
275. *Revue Générale*, 1858, XVI, pl. 17.
276. *Revue Générale*, 1858, XVI, pl. 16.
277. A. Drexler, *Beaux-Arts*, 236. (Chevonjon Frères, Paris). Photo by permission of the École Nationale Supérieure des Beaux-Arts.
278. A. Drexler, *Beaux-Arts*, 236. (Chevonjon Frères, Paris). Photo by permission of the École Nationale Supérieure des Beaux-Arts.
279. *O.C. '10–29*, 39. © S.P.A.D.E.M., Paris/V.A.G.A., New York, 1985.
280. *O.C. '10–29*, 23. © S.P.A.D.E.M., Paris/V.A.G.A., New York, 1985.
281. *O.C. '10–29*, 37. © S.P.A.D.E.M., Paris/V.A.G.A., New York, 1985.
282. *O.C. '10–29*, 189. © S.P.A.D.E.M., Paris/V.A.G.A., New York, 1985.
283. *O.C. '10–29*, 204. © S.P.A.D.E.M., Paris/V.A.G.A., New York, 1985.
284. *O.C. '10–29*, 204. © S.P.A.D.E.M., Paris/V.A.G.A., New York, 1985.
285. *O.C. '10–29*, 204. © S.P.A.D.E.M., Paris/V.A.G.A., New York, 1985.
286. Gallet, *Stately Mansions*, pl. 17.
287. *O.C. '10–29*, 90. © S.P.A.D.E.M., Paris/V.A.G.A., New York, 1985.
288. Krafft, *Plans*, 19. Photo by permission of the Frances Loeb Library, Harvard Graduate School of Design.
289. *O.C. '10–29*, 91. © S.P.A.D.E.M., Paris/V.A.G.A., New York, 1985.
290. *O.C. '10–29*, 90. © S.P.A.D.E.M., Paris/V.A.G.A., New York, 1985.
291. *O.C. '29–34*, 26. © S.P.A.D.E.M., Paris/V.A.G.A., New York, 1985.
292. N. Pevsner, *An Outline of European Architecture*, 6th edition (Harmondsworth, 1963), pl. 247. Photo by permission of Bildarchiv Foto Marburg.
294. *O.C. '10–29*, 37. © S.P.A.D.E.M., Paris/V.A.G.A., New York, 1985.
295. Drawing by Michael Dennis.
296. *O.C. '10–29*, 61. © S.P.A.D.E.M., Paris/V.A.G.A., New York, 1985.
297. *O.C. '10–29*, 64. © S.P.A.D.E.M., Paris/V.A.G.A., New York, 1985.
298. Le Corbusier, *La Ville Radieuse* (Paris, 1964), 30. © S.P.A.D.E.M., Paris/V.A.G.A., New York, 1985.
299. *O.C. '10–29*, 158. © S.P.A.D.E.M., Paris/V.A.G.A., New York, 1985.
300. *O.C. '10–29*, 159. © S.P.A.D.E.M., Paris/V.A.G.A., New York, 1985.
301. *O.C. '10–29*, 141. © S.P.A.D.E.M., Paris/V.A.G.A., New York, 1985.
302. Courtesy of Werner Seligmann.
303. *O.C. '10–29*, 142–3. © S.P.A.D.E.M., Paris/V.A.G.A., New York, 1985.
304. C. Rowe, *Mathematics of the Ideal Villa and Other Essays* (Cambridge, MA, 1976), pl. 5. © S.P.A.D.E.M., Paris/V.A.G.A., New York, 1985.
305. *O.C. '10–29*, 147. © S.P.A.D.E.M., Paris/V.A.G.A., New York, 1985.
307. *O.C. '29–34*, 101. © S.P.A.D.E.M., Paris/V.A.G.A., New York, 1985.
308. *O.C. '29–34*, 37. © S.P.A.D.E.M., Paris/V.A.G.A., New York, 1985.
309. *O.C. '57–65*, 88. © S.P.A.D.E.M., Paris/V.A.G.A., New York, 1985.
310. *O.C. '29–34*, 157.
311. *O.C. '34–38*, 51.
312. Le Corbusier, *Concerning Town Planning* (London, 1947), 22. © S.P.A.D.E.M., Paris/V.A.G.A., New York, 1985.
313. Le Corbusier, *Concerning Town Planning* (London, 1947), 23. © S.P.A.D.E.M., Paris/V.A.G.A., New York, 1985.
314. Le Corbusier, *Concerning Town Planning* (London, 1947), 24. © S.P.A.D.E.M., Paris/V.A.G.A., New York, 1985.
315. *O.C. '10–29*, 187. © S.P.A.D.E.M., Paris/V.A.G.A., New York, 1985.
316. *O.C. '10–29*, 187. © S.P.A.D.E.M., Paris/V.A.G.A., New York, 1985.
317. *O.C. '29–34*, 93. © S.P.A.D.E.M., Paris/V.A.G.A., New York, 1985.
319. Courtesy of James Stirling.
320. Courtesy of James Stirling.
321. R. Cevese, *Invito a Palladio* (Milano, 1980), 118.
322. *O.C. '29–34*, 26. © S.P.A.D.E.M., Paris/V.A.G.A., New York, 1985.
323. The Nolli plan.
324. After Sebastiano Serlio (sixth book).
325. C. Rowe and F. Koetter, *Collage City* (Cambridge, MA, 1978), 75. (Stuart Cohen and Steven Hurtt).
326. *O.C. '46–52*, 149. © S.P.A.D.E.M., Paris/V.A.G.A., New York, 1985.
327. Courtesy of Steven Peterson.
329. *O.C. '29–34*, 130. © S.P.A.D.E.M., Paris/V.A.G.A., New York, 1985.
330. B. Champigneulle, *Perret* (Paris: A.M.G., 1959), fig. 49.
336. *Henri Sauvage* (Brussels: A.A.M., 1978), 196.
337. *Monograph of the Works of McKim, Mead & White*, 1915–1920.
338. M. Raymand, *Michel Roux-Spitz*, fig. 160.

339. M. Raymand, *Michel Roux-Spitz*, figs. 161 and 162.
340. M. Raymand, *Michel Roux-Spitz*, fig. 165.
341. M. Raymand, *Michel Roux-Spitz*, fig. 164.
342. Michael Dennis (redrawn from N. Gallimberti, *Giuseppe Jappelli*, 57).
343. Michael Dennis (redrawn from N. Gallimberti, *Giuseppe Jappelli*, 61).
360. Mary Hommann, *Wooster Square Design* (New Haven, CT: New Haven Redevelopment Agency, 1965), 14.
361. Bildarchiv Foto Marburg.
363. Raymond W. Stanley (ed.), *Mr. Bulfinch's Boston* (Boston, 1963), 28.
364. After *Historic American Building Survey: Massachusetts*, no. 612.
365. William H. Pierson, Jr., *American Buildings and Their Architects: The Colonial and Neoclassical Styles* (Garden City, NY, 1970), fig. 5.
366. William H. Pierson, Jr., *American Buildings and Their Architects: The Colonial and Neoclassical Styles* (Garden City, NY, 1970), fig. 212.
367. William H. Pierson, Jr., *American Buildings and Their Architects: The Colonial and Neoclassical Styles* (Garden City, NY, 1970), fig. 214. (Thomas Jefferson Memorial Foundation).
368. William H. Pierson, Jr., *American Buildings and Their Architects: The Colonial and Neoclassical Styles* (Garden City, NY, 1970), fig. 215.
369. William H. Pierson, Jr., *American Buildings and Their Architects: The Colonial and Neoclassical Styles* (Garden City, NY, 1970), fig. 216.
370. Krafft, *Plans*, pl. 19. Photo by permission of the Frances Loeb Library, Harvard Graduate School of Design.
371. A. Braham, *The Architecture of the French Enlightenment*, fig. 306. Photo by permission of the Caisse Nationale des Monuments et des Sites.
372. Robert Auzelle and Ivan Jankovic, *Encyclopédie de l'urbanisme*, tome 1 (Paris, 1954), pl. 507.
374. Vincent Scully, *American Architecture and Urbanism* (New York, 1969), pl. 92. (Ralph Thompson. University of Virginia Information Service, Charlottesville, Virginia).
375. Thomas Jefferson Papers, Manuscripts Department, University of Virginia Library.
378. Sebastiano Serlio, *The Second Book of Architecture* (London, 1611).
379. Rollin G. Osterweis, *Three Centuries of New Haven, 1638–1938* (New Haven, CT, 1953), 315.
381. B.N.–C.E.: Ha 7c (cl. 70.B.51665).
385. Gallet, *Ledoux*, fig. 121. (Kings Maps, British Library).
386. After a drawing by Stephen Moser and Michael Markovitz.
387. Brooks M. Kelley, *New Haven Heritage* (New Haven, CT, 1974), 18.
390. Musée National du Château de Versailles.
391. Scully, *Architecture and Urbanism*, 511. (Yuji Noga, New Haven, CT).
392. Peter Blake, *God's Own Junkyard: The Planned Deterioration of America's Landscape* (New York, 1964), pl. 87.
393. Courtesy of Christian Leprette.
394. Peter Blake, *God's Own Junkyard: The Planned Deterioration of America's Landscape* (New York, 1964), pl. 1.

Plans of Paris

1. B.N.–C.P.: Ge CC1 (cl. 67.B.41331).
2. B.N.–C.P.: Ge CC1 (cl. C.9336).
3. B.N.–C.P.: Ge CC1 (cl. 66.C.28389).
4. B.N.–C.P.: AA 573 (cl. 68.E.1990).
5. B.N.–C.P.: Ge CC1 (cl. D.3321).
6. *Atlas des anciens plans de Paris.*
7. *Atlas des anciens plans de Paris.*
8. B.N.–C.P.: Ge DDa4695 (cl. F221).
9. *Atlas des anciens plans de Paris.*
10. *Atlas des anciens plans de Paris.*
11. B.N.–C.P.: Ge CC210 (cl. 74.C.67516).
12. B.N.–C.P.: Ge C3694 (cl. 77.C.82130).
13. C. N. Maire, *La Topographie de Paris, ou plan détaillé de la ville de Paris et de ses faubourgs, . . .* (Paris, 1808).
14. Maire, *Paris.*
15. Maire, *Paris.*
16. Maire, *Paris.*
17. Maire, *Paris.*

Index

Numbers in italics are *page numbers* of illustrations.

Aalto, Alvar, 212, 213
Abrégé d'architecture concernant la distribution, la décoration et la construction des bâtiments civils (J.-F. Blondel), 8
Academy of Architecture, 79
Alberti, 16
Amelot de Biseuil, Hôtel, 77
Amelot (d'), Hôtel, 99, *101*
Ancy-le-Franc, 34, *34, 36*
Angoulême (d'), Hôtel, 8, 37, *39*
Antichambre, 4, 41, 69, 157
Antiquaires, 140, 177
Anvers plan of 1933 (Le Corbusier), 205, *206*
Apartment houses, 178, 182, *183*, 203, 219, 220, 221
Appartements, 41, 52, 61, 118, 119
Architects, time-line chart of, *9–11*
L'Architecture (Ledoux), 177
Architecture in the Age of Reason (Kaufmann), 3
Architecture civile (Dubut), 177
Architecture françoise (J.-F. Blondel), 7–8, 119, 157
L'Architecture françoise (Mariette), 109
L'Architecture françoise (Marot), 7, 13, 77
Architecture françoise (Savot), 7, 52
Architecture moderne (Briseux), 7, 109
Architecture privée sous Napoléon III (Daly), 182
Argenson (d'), Hôtel, 97, *98*, 99
Arrière garde-robe, 69
L'Art de bâtir des maisons de campagne (Briseux), 7, 118–119
Artists' plan of Paris (1793), 255
Aubert, Charles, 109, 163, *168*
Auchère (l'), Hôtel, 163, *168*
Auvergne (d'), Hôtel, 97
"Aux Trois Personnages" plan of Paris (1540), 6, 29, 246
Avaux (d'), Hôtel, 61, *67*
Aviler (d'), C.-A., 4, 7, 105, *105, 106*

Babelon, J.-P., 53, 69
Bains, appartement des, 105, 109
Banker, Hôtel for a, *187*
Bantru de Serrant, Hôtel, 64
Barbier, François, *140*
Baroque *hôtels*, 5, 13, 52–78, 157, 171, 178, 203

Bastille, Place de la, 226
"Beacon Rock" (Newport), 220
Beaumarchais, Hôtel, 178, *179, 180*
Beauvais (de), Hôtel, *15*, 52, 73, *73, 74, 75, 76*
Bélanger, François-Joseph, *161*, 178, *180, 181, 193*
Bel étage, 69
Béthune (de), Hôtel, 97, *98*
Bienséance, 125
Biron (de), Hôtel, 109, *198*
Blavette, 219
Blenheim Palace, 20, 24
Blondel, François, 7
Blondel, Jacques-François, 7, 8, 109, 118, 119, *119, 120–123*, 157
Blondel, Jean-François, 109
Blunt, A., 47
Boffrand, Germain, 77, 97, 98, 99, *101*, 112, *113*, 131
Bosse, Abraham, 54, 60
Boston, 230, *230*, 231
Boudoirs, 69
Boullée, Etienne-Louis, *140*
Bourbon, Palais, 106, *108*, 109, *110, 111*
Bourbon-Condé, Duchesse de, 109
Bramante, 16
Braun plan of Paris (1540), 6, 29, 246
Bretez plan of Paris (1734–39), 6, *12, 42, 51, 62, 78, 80, 81, 82, 88, 104, 108, 109, 124, 130, 238, 252*
Bretonvilliers (de), Hôtel, 57, *60*
Briseux, Charles-Etienne, 7, 109, 112, 117, 118, *118*, 119
Brongniart, Alexandre-Théodore, *160*, 161, 163, *164, 165, 193*
Brosse, Salomon de, 41, 57, *59*, 101, *104*
Brunau, 163, *169*
Bulfinch, Charles, 229, 230, *230*, 231
Bullet, Pierre, 87, 91, *92–94*, 95
Bury (de), Château, 31, *31*

Cabinet, 41, 52, 69
Caffé Pedrocchi (Padova), 218, *222*
Cailleteau (the elder), Pierre (Lassurance), 97, 109
Callet, Hôtel, 171, *173, 174*
Ca'Pesaro (Venice), 16
Cardinal, Palais, 57, 61
Carnavalet, Hôtel, 8, 37, *38*, 54
Cartaud, Jean-Silvain, 109

Carthage II, villa at, 190, *191*
Centrosoyuz, 204, *204*
Chaise percée (chaise de commodité), 5, 69, 105
Chalons-Luxembourg, Hôtel, *58*
Chamber of Deputies, 109, *111*
Chambre, 41, 52, 69, 105
Chambre à alcôve, 69
Chambre à coucher, 69, 105
Charles IX, *10*
Charleville, 47
Chastillon, Claude, *45, 50, 51*
Chausée d'Antin, 154, *154*, 232
Chenot, Hôtel, 163, *169*
Chevalier, Jean-François, 163, *167*
Chevreuse (de), Hôtel, *58*
Châteaux, 17, 20, 31, *31*, 34, 96. See also names of specific châteaux
Citrohan, 189, *190*, 192
Clark, Jeffrey, 223–227
Colbert, Jean-Baptiste, 79
Collège des Quatre Nations, 20, 25, *26–27*
Commodité, appartement de, 96–97, 101, 105, 109, 118
Commodité, chaise de, 5, 105
Concerning Town Planning (Le Corbusier), 206, 208
Concorde (de la), Place, 9, 13. See also Louis XV, Place
Conquêtes (des), Place, 82, *84, 85*. See also Louis XIV, Place
Contant d'Ivry, 131
Convenance, 125, 141, 152
Cornell University, 236
Cotté, Robert de, 101, *102*
Cottard, Pierre, 77
Cour d'honneur, 47, 57, 61, 69, 91
Courmont, Hôtel, 163, *167*
Cours d'architecture (d'Aviler), 5, 7, 105
Cours d'architecture (F. Blondel), 7
Cours d'architecture (J.-F. Blondel), 8, 157
Courtonne, Jean, 7, 78, 101, *102, 103,* 112, *238*
Crozat, Hôtel, 91, *92–94*, 95

Daly, Cèsar, 182, *183*
Dauphine, Place, 43, 47, *50*, 66
Daviler. *See* Aviler (d')
Décor, 162, 176
Décoration, 52

Dégagement, 61, 105, 118, 148, 154
Delagrive plan of Paris (1728), 6–7, 82, 89, 109, *251*
Delamair, Pierre-Alexis, *113*
Dennis, Michael, 223–227
Dervieux, Hôtel, *161, 162, 193*
Dining room, 4, 41, 52, 69, 118, 157
Distribution, 52, 61, 105–106, 119, 126, 152, 157, 162, 176
Distribution des maisons (Blondel), 7, 118, 119, *120–123*
Dom-ino frame, *189, 190,* 192, *195, 197*, 202
Dubut, L. A., 177, *177*
Duc, J. M., *184*
Ducale, Place (Vitry-le-François), 6, 8, 9, 30, *30*, 44
Du Cerceau, Baptiste, *39*
Du Cerceau, Jacques Androuet, 37, 39, *39*
Du Cerceau, Jacques Androuet (the elder), 7, 40–41, *42*
Du Cerceau, Jean, 52, 54, *56, 57, 60, 64, 65*
Durand, J.-N.-L., 177–178
Duret de Chevry, Hôtel, *65*

Ecole Militaire, 206, *207, 208*
"Elm Street," 237, *237*, 240, 242
Elysée, Palais de l', 106
Enfilade, 20, 61, 69
Entresols, 69
Escoville (d'), Hôtel (Caen), *33*
L'Esprit nouveau, 189
Essai sur l'architecture (Laugier), 126, *127*
Estrade, Gabriel de l', 128, *131*
Estrées (d'), Hôtel, 101, *102*
Etlin, Richard, 109
Étuve, 105
Evreaux (d'), Hôtel, 91, *92–95, 95, 97, 107*
Evry (d'), Hôtel, 148, *150*

Falcony, Hôtel, *65*
Ferrare (de), Hôtel (Le Grand Ferrare), 8, 34, *34, 35,* 36, *36, 37*
Feuillade, Maréchal de la, 80
Folies, 109, 178
Fould (de M. L.), Hôtel, *184*
Fountainebleau, 4
France (de), Place, 43, 47, 50, *51*
François I, 4, 8, 9, *10*, 29

Franque, François, 114, *114, 115*
Friday Mosque (Isfahan), *75*

Gabriel, Ange-Jacques, 127, 128–140, *195*, 228
Gabriel, Jacques (the elder), 109, 128
Gabriel, Maurice, 97, *97*
Galeries, 69, 182
Garches, Villa at (Stein), 13, *196*, 199, *199*, 200, *201, 201,* 202
Garde-robe, 41, 52, 69, 105
Garot, Emile, 218, *219*
Gendre (le), Hôtel, *33*
Génie de l'architecture ou l'Analogie de cet art avec nos sensations (Le Camus de Mézières), 8, 192
Giardini, 109
Giorgio, Francesco di, *196*
Gisors, 109
Gombust plan of Paris (1652), 6, 43, 61, *80, 83, 248*
Grand Ferrare (Le), 8, 34, *34, 35,* 36, *36, 37*
Grand Marot, 7, 13, 77
Grand Trianon, 79, 136, *138, 139*
Grande salle, 69
Guimard, Hôtel, *124,* 154, *155, 156,* 157, *197,* 239

Hall of the Council of Five Hundred, 109, *111*
Hallwyl (d'), Hôtel, 148, *148, 149*
Hamlin, Talbot, 20, 91, 125
Hardouin-Mansart, Jules. See Mansart, J. H.
Hautecoeur, L., 52, 118, 119
Henri II, *10*, 30
Henri III, 4, *10*
Henri IV, 4, 8, 9, *10*, 30, 43, 44, 47
Henrichemont, 47
Henry (architect), 171, *172, 175*
Héré, Emmanuel, 131, *132*
Hôtel
  Chronology of, 263–264
  Definition of, 3–6
  Time-line chart of, *9–11*
Houston, 2
Hulme, T. E., 213
Humières (de), Hôtel, 101, *102,* 106

Ile de la Cité, 43, 47
Ile St.-Louis, 57, 70

Illustrated handbooks, 7, 52. *See also names of specific handbooks*
Ilot no. 6 plan (Paris), 205, 206
Institut, Palais de l', 206, 206
Introduction à l'architecture contenant les principes généraux de cet art (J.-F. Blondel), 8
Invalides, 206, 207, 208
Ithaca, New York, 240

Jaillot plan of Paris (1778), 7, 44, 100, 107, 125, 137, 154, 238, 239, 253
Jal, A., 185, 186
Janvry (de), Hôtel, 109
Jappelli, Giuseppi, 222
Jars (de), Hôtel, 61, 68
Jefferson, Thomas, 229, 230, 231, 231, 232, 232, 233, 234, 235, 236, 237, 243
Jouvin de Rochefort plan of Paris (1676), 249

Kaufmann, Emil, 3, 20
Krafft, J.-C., 7, 13, 176, 177
Krier, Leon, 213

Labrouste, Henri, 184
Lakanal, Hôtel, 171, 172
Lambert, Hôtel, 70, 71, 72, 72
Lassay (de), Hôtel, 108, 110
Lassurance, 97, 109
Laugier, Marc-Antoine, 126, 127, 128, 131, 162
Le Blond, A., 7, 105
Le Camus de Mézières, 8, 162, 163
Le Corbusier, 74, 188, 189–218, 189, 191–196, 198–201, 203–208, 214, 216, 218
Ledoux, Claude-Nicolas, 141, 142–151, 148, 148, 151, 152, 152–156, 154, 157, 171, 177, 197, 239
Legrand plan of Paris (1380), 66, 244
Lemercier, Jacques, 57, 59
Lemoine, Paul-Guillaume, 178, 179, 180
Le Muet, Pierre, 7, 52, 54, 55, 61, 66–68
Le Pautre, Antoine, 15, 52, 73, 73, 74, 75, 76
Leroux, Jean-Baptiste, 113
Le Vau, Louis, 20, 25, 26, 57, 64, 70, 71, 72, 72
Liancourt (de), Hôtel, 57, 59
Ligneris, Hôtel, 8, 37, 38, 54
Lipstadt, Hélène, 182
Livre d'Architecture (Du Cerceau), 7, 40–41, 40

Longhena, 16
Louis XII, 10
Louis XIII, 9, 10
Louis XIV, 4, 9, 11, 13, 79, 82
Louis XV, 9, 11, 13, 91, 109, 128, 131
Louis XVI, 9, 11, 177
Louis, Victor, 234
Louis XV, Place, 6, 125, 127, 128–136, 129–130, 132–135. *See also* Concorde, Place de la
Louis-le-Grand, Place, 6, 13, 47, 79, 80, 82–90, 85–90, 128. *See also* Vendôme, Place
Louvois, 82
Luxembourg Palace, 41, 101, 104

Maire plan of Paris (1808), 7, 125, 176, 257–261
Maison, 4
Maison de Brethaus (Bayonne), 116
Maison Carrée (Nîmes), 231–232, 231
Maison Cook, 197
Maison à loyer, 178, 182, 183, 203, 219, 220, 221
Maison de M. X., 192
Maison Plainex, 197, 199
Maison de plaisance, 109
Maisons La Roche-Albert Jeanneret, 197, 198
Manière de bien bastir pour toutes sortes de personnes (Le Muet), 7, 52
Mansart, François, 38, 61, 62, 63, 68, 238
Mansart, Jules Hardouin, 79, 80, 81, 82–90, 95–96, 96, 234, 235
Marais, Le (Paris), 8, 13, 28, 42, 43, 44, 47, 237
Mariette, Jean, 109
Marini, Girolamo, 30
Marly (de), Château, 234, 235
Marot, Jean, 7, 13, 43, 77
Massée, 61
Matignon (de), Hôtel, 78, 101, 103, 112, 238
Maupertuis, village of, 142
Mayenne (de), Hôtel, 42
Médicis, Catherine de, 44
Médicis, Marie de, 47
Meissonier, Juste-Aurèle, 114, 116
Mercier, Sebastien, 157
Merian plan of Paris (1614), 6, 43, 247
Métezeau, Clément, 58
Mique, Richard, 136

Mollet, Armand-Claude, 101, 102, 106, 107
Monaco, Hôtel, 164, 165
Monticello, 232, 232, 233
Montmorency (de), Hôtel, 152, 152, 153, 154
Mouret, Louis, 112

Nancy, 131, 132
Neoclassical *hôtels*, 5–7, 13, 118, 119, 125, 136–176, 178, 182, 197, 199
Neuf, Château (Meudon), 96
New Haven, Connecticut, 228, 237, 239, 241
Newton's Tomb, 140
Nicolas de Fer plan of Paris (1697), 43, 82, 84, 250
Nolli plan of Rome (1748), 215
Northrhine-Westphalia Art Museum (Düsseldorf), 210, 211, 218

Oakland, California, 241
Oeuvre complète (Le Corbusier), 189
Ollivier, 163, 170
Opera de la Bastille, 226, 227
Orléans, Duc de, 106
Orliane (d'), Hôtel, 163, 166, 194, 233
Orliane, Pierre d', 63, 166, 194, 233
Orme, Philibert de L', 7, 37
Ozenfant studio, 202, 203

Palace of the Soviets, 218, 218
Palais Bourbon, 106, 108, 109, 110, 111
Palais Cardinal, 57, 61
Palais de l'Elysée, 106
Palais de l'Institut, 206, 206
Palais Royal, 80, 99, 234, 234, 243
Palazzo Barbaran (Vicenza), 17, 18
Palladio, Andrea, 7, 15, 16–19, 25, 57, 136, 214, 217
Parade, appartement de, 69, 96, 101, 105, 109, 118
Paris, 4, 6, 29, 43, 91, 109, 182, 205, 231, 232, 233, 238, 239, 256. *See also names of specific districts and buildings*
Pascal, Jean-Louis, 187
Patte, Pierre, 128, 129, 130
Patte plan of Paris (1765), 128, 129, 130
Pavillon, 109
Pavillon de Bagatelle, 178, 181
Pavillon de l'Esprit Nouveau, 189
Peintre (d'un), Hôtel, 185, 186

Perrault, Claude, *14*
Perret, August, 218, *218*
Perronne, 203, *203*, 204, *219*
Peterson, Steven, 217
Petit Marot, 7, 77
Petit Trianon (Versailles), 127, 136–140, *137–139*, 157, *195*, 228
Philosophes, 140, 177
Piazza Ducale (Vigevano), *28*, 29, 44
Piranesi, Giovanni Battista, *144*, *145*
Place, 9–11 (time-line chart), 43–51, 128, 215, 230, 240. *See also names of specific squares*
Plans of Paris, 6, 7, 43, 244–262. *See also names of specific plans*
Plans, coupes, élévations des plus belles maisons ... à Paris (Krafft and Ransonnette), 7, 176
Les Plus excellents bastiments de France (Du Cerceau), 7, 41
Poché, 4–5
Pont Neuf, 43, 47, 66
Porte-cochère, 57, 73, 75, 91
Porte de France, 50
Poyet, Bernard, 109, 131, 171, *173*, *174*
Précis (Durand), 177
Promenade architecturale, 197, 199, 201

Rambouillet (de), Hôtel, *53*
Rambouillet, Marquise de, 53, *53*, 54, 61, 69
Ramée, Jean-Jacques, 234
Ransonnette, N., 7, *13*, 176, 177
Recueil (Durand), 177
Recueil (Marot), 7, 77
Régence period, 7
Reigns, time-line chart of, 9–11
Révolution (de la), Place, *9*
Revue générale de l'architecture et des travaux publics (Daly), 182
Richelieu, 47, 57, 61
Richelieu district (Paris), *13*, 57, 61
Rococo *hôtels*, 5, *13*, 41, 91–127, 157, 197
Rohan (de), Hôtel, *113*
Roman house type, 17, *18*
Romma Interotta, 217
Rouillé (de), Hôtel, 109
Rousseau, Pierre, *158*, *159*, 233
Roux-Spitz, Michel, 218, 220, *221*

Rowe, Colin, 199, 217
Royale, Place (Bordeaux), 128
Royale, Place (Nancy), 131, *132*
Royale, Place (Paris), 6, 8, 30, 42, 43, 44, *45*, *46*, 47. *See also* Vosges, Place des
Rue St.-Honoré, *107*
Ruelle, 69

Saalman, Howard, 87
Ste.-Foix (de), Hôtel, *160*
St.-Germain, Faubourg (Paris), 41, 78, 91, 96, 100, 237
St.-Honoré, Faubourg (Paris), 82, 96
Saint Peter's (Rome), *16*
Salle, 41, 52, 105
Salle à manger, 41, 52, 118, 157
Salm (de), Hôtel, *158*, *159*, 233
Salon, 69, 178
Salon de compagnie, 157
Salvation Army building (Le Corbusier), 203, *203*, 204
Sant' Andrea (Mantua), *16*
Sauvage, Henri, 220
Savot, Louis, 7, 52, 61
Scully, Vincent, 229
Séguier, Hôtel, *64*
Sennett, Richard, 1
Sens (de), Hôtel, *32*
Serlio, Sebastiano, 7, 34–37, 40, *215*, 237
Serre-papier, 69
Société, appartement de, 118
Soubise (de), Hôtel, *112*, *113*
Squares, 9–11 (time-line chart), 43–51, 128, 215, 230, 240. *See also names of specific squares*
Stirling, James, 210, *211*, 218
Sully, Duc de, 43
Sully (de), Hôtel, 52, 54, *56*, 57

Tablino della Carita (Venice), 214
Temple of Terpsichore (Hôtel Guimard), 124, 154, *155*, *156*, 157, 197, 239
Thélusson (de), Hôtel, 141, *144–147*
Theoretical treatises, 7, 37, 52, 105, 125. *See also names of specific treatises*
Thion, *219*
Thiriot, Jean, *65*
Tontine Crescent (Boston), 230, *230*, 231
Tournelles (des), Hôtel, 43, *45*

Traité de perspective pratique avec les remarques sur l'architecture (Courtonne), 7, 112
Tubeuf, Hôtel, 61, 66
Tuileries, 88
Turgot plan of Paris (1734–39), 6, *12*, 42, *51*, 62, *78*, *80*, *81*, *82*, *88*, *104*, *108*, *109*, *124*, *130*, *238*, *252*

University of California at Santa Barbara Art Museum, 223–225
University of Virginia, 234, *235*, *236*, 243
Uzès (d'), Hôtel, 148, *151*, 152

Vanbrugh, Sir John, 24
Varanjeville (de), Hôtel, 97, *97*
Vassale, Hôtel, 171, *174*
Vasserot plan of Paris (1827–36), 7
Vaux-le-Vicomte, 20, *25*
Vendôme (de), Hôtel, 82, *83*
Vendôme, Place, *9*, 90, 206, *206*. *See also* Louis-le-Grand, Place
Verneuil (de), Château, 41
Verniquet plan of Paris (1791–99), 7, *254*
Vers une architecture (Le Corbusier), 189
Versailles, *1*, 9, 20, *21–23*, 79, 209, *241*. *See also* Grand Trianon; Petit Trianon
Vestibule, 69, 75
Victoires (des), Place, 79, 80, *80*, *81*, 82, 128
Villa, 182
Villa Foscari, 17, *19*
Villa of Light (Croissy), *184*
Villa Meyer, 192, *193*, *194*, 195
Villa Pisani (Montagnana), *18*
Villa Savoye, *74*, *75*, 195, *207*, 214
Villa Stein (Garches), *13*, 196, 199, *199*, 200, 201, *201*, 202
Villa Trissino (Meledo), 17, *19*
Villandry (de), Château, 31, *31*
Ville contemporaine, 188, 189, *191*, 196, 209
Villefranche (de), Hôtel, 114, *114*
Ville radieuse, 189–190, 195, 197, 204, 208
Villeroy (de), Hôtel, *113*
Villers-Cotterets, 114, *115*, 157
Virginia State Capitol, 231, *231*
Vitry-le-François, 6, 8, *9*, 30, *30*, 44
Voison plan for Paris (1925), 208, *216*

Vosges (des), Place, 8, 9, *48*
Vrillière (de la), Hôtel, 61, *62, 63,* 80, 82, *238*

Ward, W. H., 114
White House, *228*
Wittkower, Rudolf, 16–17
Woodstock, Robert, *217*